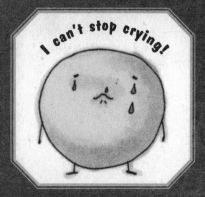

I can't stop crying!

Ken-ichi Sakura

It's the second anniversary of *Dragon Drive*! I remember writing the first chapter in the meeting room on the 10th floor of the Shueisha building just like it was yesterday. I couldn't have gotten this far without the support of lots of people.

Thank you, everyone!
Thank you for reading!
Thank you so much!
I'm going to keep trying my best!
I'll try my best at putting out the trash, too!

Ken-ichi Sakura's manga debut was *Fabre Tanteiki*, which was published in a special edition of *Monthly Shonen Jump* in 2000. Serialization of *Dragon Drive* began in the March 2001 issue of *Monthly Shonen Jump* and the hugely successful series has inspired video games and an animated TV show. Sakura's latest title, *Kotokuri*, began running in the March 2006 issue of *Monthly Shonen Jump*. *Dragon Drive* and *Kotokuri* have both become tremendously popular in Japan because of Sakura's unique sense of humor and dynamic portrayal of feisty teen characters.

DRAGON DRIVE

DRAGON DRIVE
VOLUME 6

The SHONEN JUMP Manga Edition

STORY AND ART BY
KEN-ICHI SAKURA

Translation/Martin Hunt, HC Language Solutions, Inc.
English Adaptation/Ian Reid, HC Language Solutions, Inc.
Touch-up Art & Lettering/Jim Keefe
Design/Sam Elzway
Editor/Shaenon K. Garrity

Editor in Chief, Books/Alvin Lu
Editor in Chief, Magazines/Marc Weidenbaum
VP of Publishing Licensing/Rika Inouye
VP of Sales/Gonzalo Ferreyra
Sr. VP of Marketing/Liza Coppola
Publisher/Hyoe Narita

Printed in the U.S.A.

Published by VIZ Media, LLC
P.O. Box 77010
San Francisco, CA 94107

SHONEN JUMP Manga Edition
10 9 8 7 6 5 4 3 2 1
First printing, February 2008

THE WORLD'S
MOST POPULAR MANGA

www.viz.com

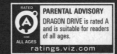

www.shonenjump.com

DRAGON DRIVE

SHONEN JUMP MANGA EDITION

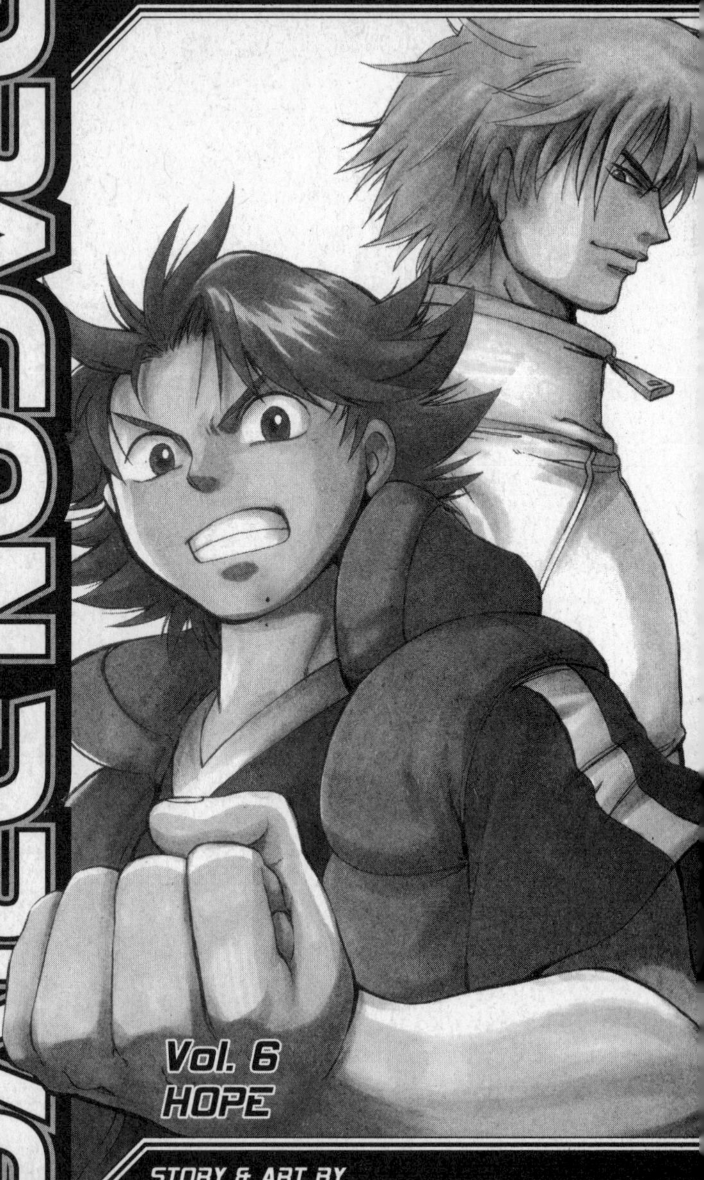

Vol. 6
HOPE

STORY & ART BY
KEN-ICHI SAKURA
IN COLLABORATION WITH BANDAI • CHAN'S • ORG

CHARACTERS

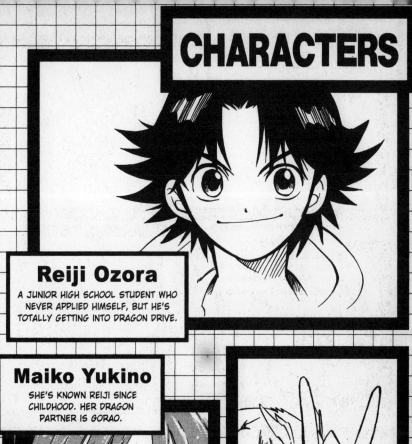

Reiji Ozora

A JUNIOR HIGH SCHOOL STUDENT WHO NEVER APPLIED HIMSELF, BUT HE'S TOTALLY GETTING INTO DRAGON DRIVE.

Maiko Yukino

SHE'S KNOWN REIJI SINCE CHILDHOOD. HER DRAGON PARTNER IS GORAO.

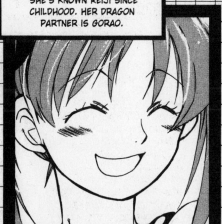

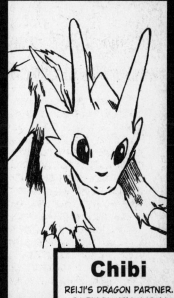

Chibi

REIJI'S DRAGON PARTNER. IN RIKYU, HE'S KNOWN AS SENKOKURA.

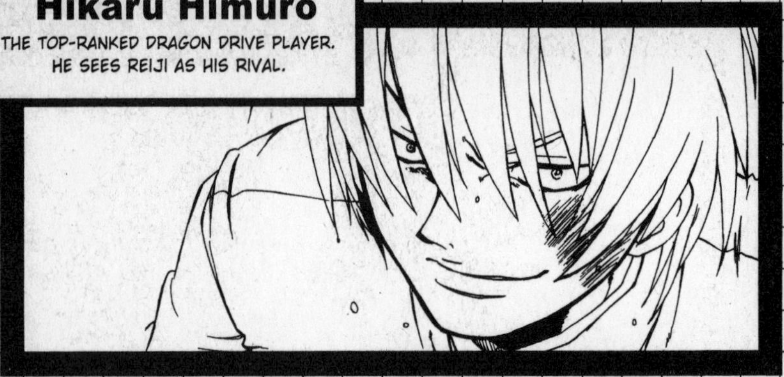

Hikaru Himuro

THE TOP-RANKED DRAGON DRIVE PLAYER. HE SEES REIJI AS HIS RIVAL.

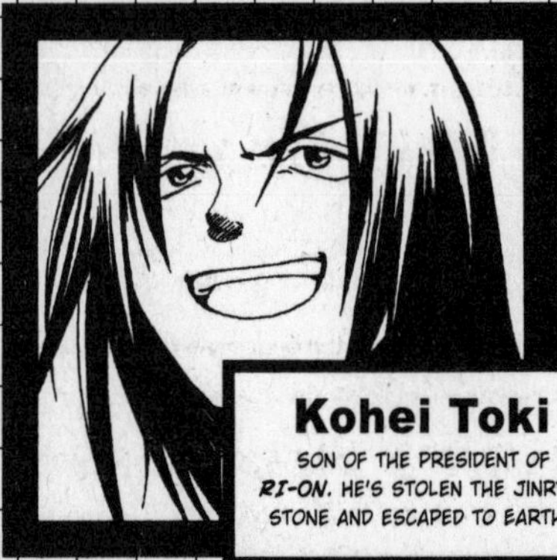

Kohei Toki

SON OF THE PRESIDENT OF *RI-ON*. HE'S STOLEN THE JINRYU STONE AND ESCAPED TO EARTH.

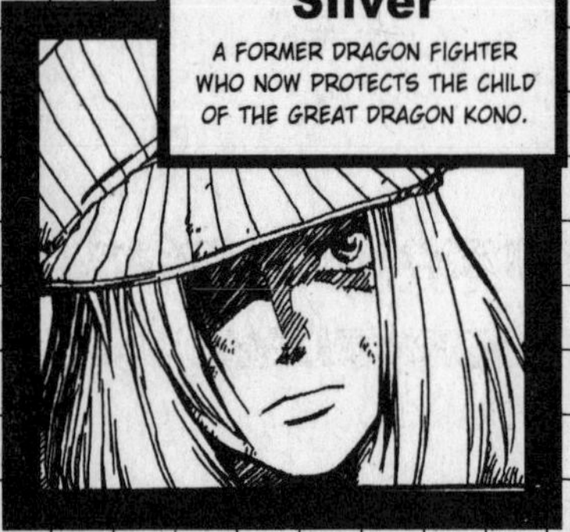

Silver

A FORMER DRAGON FIGHTER WHO NOW PROTECTS THE CHILD OF THE GREAT DRAGON KONO.

STORY

DRAGON DRIVE IS A VIRTUAL REALITY GAME THAT ONLY KIDS CAN PLAY. THE THRILL OF THE GAME GRIPS REIJI, A BOY WHO WAS NEVER REALLY GOOD AT ANYTHING. WHILE TRAINING IN A SPECIAL ROOM ONE DAY, REIJI AND HIS FRIENDS ARE WHISKED AWAY TO RIKYU, AN ALTERNATE EARTH. THERE, HE LEARNS THAT *RI-ON*, THE ORGANIZATION RUNNING DRAGON DRIVE, IS PLOTTING TO CONQUER BOTH RIKYU AND EARTH. *RI-ON* IS USING CHILDREN TO GET THE JINRYU STONE, WHICH HAS THE POWER TO CONTROL DRAGONS. TO SAVE BOTH WORLDS, REIJI ENTERS THE DRAGONIC HEAVEN COMPETITION IN RIKYU. THE BATTLE FOR THE GRAND PRIZE, THE JINRYU STONE, ENDS WITH KOHEI TOKI SEIZING THE STONE THROUGH UNDERHANDED TACTICS. HOWEVER, THE STONE THAT KOHEI TAKES IS JUST THE KEY TO ACCESS THE SHRINE WHERE THE REAL JINRYU STONE LIES. TO STOP *RI-ON'S* PLAN AND SAVE RIKYU, REIJI SEEKS THE LEGENDARY DRAGON SHINSABER...

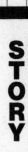

Vol. 6 HOPE
CONTENTS

DRAGON DRIVE

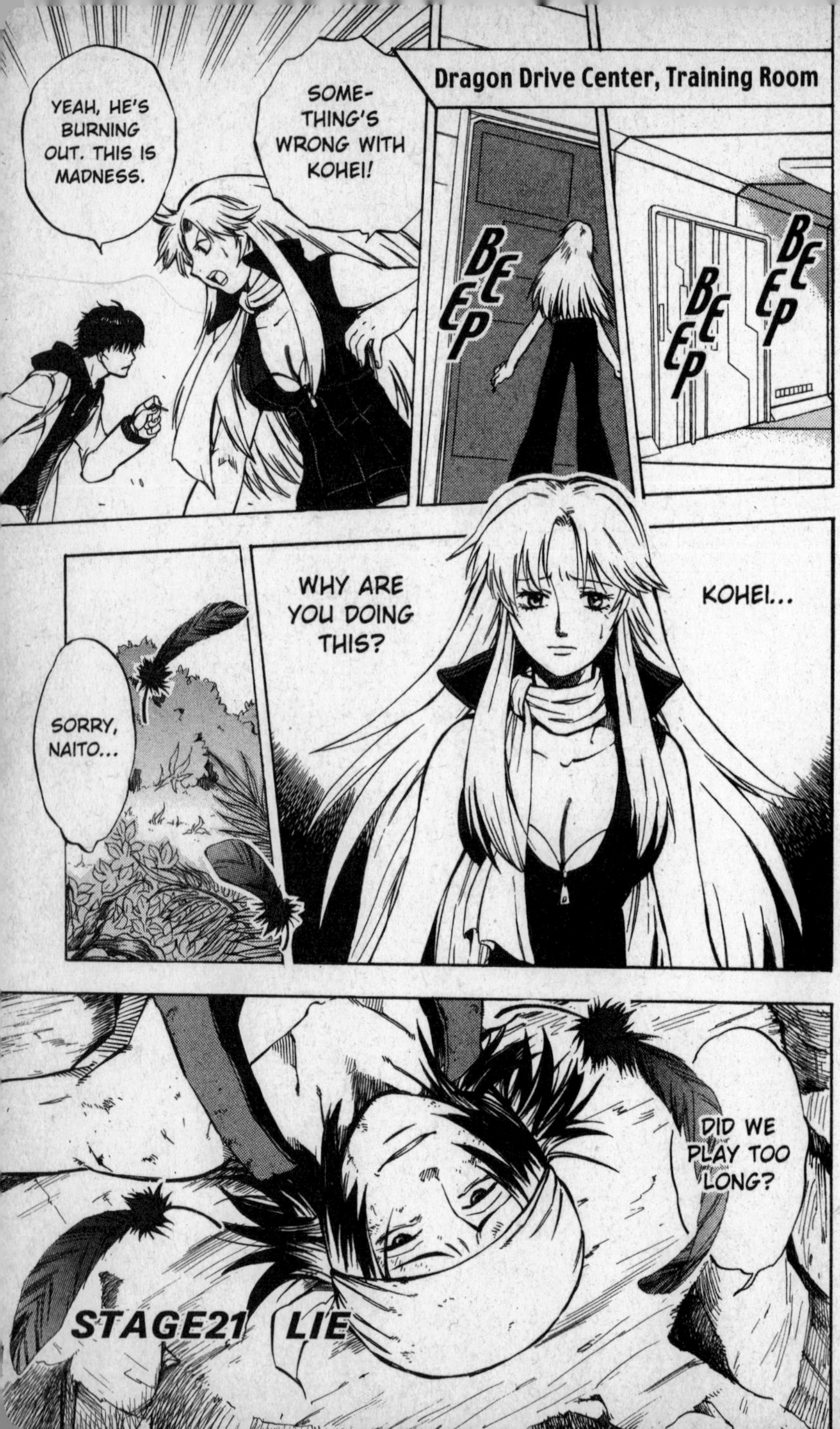
Dragon Drive Center, Training Room
BEEP
BEEP
BEEP
SOME-THING'S WRONG WITH KOHEI!
YEAH, HE'S BURNING OUT. THIS IS MADNESS.
KOHEI...
WHY ARE YOU DOING THIS?
SORRY, NAITO...
DID WE PLAY TOO LONG?
STAGE21 LIE

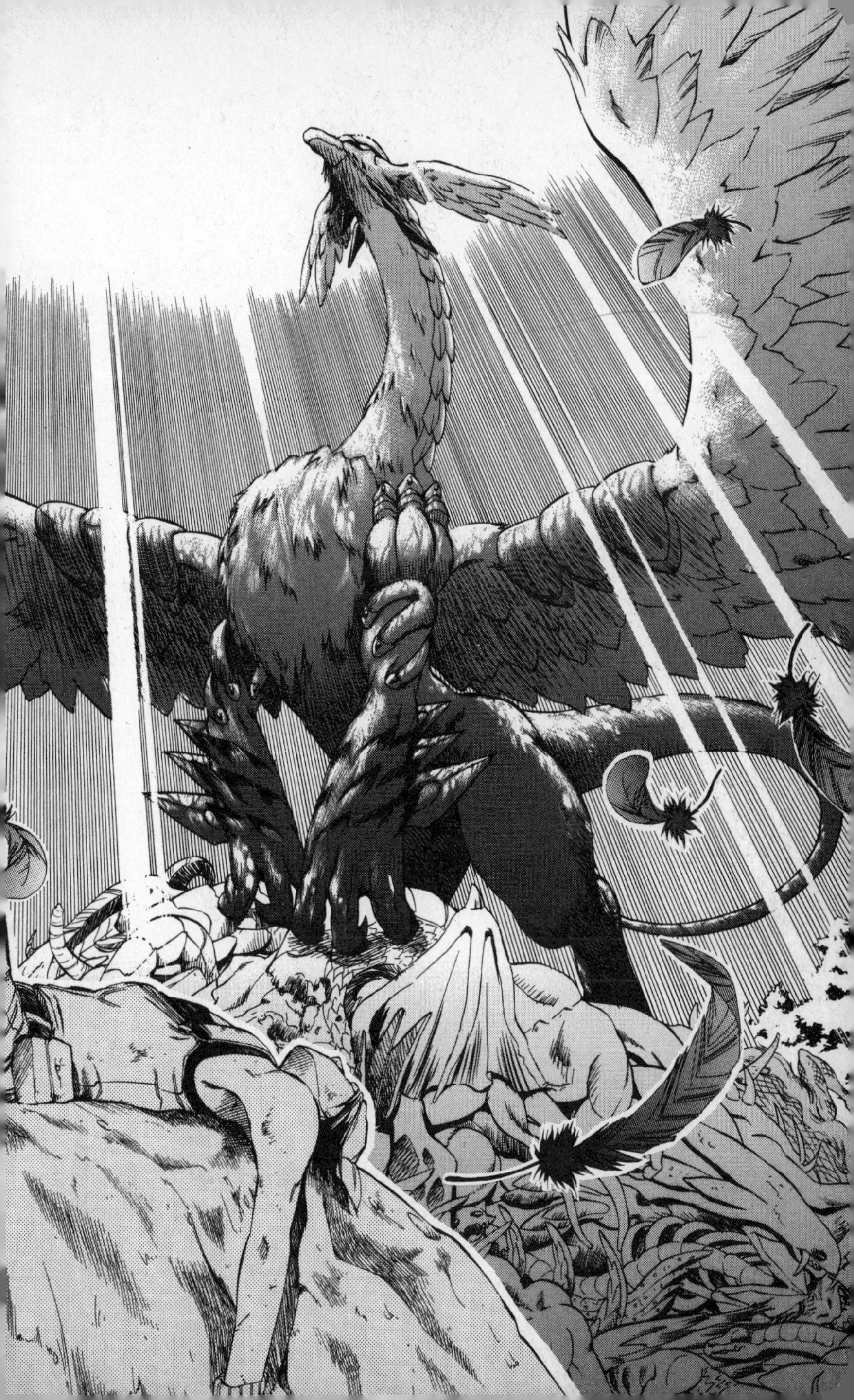

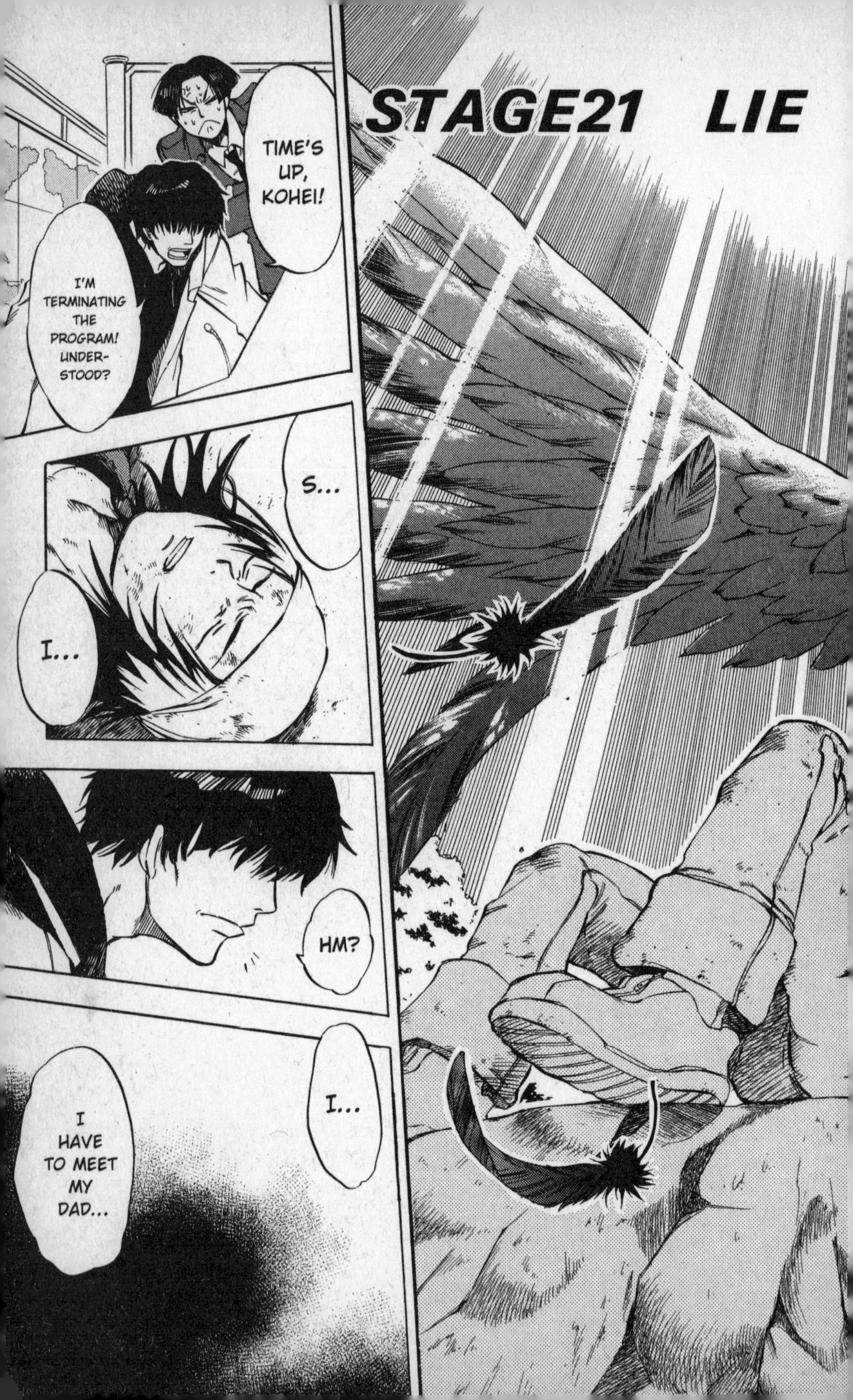
STAGE21 LIE
TIME'S UP, KOHEI!
I'M TERMINATING THE PROGRAM! UNDERSTOOD?
S...
I...
HM?
I...
I HAVE TO MEET MY DAD...

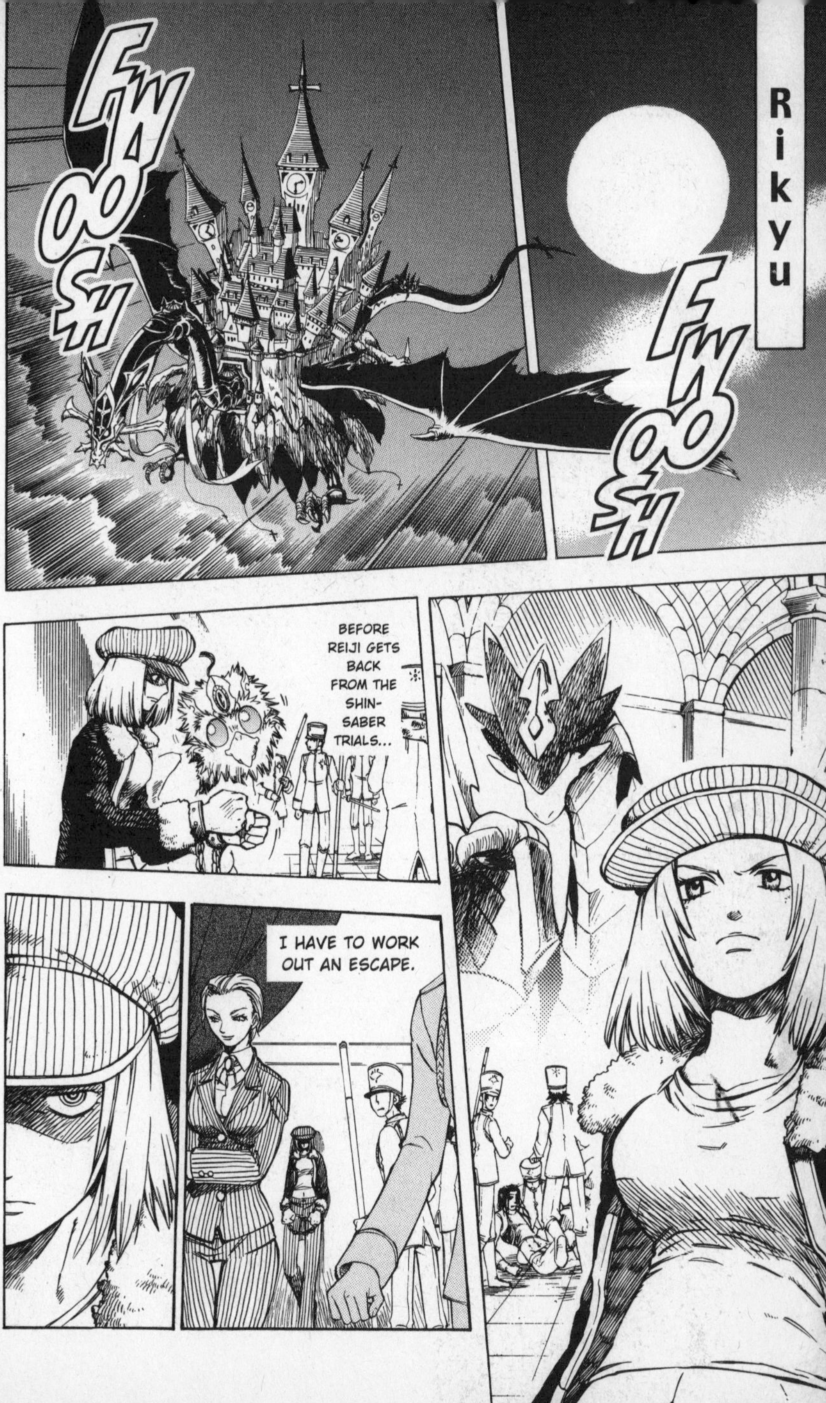
Rikyu
FWOOSH
FWOOSH
BEFORE REIJI GETS BACK FROM THE SHIN-SABER TRIALS...
I HAVE TO WORK OUT AN ESCAPE.

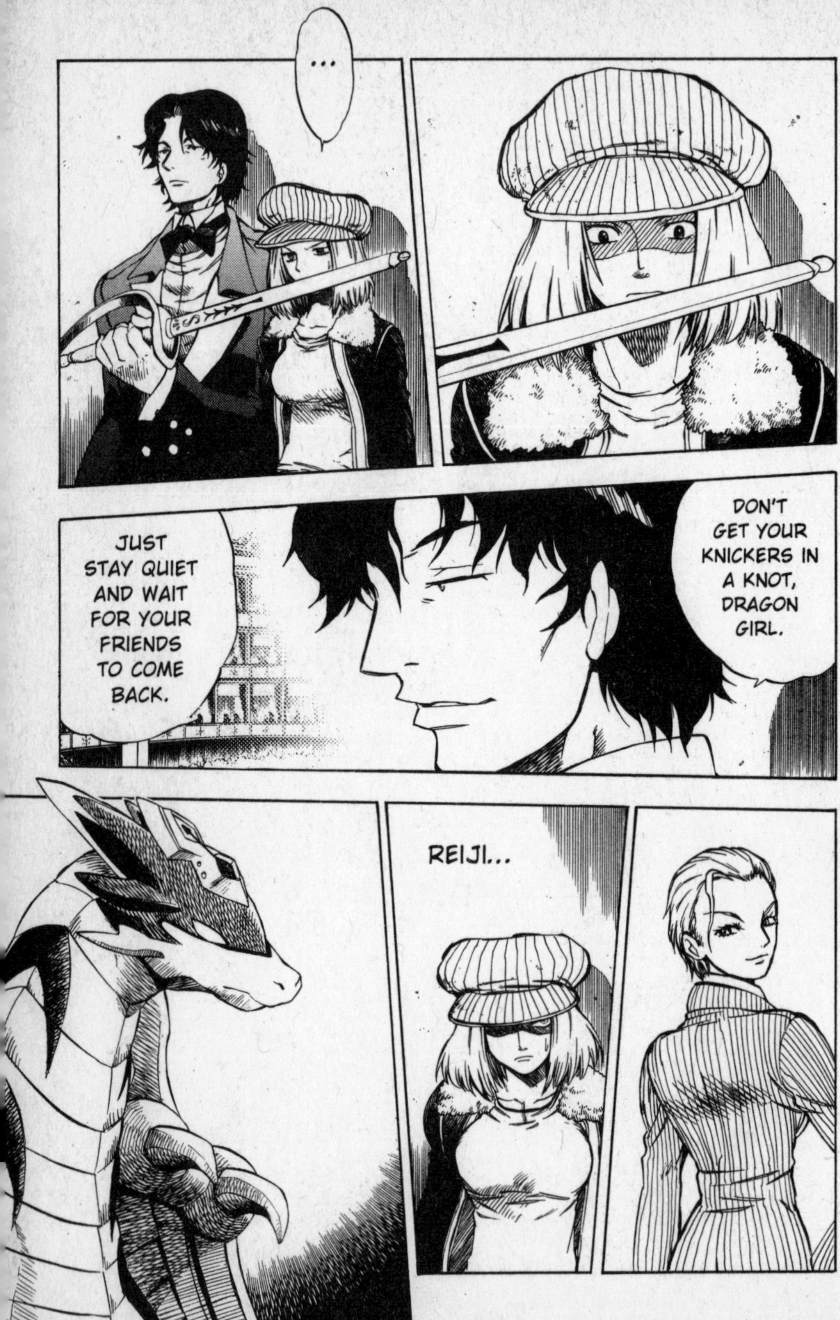
...
DON'T GET YOUR KNICKERS IN A KNOT, DRAGON GIRL.
JUST STAY QUIET AND WAIT FOR YOUR FRIENDS TO COME BACK.
REIJI...

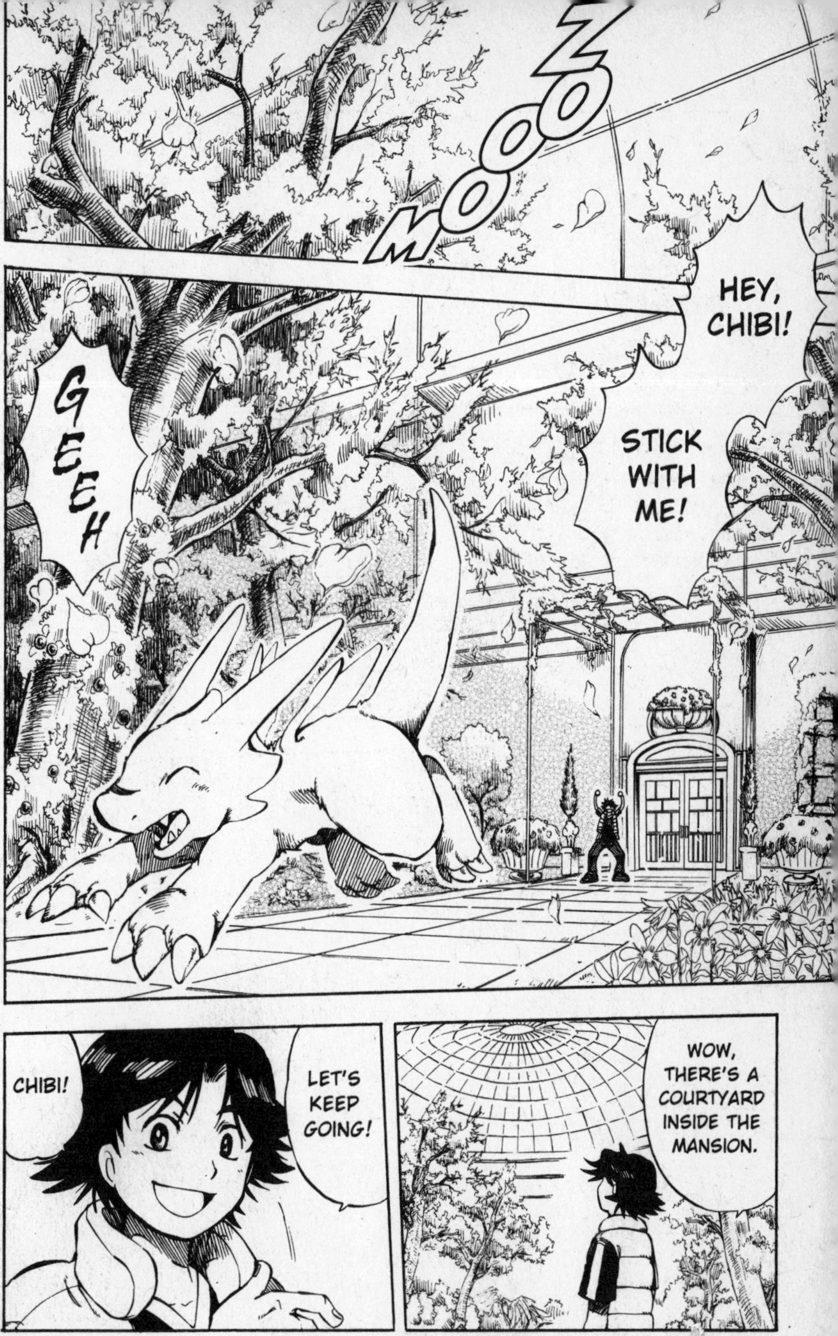
MOOOOZ
HEY, CHIBI!
STICK WITH ME!
GEEH
WOW, THERE'S A COURTYARD INSIDE THE MANSION.
LET'S KEEP GOING!
CHIBI!

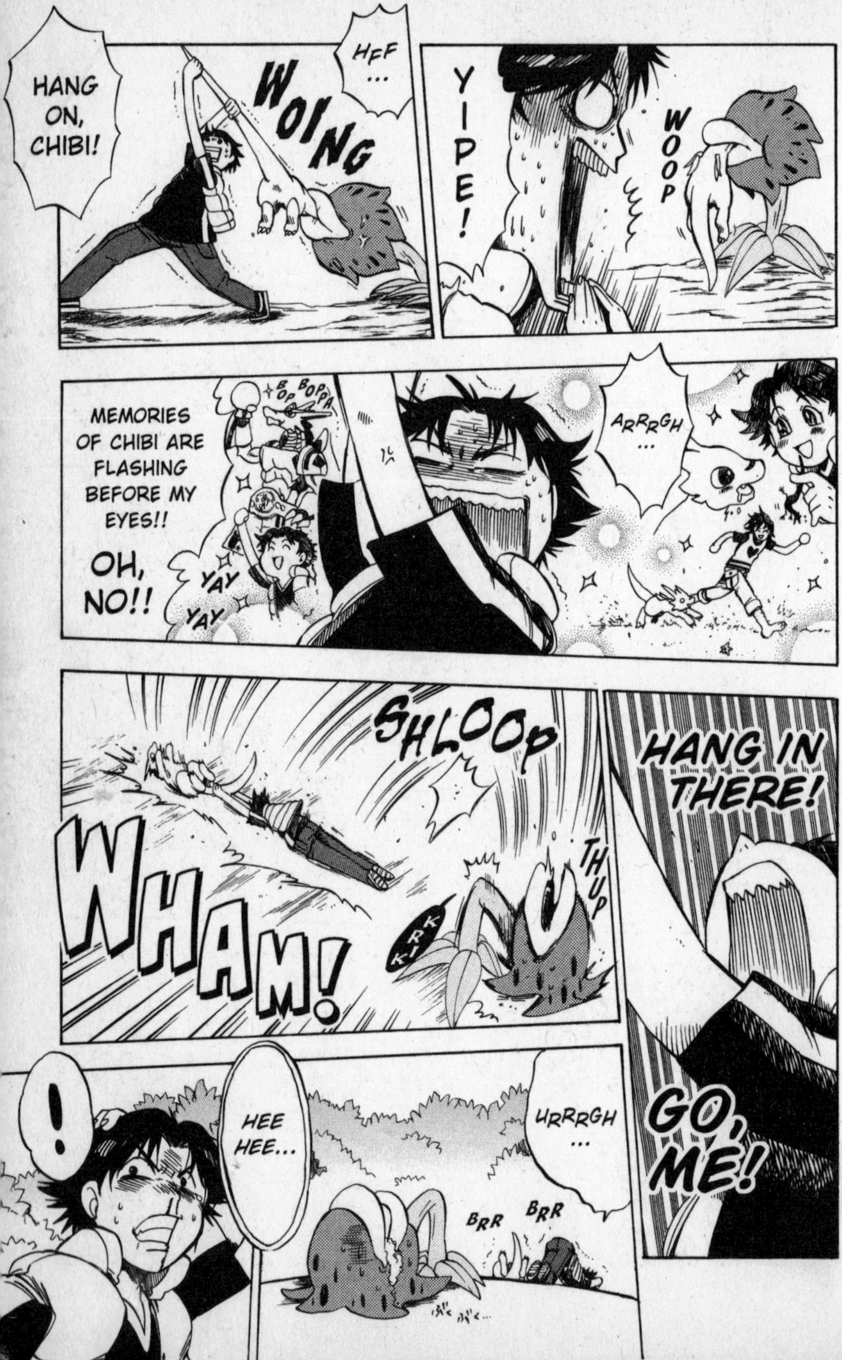
WOOOP
YIPE!
HFF...
WOING
HANG ON, CHIBI!
ARRRGH...
MEMORIES OF CHIBI ARE FLASHING BEFORE MY EYES!!
BOP BOPPA
YAY YAY
OH, NO!!
HANG IN THERE!
GO, ME!
SHLOOP
THUP
KRI KRI
WHAM!
URRRGH...
BRR
BRR
HEE HEE...
!

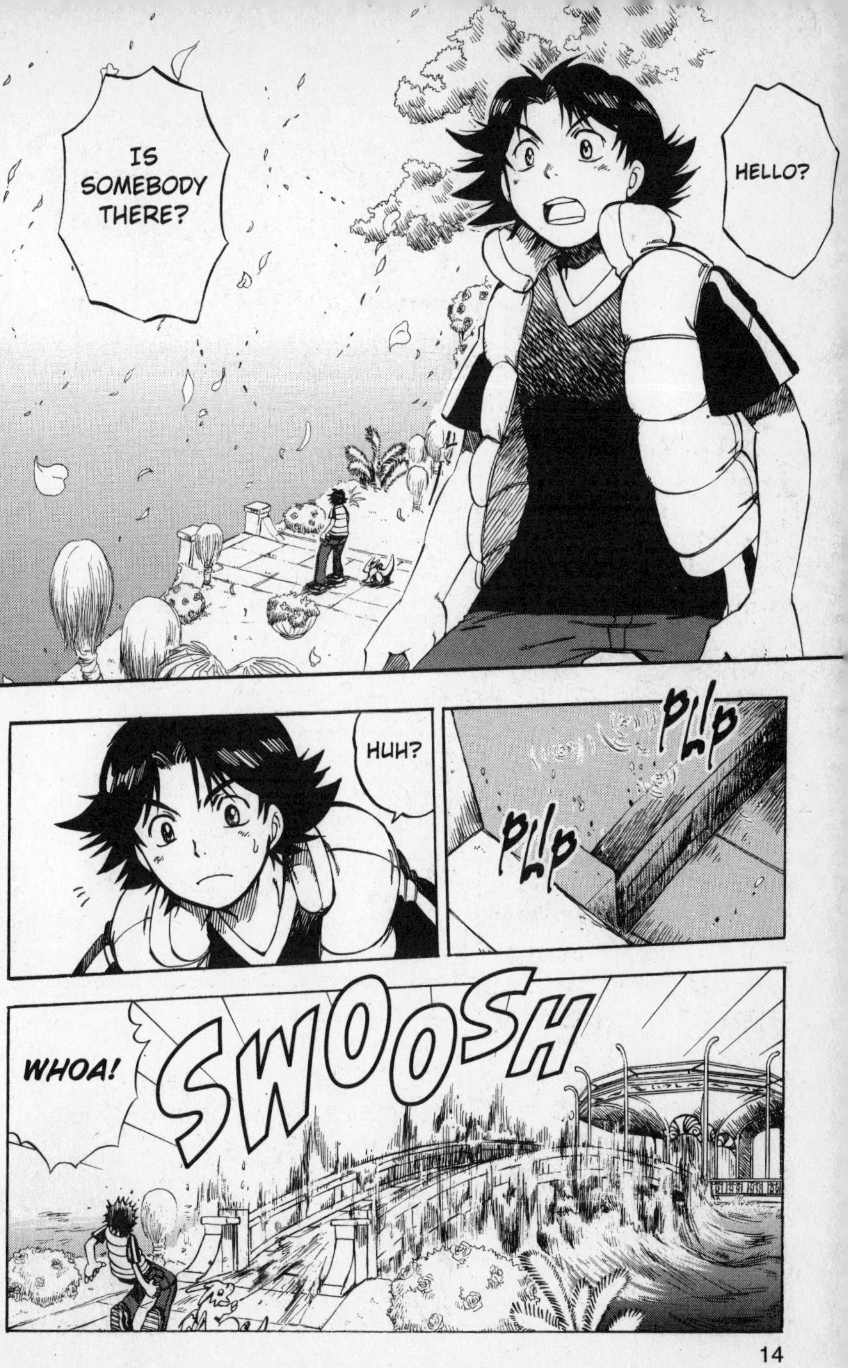
HELLO?
IS SOMEBODY THERE?
PLIP
PLIP
HUH?
SWOOSH
WHOA!

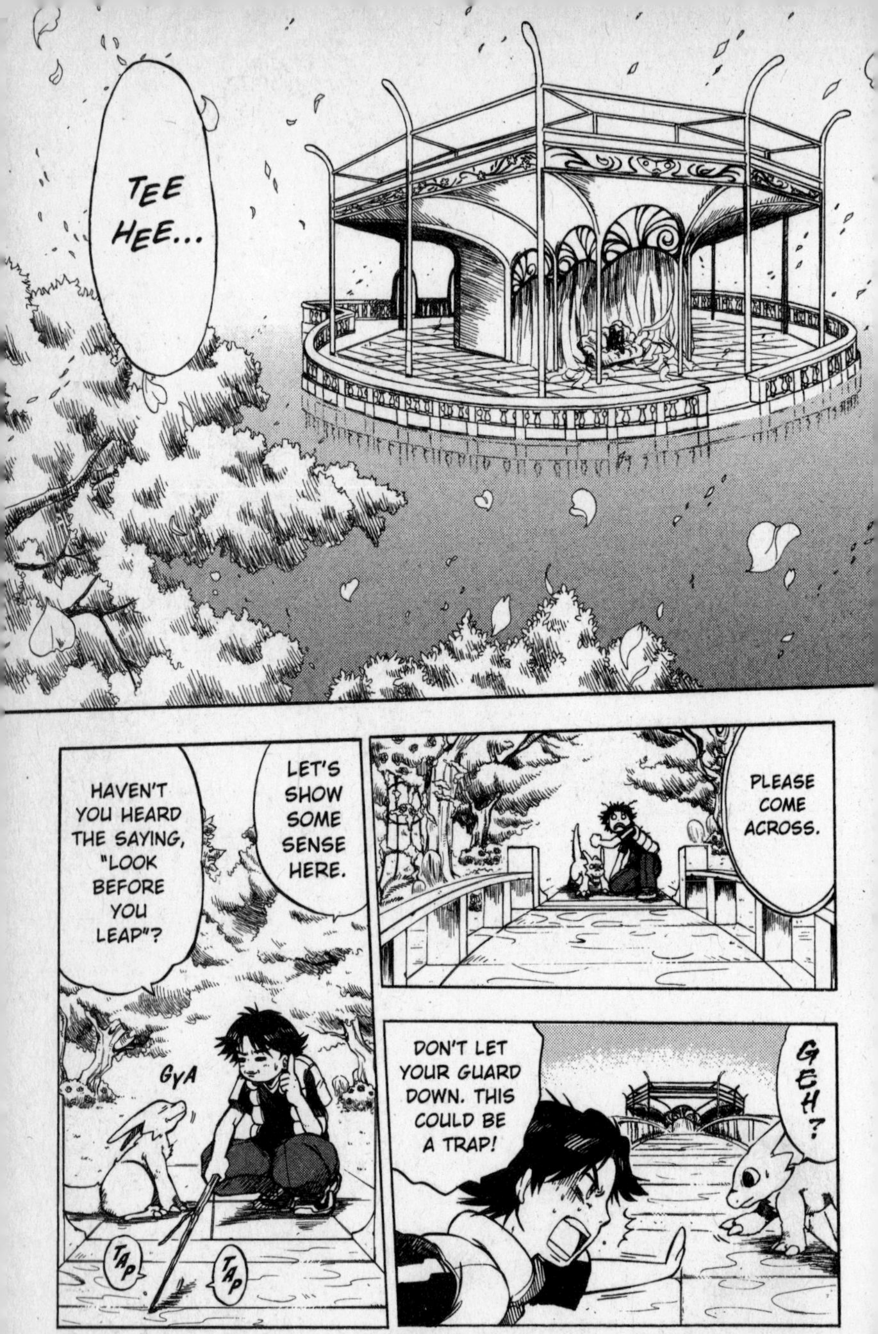
TEE HEE...
PLEASE COME ACROSS.
GEH?
DON'T LET YOUR GUARD DOWN. THIS COULD BE A TRAP!
LET'S SHOW SOME SENSE HERE.
HAVEN'T YOU HEARD THE SAYING, "LOOK BEFORE YOU LEAP"?
GYA
TAP
TAP

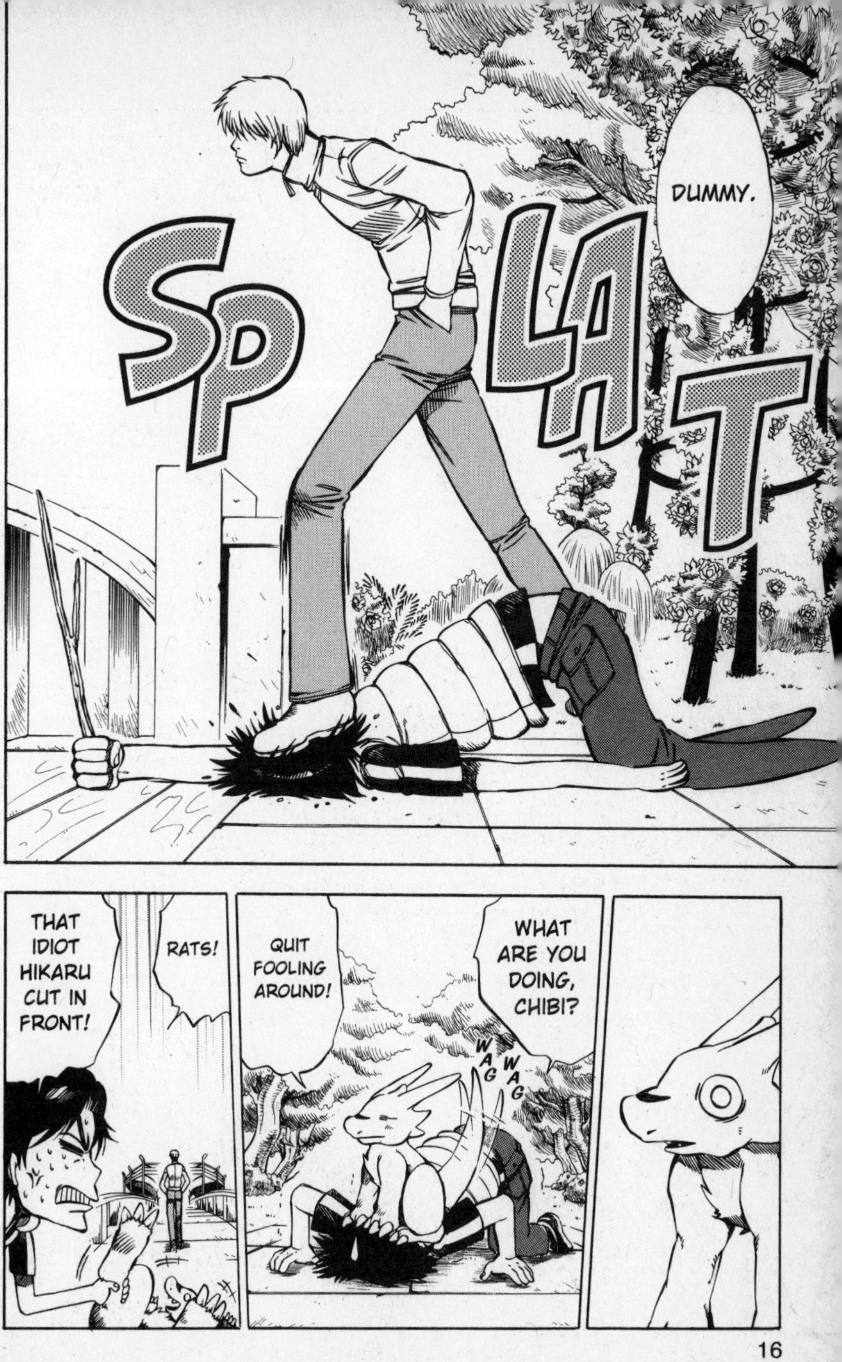
DUMMY.
SPLAT
WHAT ARE YOU DOING, CHIBI?
WAG WAG
QUIT FOOLING AROUND!
RATS!
THAT IDIOT HIKARU CUT IN FRONT!

READ THIS WAY

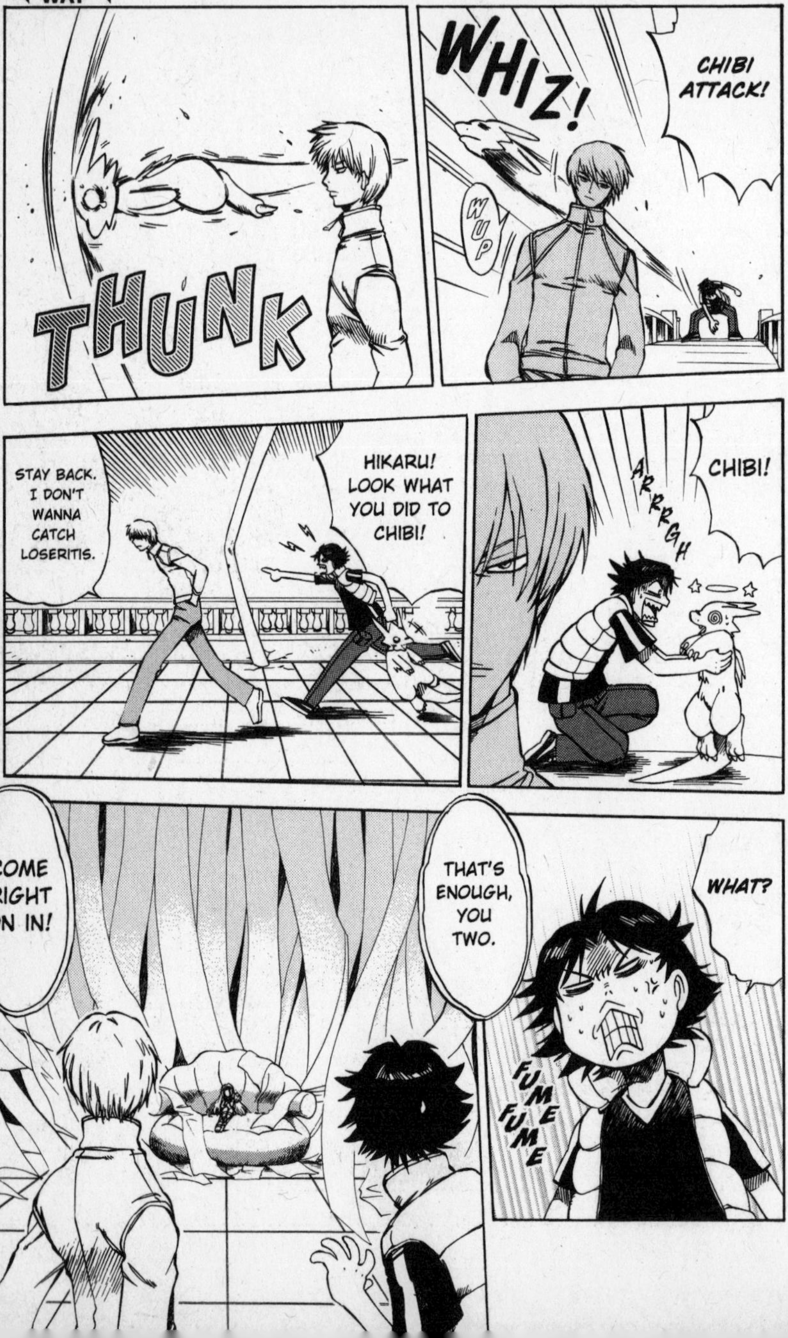
CHIBI ATTACK!
WHIZ!
WUP
THUNK
CHIBI!
ARRRGH
HIKARU! LOOK WHAT YOU DID TO CHIBI!
STAY BACK. I DON'T WANNA CATCH LOSERITIS.
WHAT?
FUME FUME
THAT'S ENOUGH, YOU TWO.
COME RIGHT ON IN!

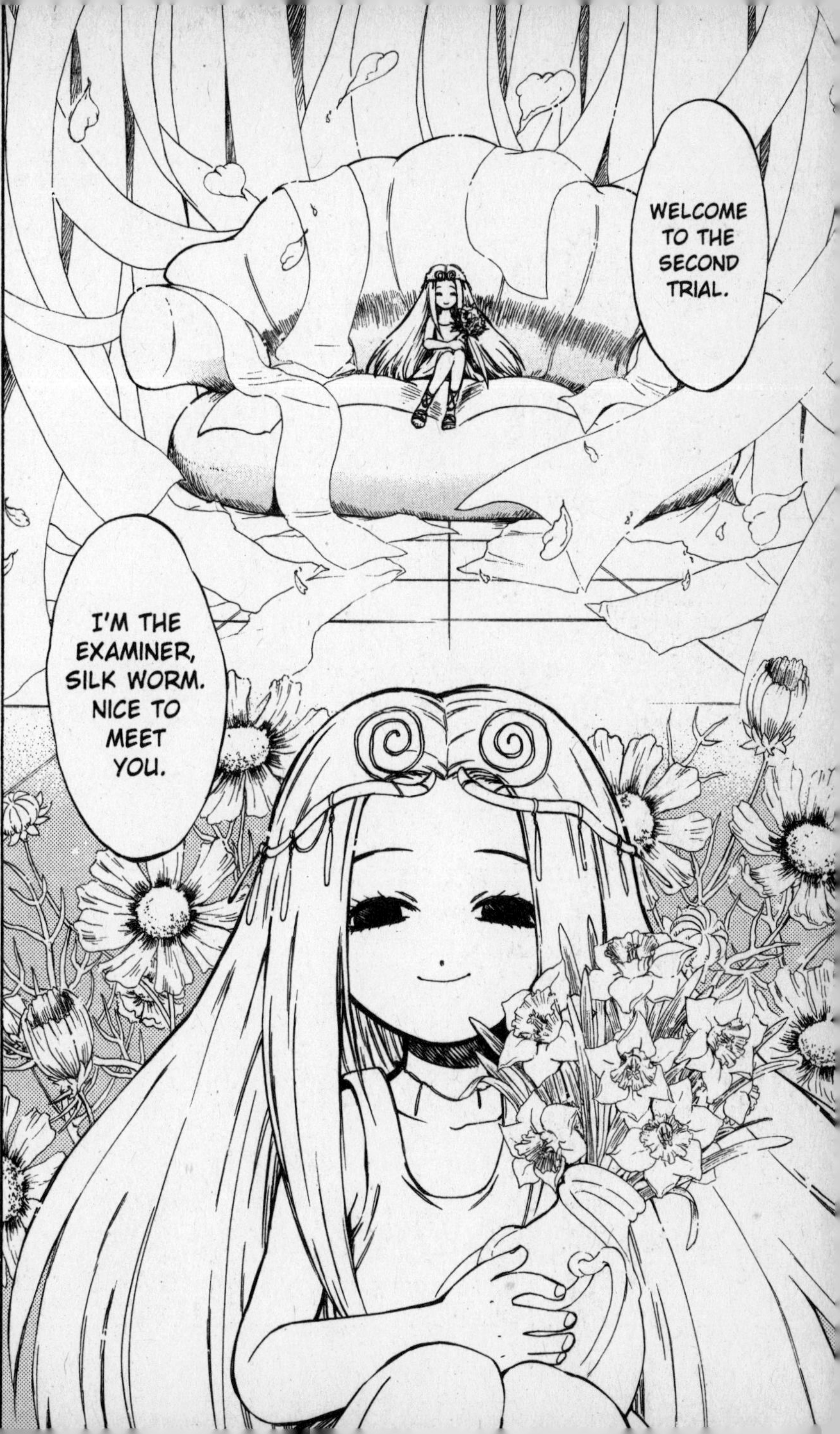
WELCOME TO THE SECOND TRIAL.
I'M THE EXAMINER, SILK WORM. NICE TO MEET YOU.

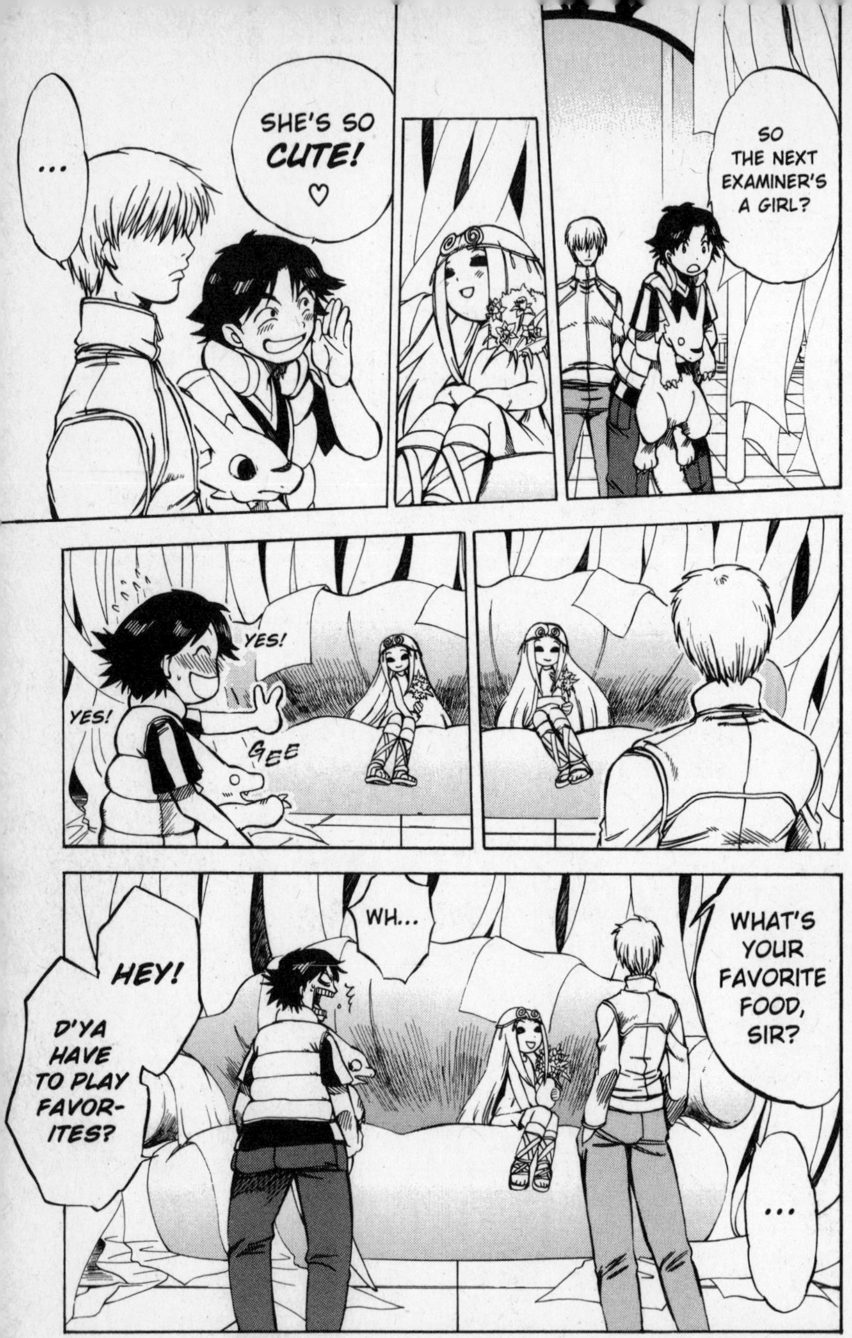
SO THE NEXT EXAMINER'S A GIRL?
SHE'S SO CUTE! ♡
...
YES!
YES!
GEE
WHAT'S YOUR FAVORITE FOOD, SIR?
...
WH...
HEY!
D'YA HAVE TO PLAY FAVOR-ITES?

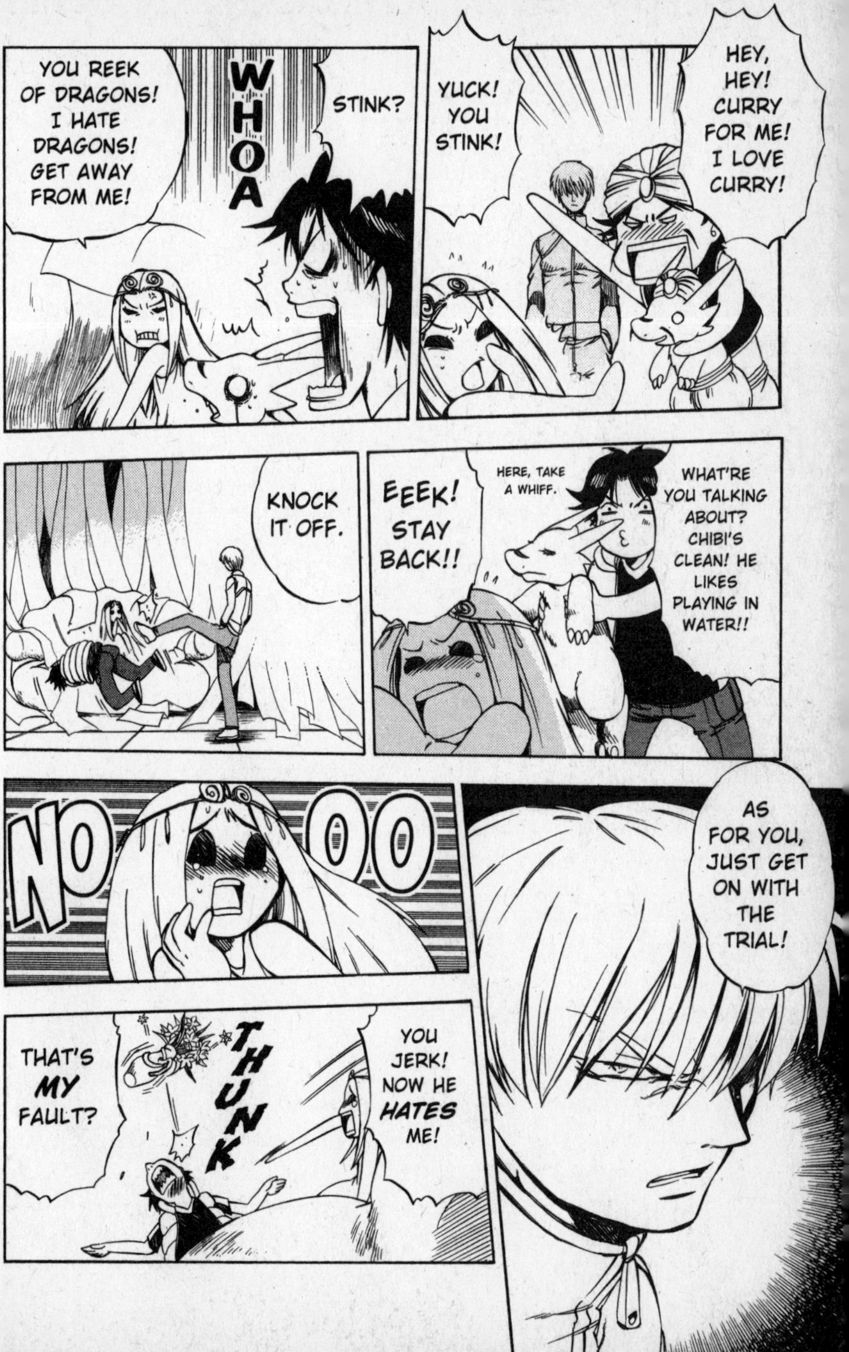
HEY, HEY! CURRY FOR ME! I LOVE CURRY!
YUCK! YOU STINK!
STINK?
WHOA
YOU REEK OF DRAGONS! I HATE DRAGONS! GET AWAY FROM ME!
WHAT'RE YOU TALKING ABOUT? CHIBI'S CLEAN! HE LIKES PLAYING IN WATER!!
HERE, TAKE A WHIFF.
EEEK! STAY BACK!!
KNOCK IT OFF.
AS FOR YOU, JUST GET ON WITH THE TRIAL!
NOOOO
YOU JERK! NOW HE HATES ME!
THUNK
THAT'S MY FAULT?

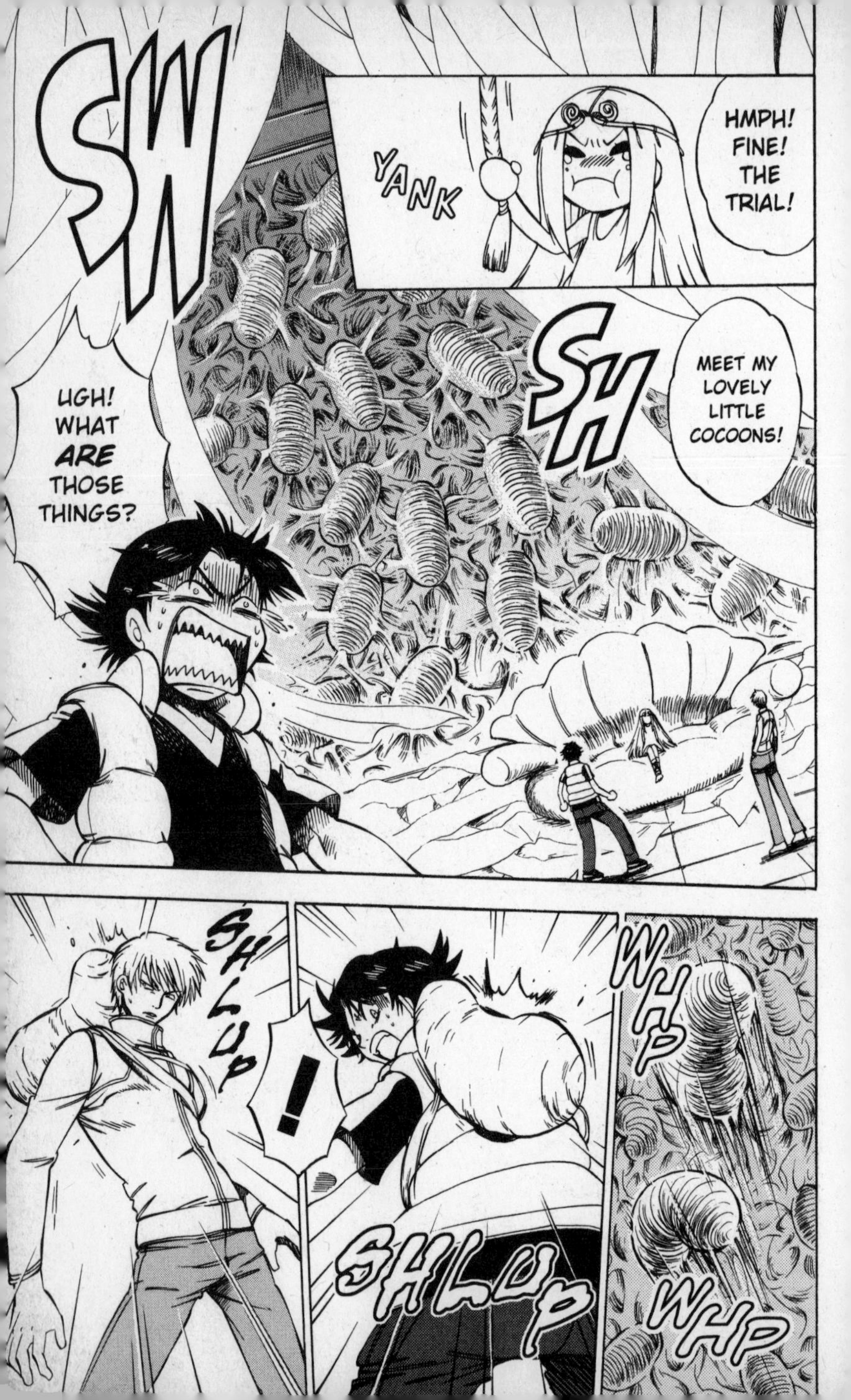
HMPH! FINE! THE TRIAL!
YANK
SW
MEET MY LOVELY LITTLE COCOONS!
SH
UGH! WHAT ARE THOSE THINGS?
WHP
WHP
SHLUP
!
SHLUP

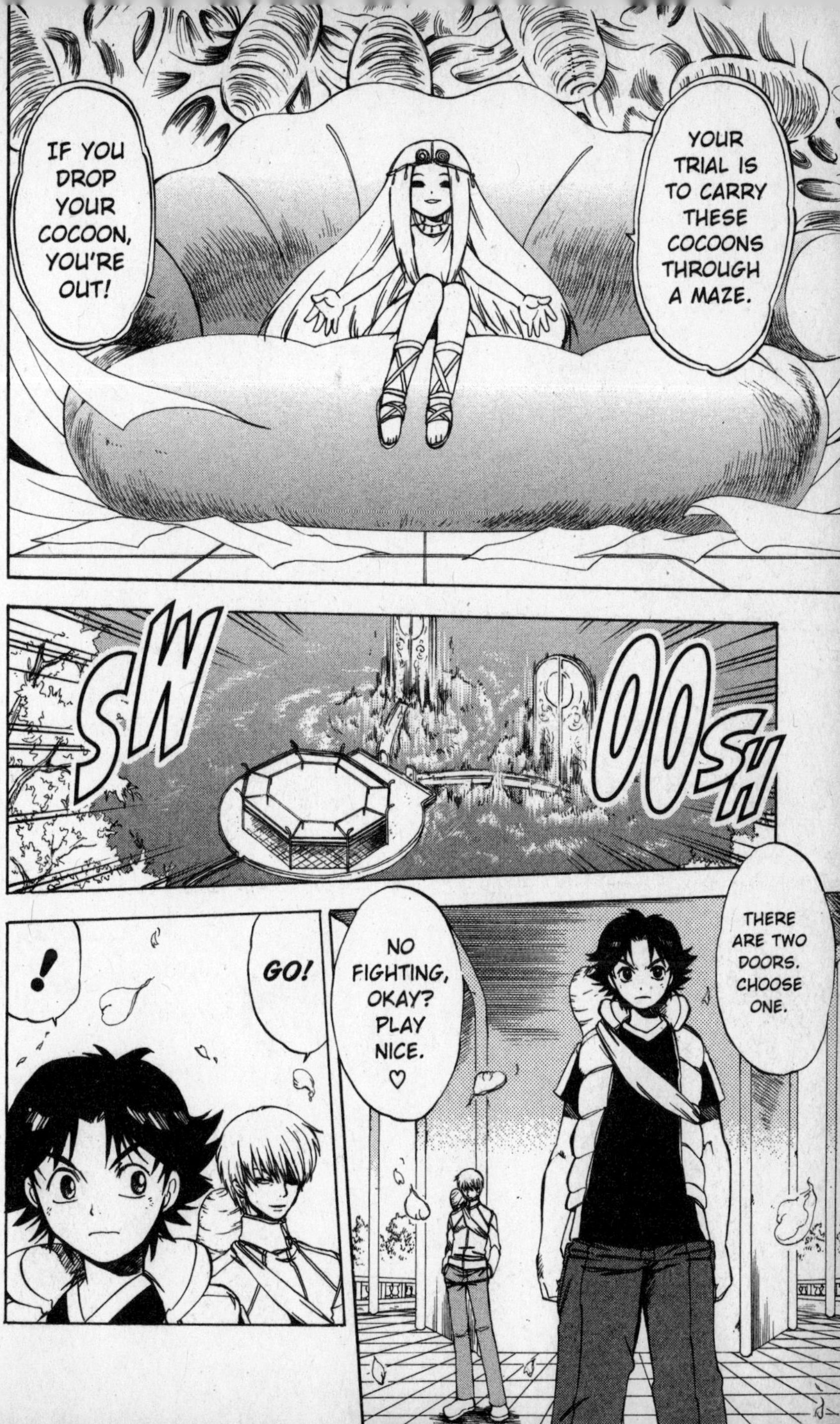
YOUR TRIAL IS TO CARRY THESE COCOONS THROUGH A MAZE.
IF YOU DROP YOUR COCOON, YOU'RE OUT!
SHWOOSH
THERE ARE TWO DOORS. CHOOSE ONE.
NO FIGHTING, OKAY? PLAY NICE. ♥
GO!
!

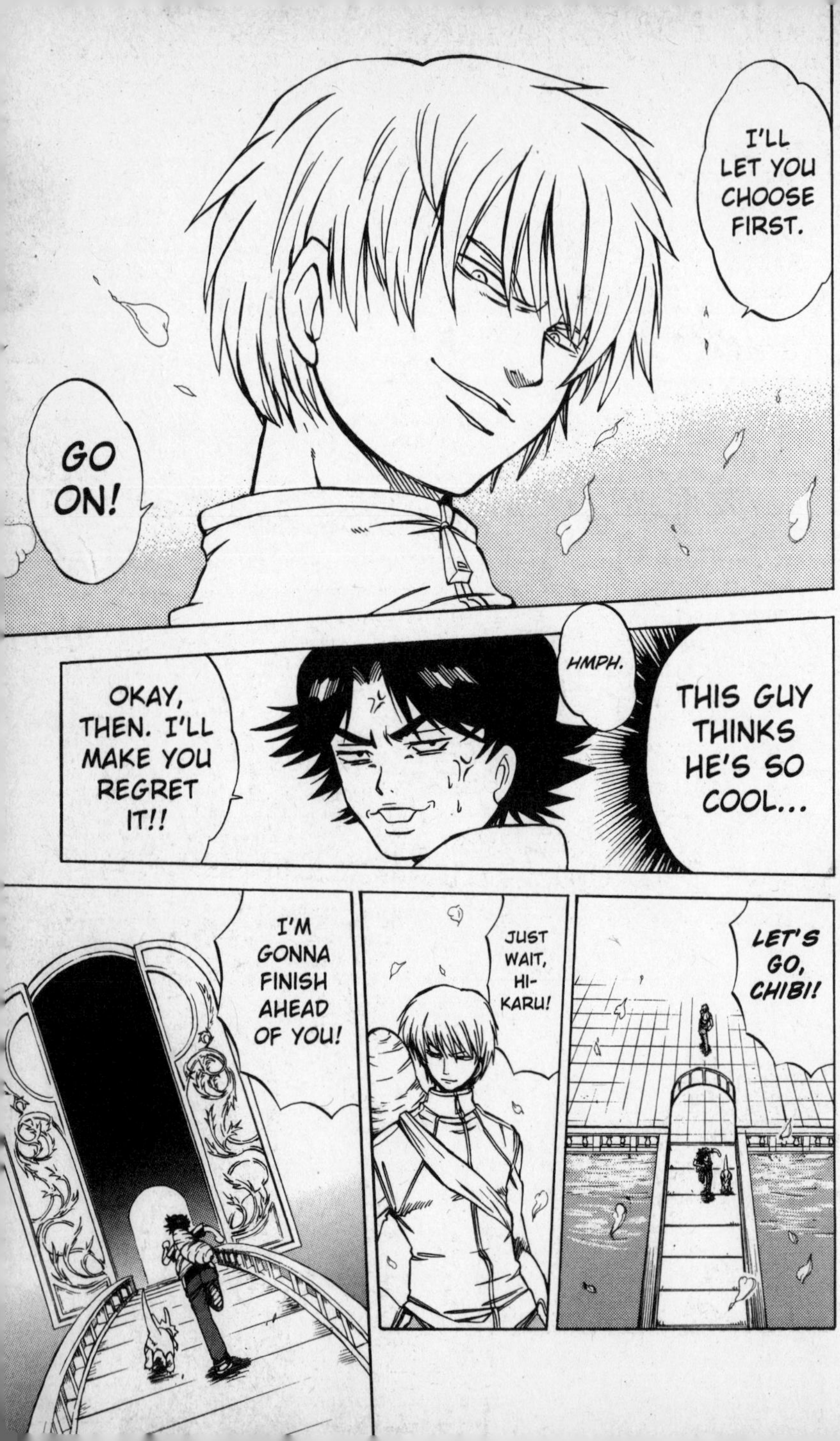
I'LL LET YOU CHOOSE FIRST.
GO ON!
HMPH.
THIS GUY THINKS HE'S SO COOL...
OKAY, THEN. I'LL MAKE YOU REGRET IT!!
LET'S GO, CHIBI!
JUST WAIT, HI-KARU!
I'M GONNA FINISH AHEAD OF YOU!

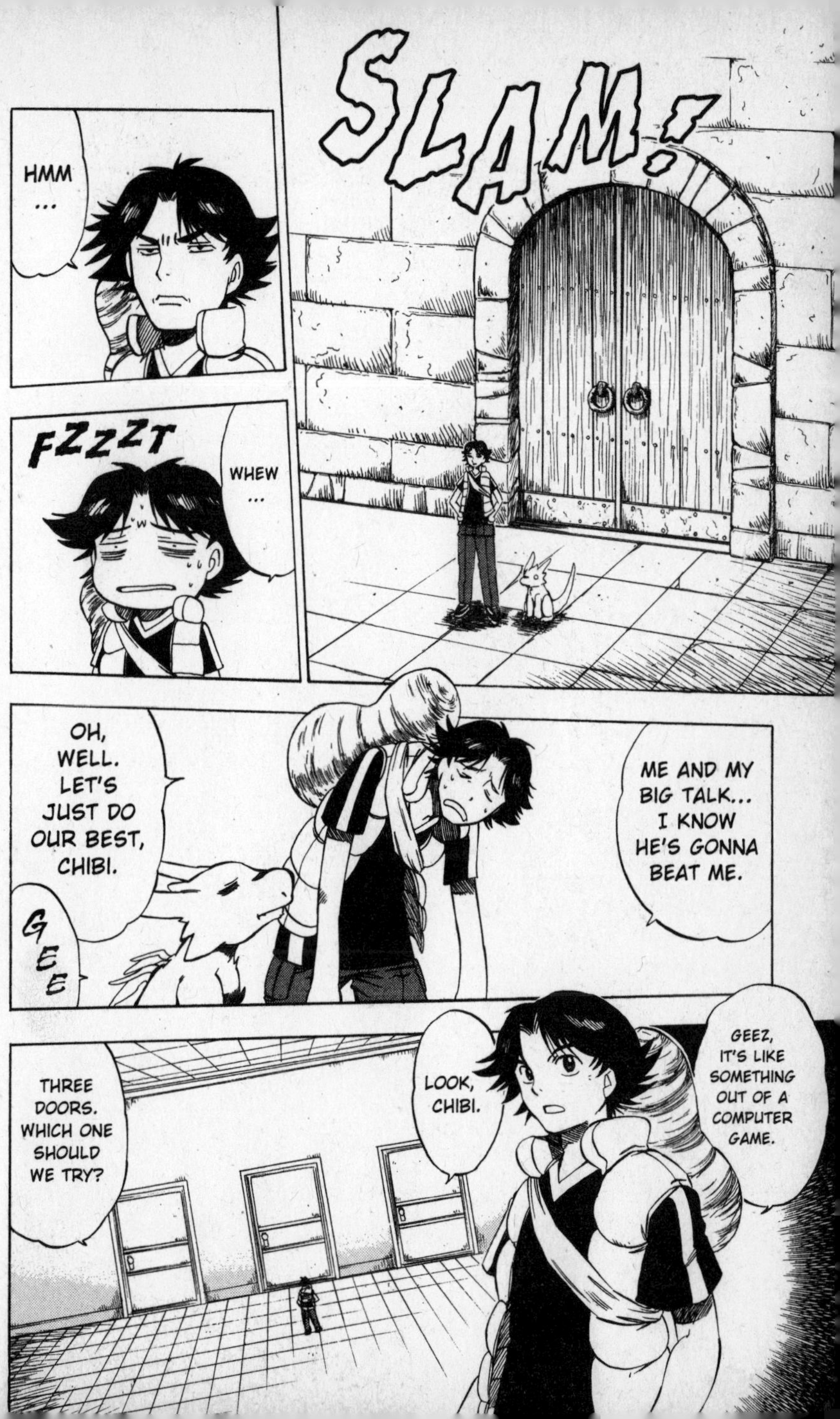
SLAM!
HMM ...
FZZZT
WHEW ...
ME AND MY BIG TALK... I KNOW HE'S GONNA BEAT ME.
OH, WELL. LET'S JUST DO OUR BEST, CHIBI.
GEE
GEEZ, IT'S LIKE SOMETHING OUT OF A COMPUTER GAME.
LOOK, CHIBI.
THREE DOORS. WHICH ONE SHOULD WE TRY?

READ THIS WAY

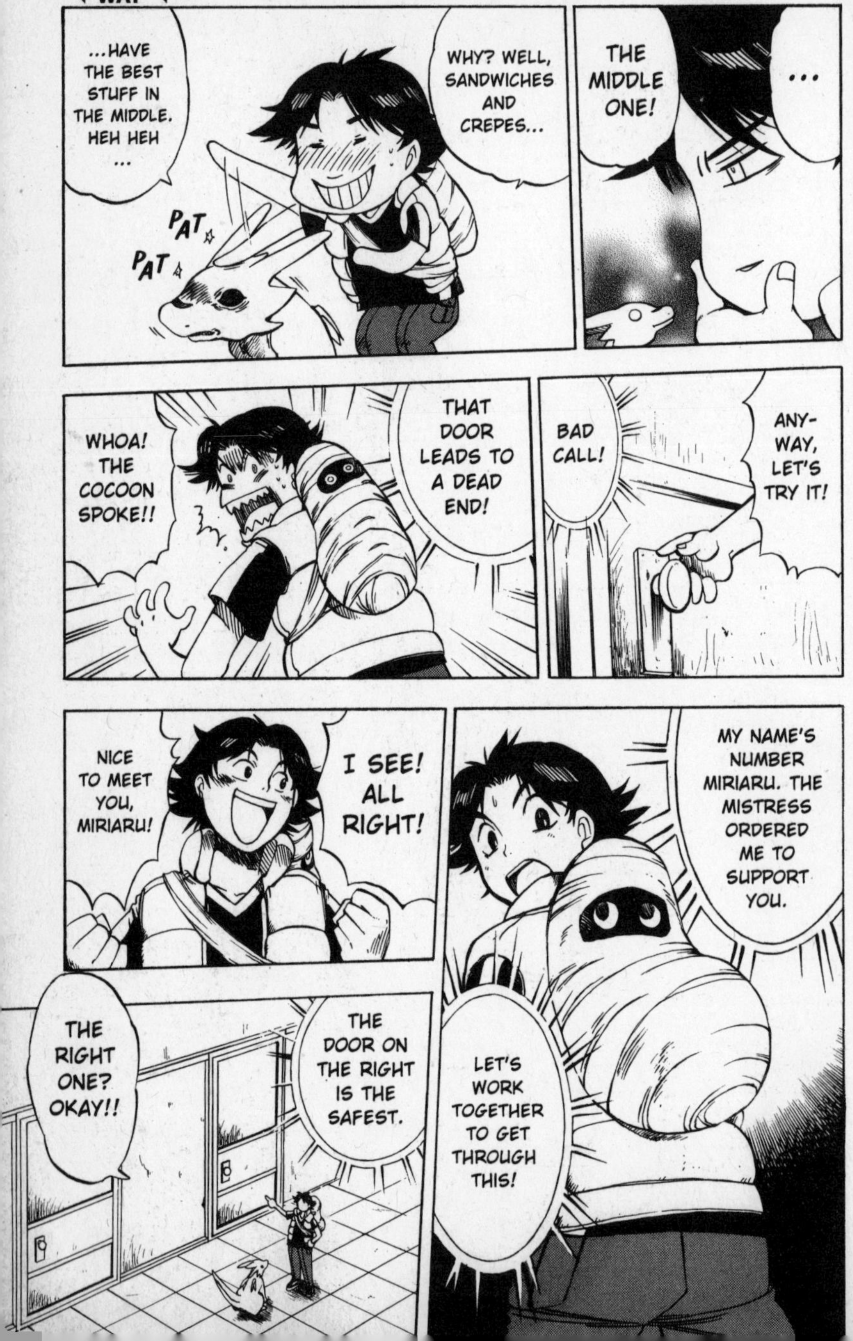
...
THE MIDDLE ONE!
WHY? WELL, SANDWICHES AND CREPES...
...HAVE THE BEST STUFF IN THE MIDDLE. HEH HEH ...
PAT
PAT
ANY-WAY, LET'S TRY IT!
BAD CALL!
THAT DOOR LEADS TO A DEAD END!
WHOA! THE COCOON SPOKE!!
MY NAME'S NUMBER MIRIARU. THE MISTRESS ORDERED ME TO SUPPORT YOU.
LET'S WORK TOGETHER TO GET THROUGH THIS!
I SEE! ALL RIGHT!
NICE TO MEET YOU, MIRIARU!
THE DOOR ON THE RIGHT IS THE SAFEST.
THE RIGHT ONE? OKAY!!

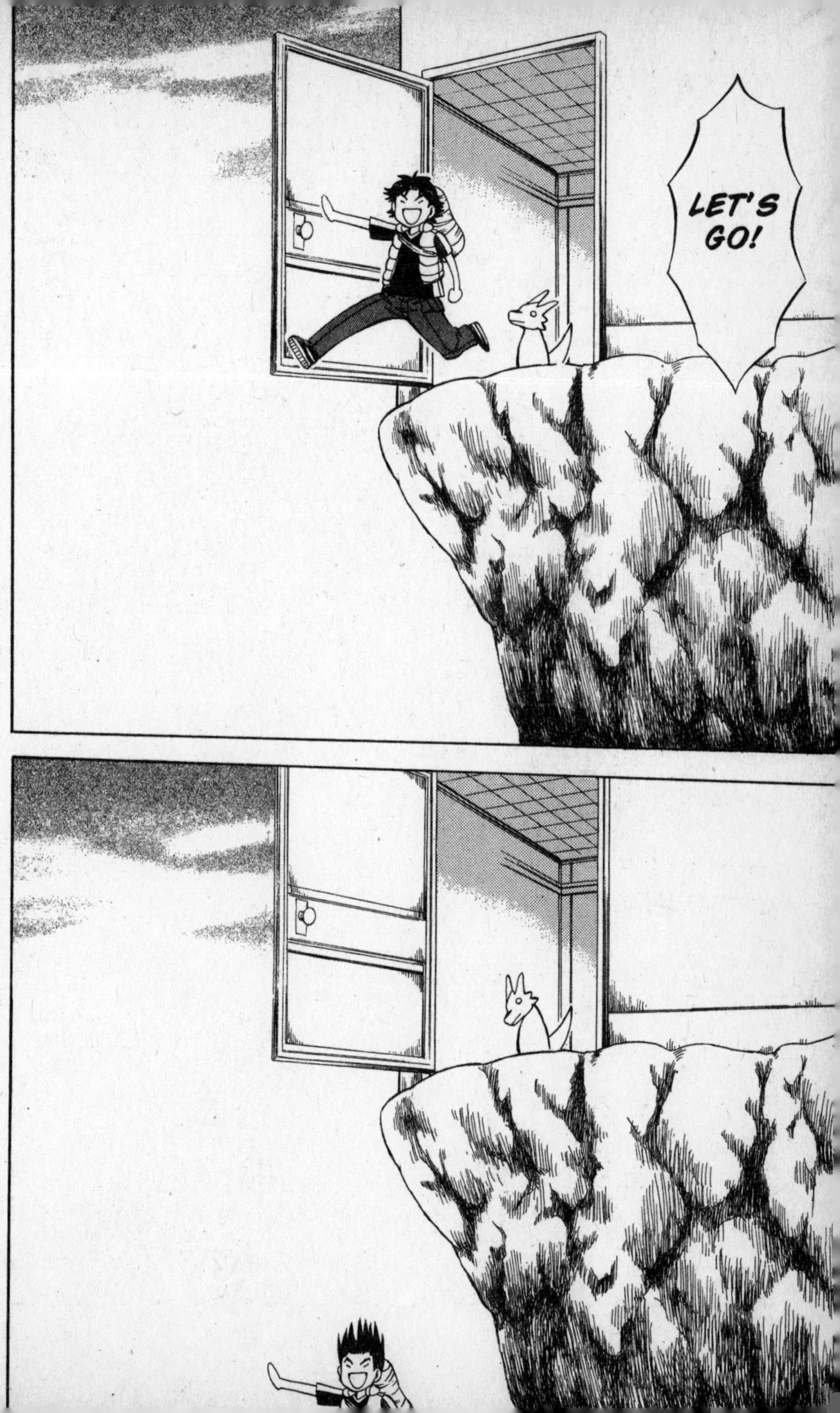
LET'S GO!

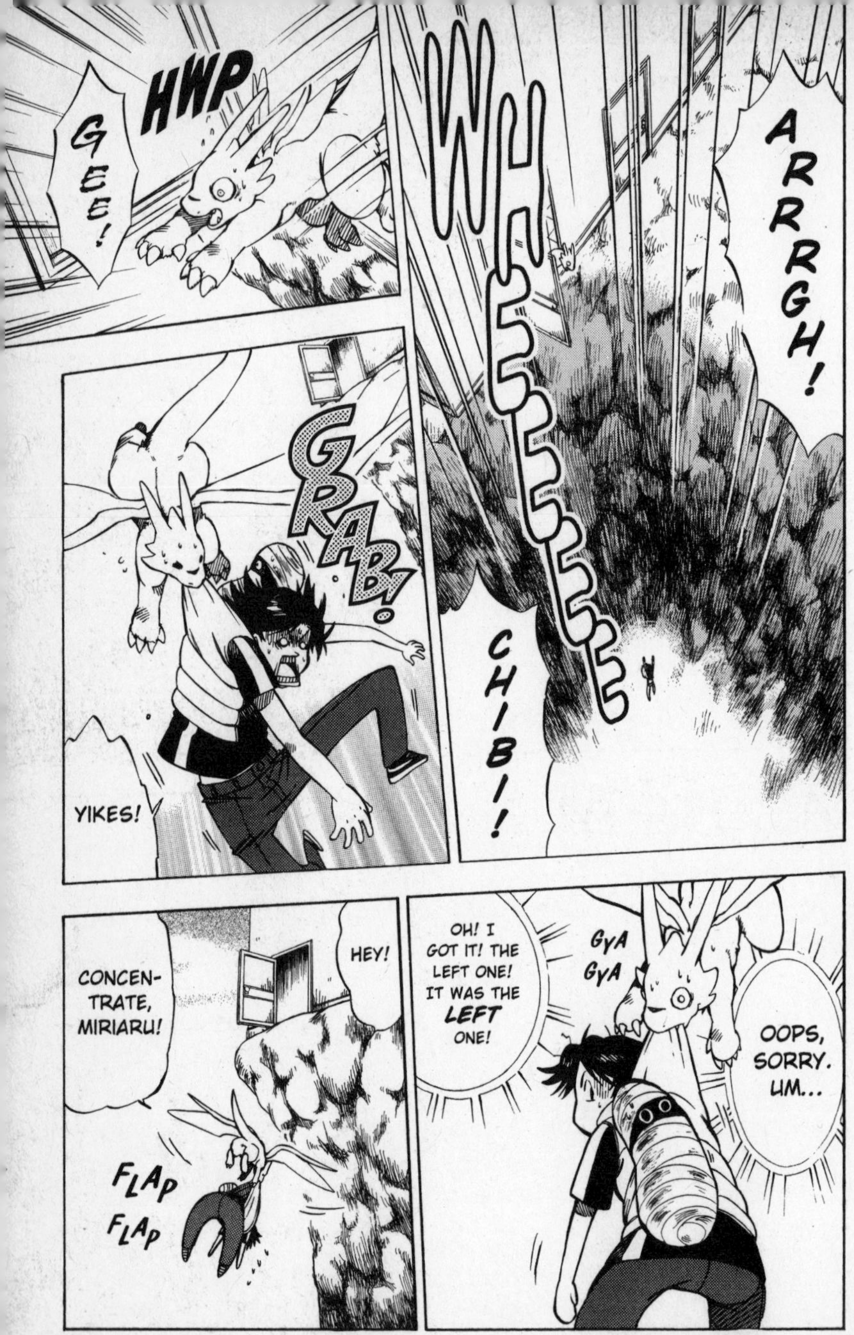
ARRRGH!
WHEEEEEEE
CHIBI!!
HWP
GEE!
GRAB!
YIKES!
GYA GYA
OOPS, SORRY. UM...
OH! I GOT IT! THE LEFT ONE! IT WAS THE **LEFT** ONE!
HEY!
CONCENTRATE, MIRIARU!
FLAP FLAP

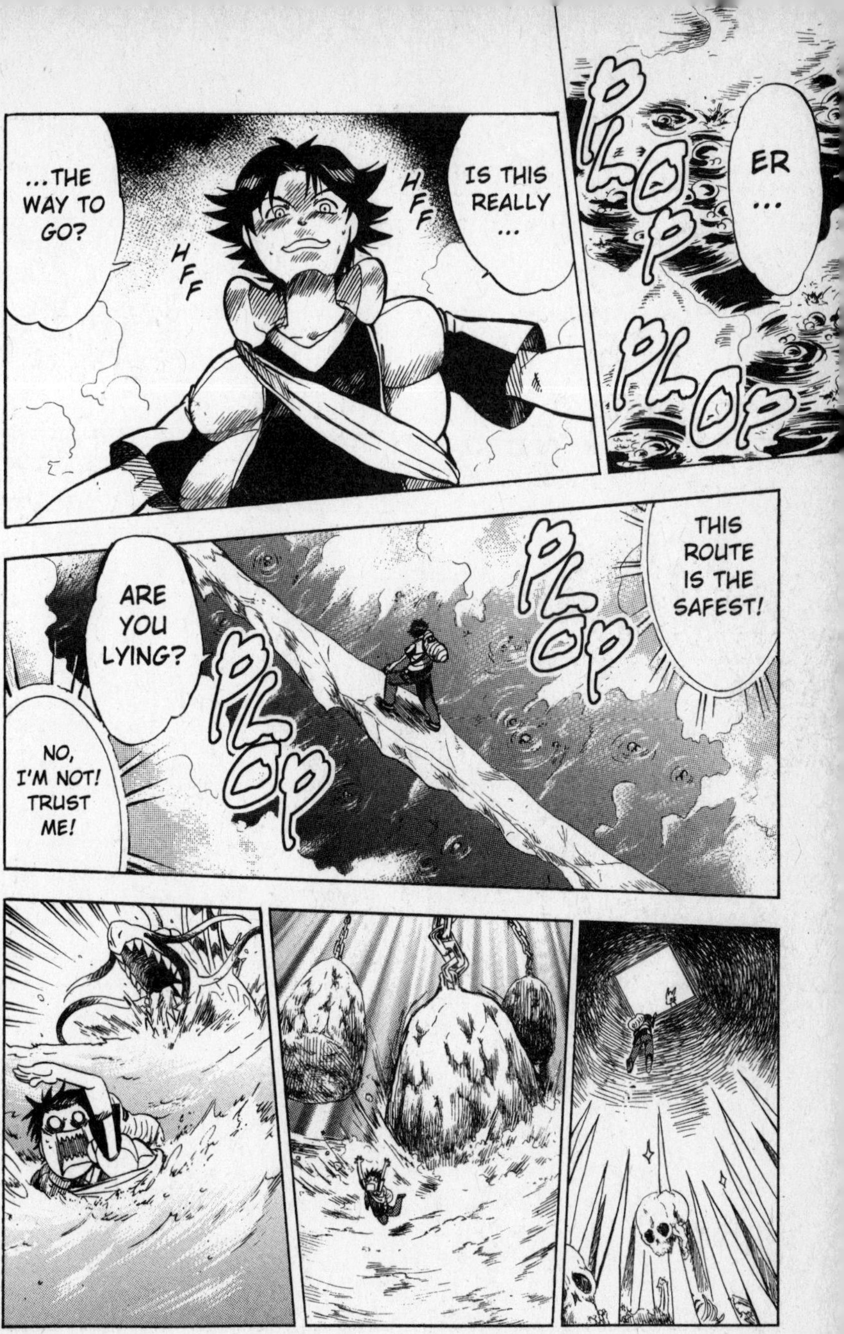
ER ...
PLOP
PLOP
IS THIS REALLY ...
HFF
...THE WAY TO GO?
HFF
THIS ROUTE IS THE SAFEST!
PLOP
ARE YOU LYING?
PLOP
NO, I'M NOT! TRUST ME!

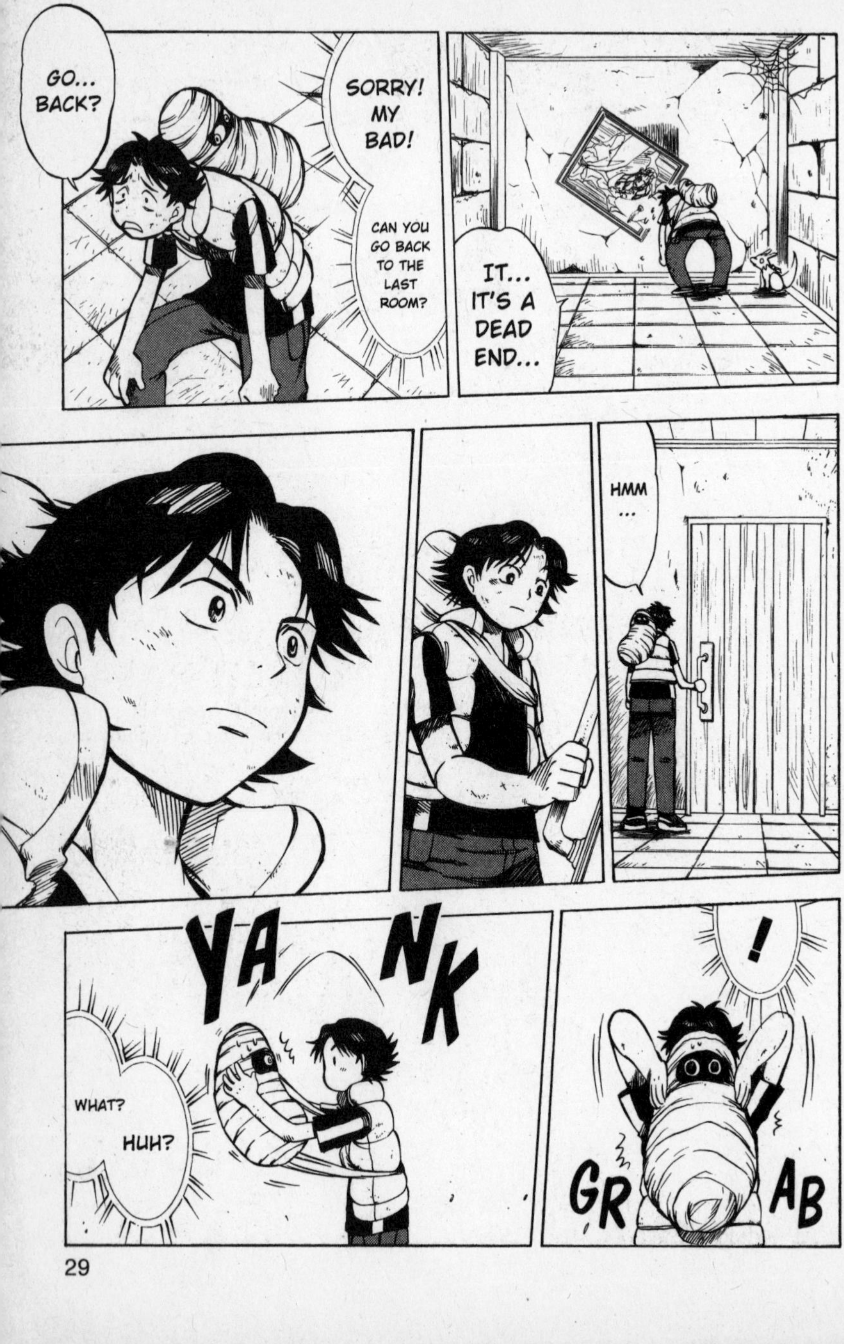

IT... IT'S A DEAD END...
SORRY! MY BAD!
CAN YOU GO BACK TO THE LAST ROOM?
GO... BACK?
HMM ...
!
GRAB
YANK
WHAT?
HUH?

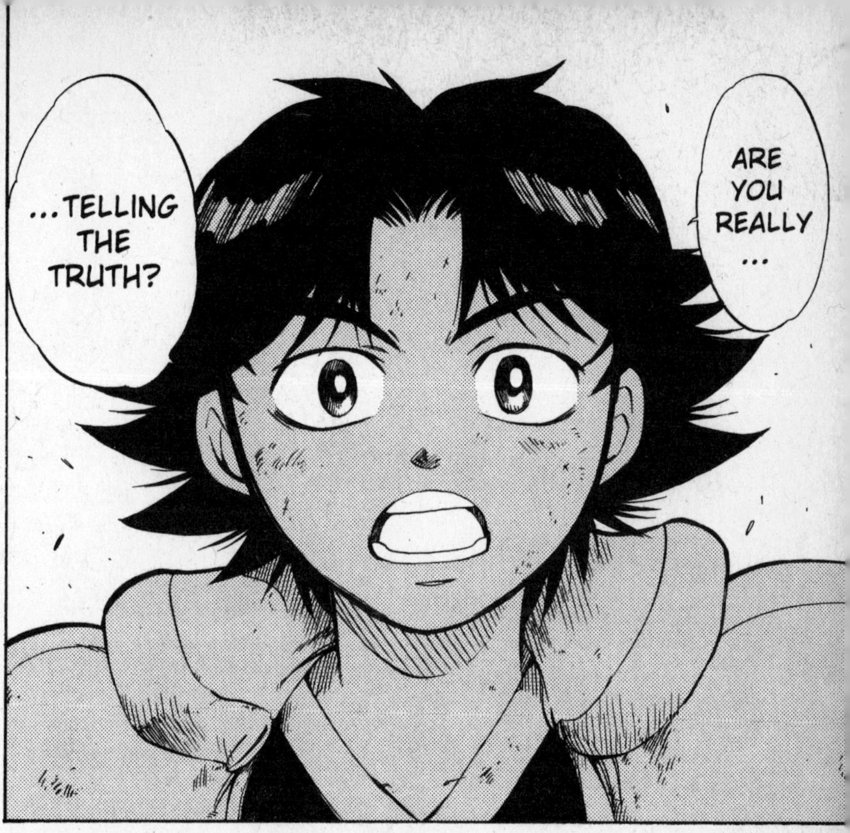
ARE YOU REALLY ...
...TELLING THE TRUTH?

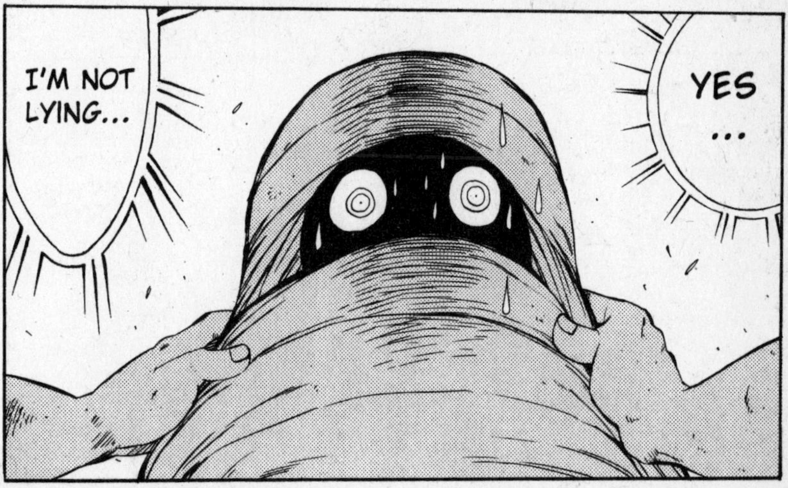
YES ...
I'M NOT LYING...

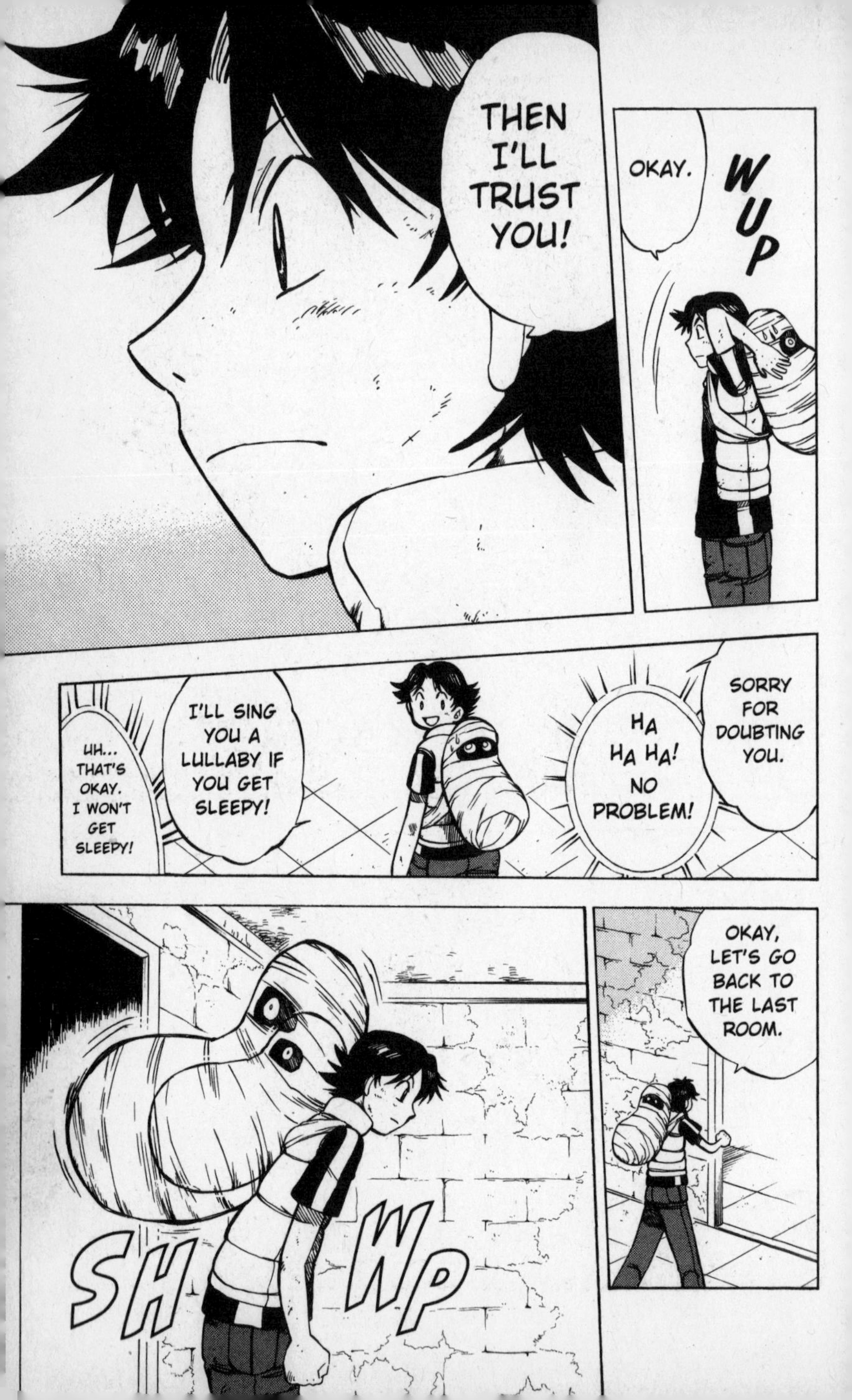
OKAY.
WUP
THEN I'LL TRUST YOU!
SORRY FOR DOUBTING YOU.
HA HA HA! NO PROBLEM!
I'LL SING YOU A LULLABY IF YOU GET SLEEPY!
UH... THAT'S OKAY. I WON'T GET SLEEPY!
OKAY, LET'S GO BACK TO THE LAST ROOM.
SHWP

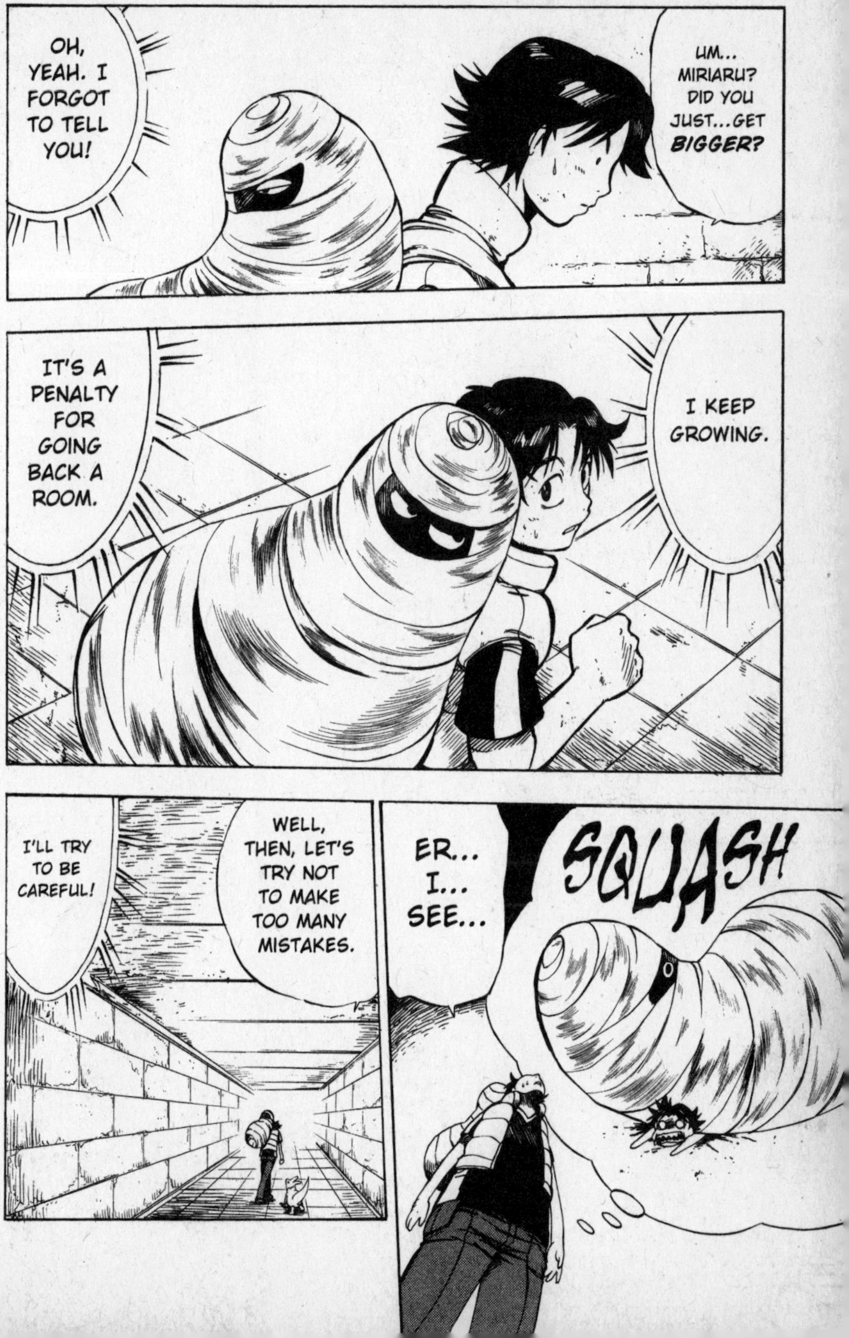
UM... MIRIARU? DID YOU JUST...GET BIGGER?
OH, YEAH. I FORGOT TO TELL YOU!
I KEEP GROWING.
IT'S A PENALTY FOR GOING BACK A ROOM.
SQUASH
ER... I... SEE...
WELL, THEN, LET'S TRY NOT TO MAKE TOO MANY MISTAKES.
I'LL TRY TO BE CAREFUL!

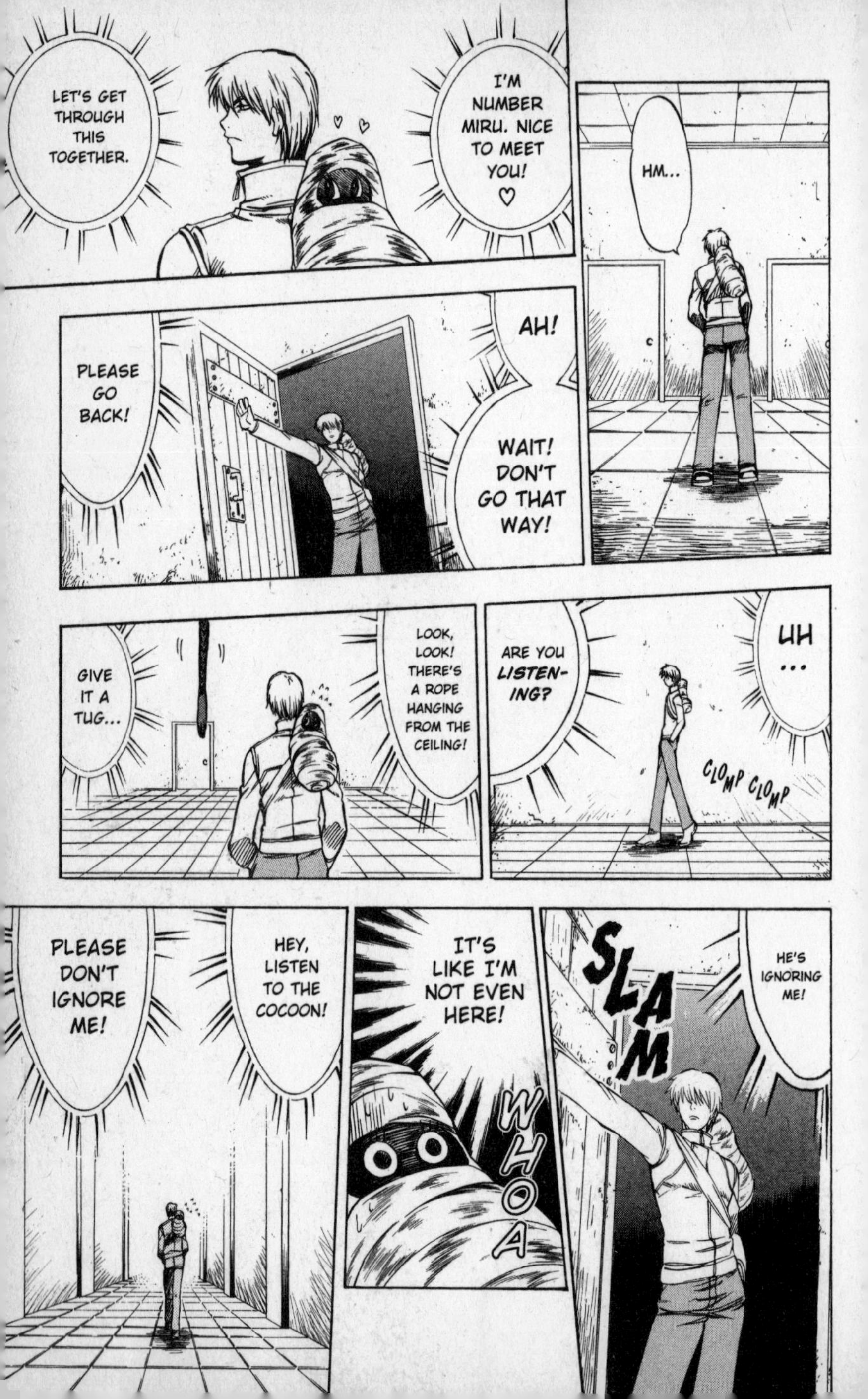
HM...
I'M NUMBER MIRU. NICE TO MEET YOU! ♡
LET'S GET THROUGH THIS TOGETHER.
AH!
WAIT! DON'T GO THAT WAY!
PLEASE GO BACK!
UH...
ARE YOU *LISTENING?*
CLOMP CLOMP
LOOK, LOOK! THERE'S A ROPE HANGING FROM THE CEILING!
GIVE IT A TUG...
HE'S IGNORING ME!
SLAM
IT'S LIKE I'M NOT EVEN HERE!
WHOA
HEY, LISTEN TO THE COCOON!
PLEASE DON'T IGNORE ME!

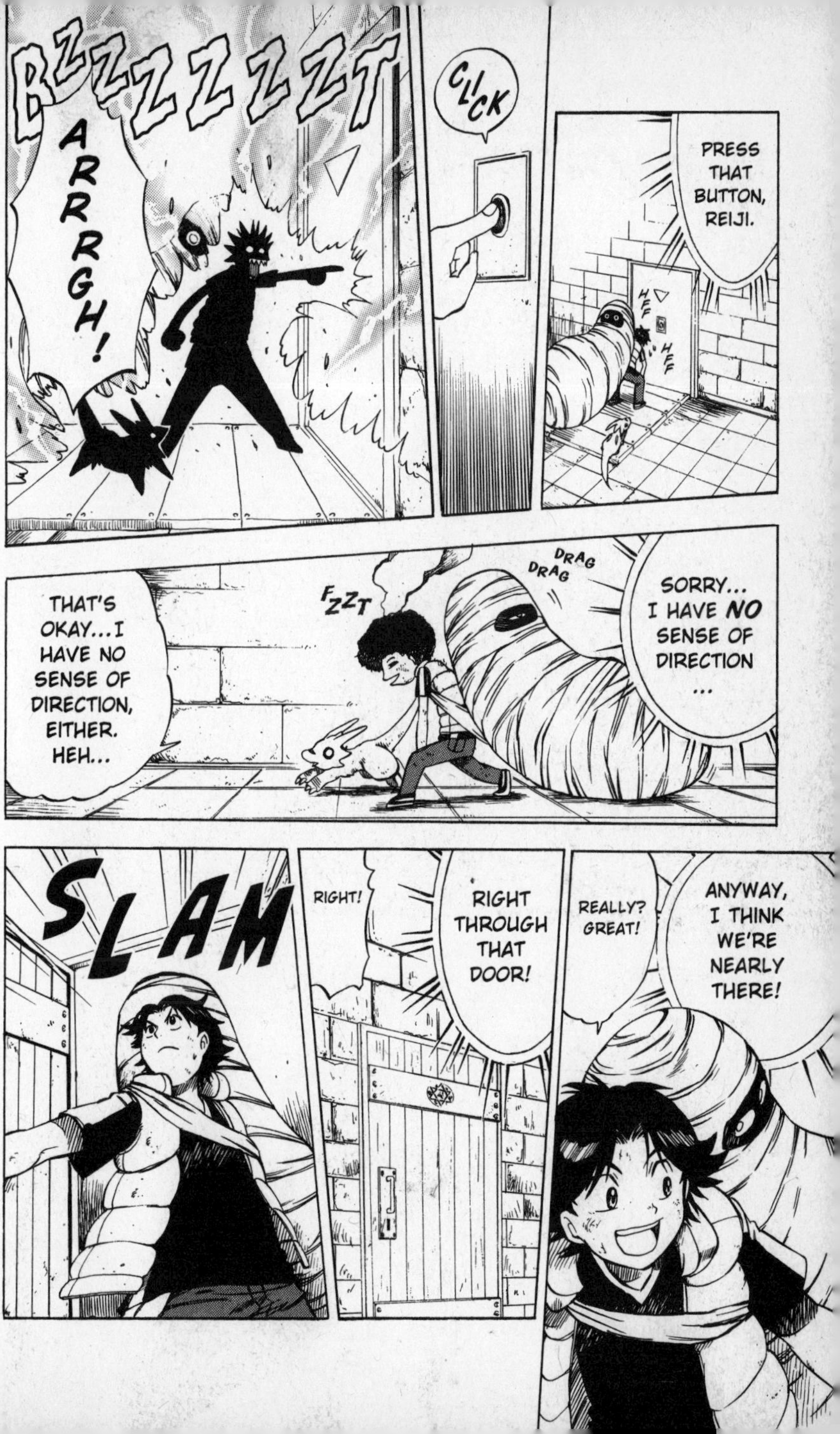
PRESS THAT BUTTON, REIJI.
HFF
HFF
CLICK
BZZZZZZZT
ARRRGH!
SORRY... I HAVE **NO** SENSE OF DIRECTION ...
DRAG DRAG
FZZT
THAT'S OKAY...I HAVE NO SENSE OF DIRECTION, EITHER. HEH...
ANYWAY, I THINK WE'RE NEARLY THERE!
REALLY? GREAT!
RIGHT THROUGH THAT DOOR!
RIGHT!
SLAM

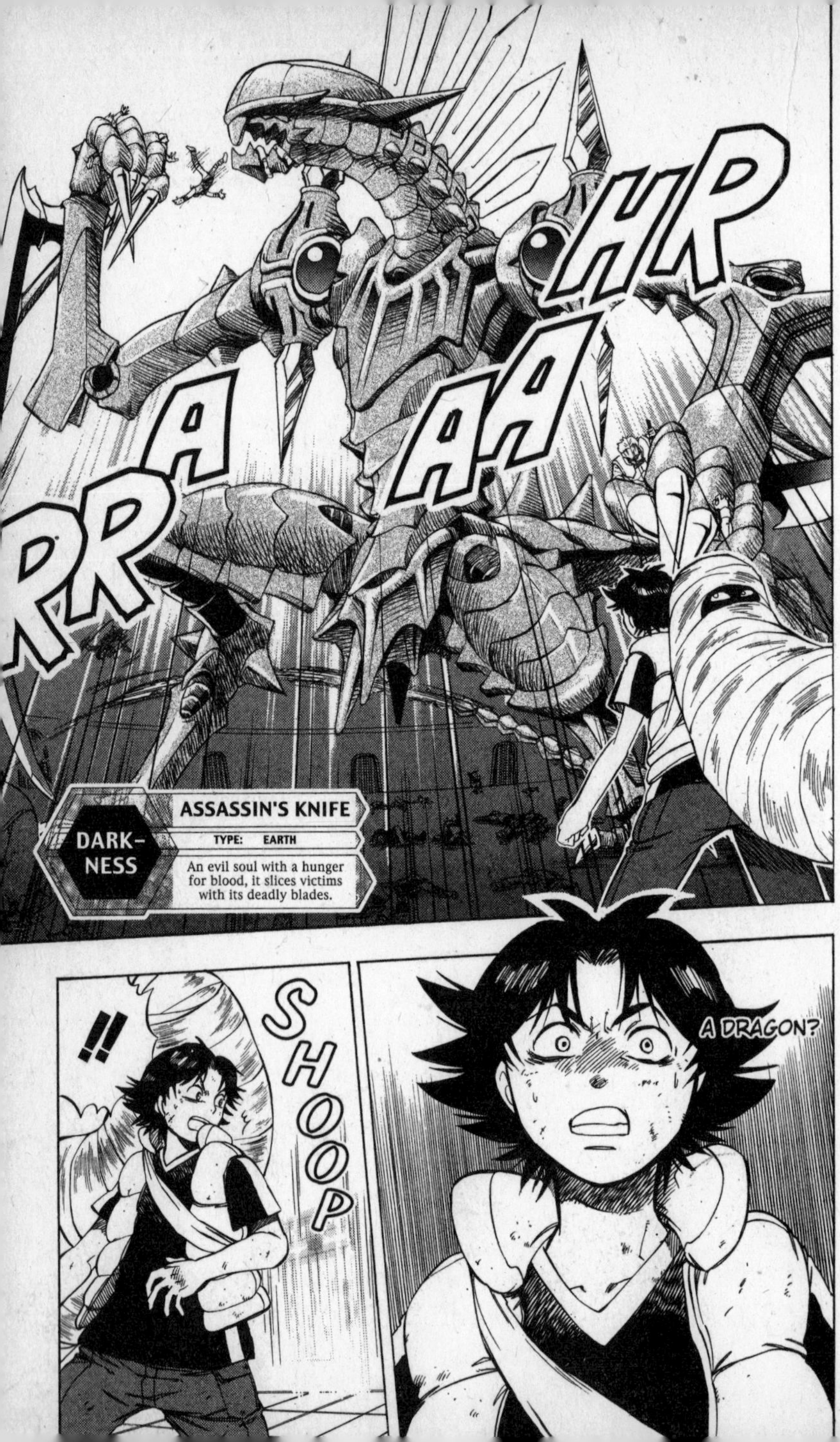
RRAAAAHR
ASSASSIN'S KNIFE
DARK-NESS
TYPE: EARTH
An evil soul with a hunger for blood, it slices victims with its deadly blades.
A DRAGON?
!!
SHOOP

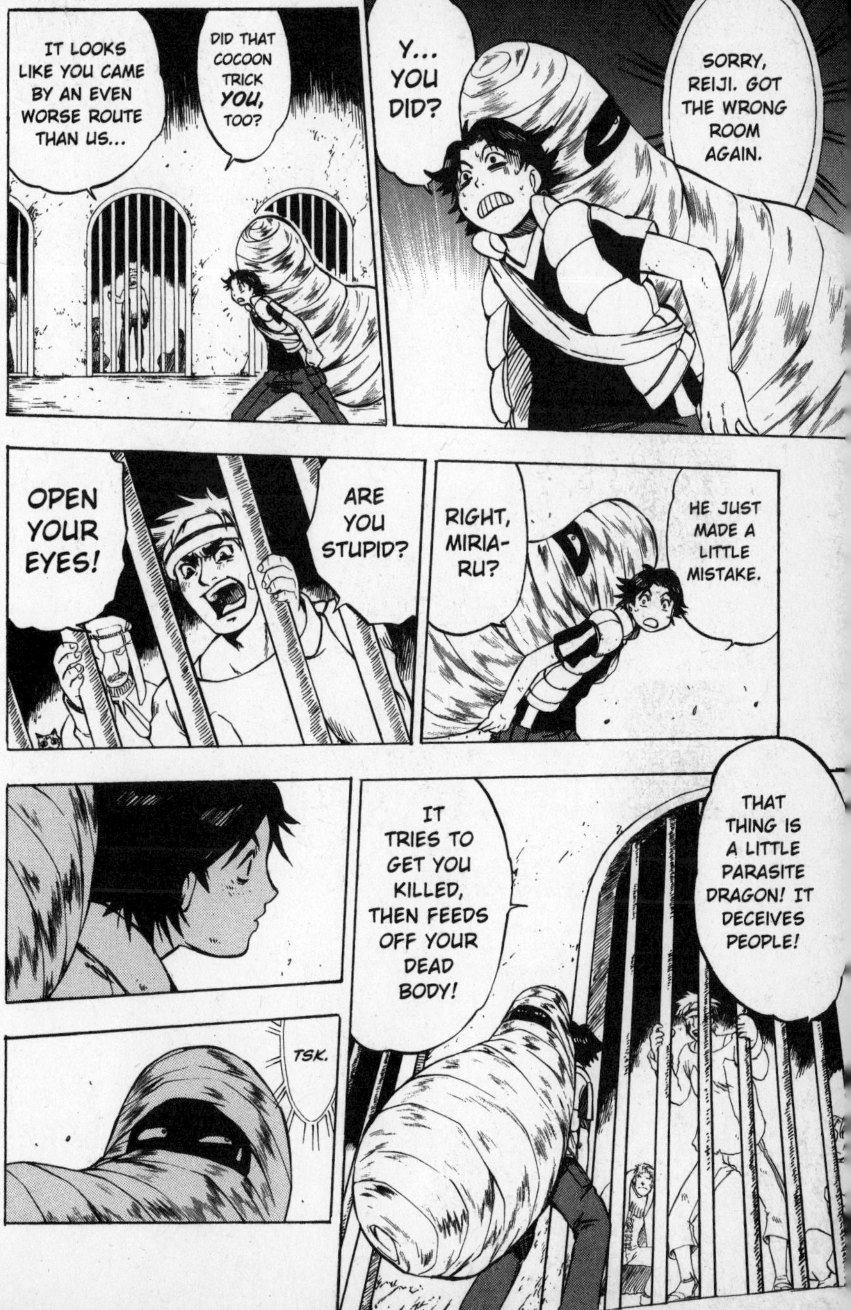
SORRY, REIJI. GOT THE WRONG ROOM AGAIN.
Y... YOU DID?
DID THAT COCOON TRICK *YOU,* TOO?
IT LOOKS LIKE YOU CAME BY AN EVEN WORSE ROUTE THAN US...
HE JUST MADE A LITTLE MISTAKE.
RIGHT, MIRIA-RU?
ARE YOU STUPID?
OPEN YOUR EYES!
THAT THING IS A LITTLE PARASITE DRAGON! IT DECEIVES PEOPLE!
IT TRIES TO GET YOU KILLED, THEN FEEDS OFF YOUR DEAD BODY!
TSK.

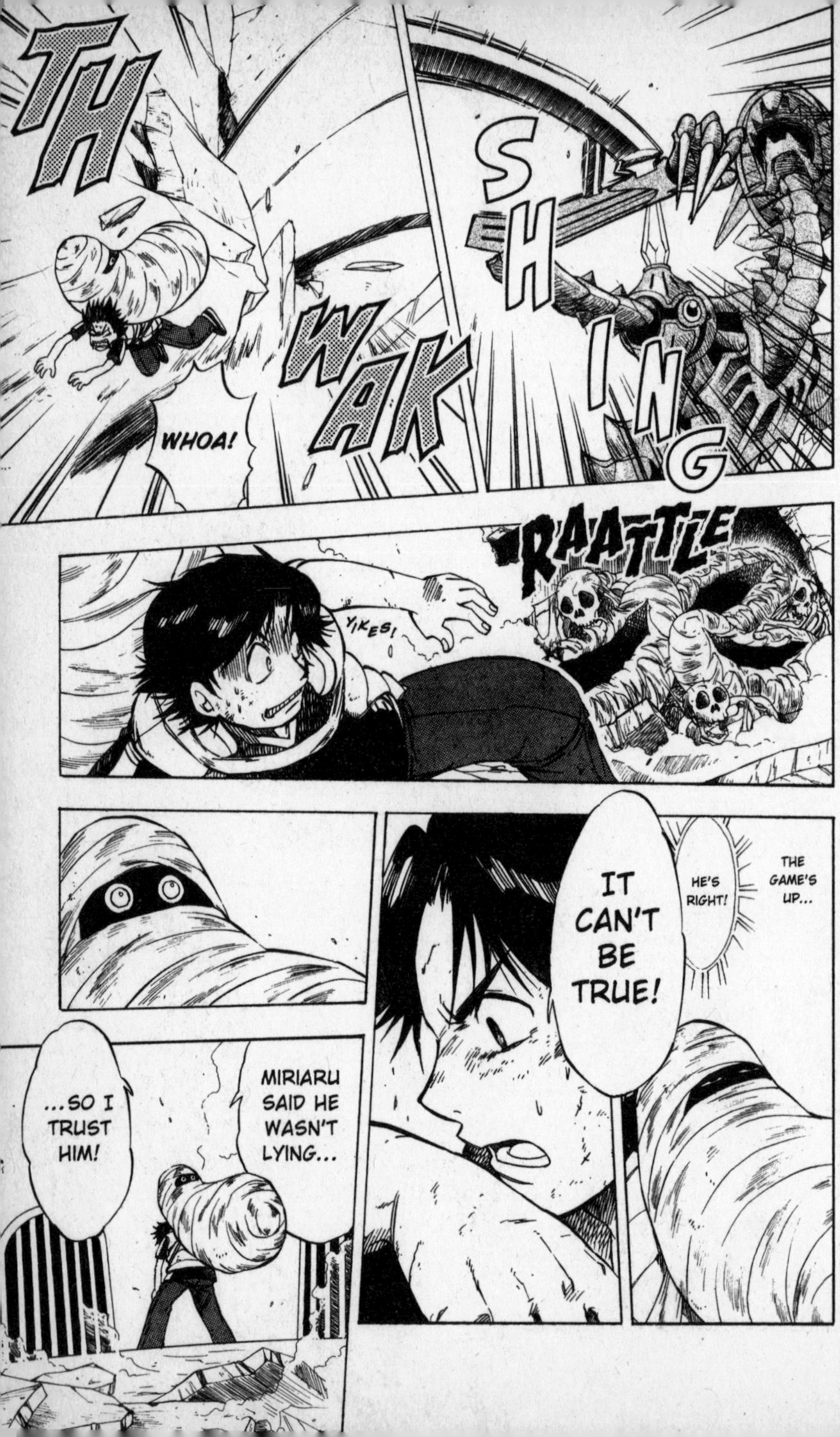
SHING
TH
WAK
WHOA!
RAATTLE
YIKES!
THE GAME'S UP...
HE'S RIGHT!
IT CAN'T BE TRUE!
MIRIARU SAID HE WASN'T LYING...
...SO I TRUST HIM!

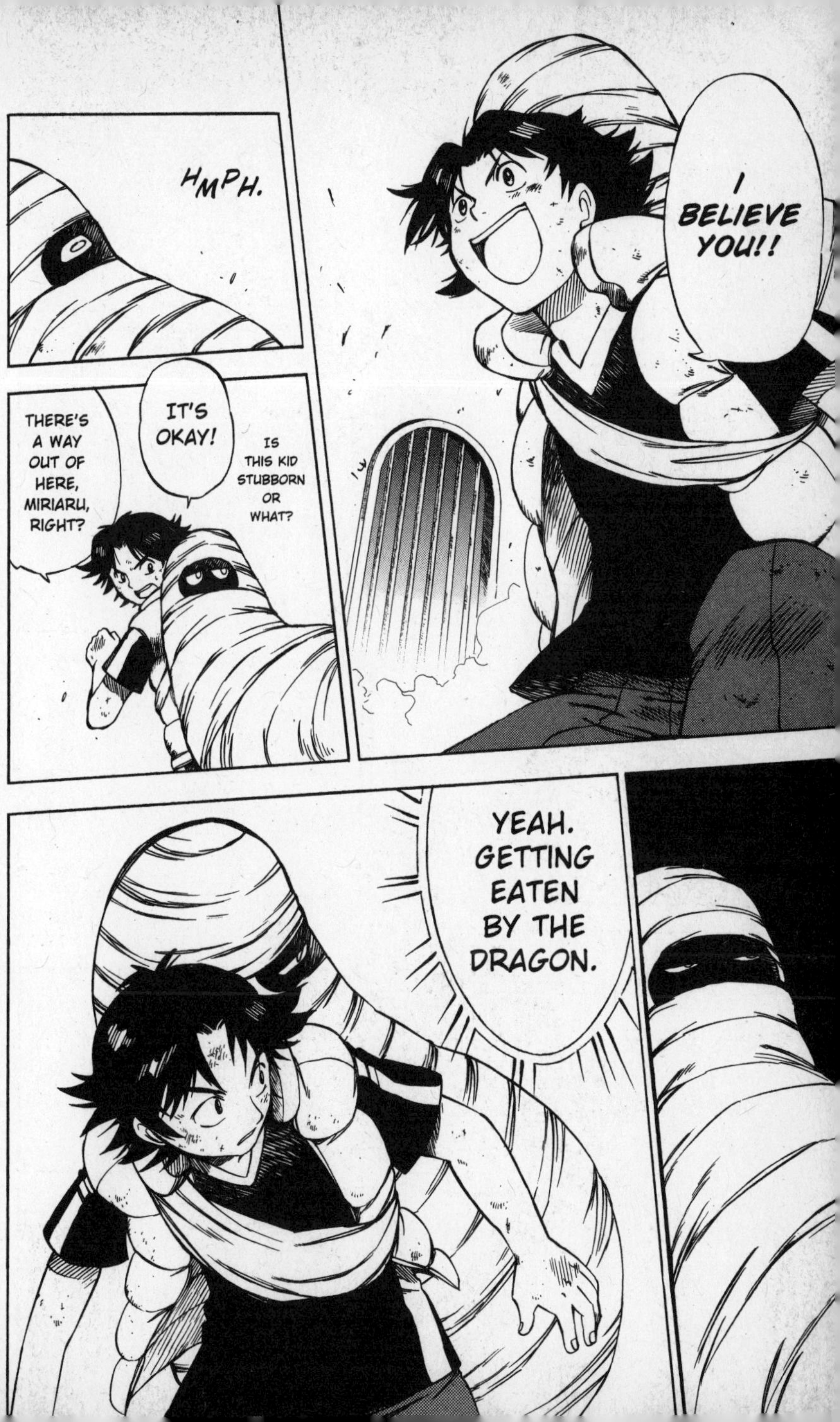
I BELIEVE YOU!!
HMPH.
IS THIS KID STUBBORN OR WHAT?
IT'S OKAY!
THERE'S A WAY OUT OF HERE, MIRIARU, RIGHT?
YEAH. GETTING EATEN BY THE DRAGON.

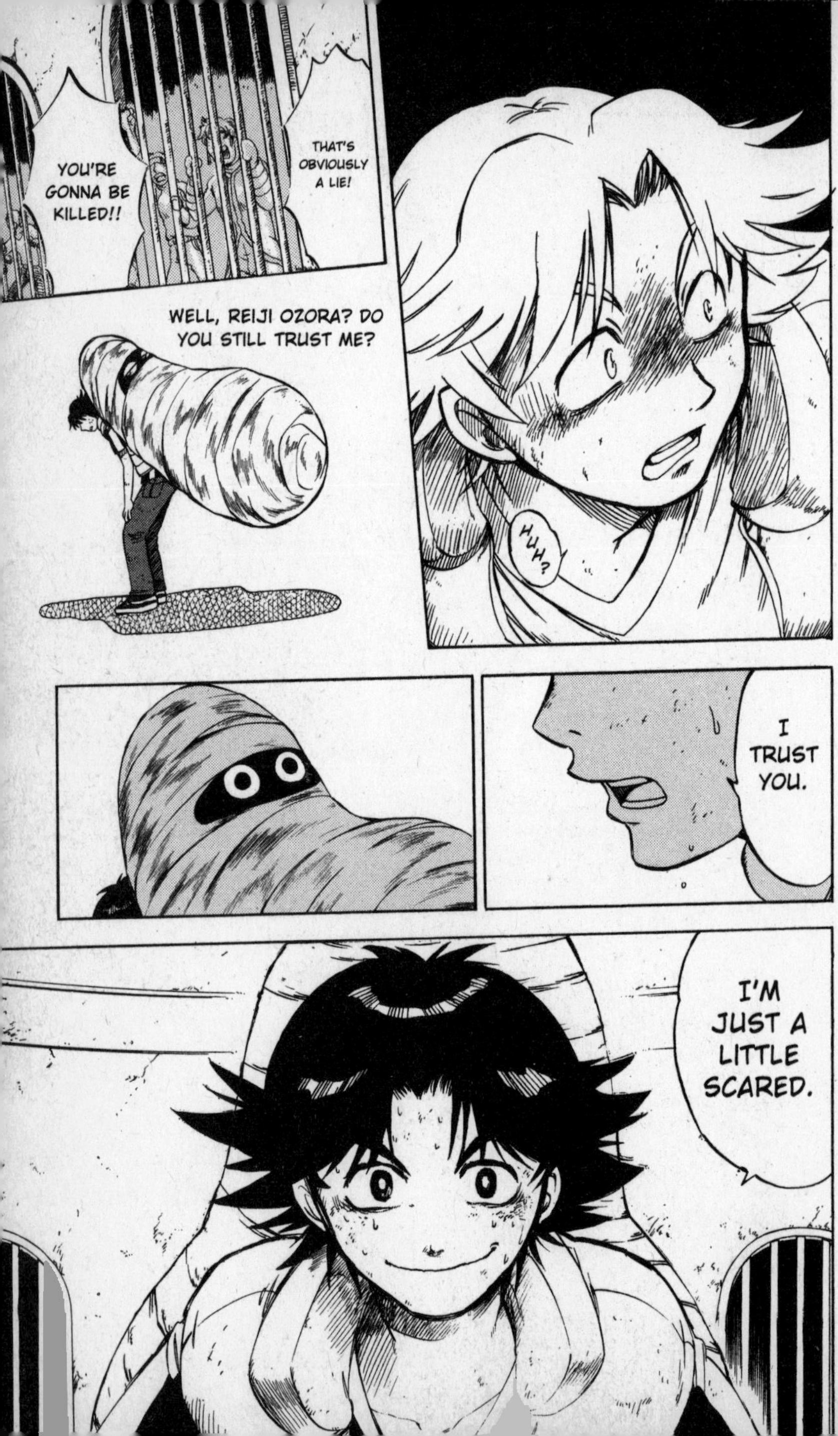
HUH?
THAT'S OBVIOUSLY A LIE!
YOU'RE GONNA BE KILLED!!
WELL, REIJI OZORA? DO YOU STILL TRUST ME?
I TRUST YOU.
I'M JUST A LITTLE SCARED.

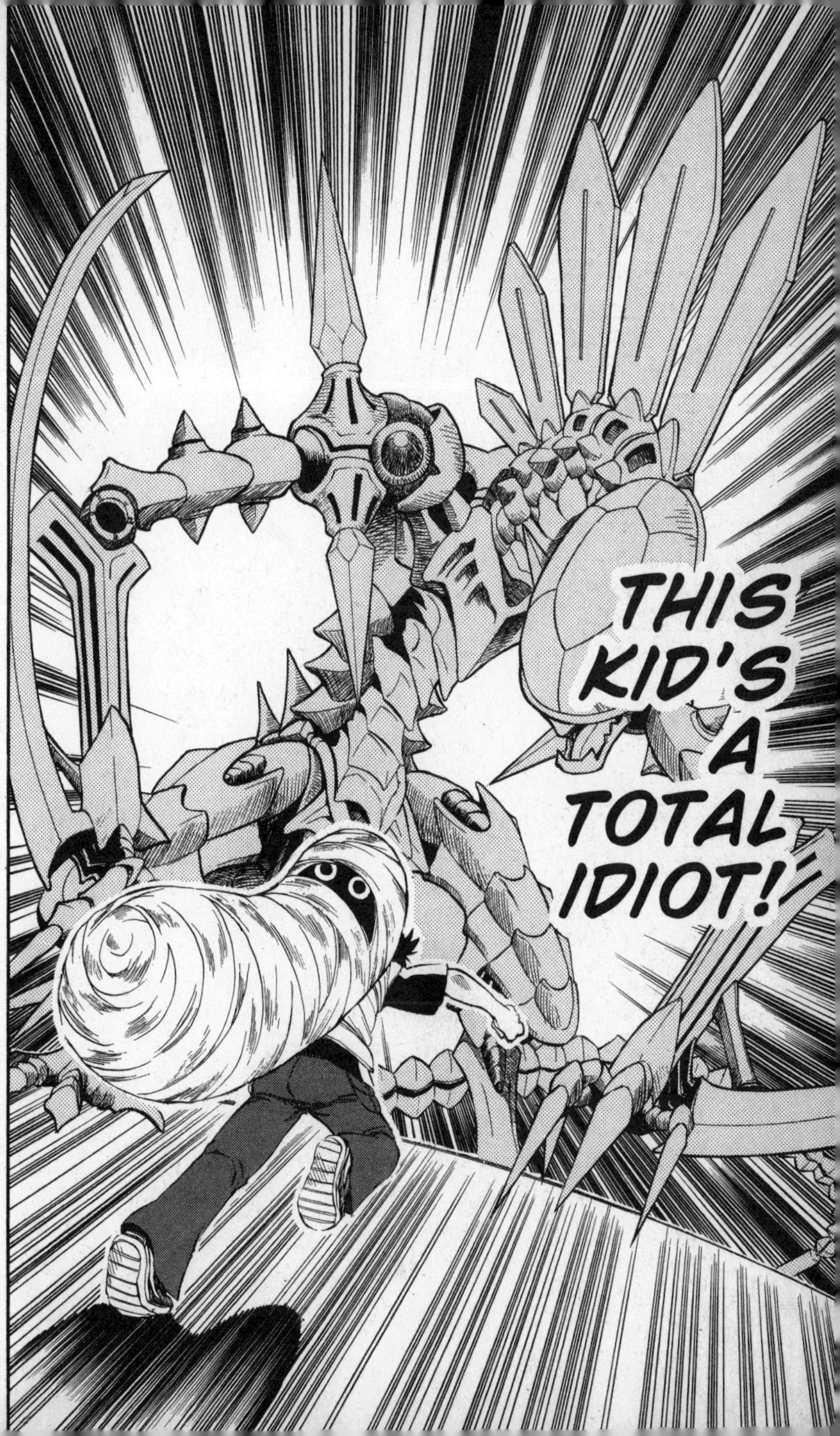
THIS KID'S A TOTAL IDIOT!

READ THIS WAY

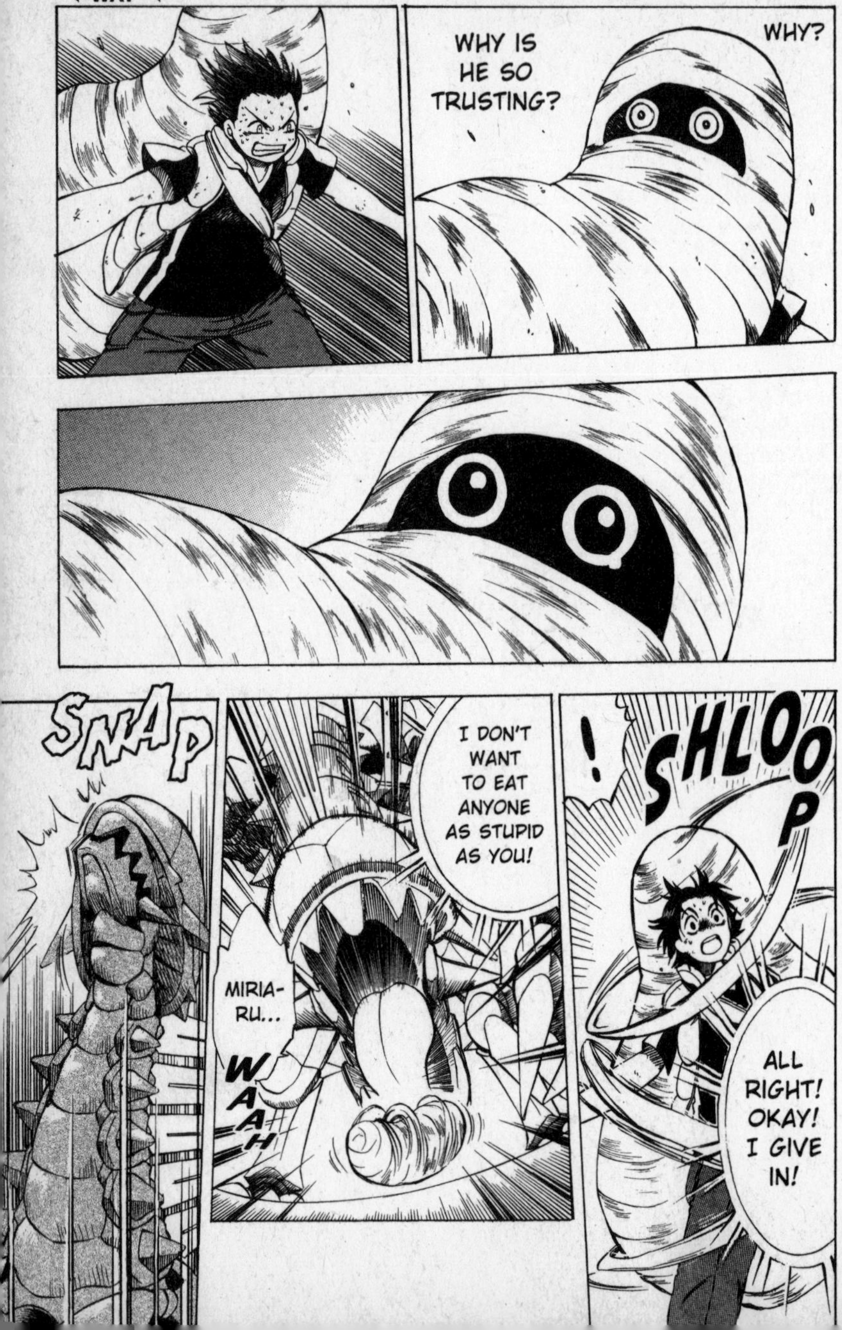
WHY?
WHY IS HE SO TRUSTING?
SHLOOP
!
ALL RIGHT! OKAY! I GIVE IN!
I DON'T WANT TO EAT ANYONE AS STUPID AS YOU!
MIRIA-RU...
WAAH
SNAP

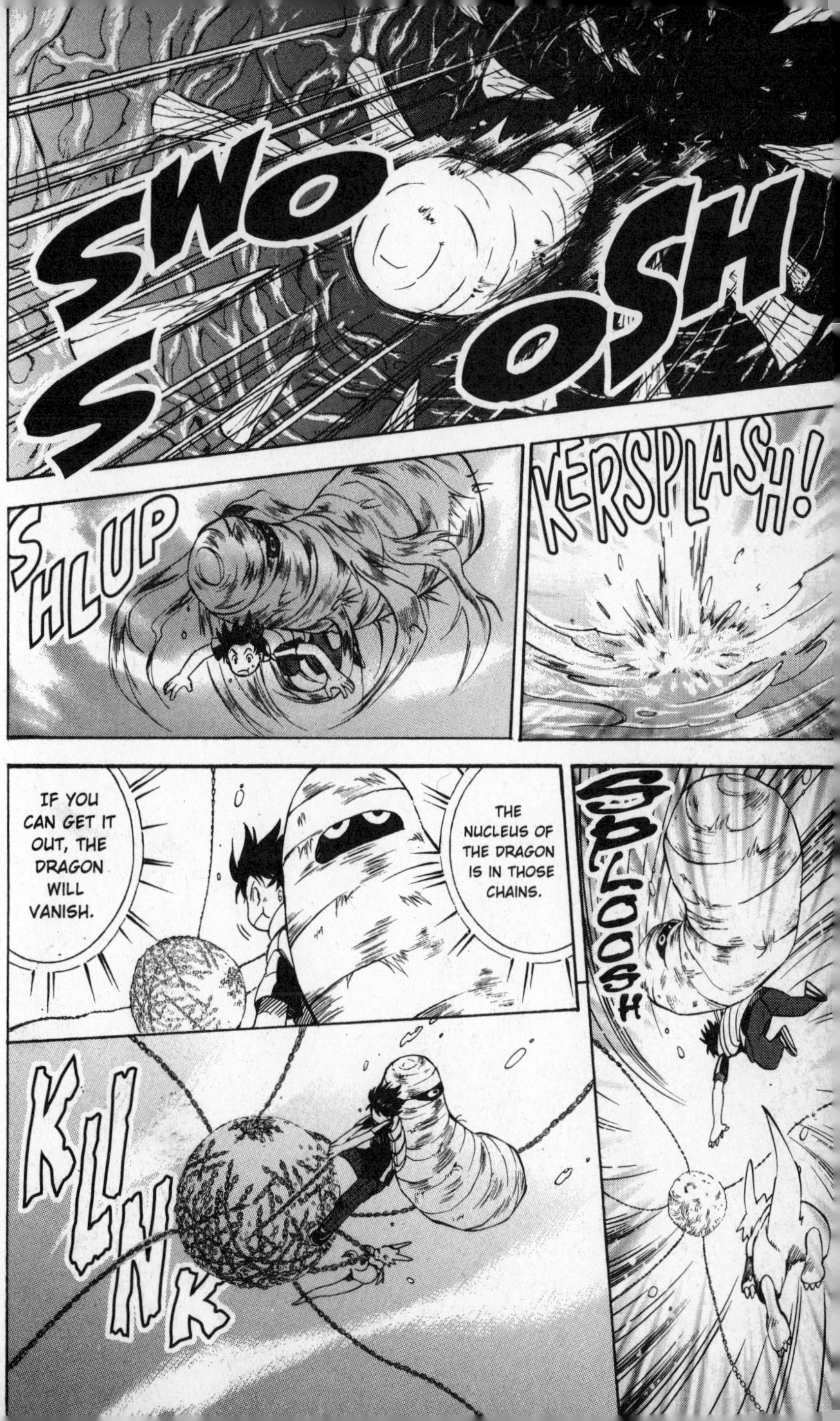
SWOOSH
KERSPLASH!
SHLUP
SPLOOOSH
THE NUCLEUS OF THE DRAGON IS IN THOSE CHAINS.
IF YOU CAN GET IT OUT, THE DRAGON WILL VANISH.
KLINK

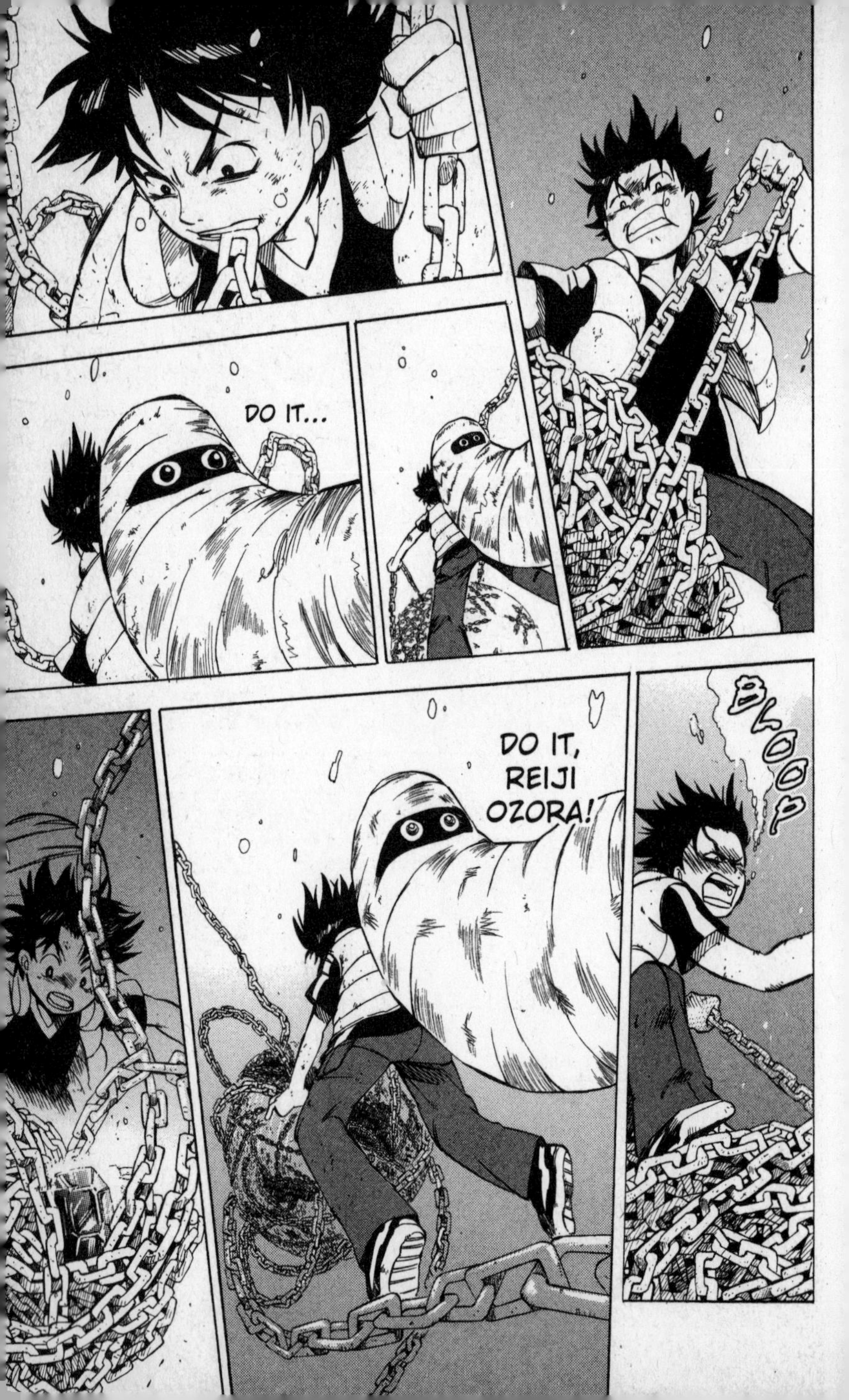
DO IT...
BLOOOP
DO IT, REIJI OZORA!

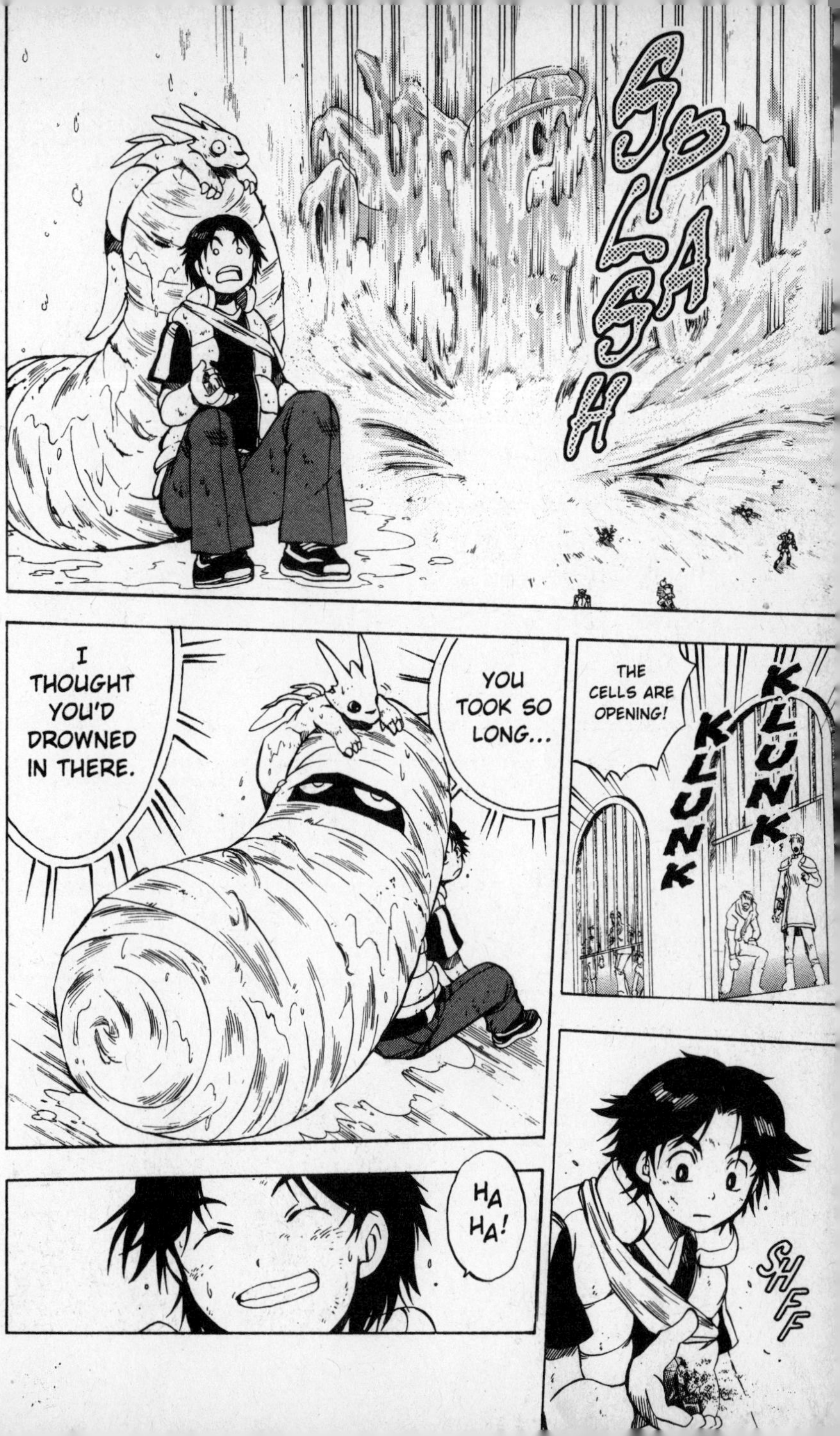
SPLASH
KLUNK KLUNK
THE CELLS ARE OPENING!
KLUNK
YOU TOOK SO LONG...
I THOUGHT YOU'D DROWNED IN THERE.
SHFF
HA HA!

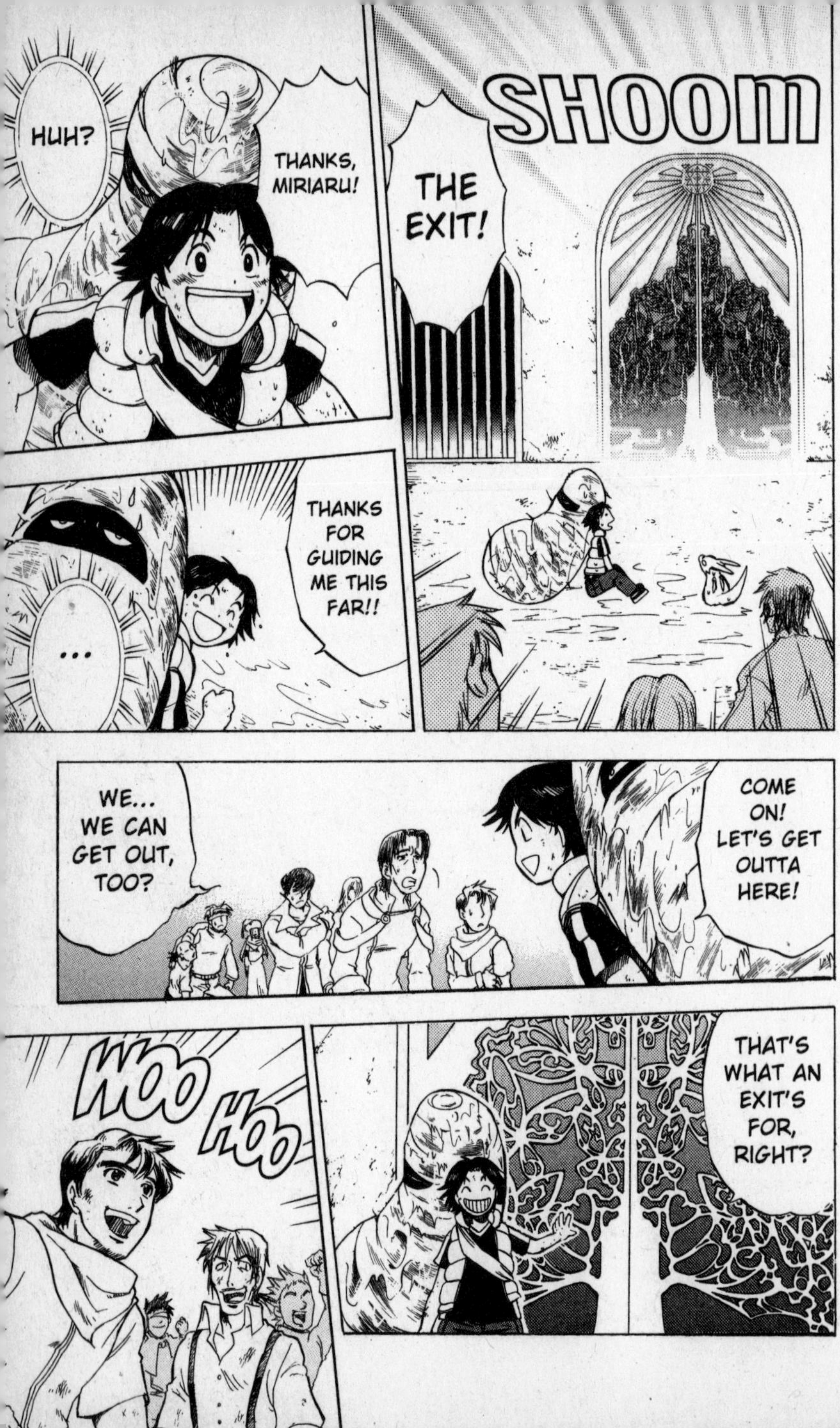
SHOOM
THE EXIT!
THANKS, MIRIARU!
HUH?
THANKS FOR GUIDING ME THIS FAR!!
...
COME ON! LET'S GET OUTTA HERE!
WE... WE CAN GET OUT, TOO?
THAT'S WHAT AN EXIT'S FOR, RIGHT?
WOO HOO

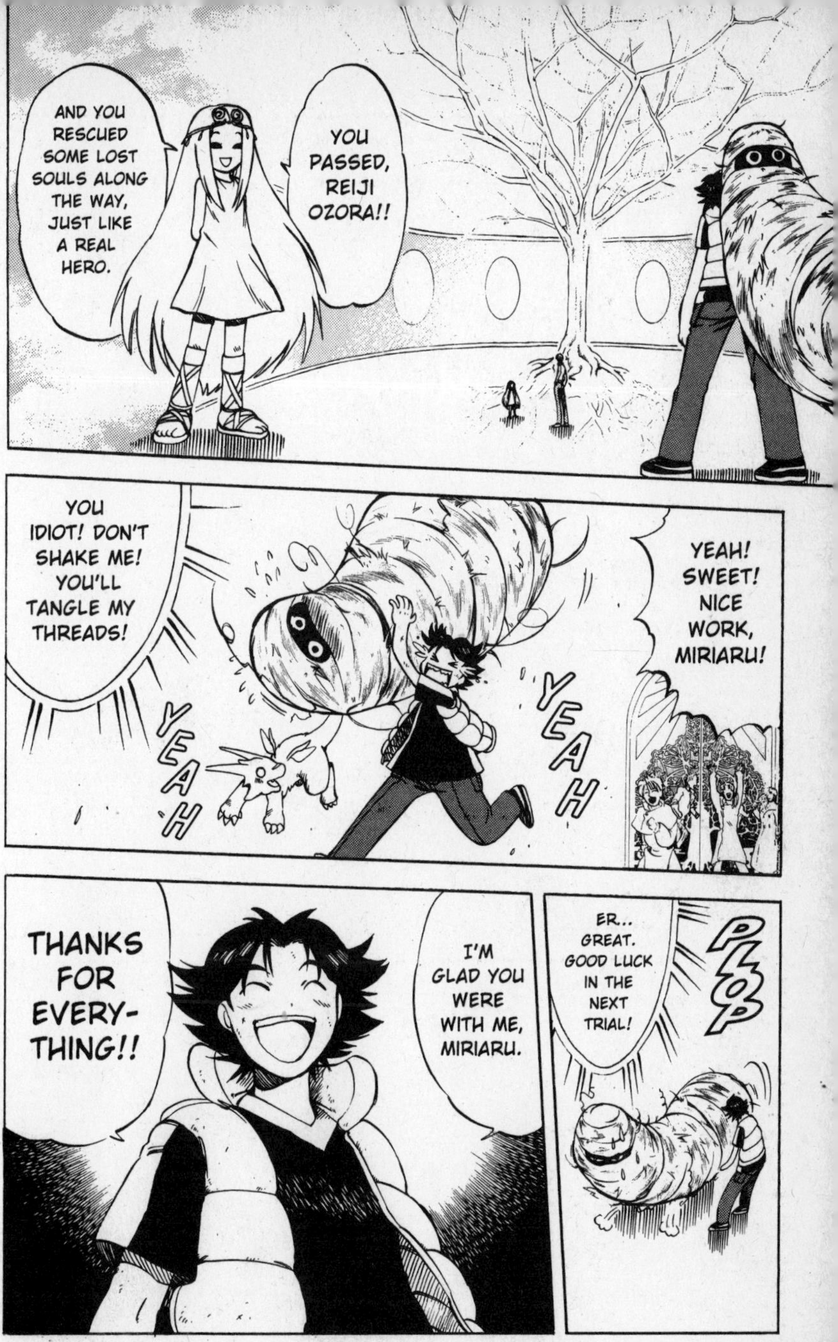
YOU PASSED, REIJI OZORA!!
AND YOU RESCUED SOME LOST SOULS ALONG THE WAY, JUST LIKE A REAL HERO.
YEAH! SWEET! NICE WORK, MIRIARU!
YEAH
YOU IDIOT! DON'T SHAKE ME! YOU'LL TANGLE MY THREADS!
YEAH
ER... GREAT. GOOD LUCK IN THE NEXT TRIAL!
PLOP
I'M GLAD YOU WERE WITH ME, MIRIARU.
THANKS FOR EVERY-THING!!

READ THIS WAY

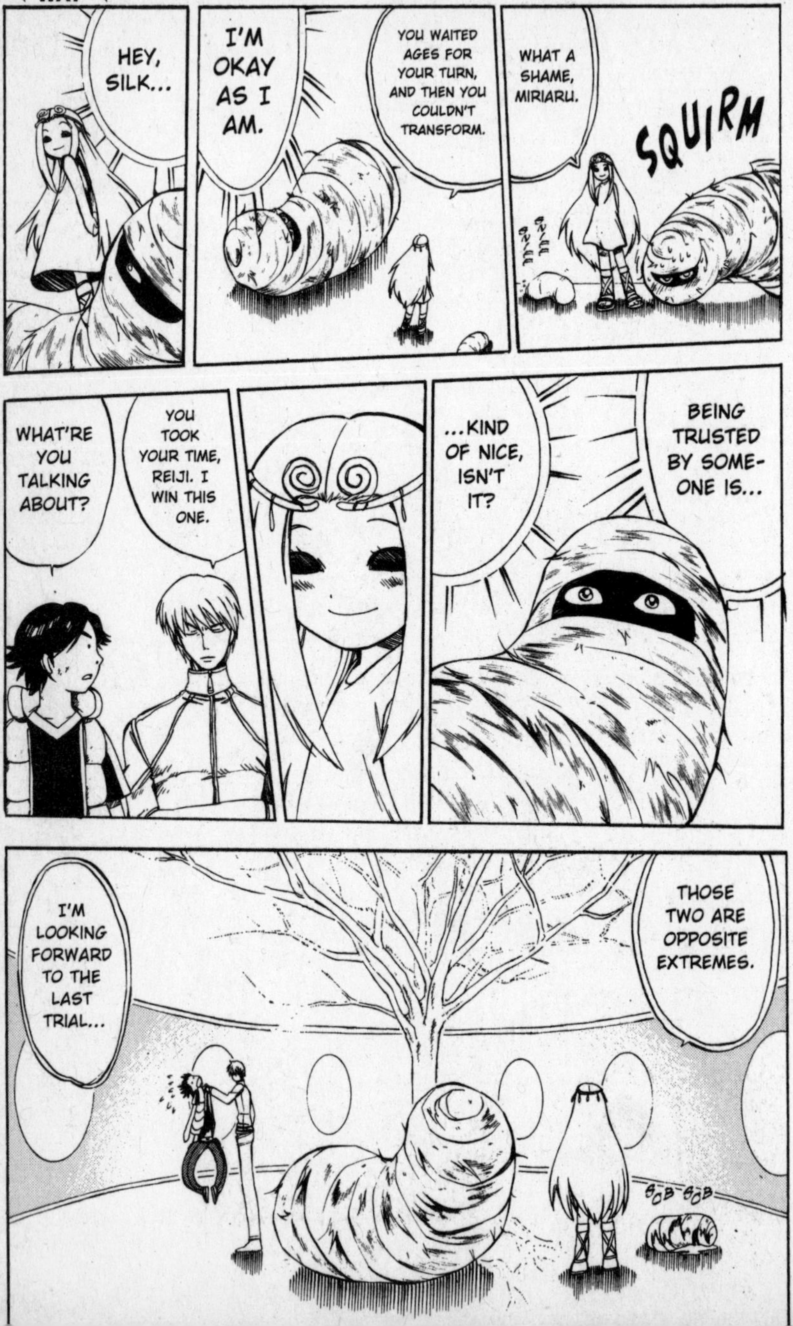
WHAT A SHAME, MIRIARU.
SQUIRM
YOU WAITED AGES FOR YOUR TURN, AND THEN YOU COULDN'T TRANSFORM.
I'M OKAY AS I AM.
HEY, SILK...
BEING TRUSTED BY SOME-ONE IS...
...KIND OF NICE, ISN'T IT?
YOU TOOK YOUR TIME, REIJI. I WIN THIS ONE.
WHAT'RE YOU TALKING ABOUT?
THOSE TWO ARE OPPOSITE EXTREMES.
I'M LOOKING FORWARD TO THE LAST TRIAL...
SOB SOB

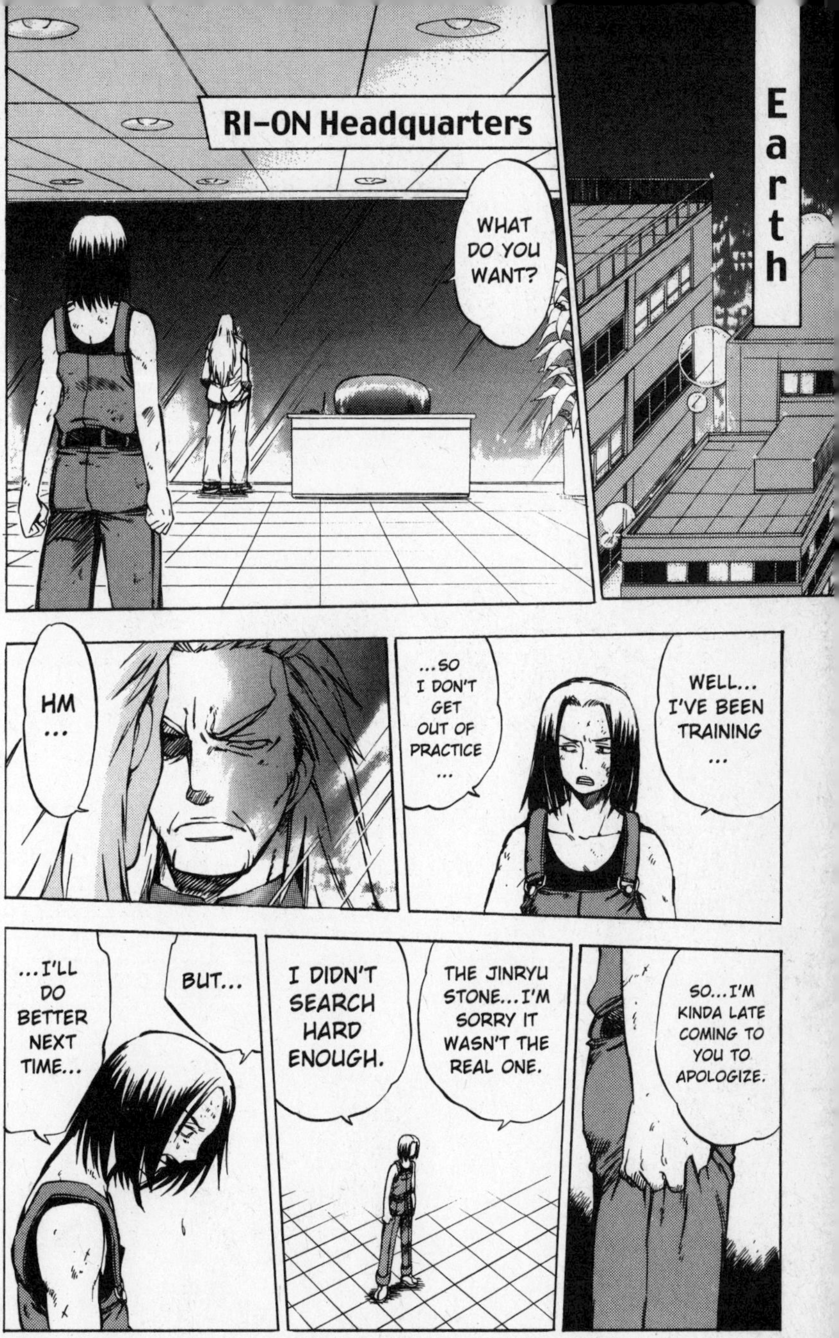
Earth
RI-ON Headquarters
WHAT DO YOU WANT?
WELL... I'VE BEEN TRAINING...
...SO I DON'T GET OUT OF PRACTICE...
HM...
SO...I'M KINDA LATE COMING TO YOU TO APOLOGIZE.
THE JINRYU STONE...I'M SORRY IT WASN'T THE REAL ONE.
I DIDN'T SEARCH HARD ENOUGH.
BUT...
...I'LL DO BETTER NEXT TIME...

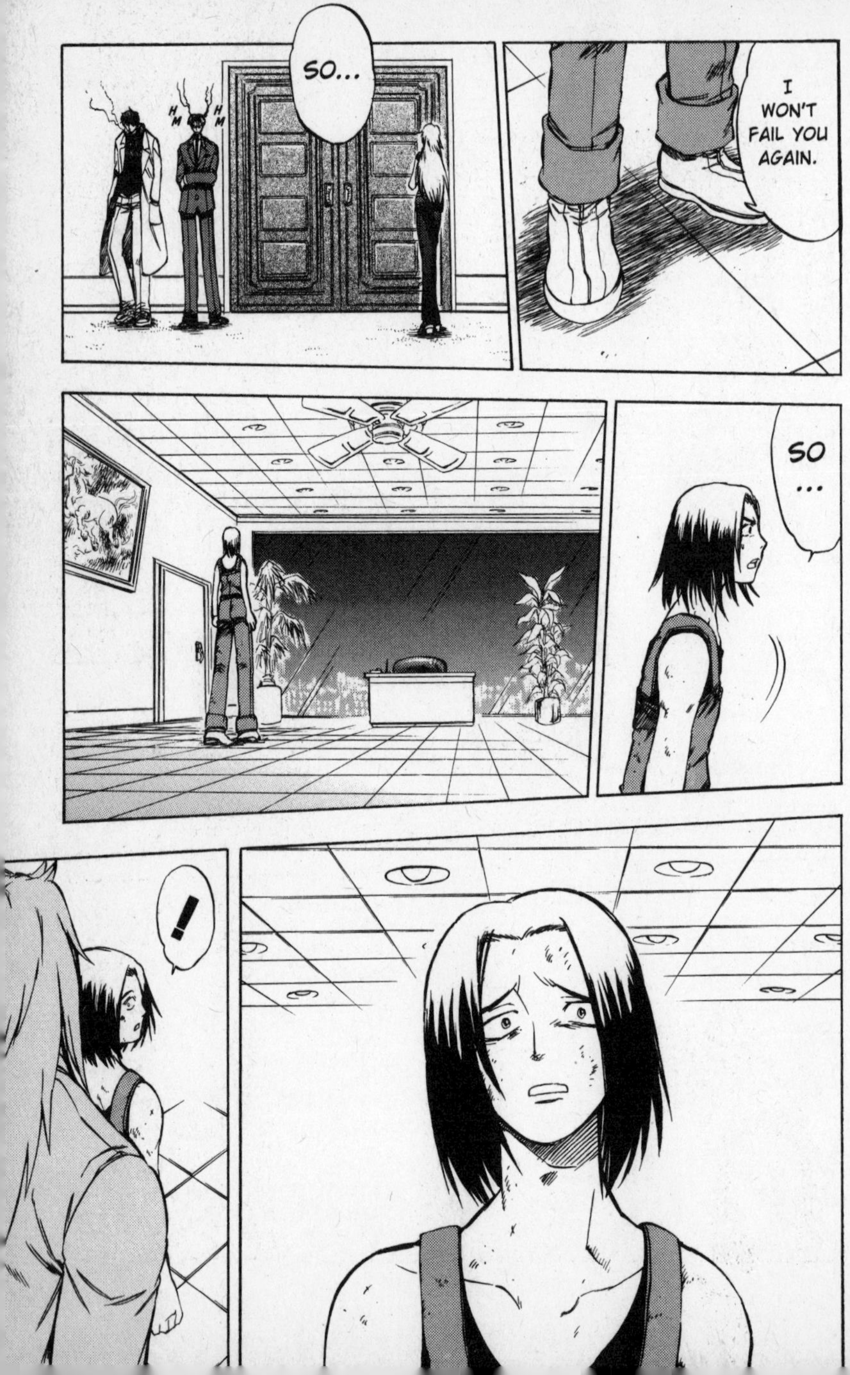
I WON'T FAIL YOU AGAIN.
SO...
HM HM
SO ...
!

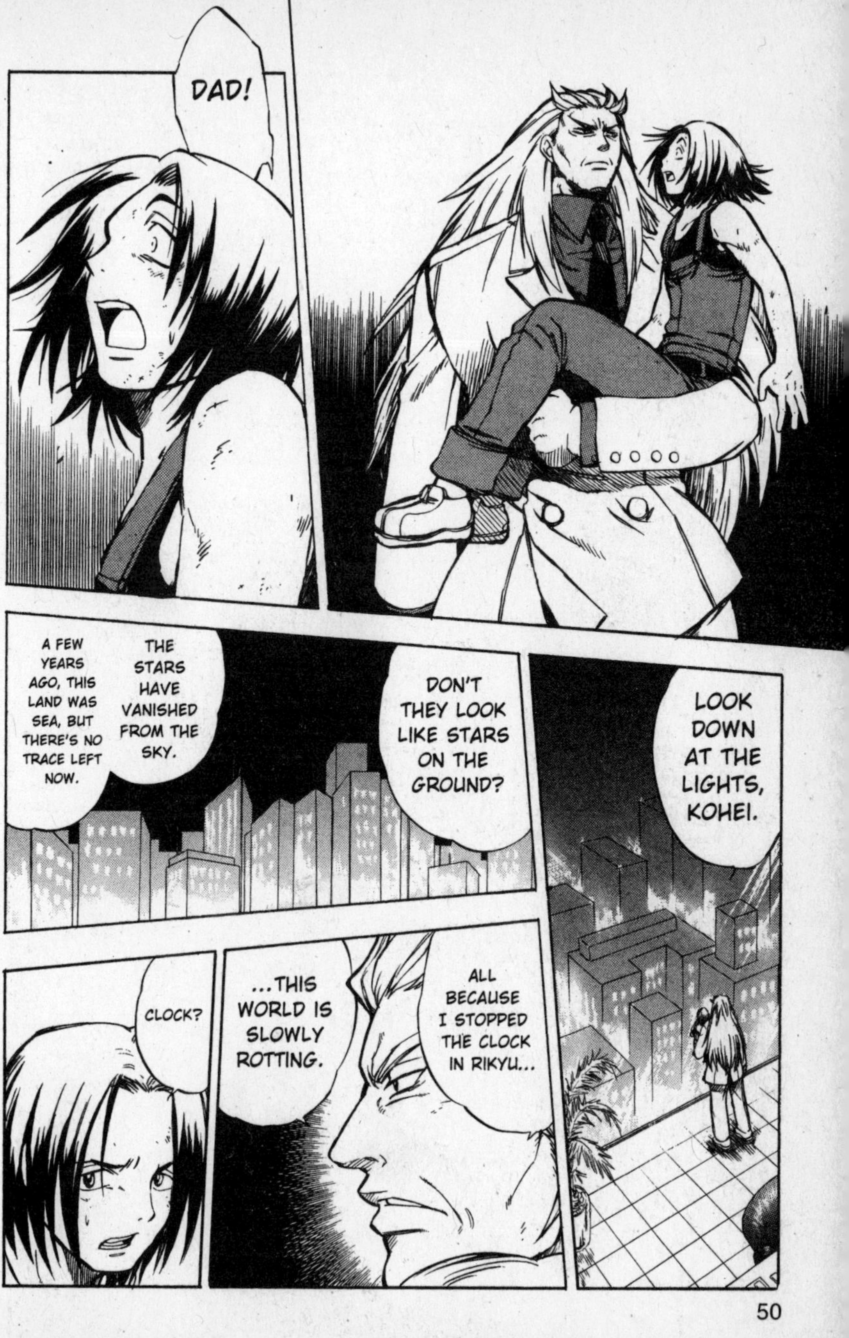
DAD!
LOOK DOWN AT THE LIGHTS, KOHEI.
DON'T THEY LOOK LIKE STARS ON THE GROUND?
THE STARS HAVE VANISHED FROM THE SKY.
A FEW YEARS AGO, THIS LAND WAS SEA, BUT THERE'S NO TRACE LEFT NOW.
ALL BECAUSE I STOPPED THE CLOCK IN RIKYU...
...THIS WORLD IS SLOWLY ROTTING.
CLOCK?

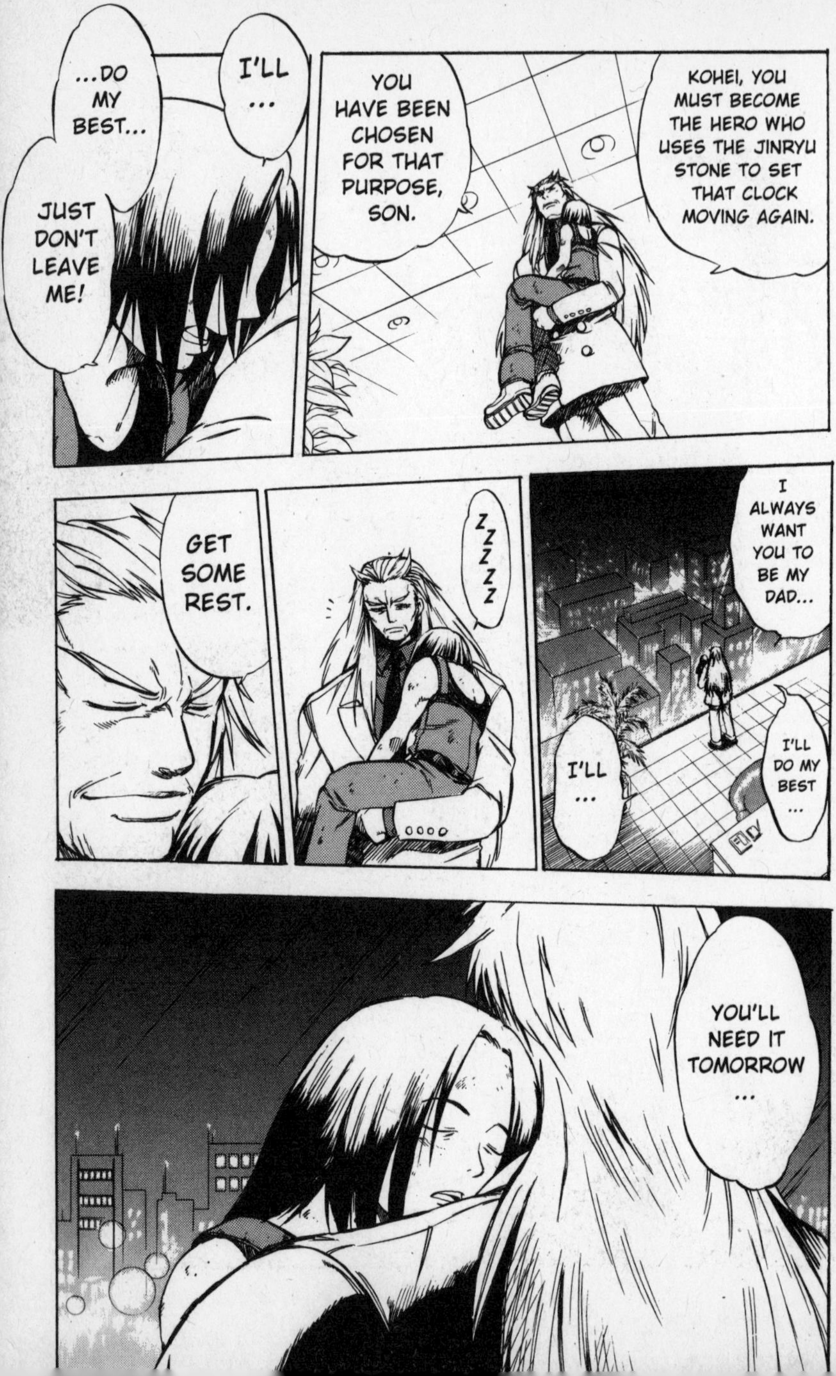
KOHEI, YOU MUST BECOME THE HERO WHO USES THE JINRYU STONE TO SET THAT CLOCK MOVING AGAIN.
YOU HAVE BEEN CHOSEN FOR THAT PURPOSE, SON.
I'LL ...
...DO MY BEST...
JUST DON'T LEAVE ME!
I ALWAYS WANT YOU TO BE MY DAD...
I'LL DO MY BEST ...
I'LL ...
ZZZZZ
GET SOME REST.
YOU'LL NEED IT TOMORROW ...

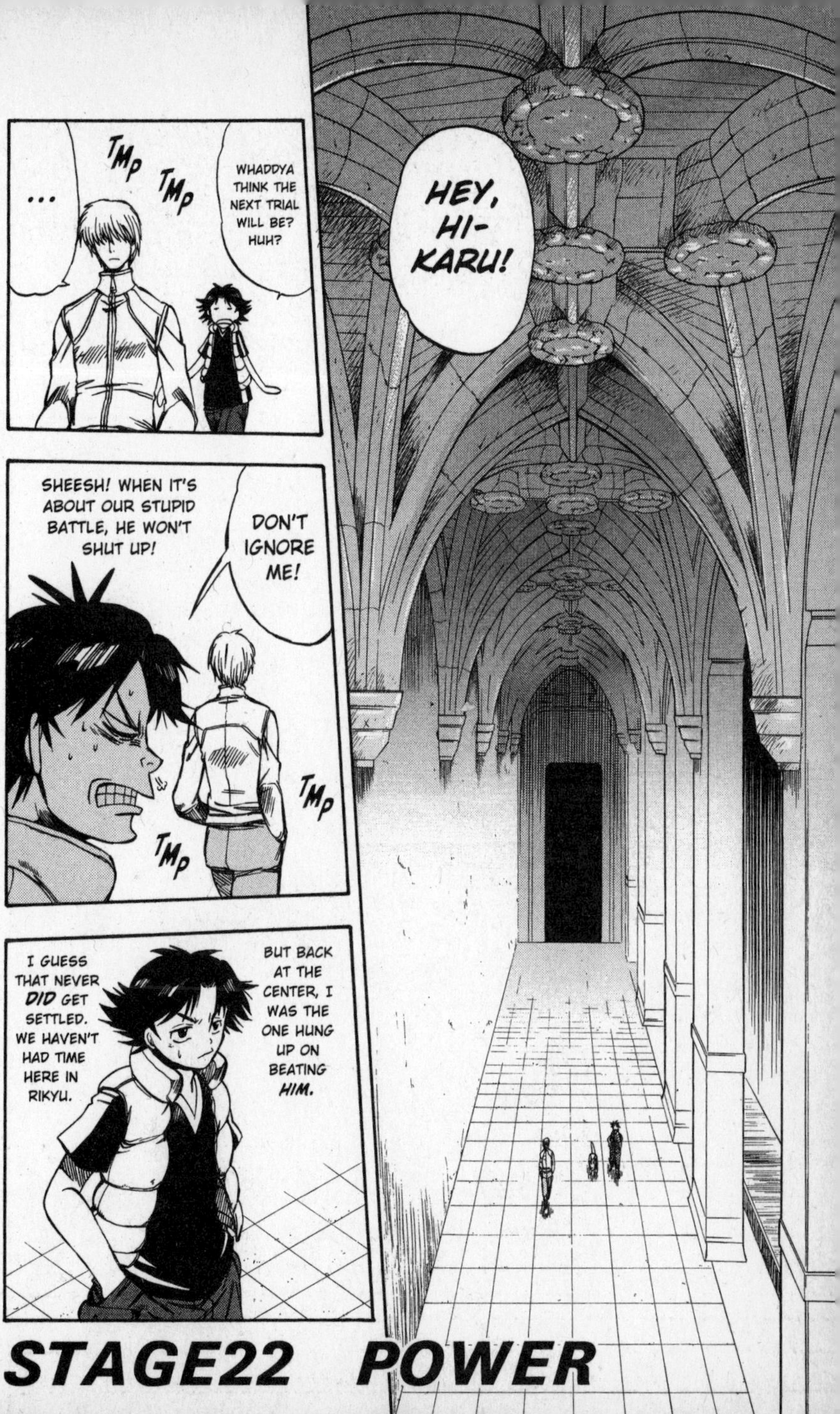
HEY, HI-KARU!
WHADDYA THINK THE NEXT TRIAL WILL BE? HUH?
TMP TMP
...
DON'T IGNORE ME!
SHEESH! WHEN IT'S ABOUT OUR STUPID BATTLE, HE WON'T SHUT UP!
TMP TMP
BUT BACK AT THE CENTER, I WAS THE ONE HUNG UP ON BEATING HIM.
I GUESS THAT NEVER DID GET SETTLED. WE HAVEN'T HAD TIME HERE IN RIKYU.

STAGE22 POWER

READ THIS WAY

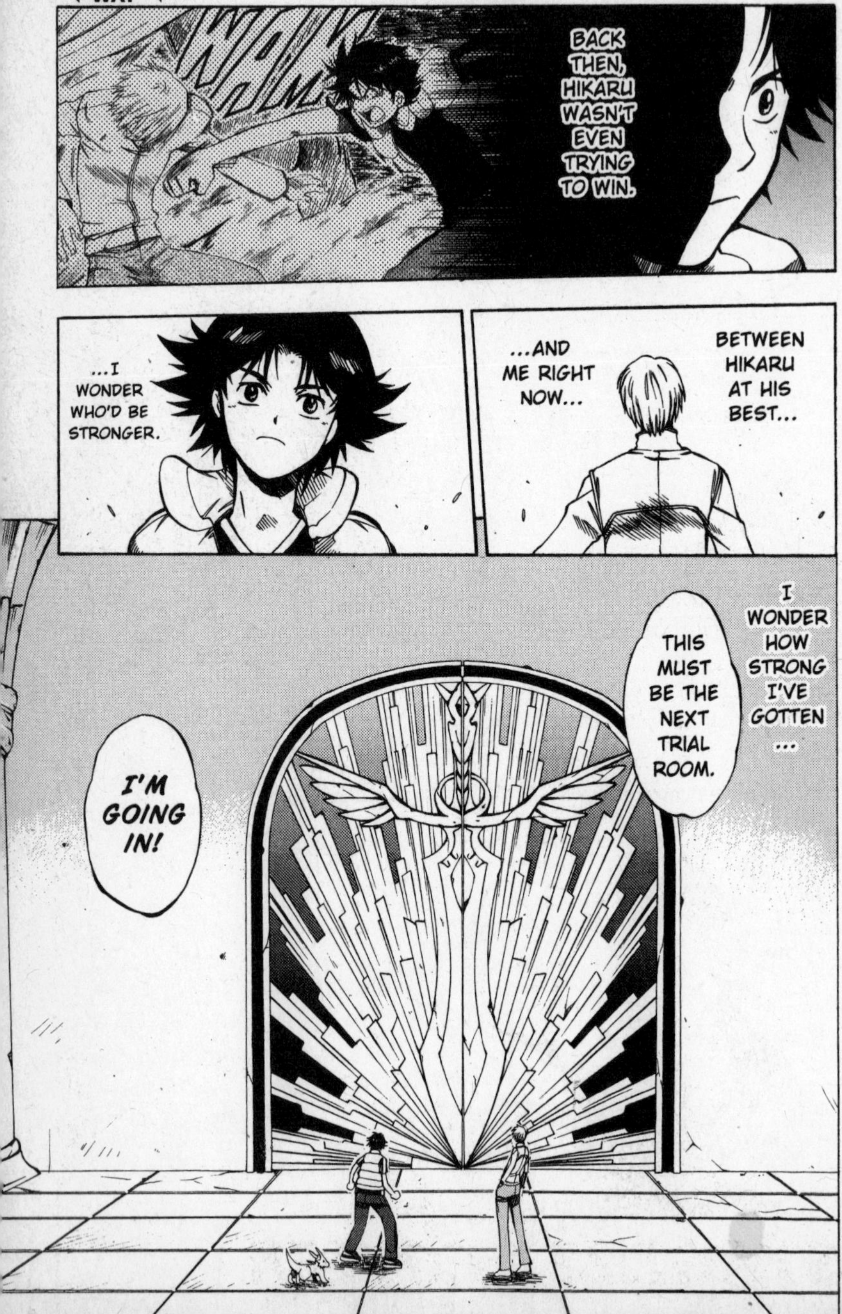
BACK THEN, HIKARU WASN'T EVEN TRYING TO WIN.
BETWEEN HIKARU AT HIS BEST...
...AND ME RIGHT NOW...
...I WONDER WHO'D BE STRONGER.
I WONDER HOW STRONG I'VE GOTTEN...
THIS MUST BE THE NEXT TRIAL ROOM.
I'M GOING IN!

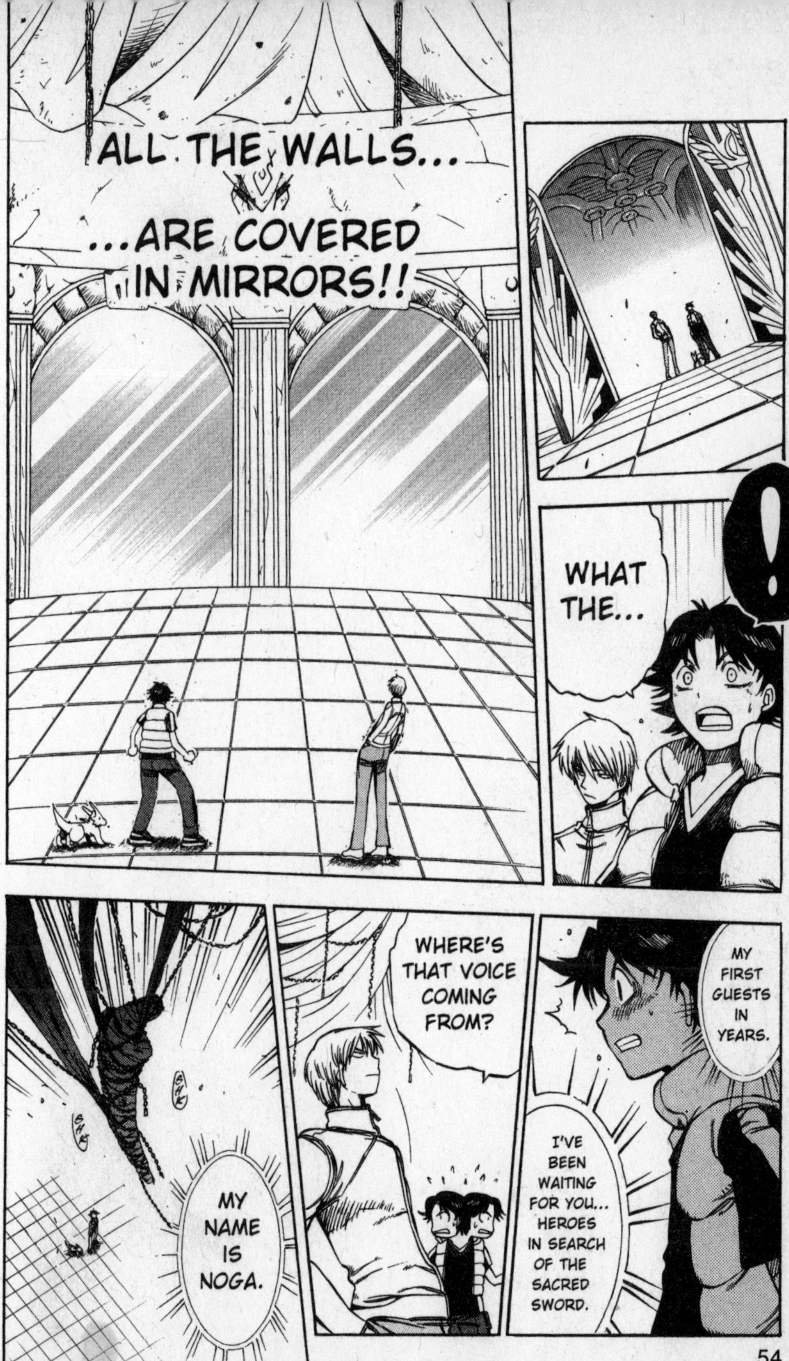
WHAT THE...
ALL THE WALLS...
...ARE COVERED IN MIRRORS!!
MY FIRST GUESTS IN YEARS.
I'VE BEEN WAITING FOR YOU... HEROES IN SEARCH OF THE SACRED SWORD.
WHERE'S THAT VOICE COMING FROM?
SHK
SHK
MY NAME IS NOGA.

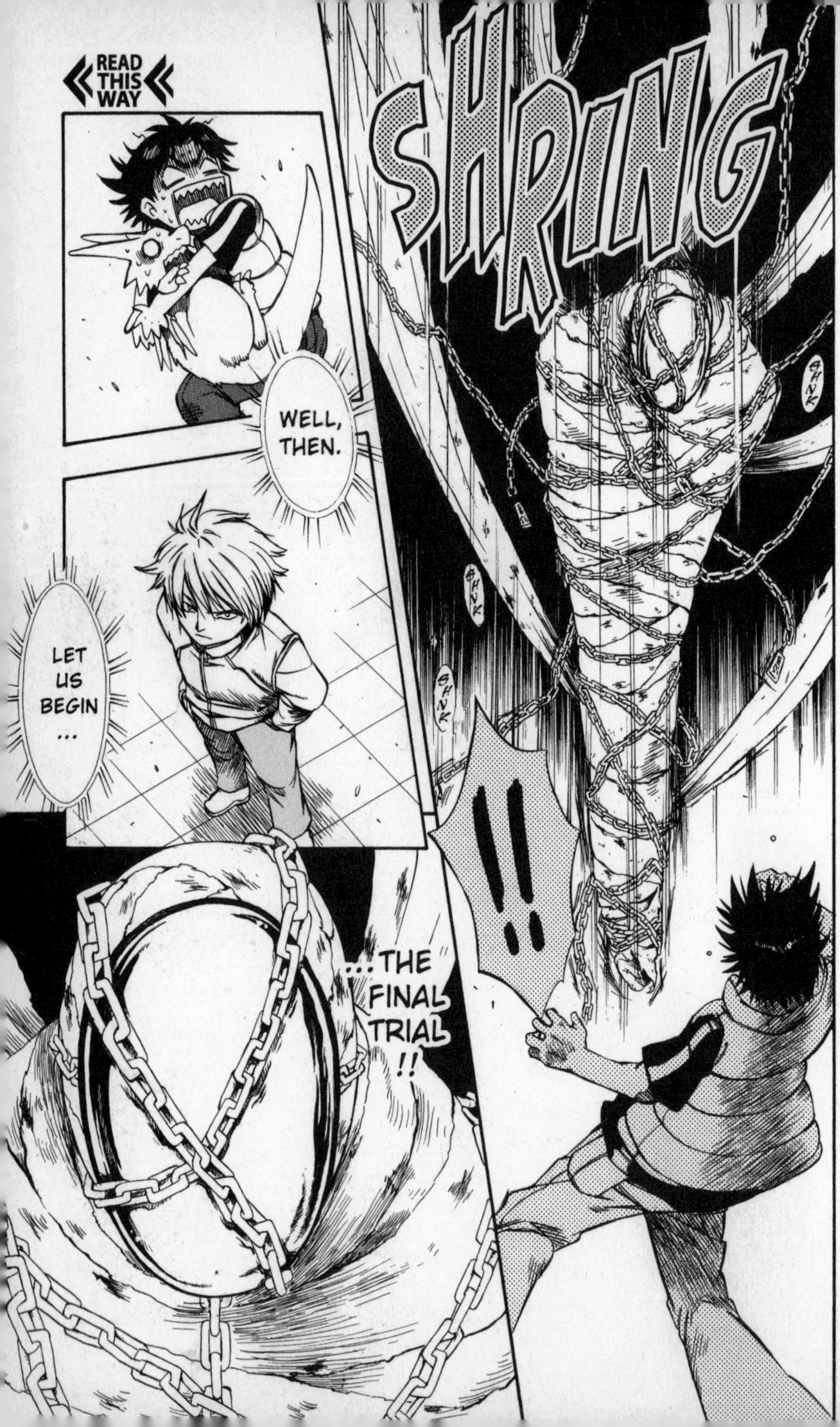
READ THIS WAY
SHRING
SHNK
SHNK
SHNK
!!
WELL, THEN.
LET US BEGIN ...
...THE FINAL TRIAL !!

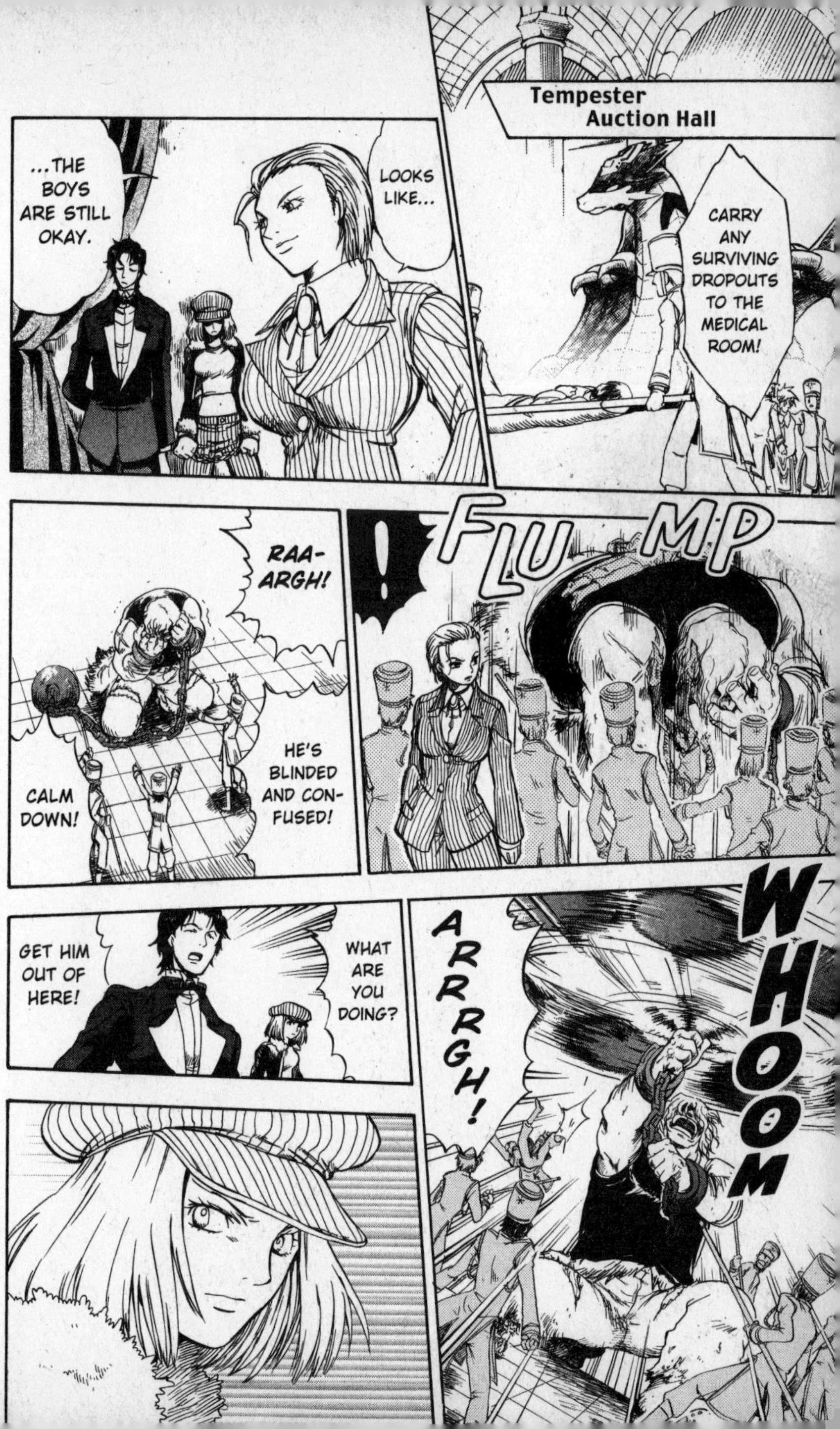
Tempester Auction Hall
CARRY ANY SURVIVING DROPOUTS TO THE MEDICAL ROOM!
LOOKS LIKE...
...THE BOYS ARE STILL OKAY.
!
FLUMP
RAA-ARGH!
HE'S BLINDED AND CONFUSED!
CALM DOWN!
WHOOM
ARRRGH!
WHAT ARE YOU DOING?
GET HIM OUT OF HERE!

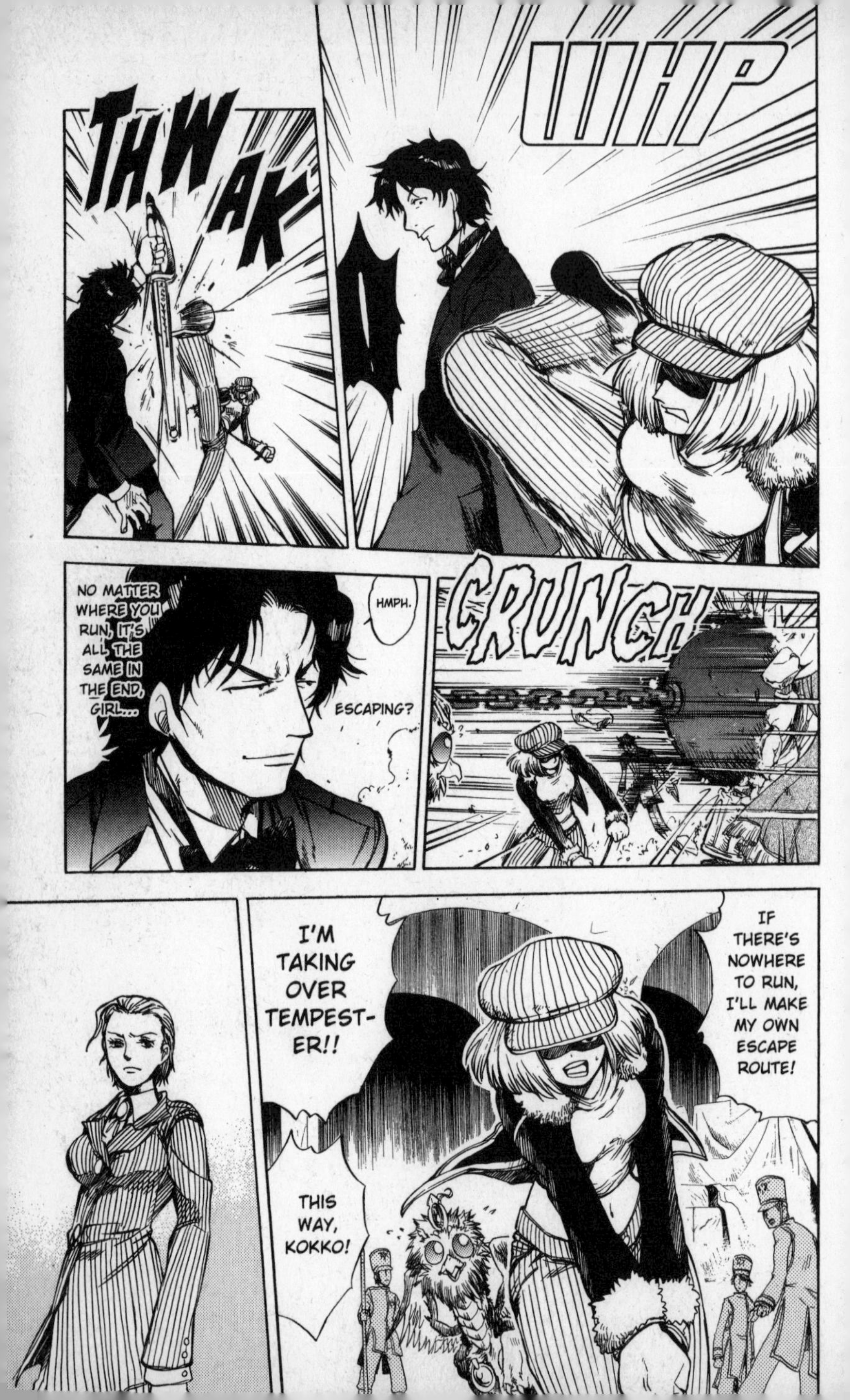
WHP
THWAK
CRUNCH
HMPH.
ESCAPING?
NO MATTER WHERE YOU RUN, IT'S ALL THE SAME IN THE END, GIRL...
IF THERE'S NOWHERE TO RUN, I'LL MAKE MY OWN ESCAPE ROUTE!
I'M TAKING OVER TEMPEST-ER!!
THIS WAY, KOKKO!

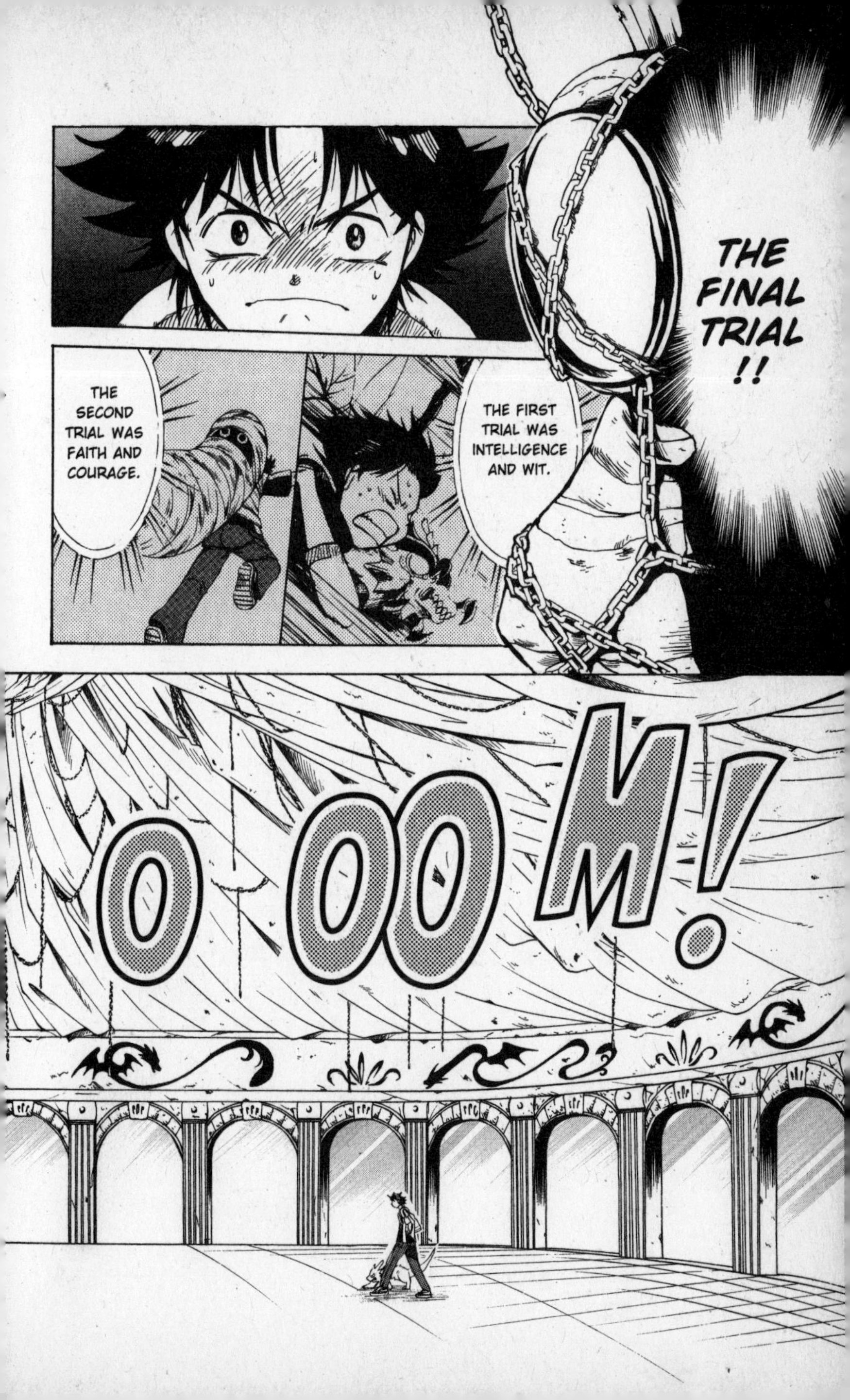
THE FIRST TRIAL WAS INTELLIGENCE AND WIT.
THE SECOND TRIAL WAS FAITH AND COURAGE.
THE FINAL TRIAL!!
O OOM!

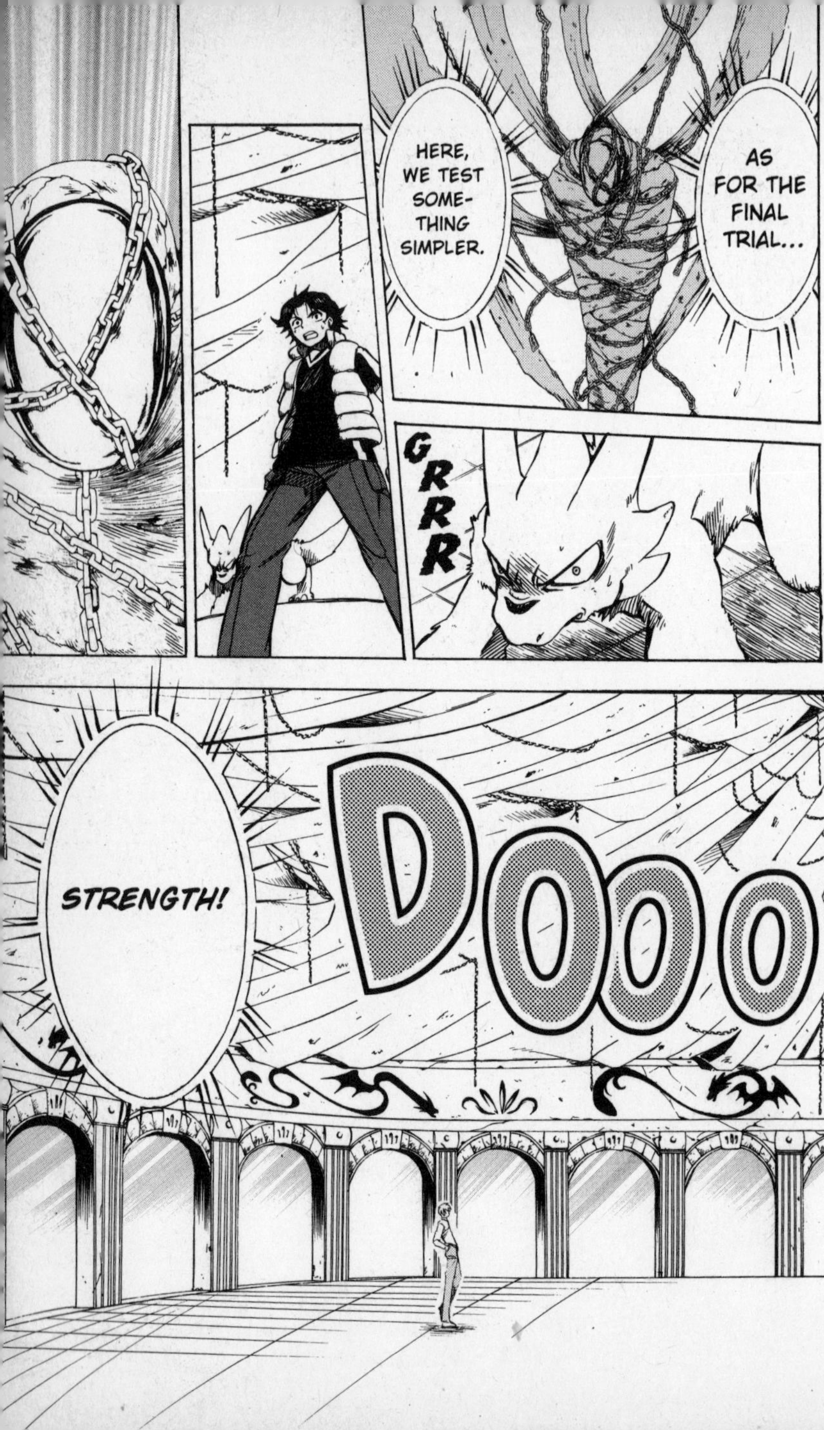
AS FOR THE FINAL TRIAL...
HERE, WE TEST SOME-THING SIMPLER.
GRRR
DOOO
STRENGTH!

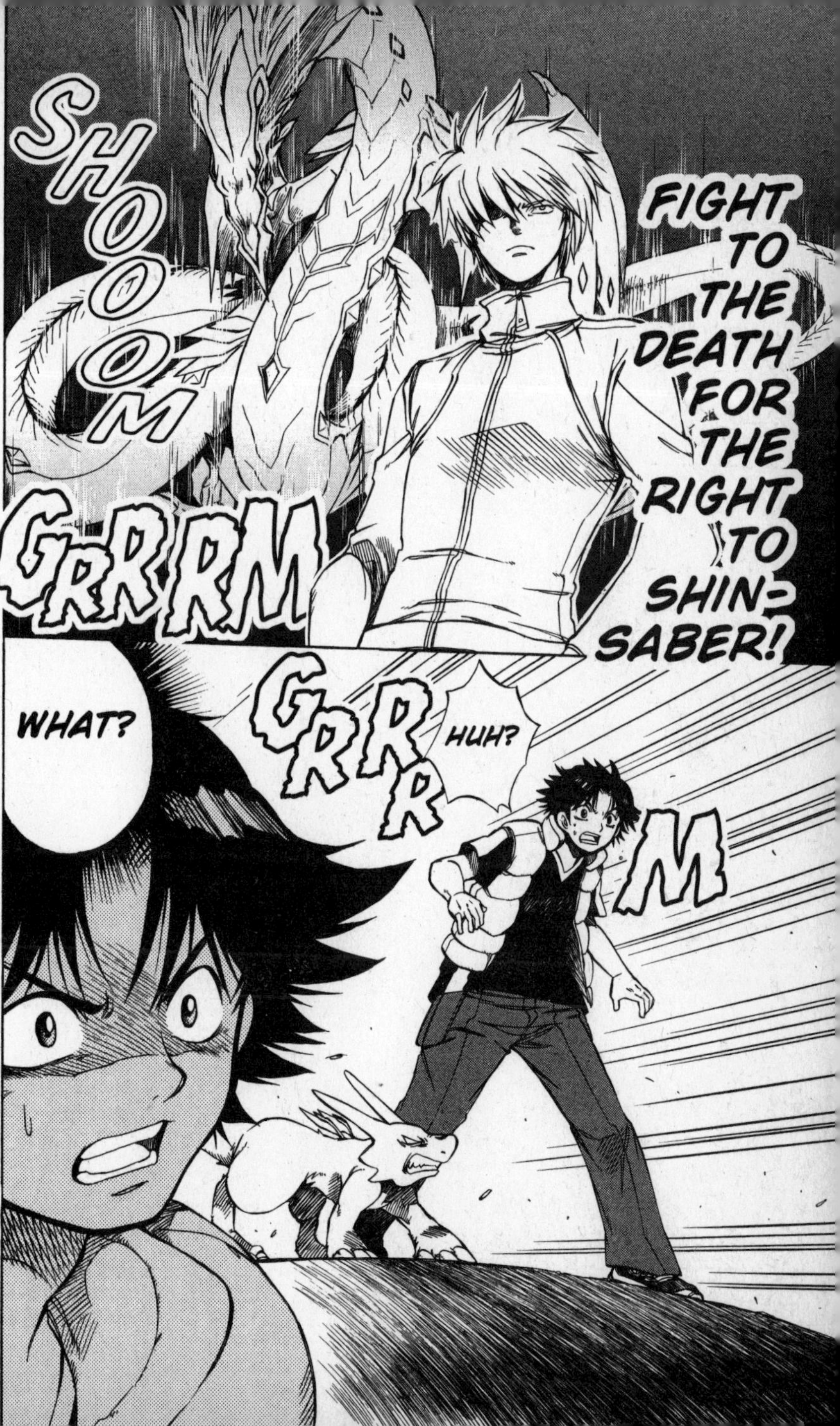
FIGHT TO THE DEATH FOR THE RIGHT TO SHIN-SABER!
SHOOOOM
GRRRM
HUH?
GRRRM
WHAT?

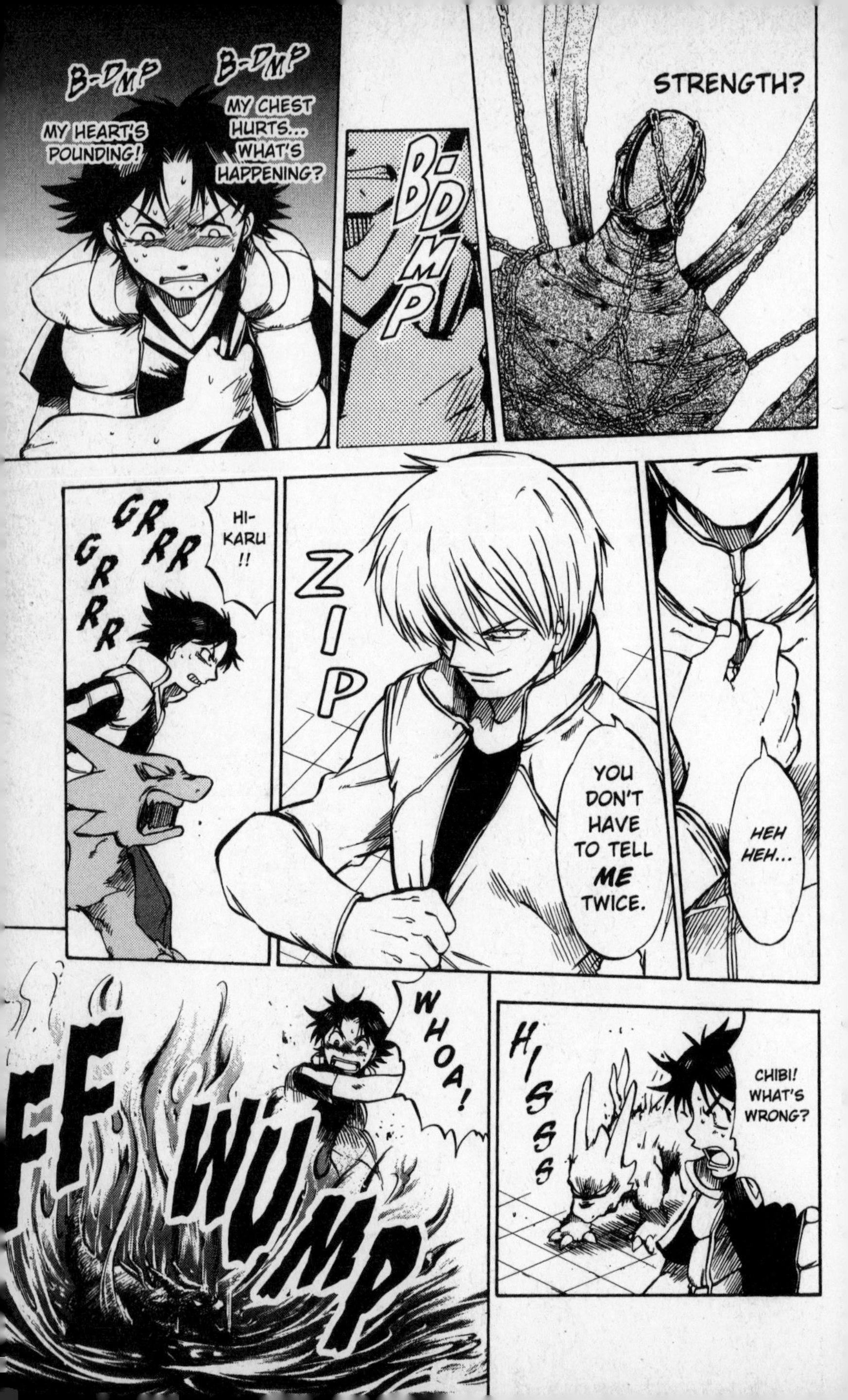
STRENGTH?
B-DMP
B-DMP
MY CHEST HURTS... WHAT'S HAPPENING?
B-DMP
MY HEART'S POUNDING!
HEH HEH...
YOU DON'T HAVE TO TELL ME TWICE.
ZIP
HI-KARU!!
GRRR
GRRR
CHIBI! WHAT'S WRONG?
HISSS
WHOA!
FFWUMP

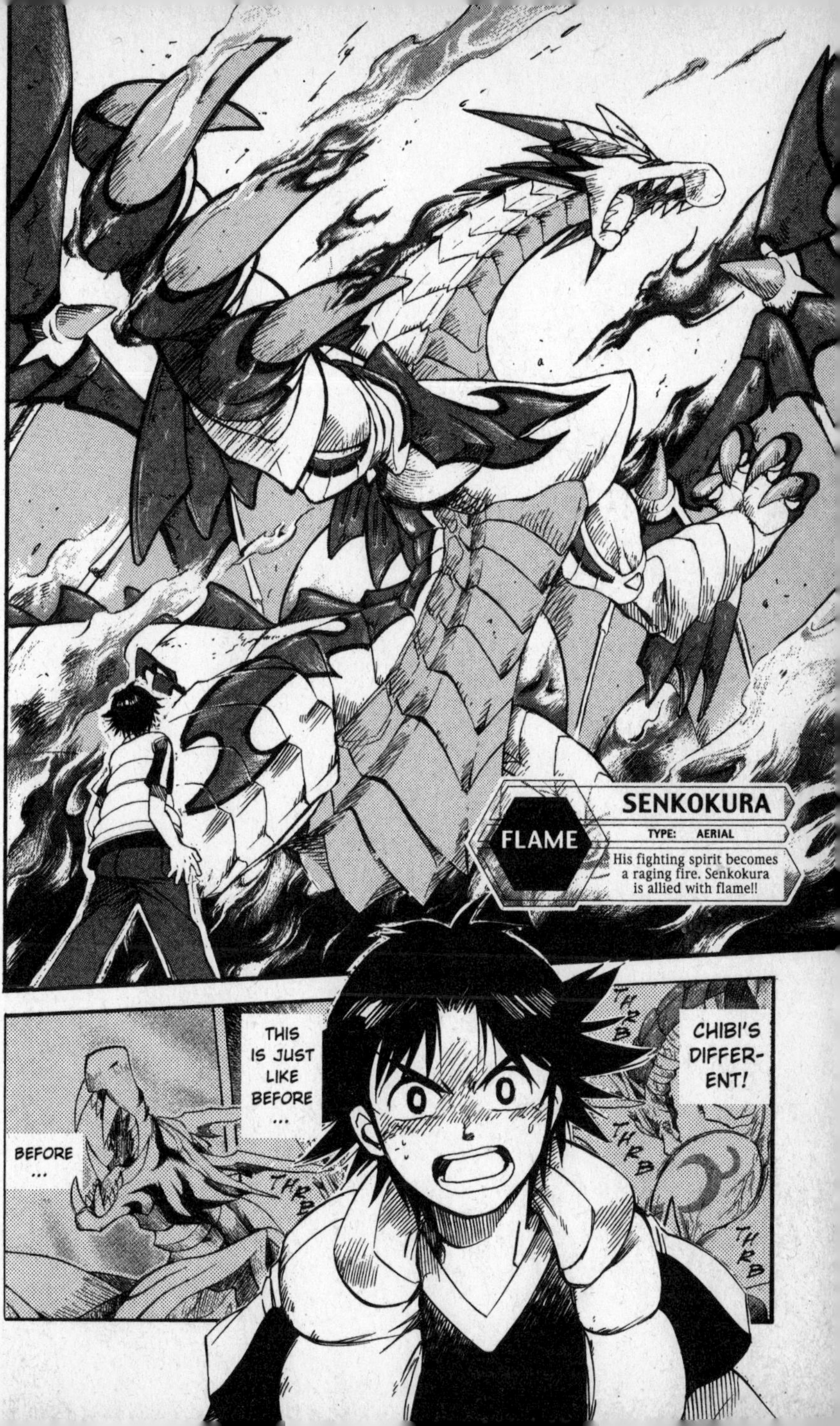
SENKOKURA
FLAME
TYPE: AERIAL
His fighting spirit becomes a raging fire. Senkokura is allied with flame!!
CHIBI'S DIFFER-ENT!
THRB
THRB
THRB
THIS IS JUST LIKE BEFORE ...
THRB
BEFORE ...

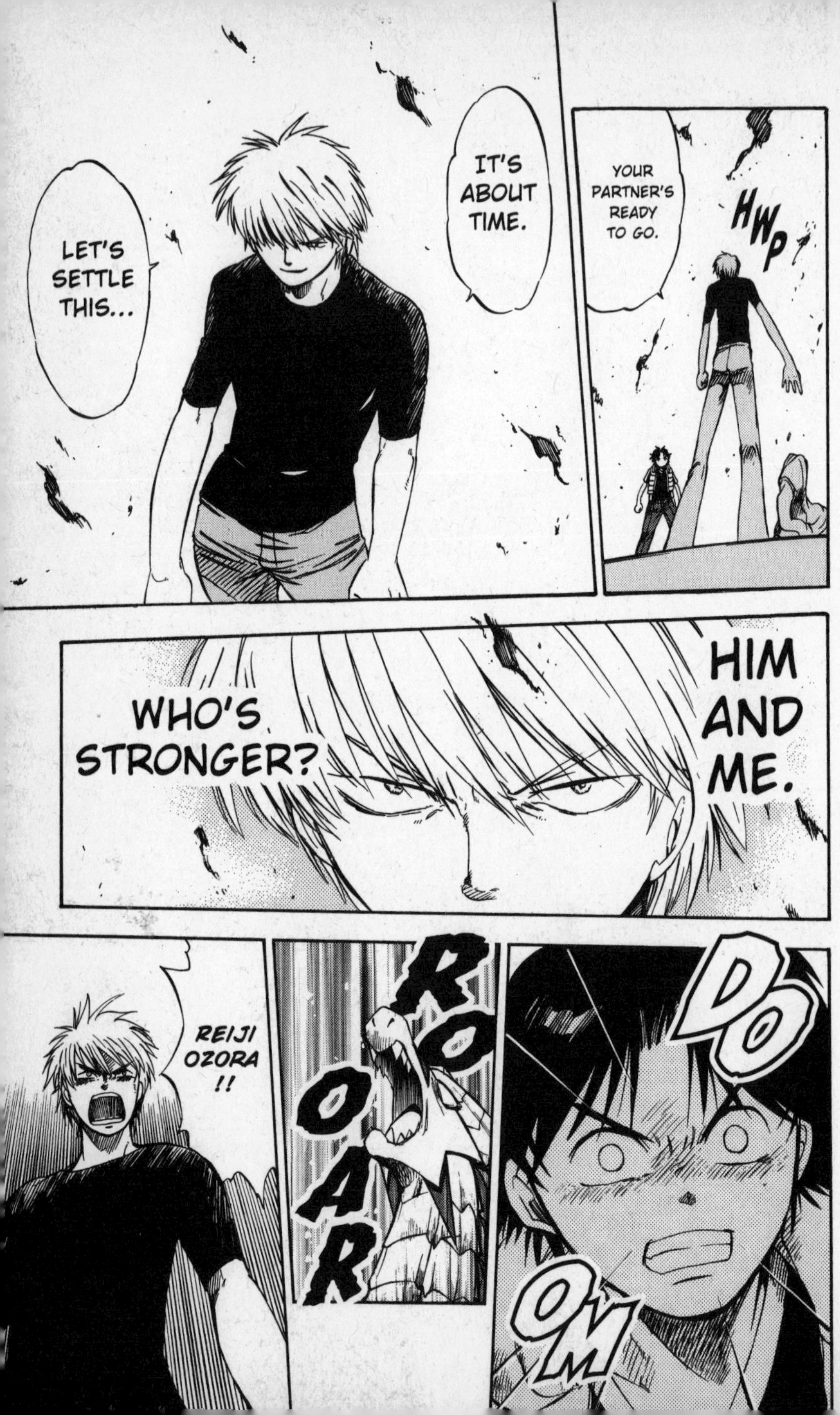
YOUR PARTNER'S READY TO GO.
HWP
IT'S ABOUT TIME.
LET'S SETTLE THIS...
HIM AND ME.
WHO'S STRONGER?
DOOM
ROOAR
REIJI OZORA !!

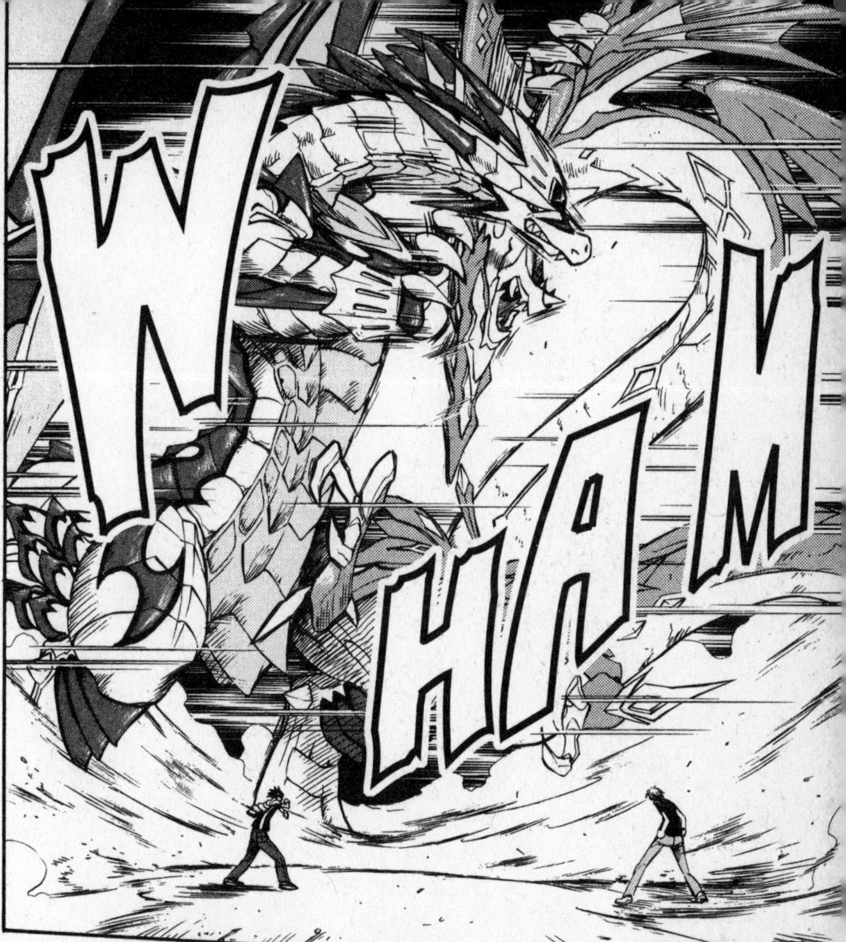
WHAM
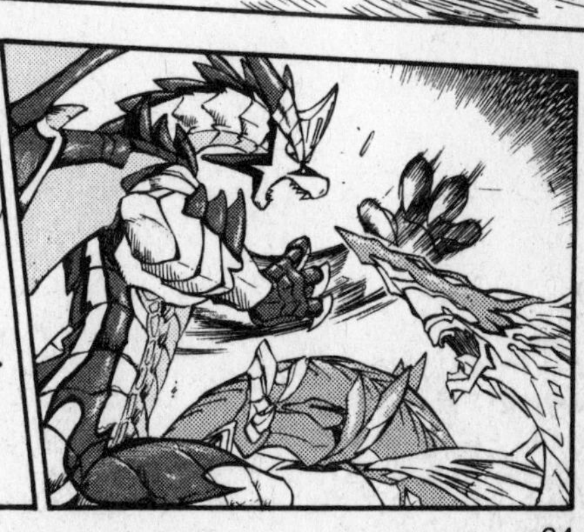
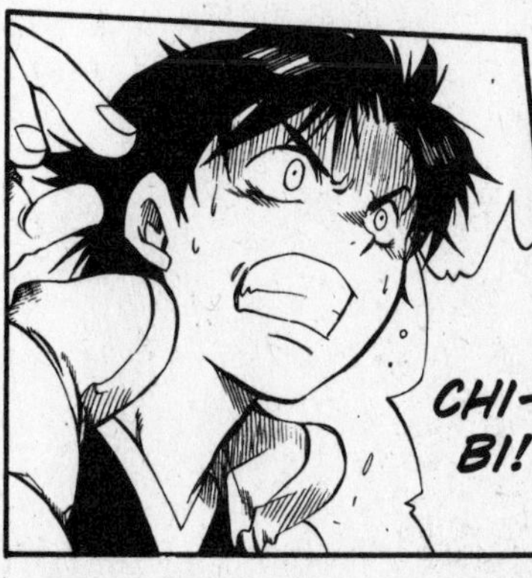
CHI-
BI!

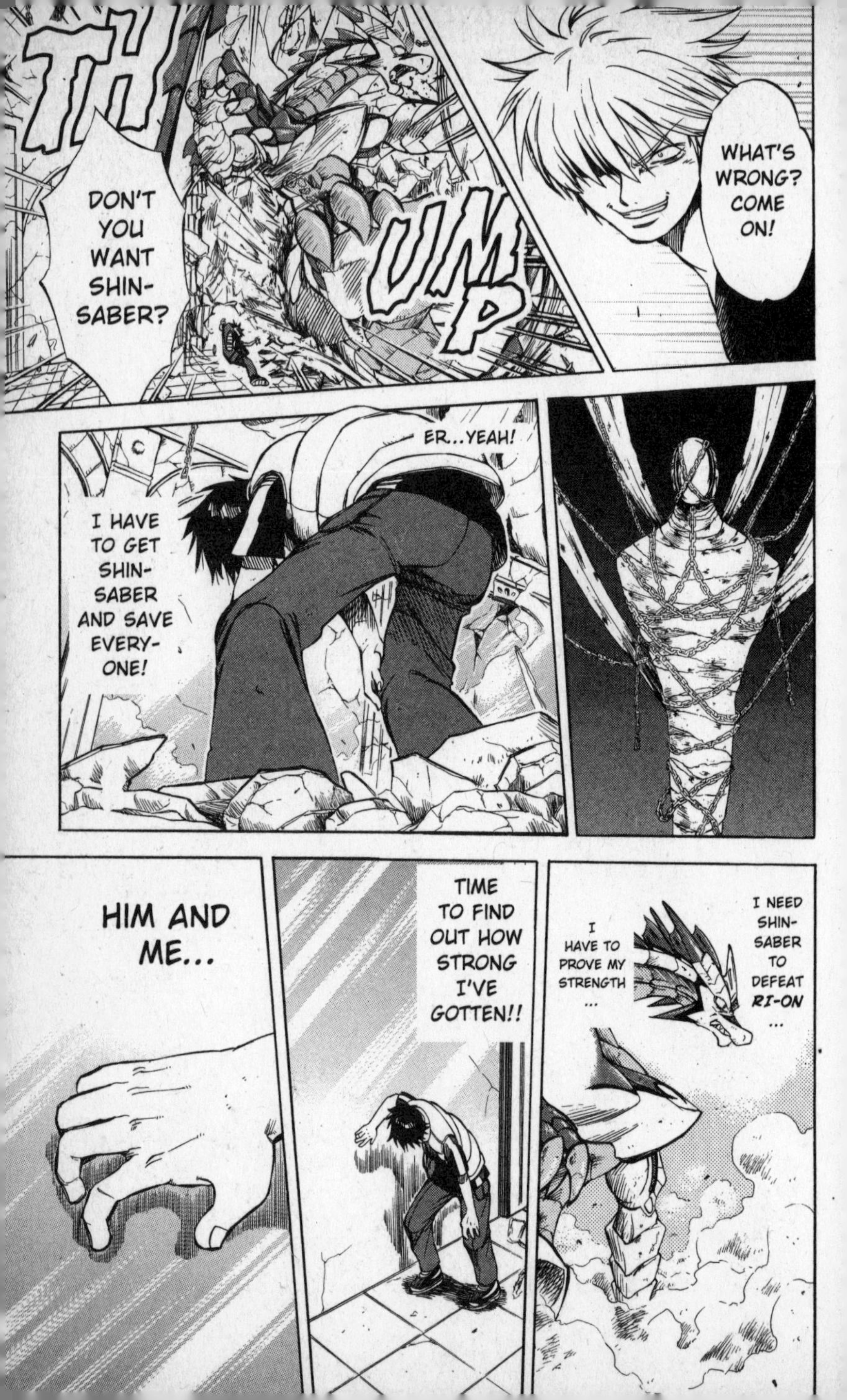
WHAT'S WRONG? COME ON!
THUMP
DON'T YOU WANT SHIN-SABER?
ER...YEAH!
I HAVE TO GET SHIN-SABER AND SAVE EVERY-ONE!
I NEED SHIN-SABER TO DEFEAT RI-ON...
I HAVE TO PROVE MY STRENGTH...
TIME TO FIND OUT HOW STRONG I'VE GOTTEN!!
HIM AND ME...

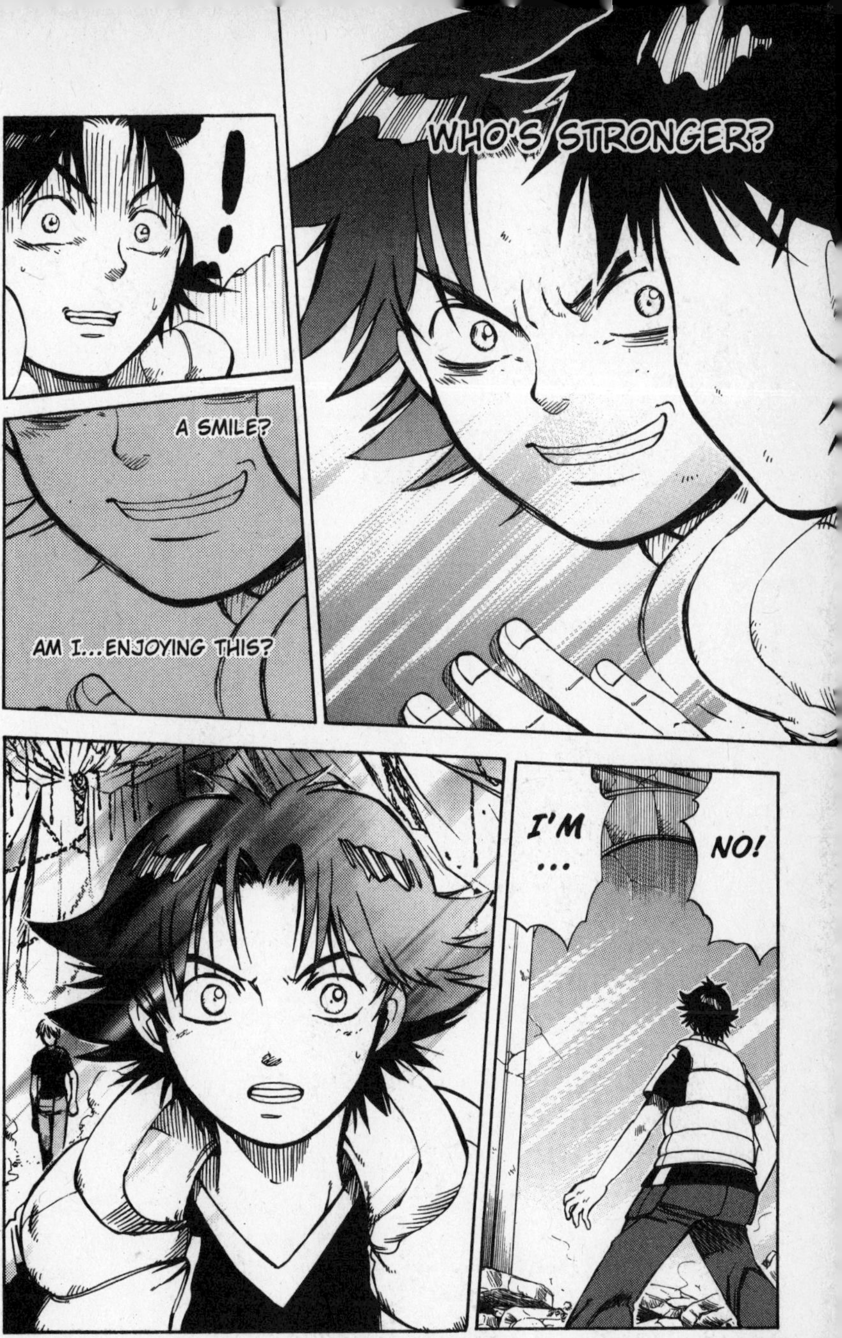
WHO'S STRONGER?
!
A SMILE?
AM I...ENJOYING THIS?
I'M ...
NO!

READ THIS WAY

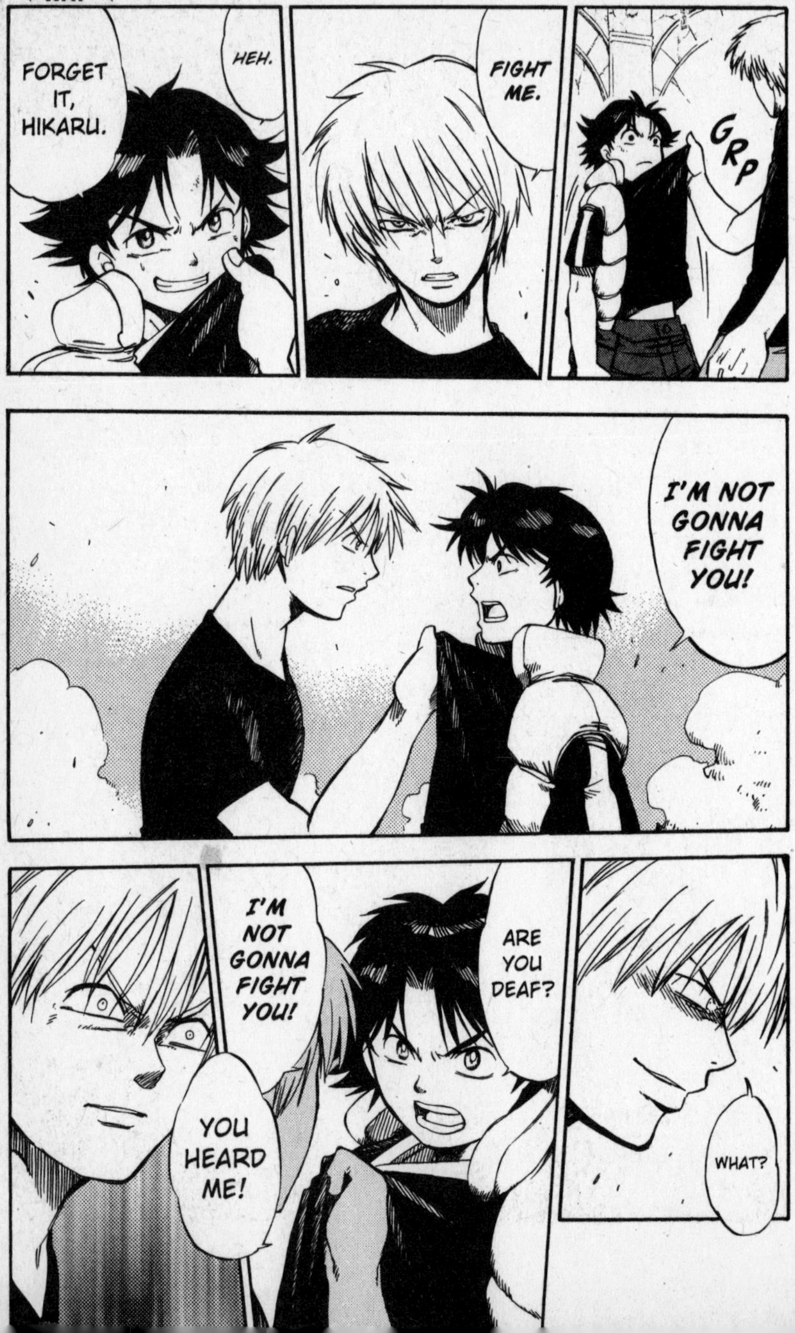

GRP
FIGHT ME.
HEH.
FORGET IT, HIKARU.
I'M NOT GONNA FIGHT YOU!
WHAT?
ARE YOU DEAF?
I'M NOT GONNA FIGHT YOU!
YOU HEARD ME!

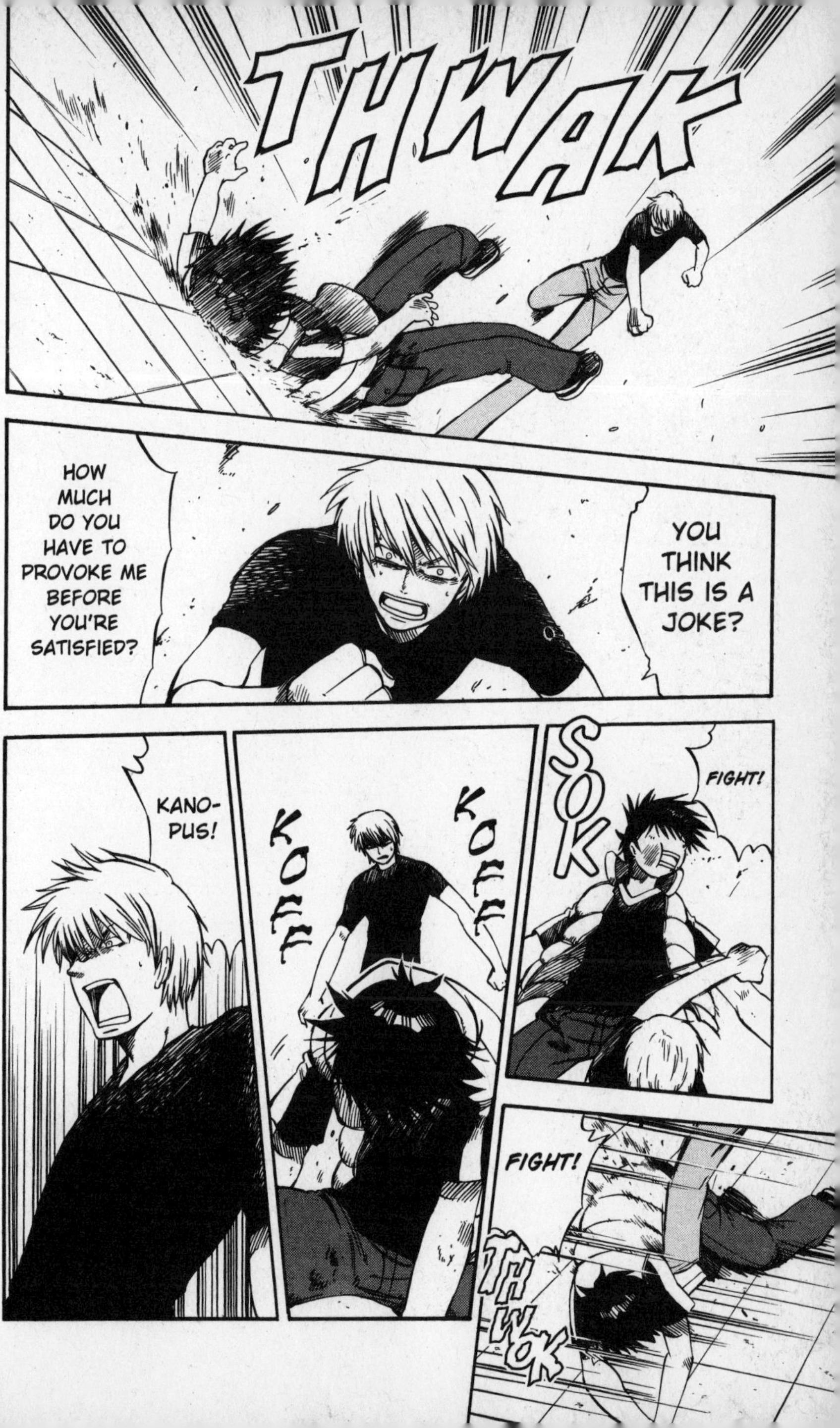
THWAK
YOU THINK THIS IS A JOKE?
HOW MUCH DO YOU HAVE TO PROVOKE ME BEFORE YOU'RE SATISFIED?
SOK
FIGHT!
FIGHT!
THWOK
KOFF
KOFF
KANO-PUS!

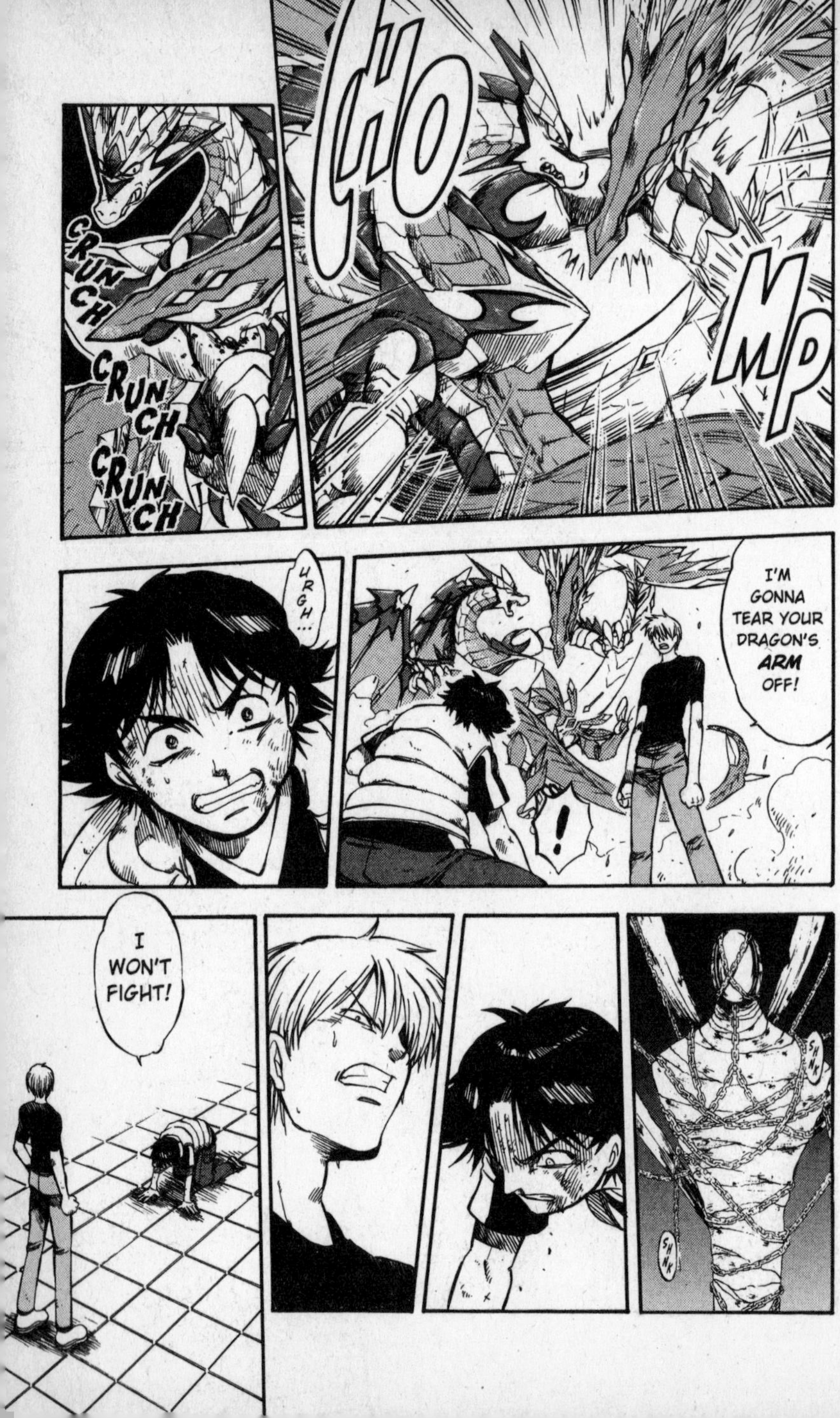
CHOMP
CRUNCH
CRUNCH
CRUNCH
I'M GONNA TEAR YOUR DRAGON'S **ARM** OFF!
!
URGH...
SHNK
SHNK
I WON'T FIGHT!

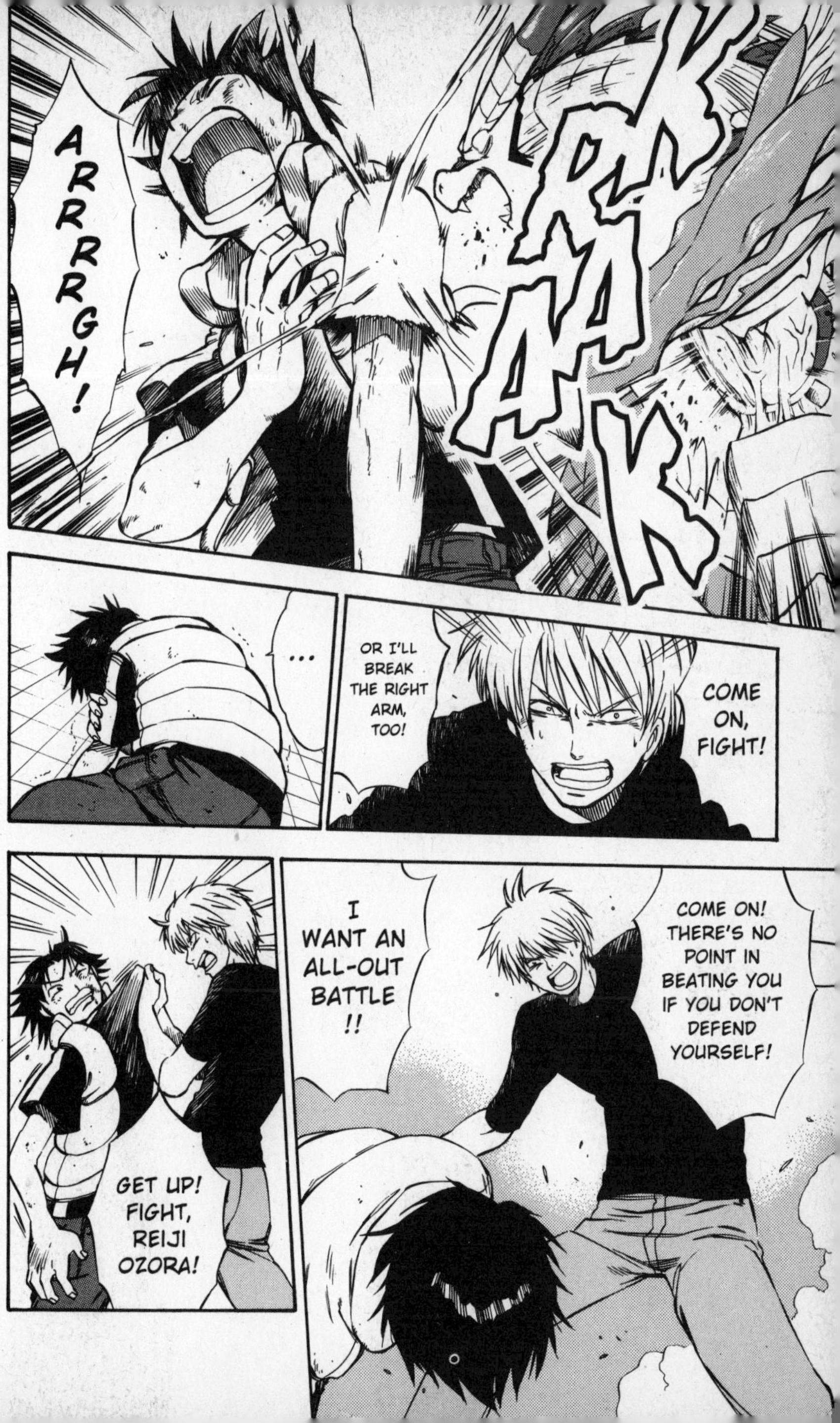
KRAAK
ARRRRGH!
COME ON, FIGHT!
OR I'LL BREAK THE RIGHT ARM, TOO!
...
COME ON! THERE'S NO POINT IN BEATING YOU IF YOU DON'T DEFEND YOURSELF!
I WANT AN ALL-OUT BATTLE !!
GET UP! FIGHT, REIJI OZORA!

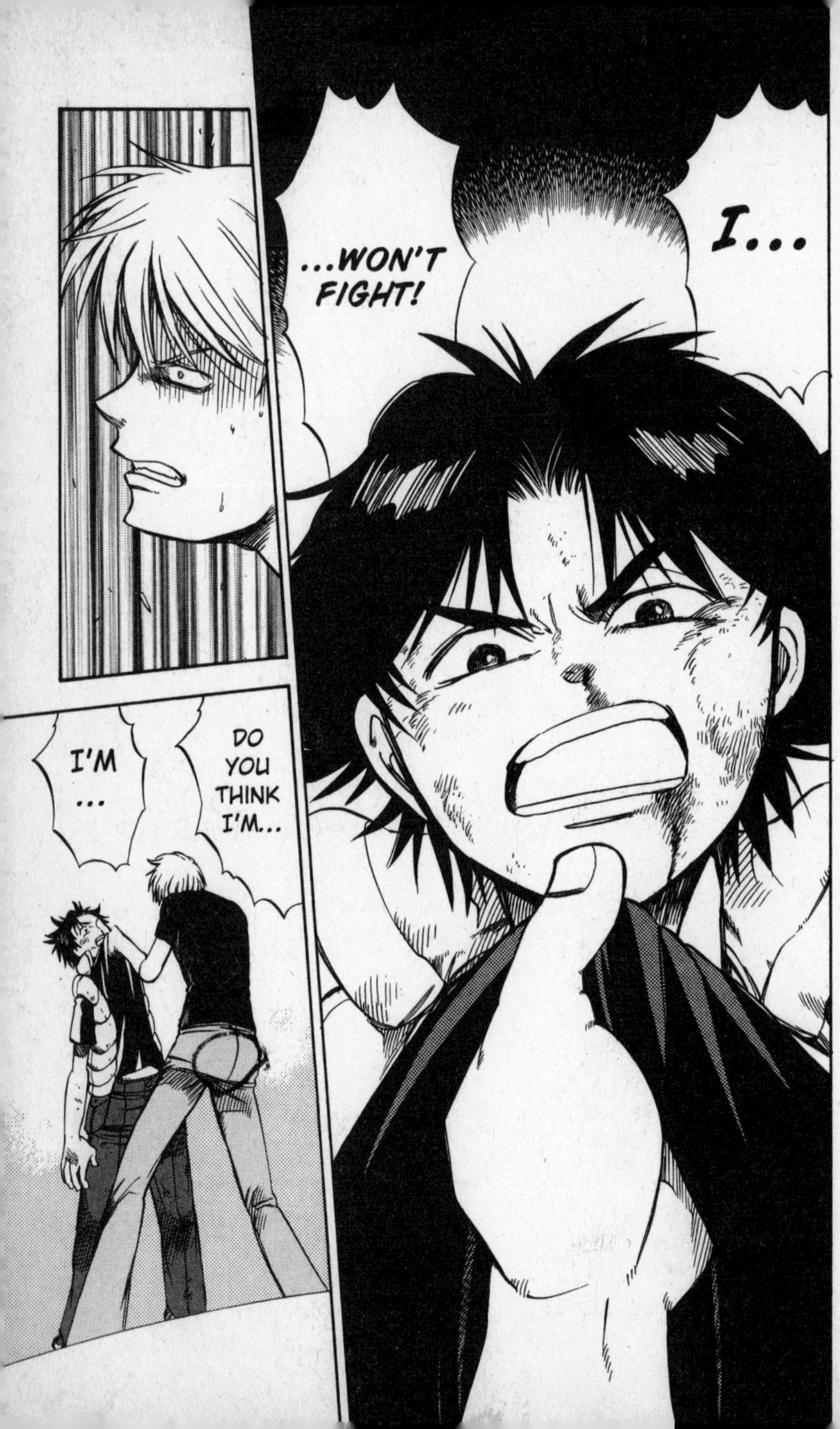
I...
...WON'T FIGHT!
DO YOU THINK I'M...
I'M ...

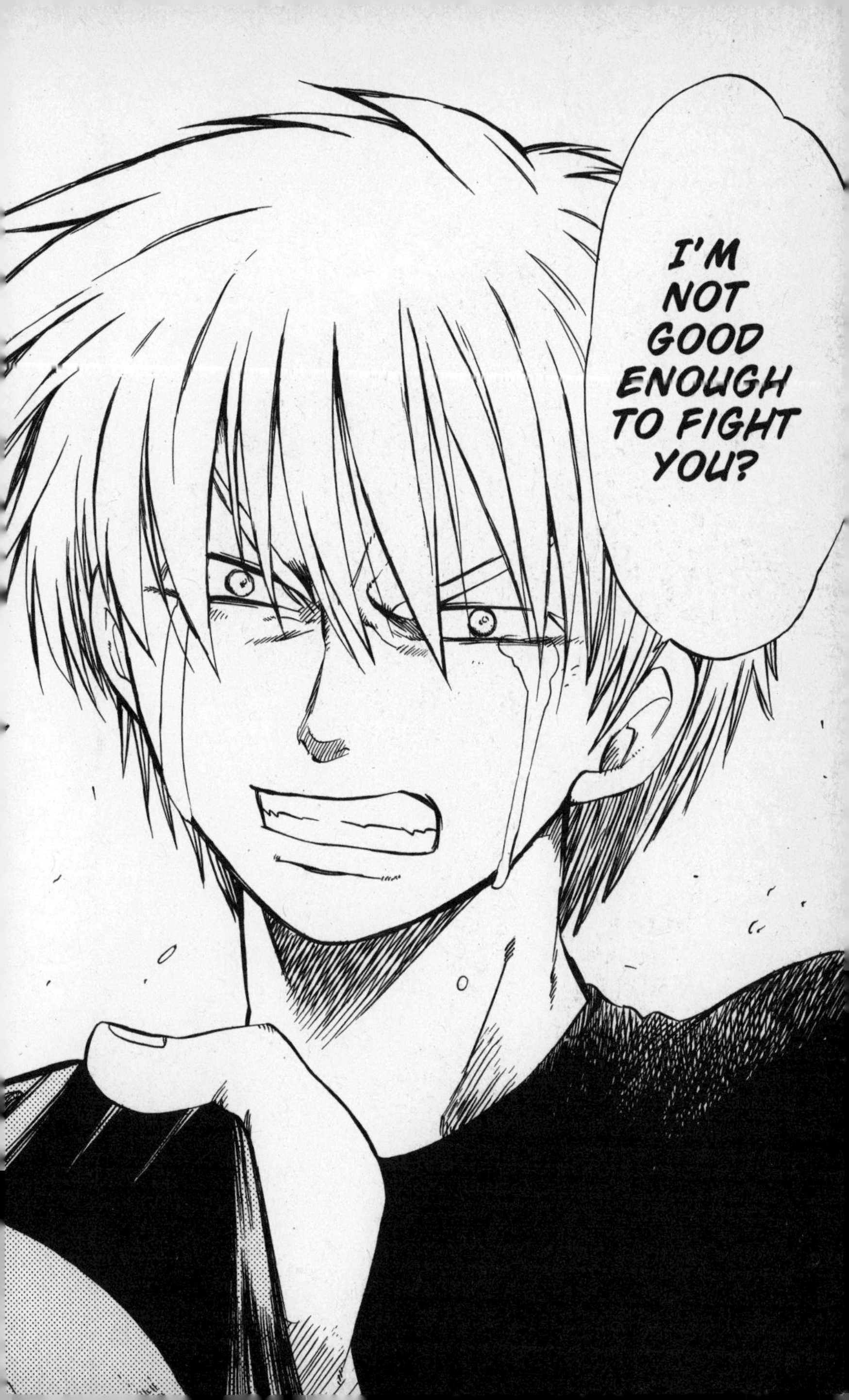
I'M NOT GOOD ENOUGH TO FIGHT YOU?

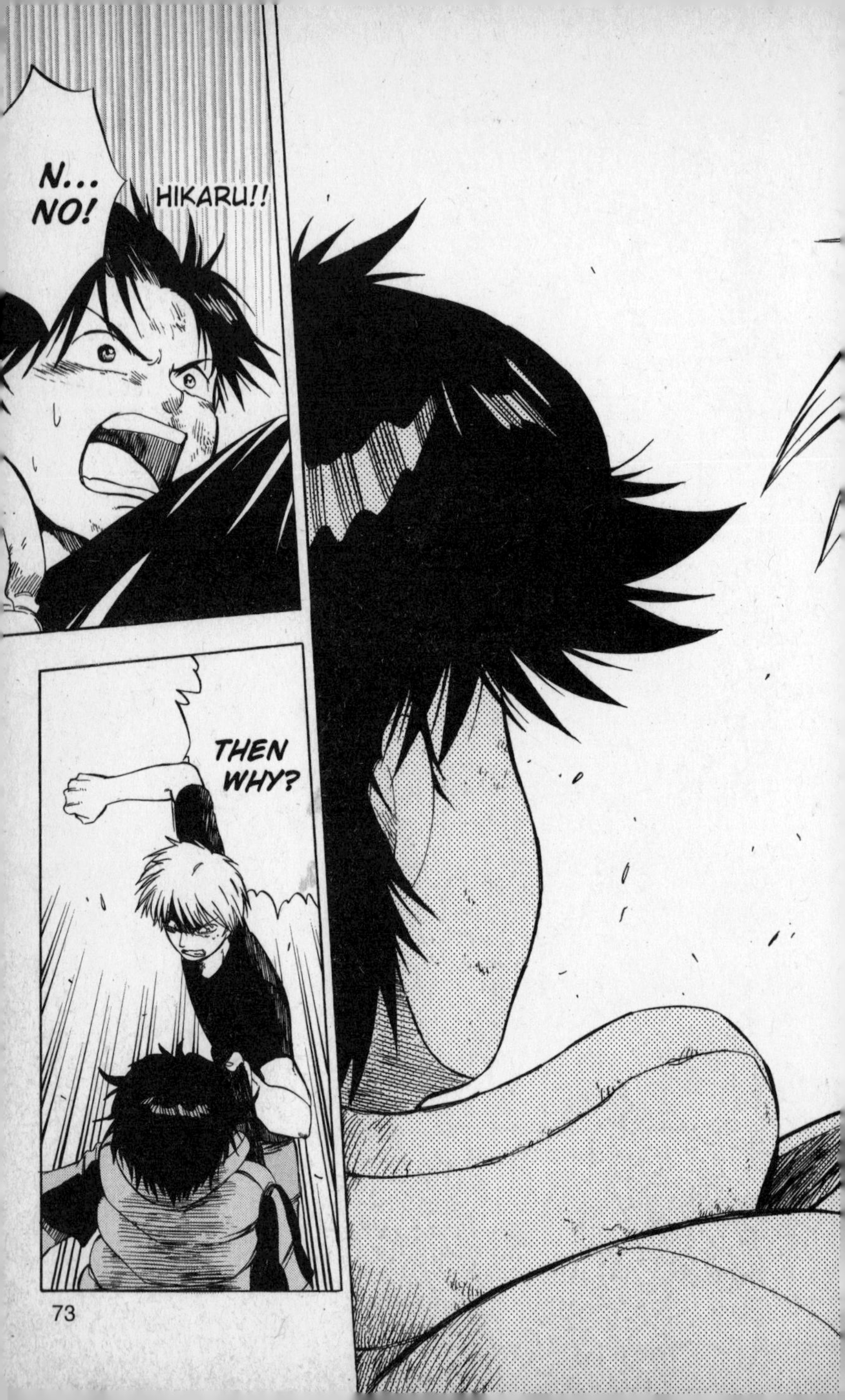
HIKARU!!
N... NO!
THEN WHY?

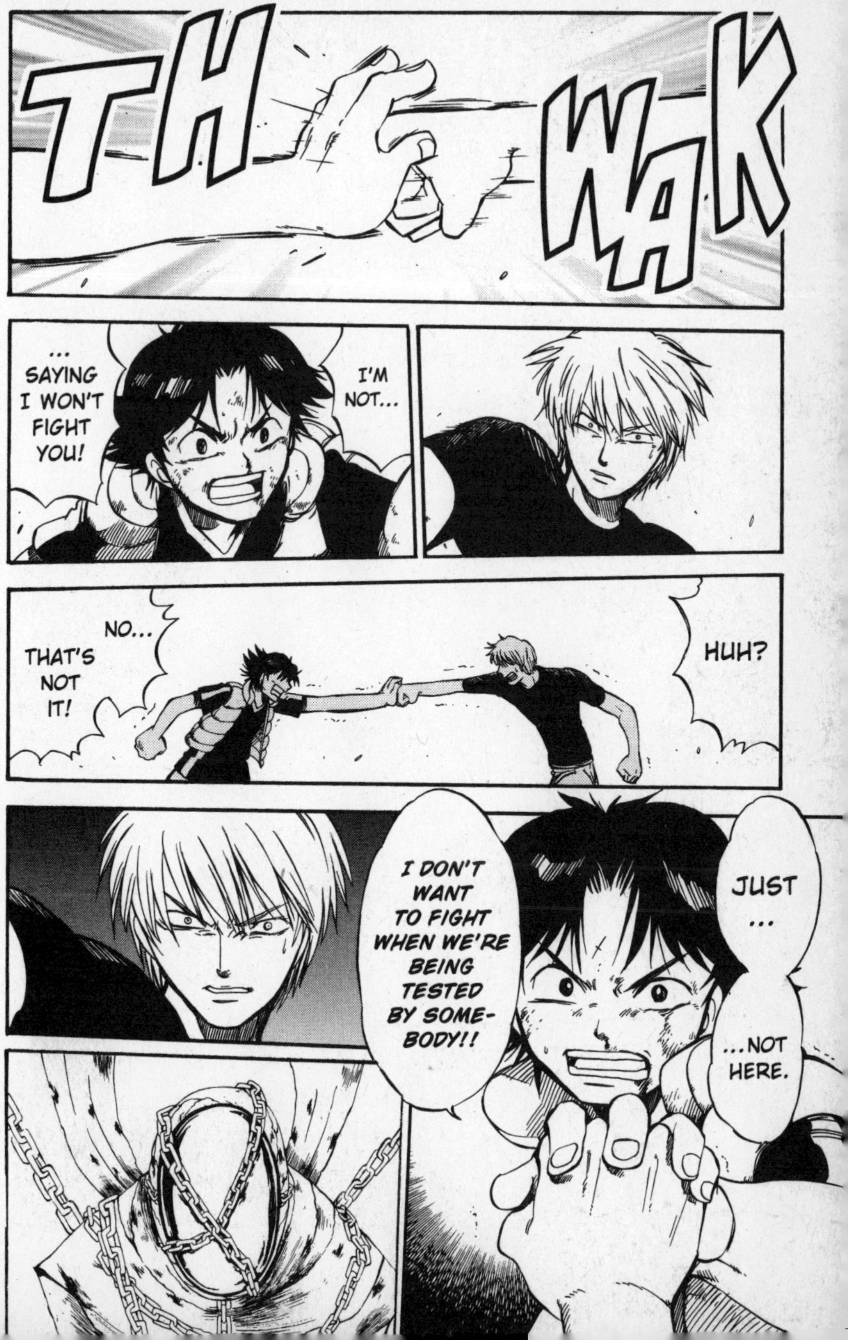
THWAK
I'M NOT...
...SAYING I WON'T FIGHT YOU!
HUH?
NO...
THAT'S NOT IT!
JUST...
...NOT HERE.
I DON'T WANT TO FIGHT WHEN WE'RE BEING TESTED BY SOME-BODY!!

READ THIS WAY

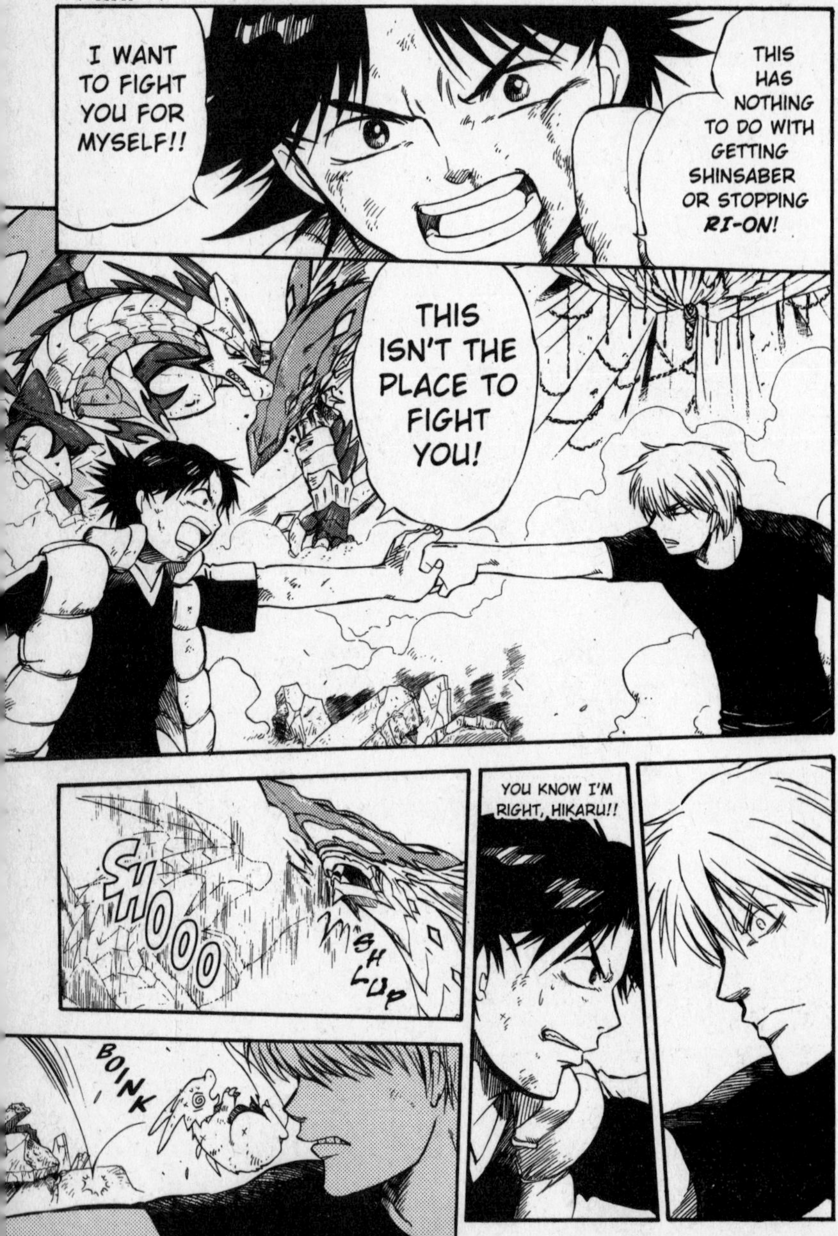
THIS HAS NOTHING TO DO WITH GETTING SHINSABER OR STOPPING RI-ON!
I WANT TO FIGHT YOU FOR MYSELF!!
THIS ISN'T THE PLACE TO FIGHT YOU!
YOU KNOW I'M RIGHT, HIKARU!!
SHOOO
SHLUP
BOINK

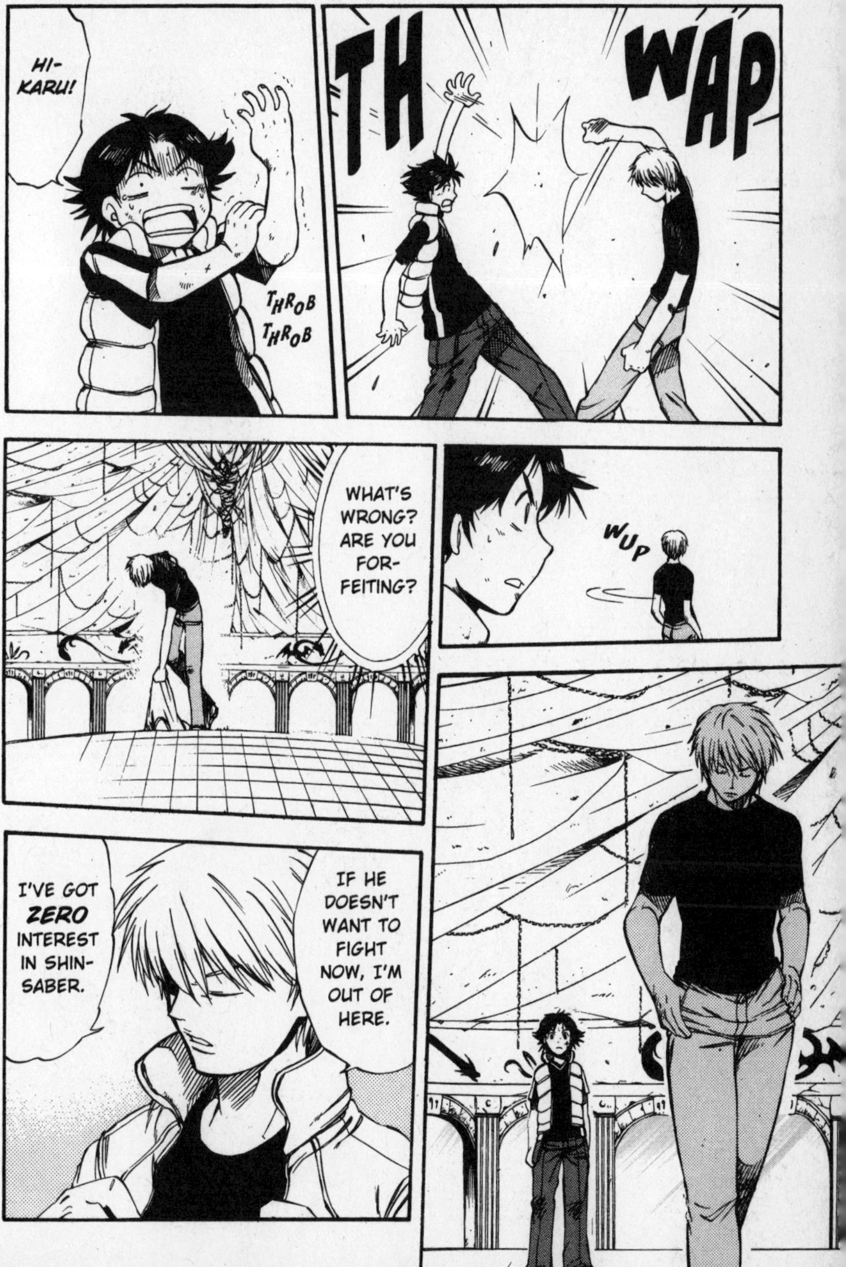
THWAP
HI-KARU!
THROB THROB
WUP
WHAT'S WRONG? ARE YOU FOR-FEITING?
IF HE DOESN'T WANT TO FIGHT NOW, I'M OUT OF HERE.
I'VE GOT **ZERO** INTEREST IN SHIN-SABER.

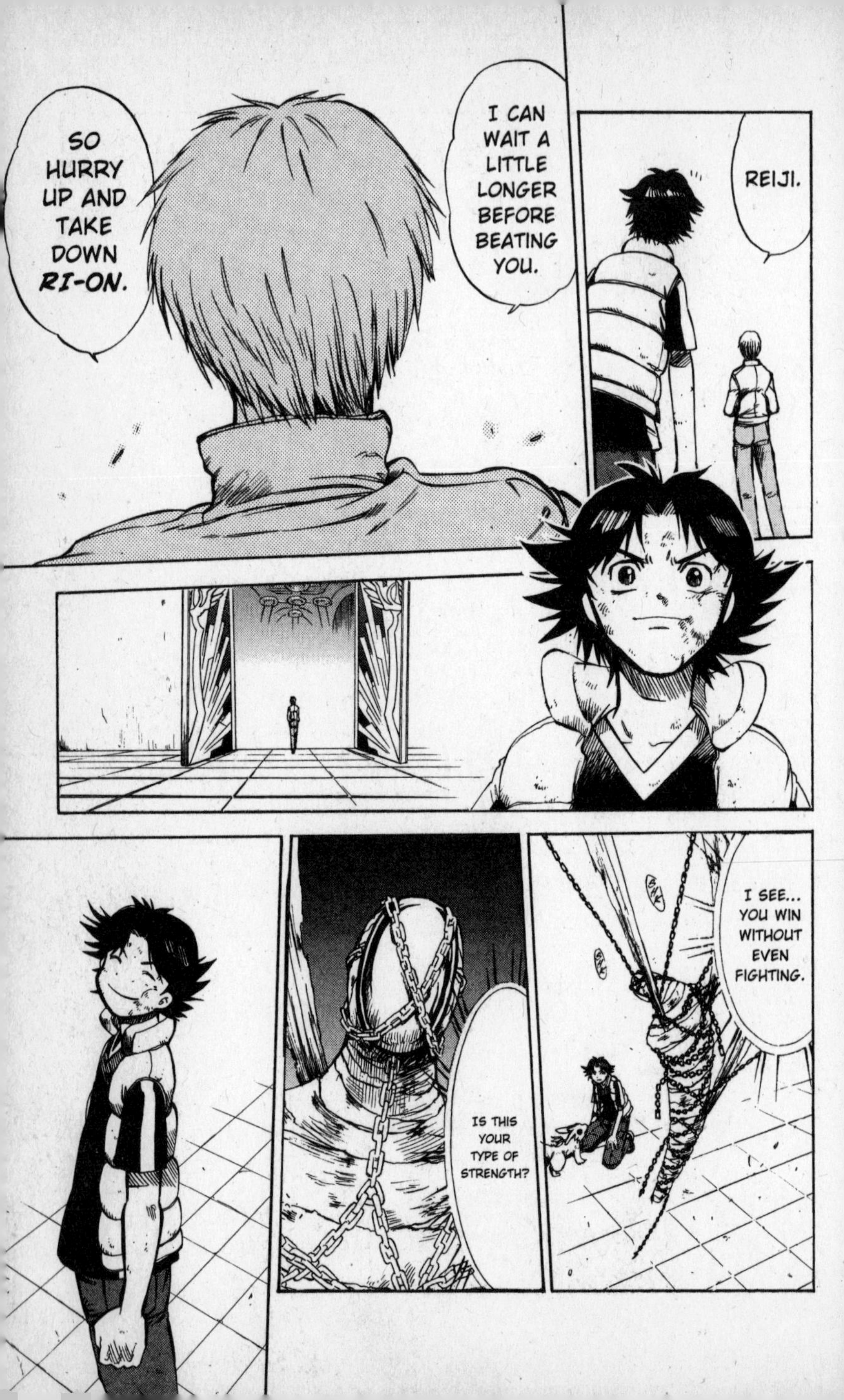
REIJI.
I CAN WAIT A LITTLE LONGER BEFORE BEATING YOU.
SO HURRY UP AND TAKE DOWN *RI-ON*.
SNK
SNK
I SEE... YOU WIN WITHOUT EVEN FIGHTING.
IS THIS YOUR TYPE OF STRENGTH?

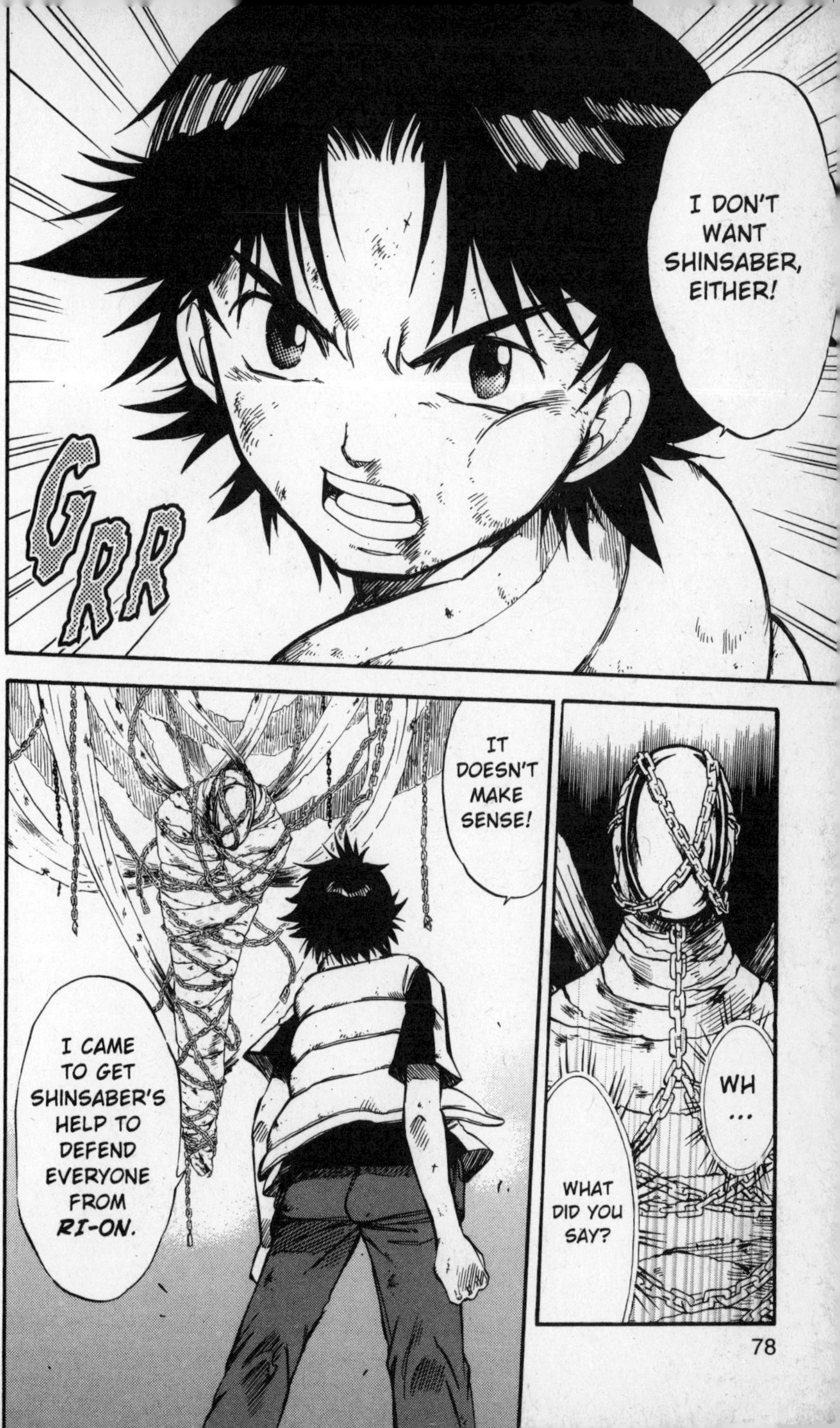
I DON'T WANT SHINSABER, EITHER!
GRR
WH ...
WHAT DID YOU SAY?
IT DOESN'T MAKE SENSE!
I CAME TO GET SHINSABER'S HELP TO DEFEND EVERYONE FROM *RI-ON*.

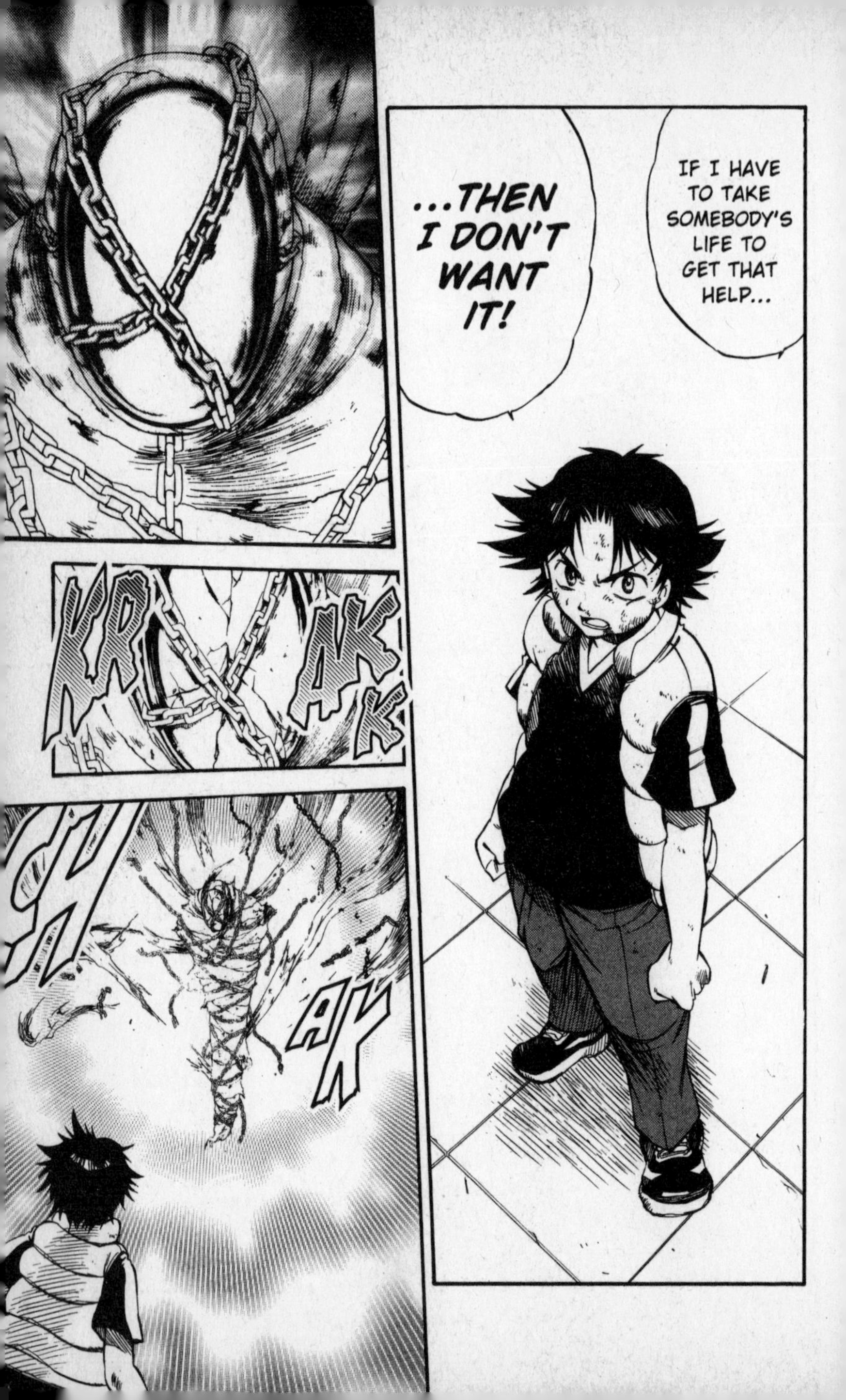
IF I HAVE TO TAKE SOMEBODY'S LIFE TO GET THAT HELP...
...THEN I DON'T WANT IT!
KRAKK
AK

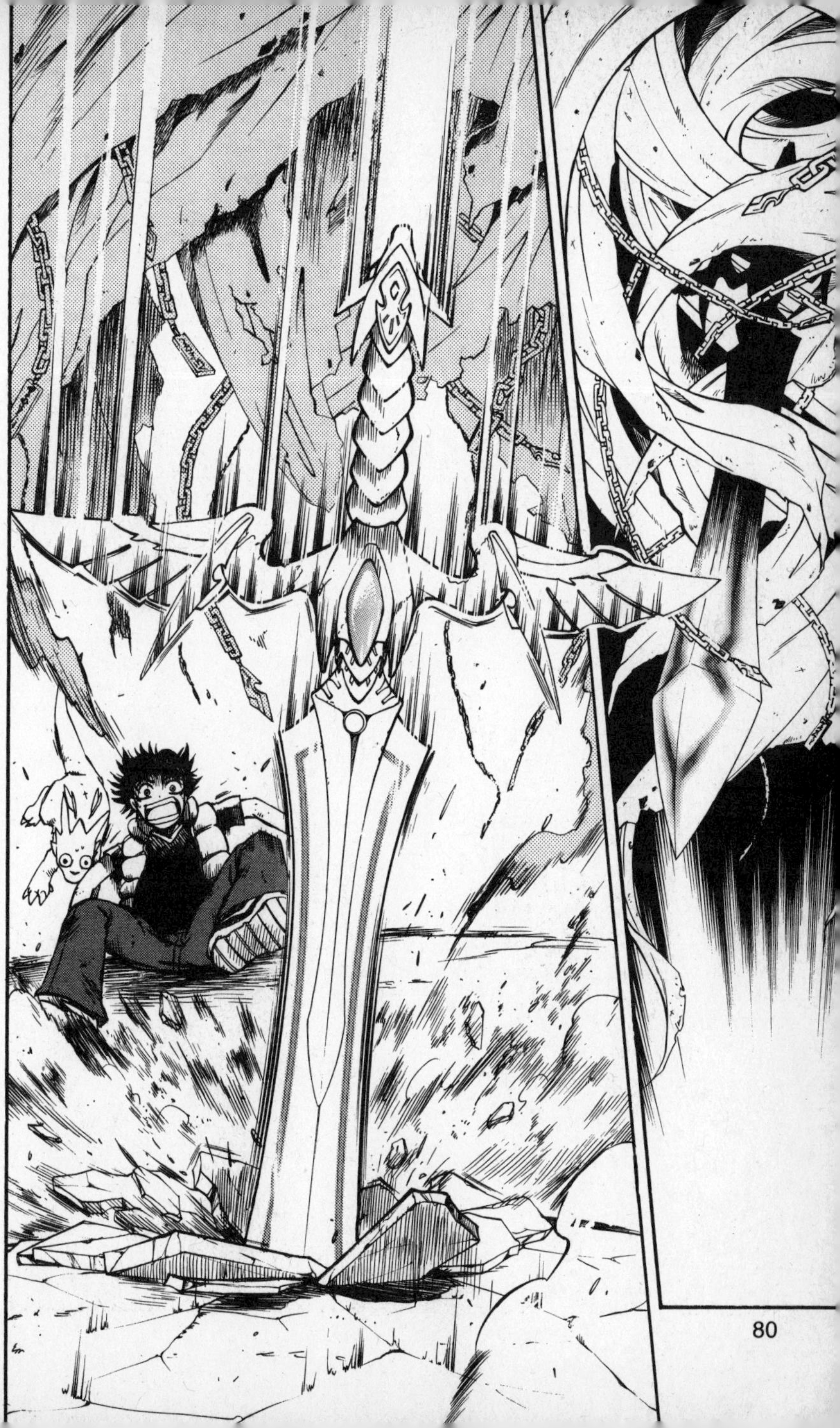

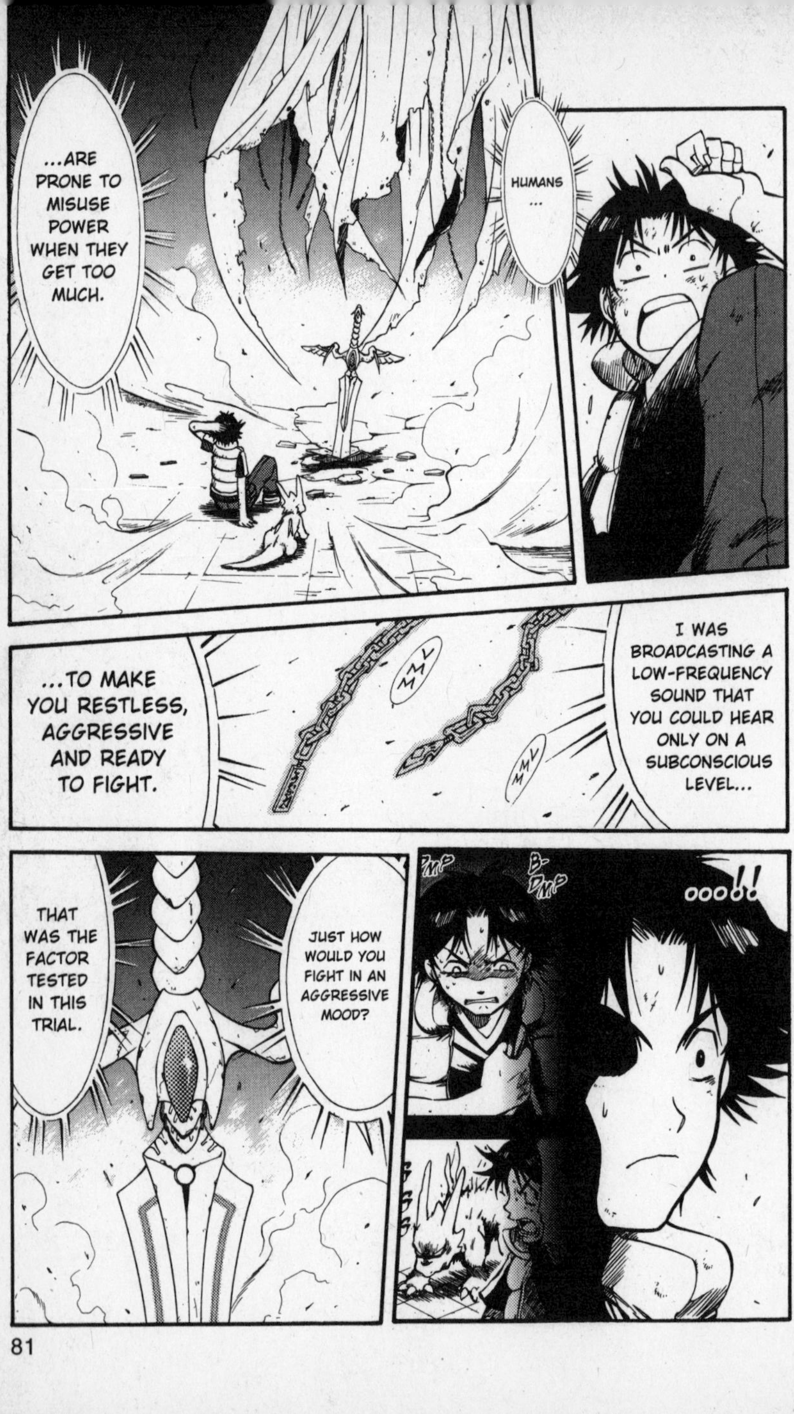
HUMANS ...
...ARE PRONE TO MISUSE POWER WHEN THEY GET TOO MUCH.
I WAS BROADCASTING A LOW-FREQUENCY SOUND THAT YOU COULD HEAR ONLY ON A SUBCONSCIOUS LEVEL...
...TO MAKE YOU RESTLESS, AGGRESSIVE AND READY TO FIGHT.
OOO..!!
B-DMP
DMP
JUST HOW WOULD YOU FIGHT IN AN AGGRESSIVE MOOD?
THAT WAS THE FACTOR TESTED IN THIS TRIAL.

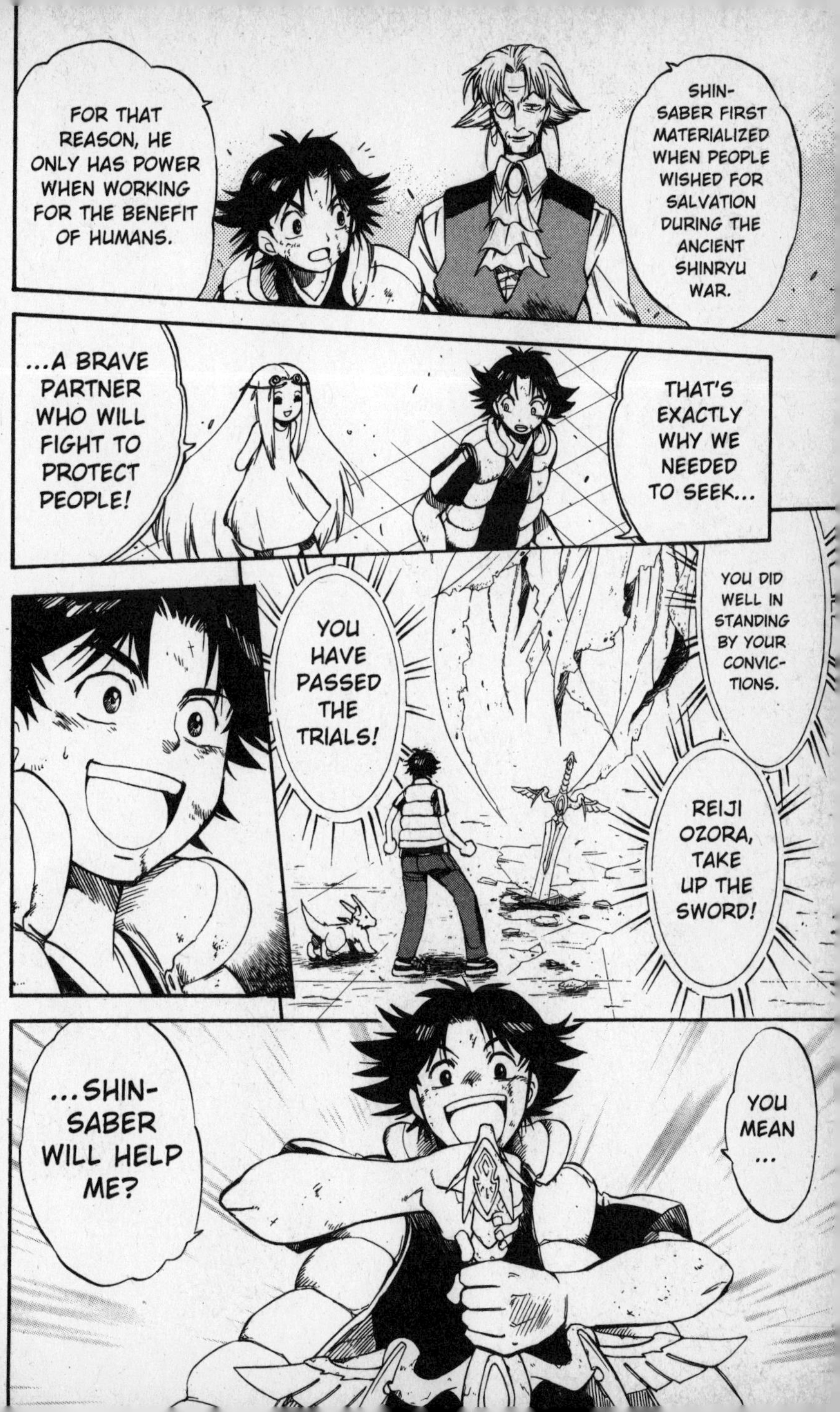
SHIN-SABER FIRST MATERIALIZED WHEN PEOPLE WISHED FOR SALVATION DURING THE ANCIENT SHINRYU WAR.
FOR THAT REASON, HE ONLY HAS POWER WHEN WORKING FOR THE BENEFIT OF HUMANS.
THAT'S EXACTLY WHY WE NEEDED TO SEEK...
...A BRAVE PARTNER WHO WILL FIGHT TO PROTECT PEOPLE!
YOU DID WELL IN STANDING BY YOUR CONVIC-TIONS.
YOU HAVE PASSED THE TRIALS!
REIJI OZORA, TAKE UP THE SWORD!
YOU MEAN...
...SHIN-SABER WILL HELP ME?

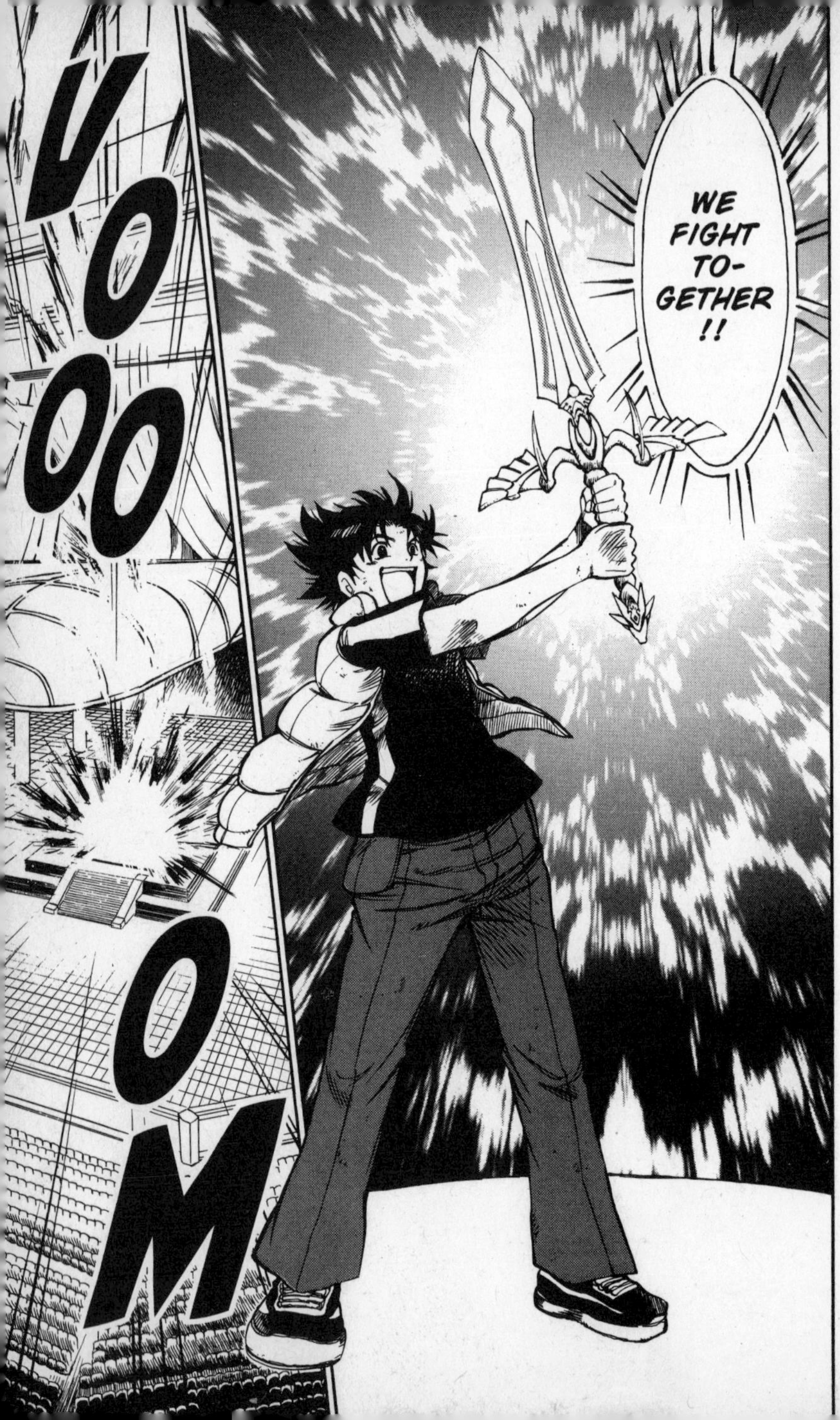
WE FIGHT TO-GETHER !!
VOOOOM

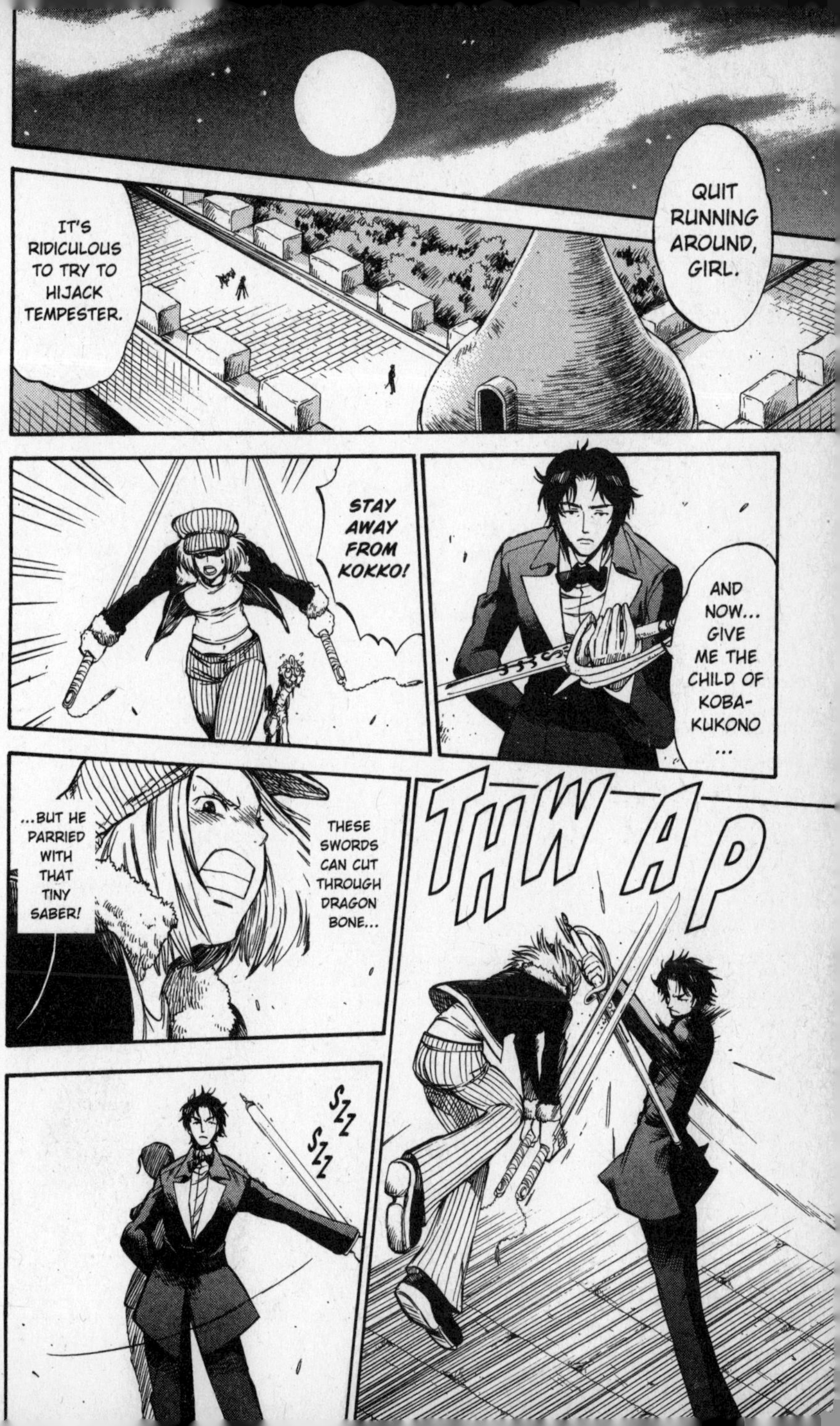
QUIT RUNNING AROUND, GIRL.
IT'S RIDICULOUS TO TRY TO HIJACK TEMPESTER.
AND NOW... GIVE ME THE CHILD OF KOBA-KUKONO...
STAY AWAY FROM KOKKO!
THWAP
THESE SWORDS CAN CUT THROUGH DRAGON BONE...
...BUT HE PARRIED WITH THAT TINY SABER!
SZZ SZZ

READ THIS WAY

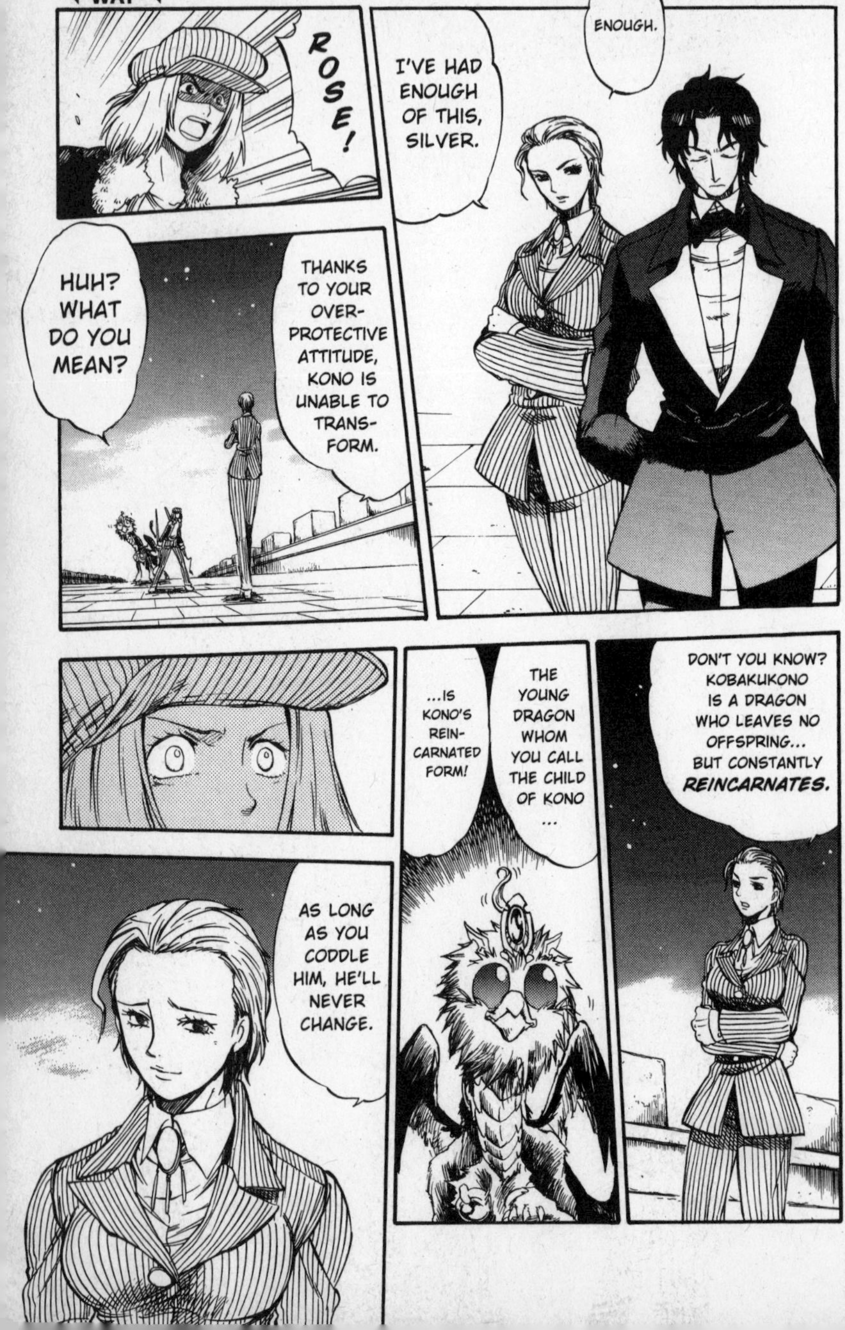
ENOUGH.
I'VE HAD ENOUGH OF THIS, SILVER.
ROSE!
THANKS TO YOUR OVER-PROTECTIVE ATTITUDE, KONO IS UNABLE TO TRANS-FORM.
HUH? WHAT DO YOU MEAN?
DON'T YOU KNOW? KOBAKUKONO IS A DRAGON WHO LEAVES NO OFFSPRING... BUT CONSTANTLY ***REINCARNATES.***
THE YOUNG DRAGON WHOM YOU CALL THE CHILD OF KONO ...
...IS KONO'S REIN-CARNATED FORM!
AS LONG AS YOU CODDLE HIM, HE'LL NEVER CHANGE.

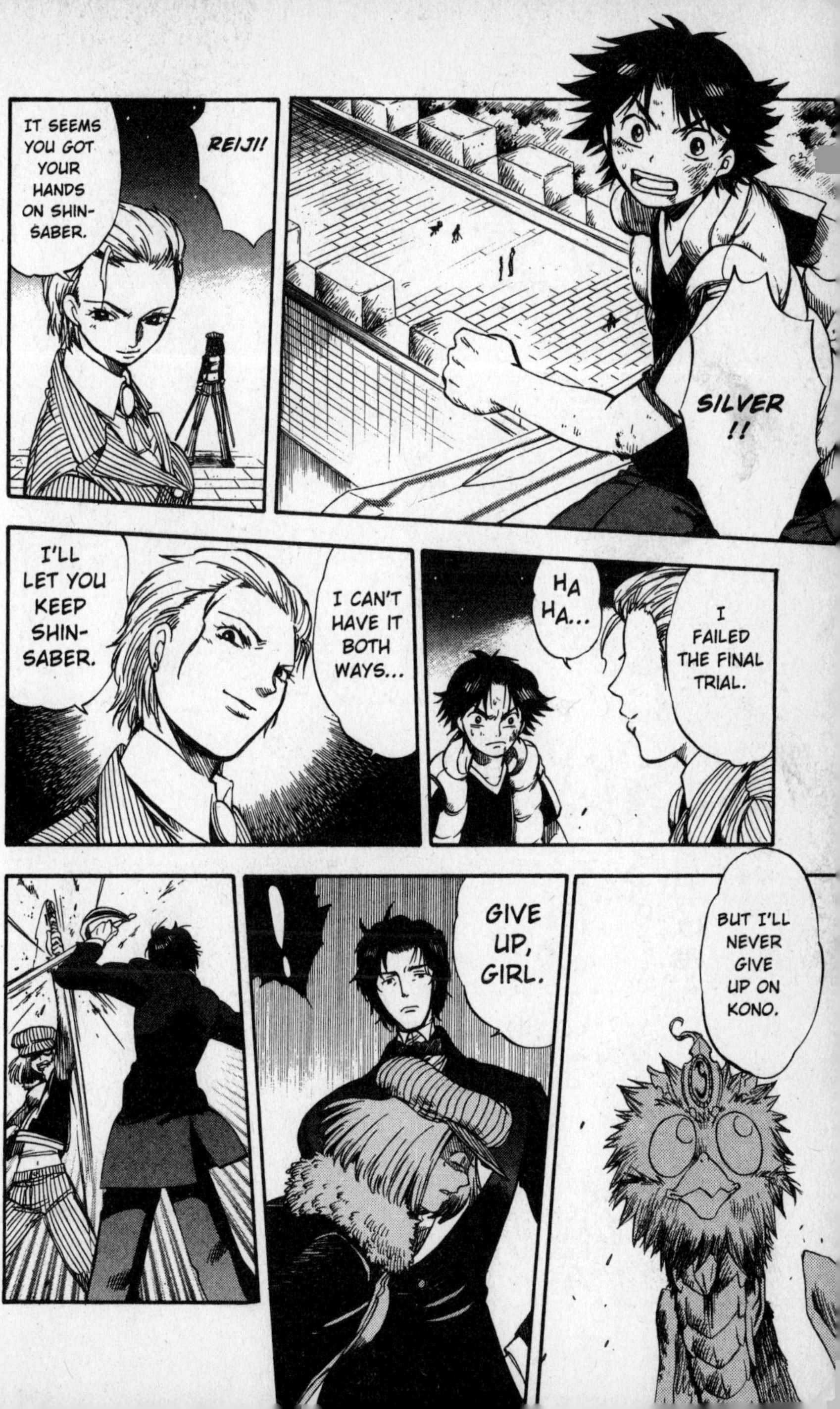
SILVER !!
REIJI!
IT SEEMS YOU GOT YOUR HANDS ON SHIN-SABER.
I FAILED THE FINAL TRIAL.
HA HA...
I CAN'T HAVE IT BOTH WAYS...
I'LL LET YOU KEEP SHIN-SABER.
BUT I'LL NEVER GIVE UP ON KONO.
!
GIVE UP, GIRL.

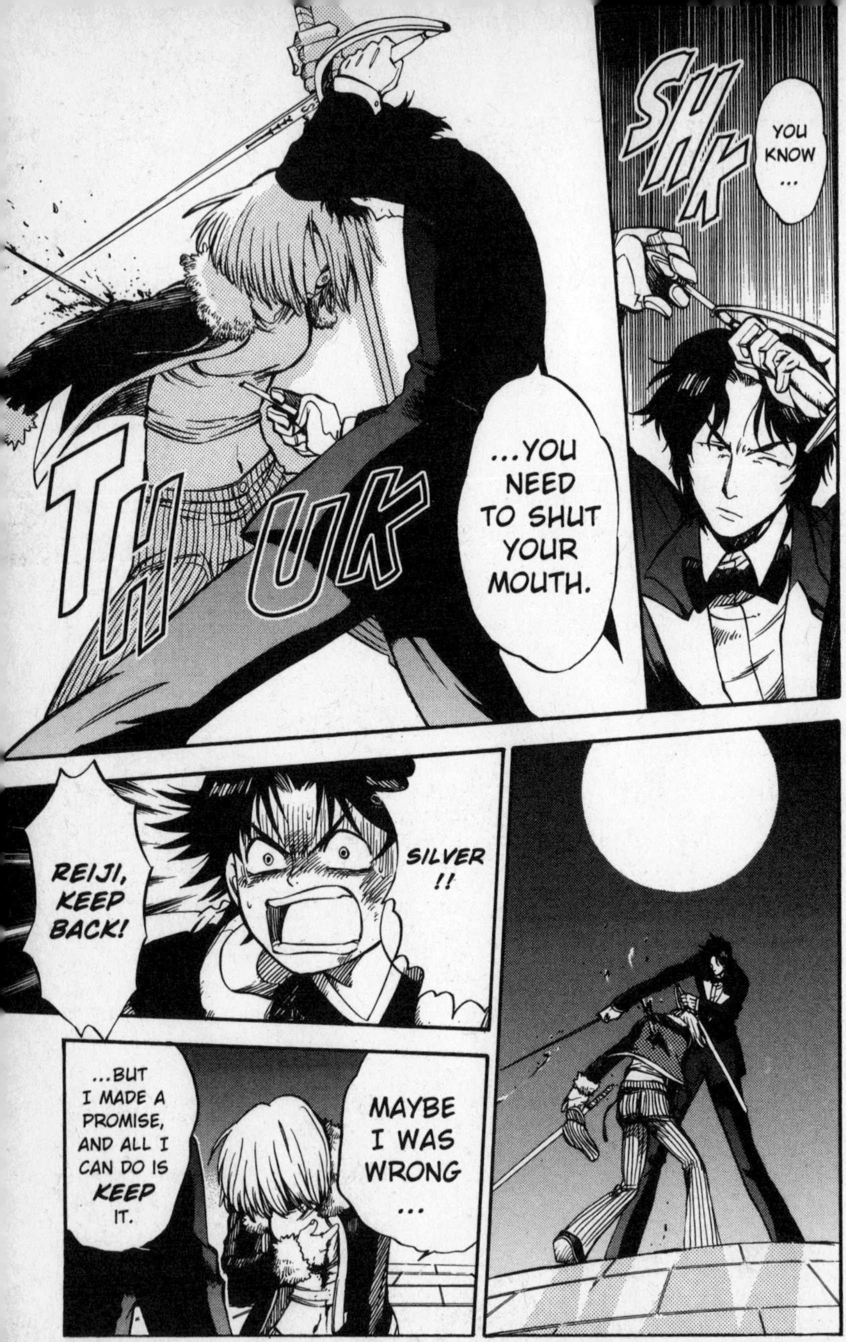
SHK
YOU KNOW...
...YOU NEED TO SHUT YOUR MOUTH.
THUK
SILVER!!
REIJI, KEEP BACK!
MAYBE I WAS WRONG...
...BUT I MADE A PROMISE, AND ALL I CAN DO IS KEEP IT.

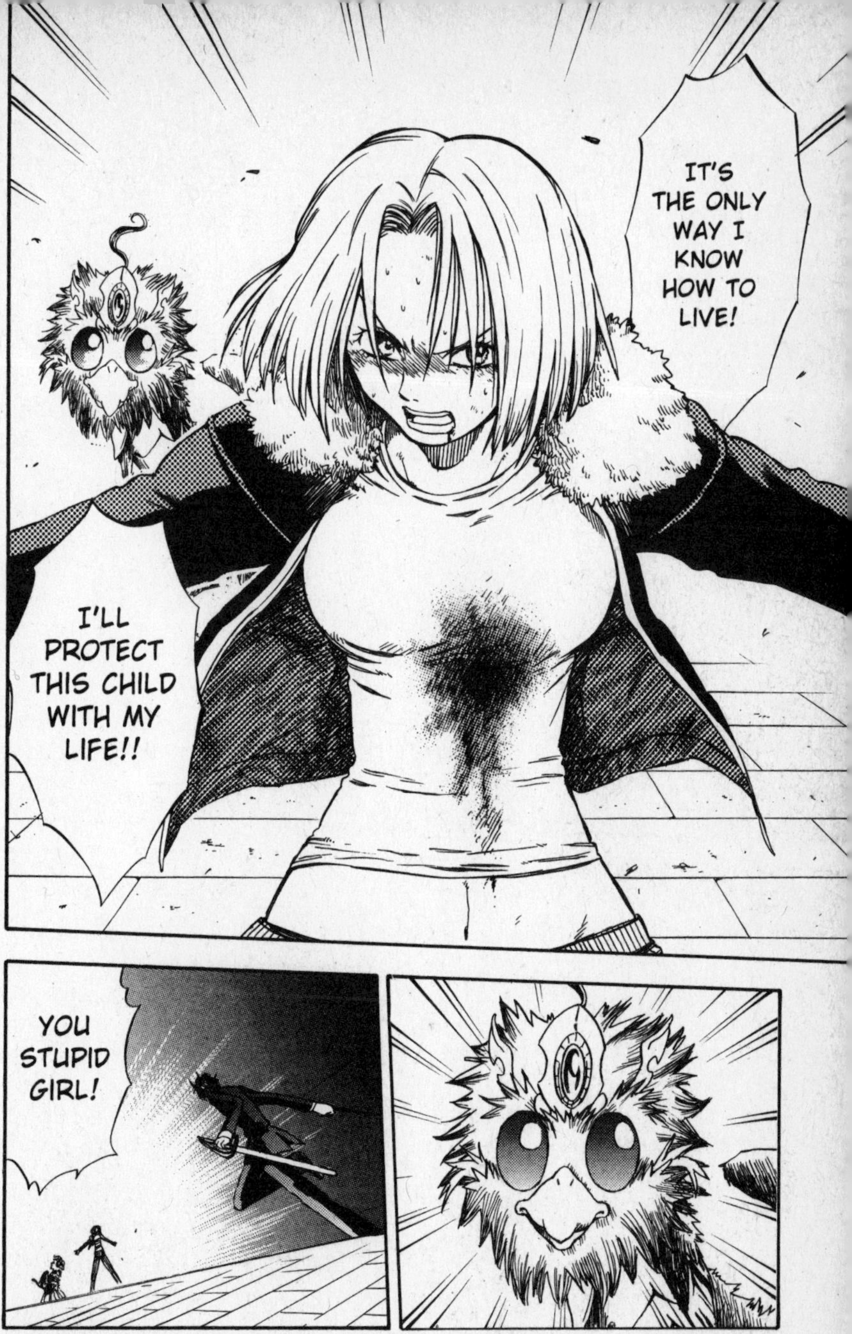
IT'S THE ONLY WAY I KNOW HOW TO LIVE!
I'LL PROTECT THIS CHILD WITH MY LIFE!!
YOU STUPID GIRL!

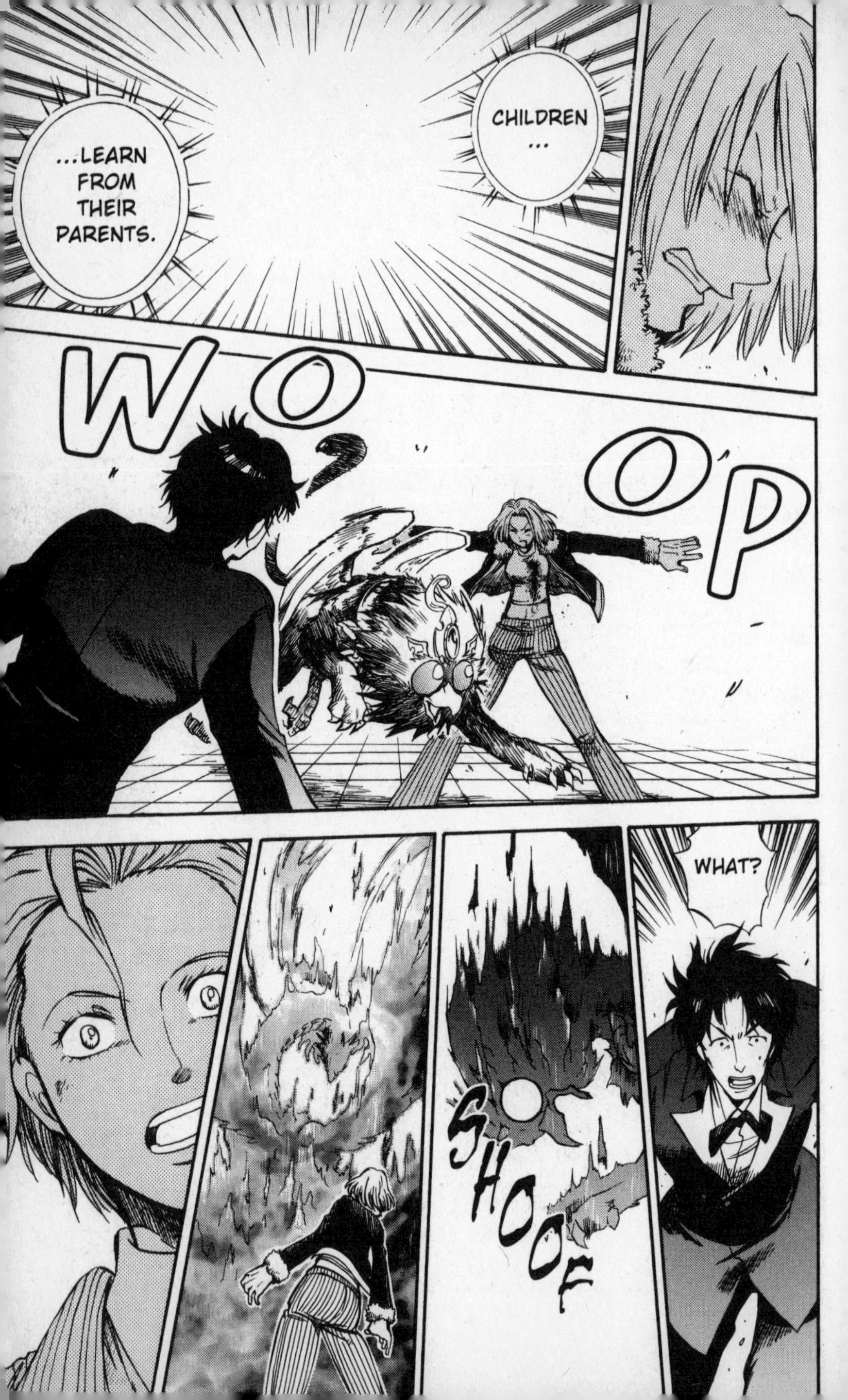
CHILDREN ...
...LEARN FROM THEIR PARENTS.
WOOP
WHAT?
SHOOF

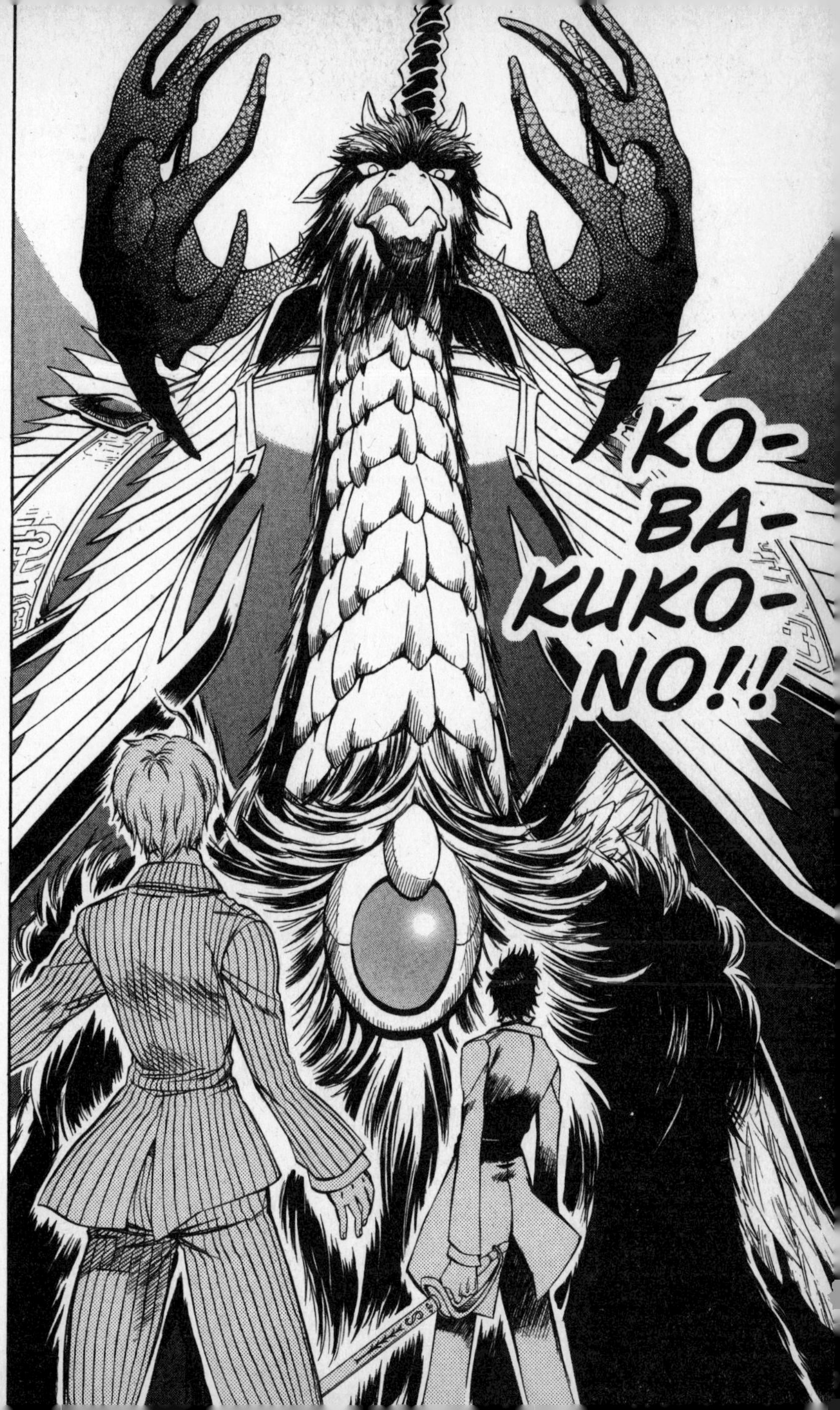
KO-
BA-
KUKO-
NO!!!

READ THIS WAY

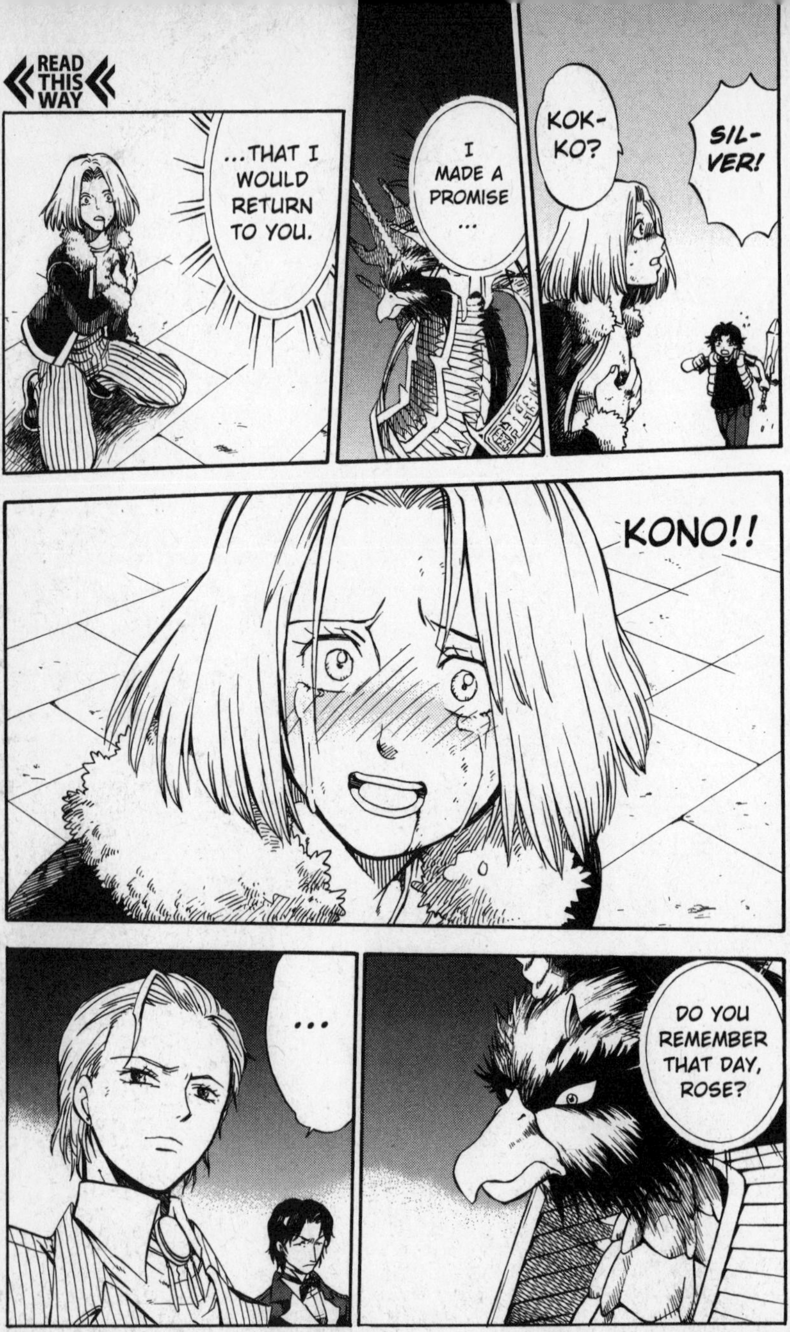
SIL-VER!
KOK-KO?
I MADE A PROMISE ...
...THAT I WOULD RETURN TO YOU.
KONO!!
DO YOU REMEMBER THAT DAY, ROSE?
...

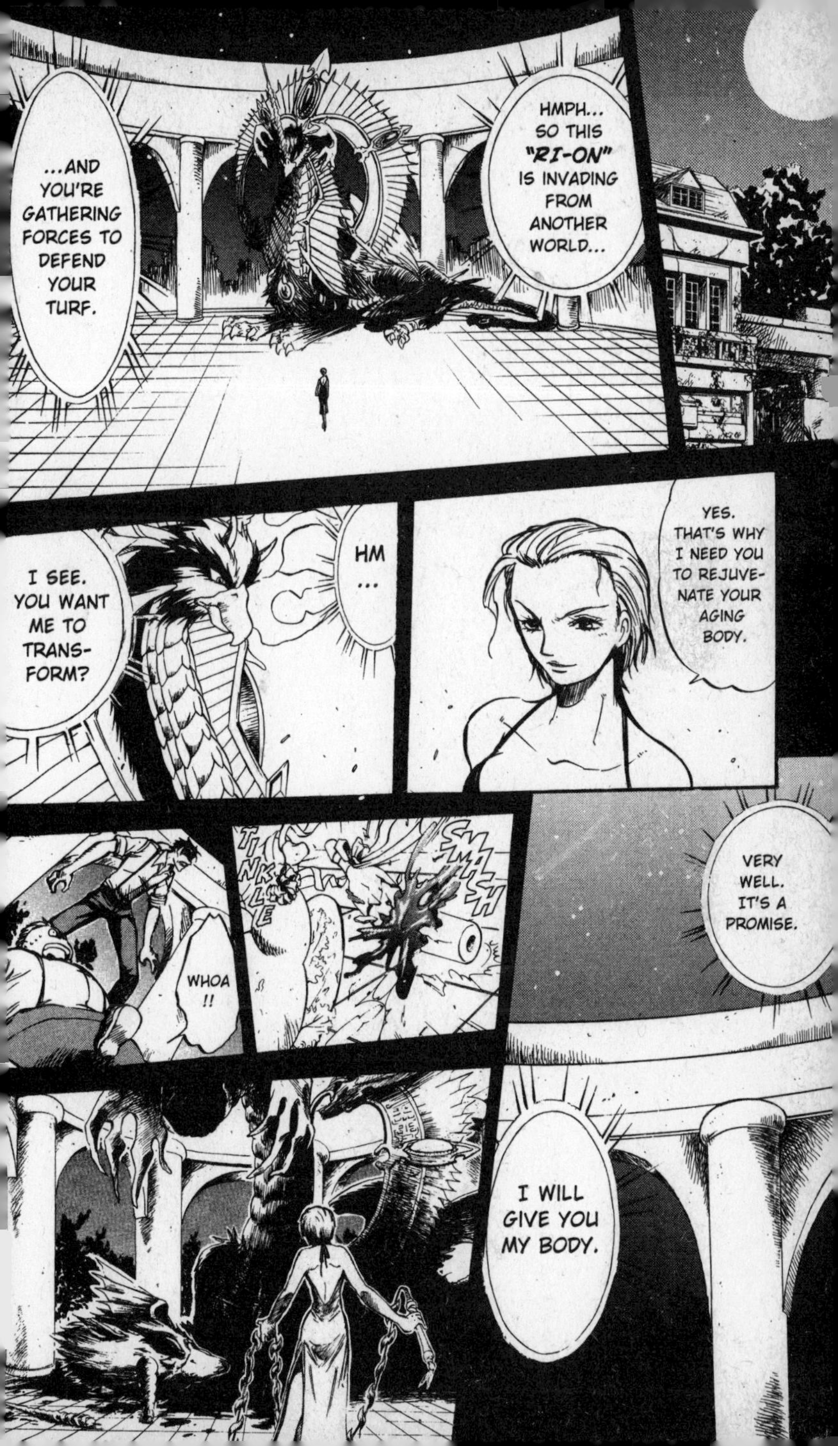
HMPH... SO THIS "RI-ON" IS INVADING FROM ANOTHER WORLD...
...AND YOU'RE GATHERING FORCES TO DEFEND YOUR TURF.
YES. THAT'S WHY I NEED YOU TO REJUVE-NATE YOUR AGING BODY.
HM ...
I SEE. YOU WANT ME TO TRANS-FORM?
VERY WELL. IT'S A PROMISE.
SMASH
TINKLE
WHOA !!
I WILL GIVE YOU MY BODY.

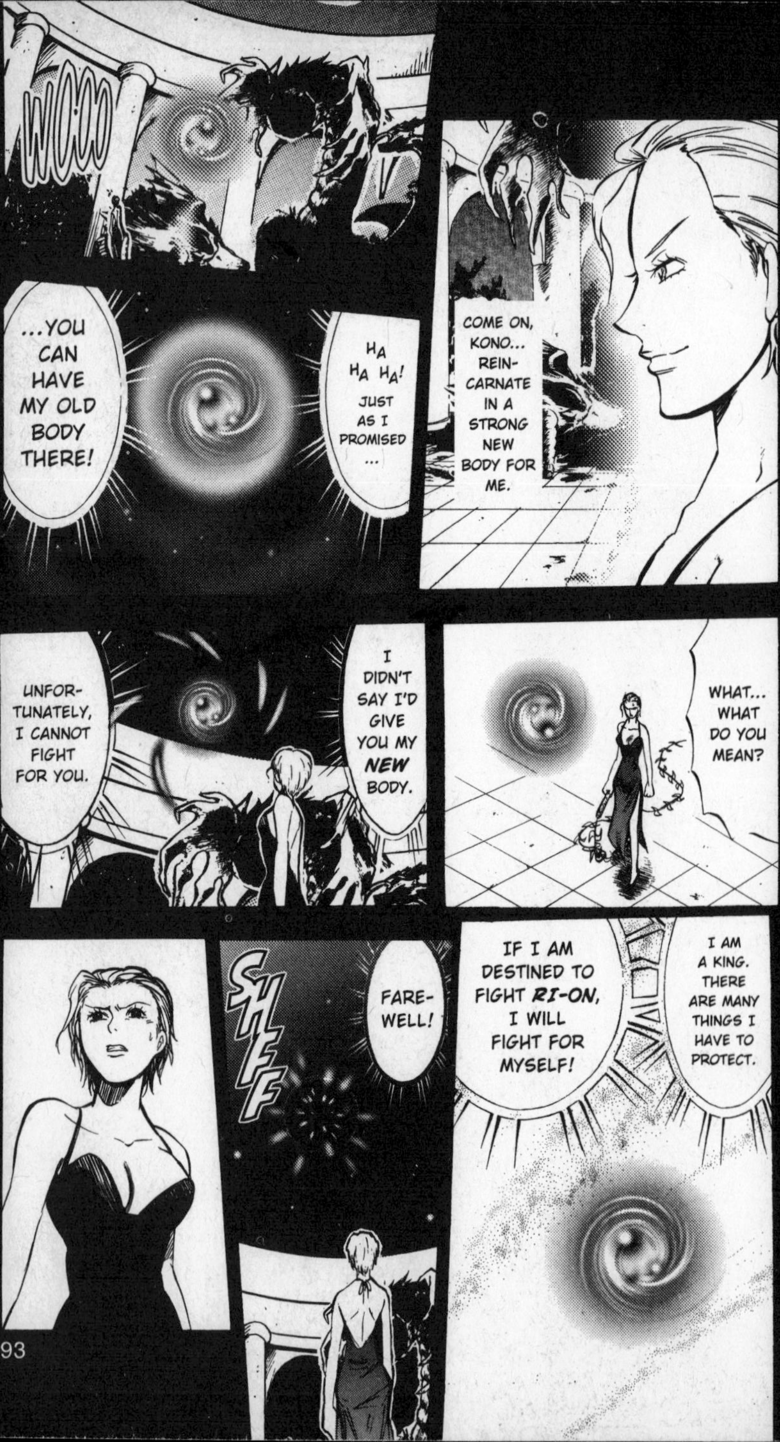
COME ON, KONO... REIN-CARNATE IN A STRONG NEW BODY FOR ME.
WOOO
HA HA HA! JUST AS I PROMISED...
...YOU CAN HAVE MY OLD BODY THERE!
WHAT... WHAT DO YOU MEAN?
I DIDN'T SAY I'D GIVE YOU MY NEW BODY.
UNFOR-TUNATELY, I CANNOT FIGHT FOR YOU.
I AM A KING. THERE ARE MANY THINGS I HAVE TO PROTECT.
IF I AM DESTINED TO FIGHT RI-ON, I WILL FIGHT FOR MYSELF!
FARE-WELL!
SHFF

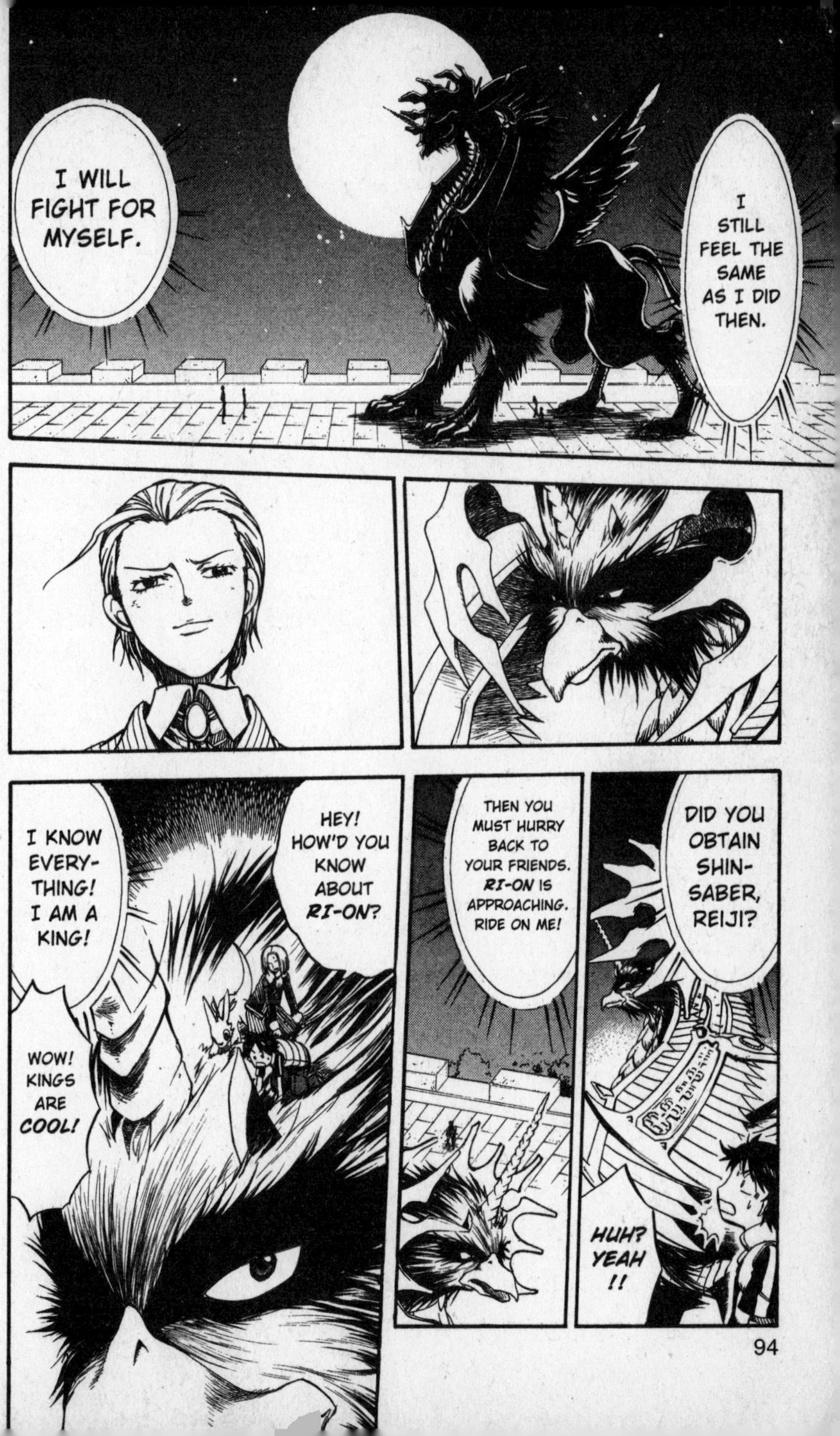
I STILL FEEL THE SAME AS I DID THEN.
I WILL FIGHT FOR MYSELF.
DID YOU OBTAIN SHIN-SABER, REIJI?
HUH? YEAH !!
THEN YOU MUST HURRY BACK TO YOUR FRIENDS. RI-ON IS APPROACHING. RIDE ON ME!
HEY! HOW'D YOU KNOW ABOUT RI-ON?
I KNOW EVERY-THING! I AM A KING!
WOW! KINGS ARE COOL!

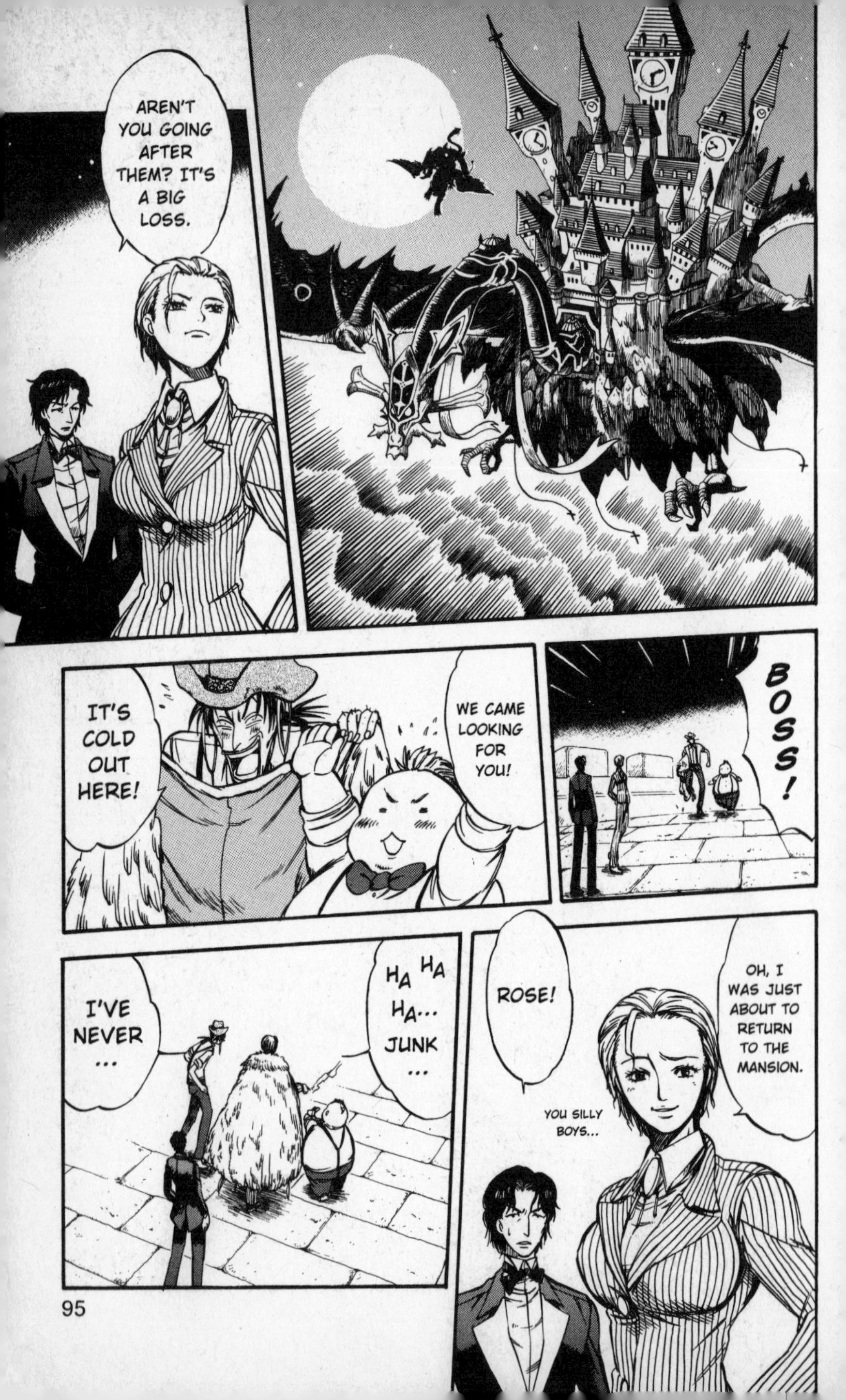
AREN'T YOU GOING AFTER THEM? IT'S A BIG LOSS.
BOSS!
WE CAME LOOKING FOR YOU!
IT'S COLD OUT HERE!
ROSE!
OH, I WAS JUST ABOUT TO RETURN TO THE MANSION.
YOU SILLY BOYS...
HA HA HA... JUNK...
I'VE NEVER...

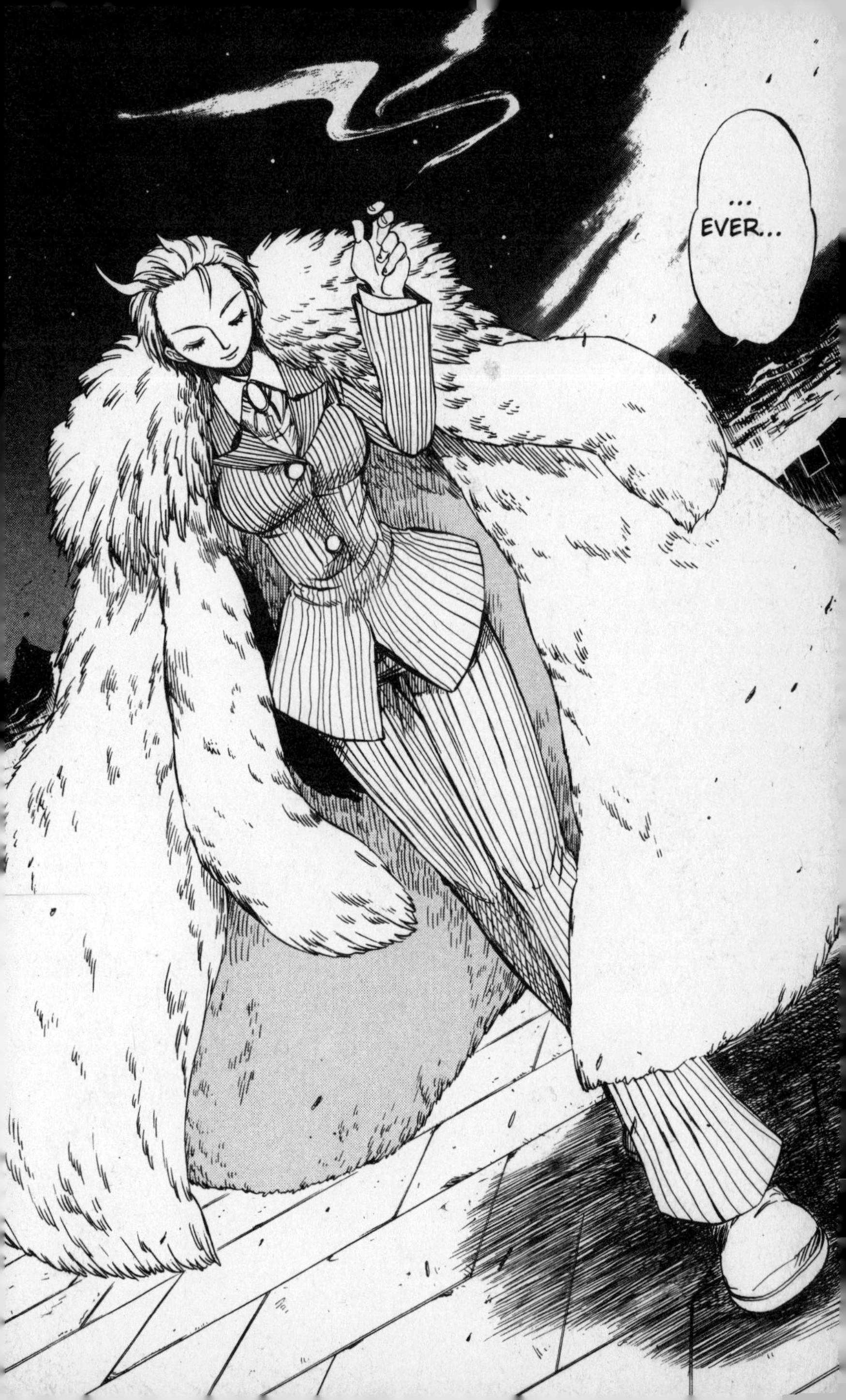
...
EVER...

READ THIS WAY

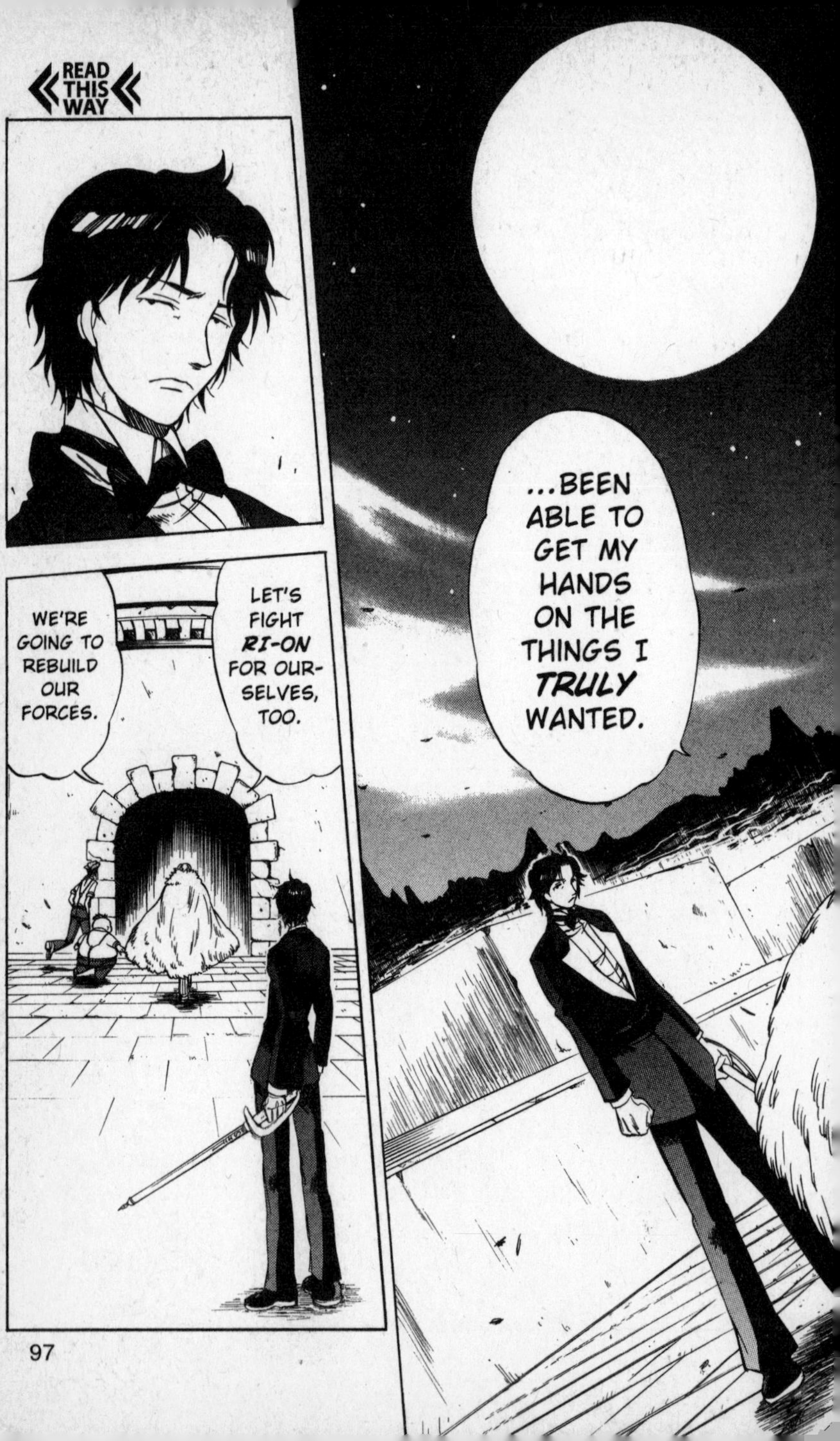
...BEEN ABLE TO GET MY HANDS ON THE THINGS I *TRULY* WANTED.
LET'S FIGHT *RI-ON* FOR OUR-SELVES, TOO.
WE'RE GOING TO REBUILD OUR FORCES.

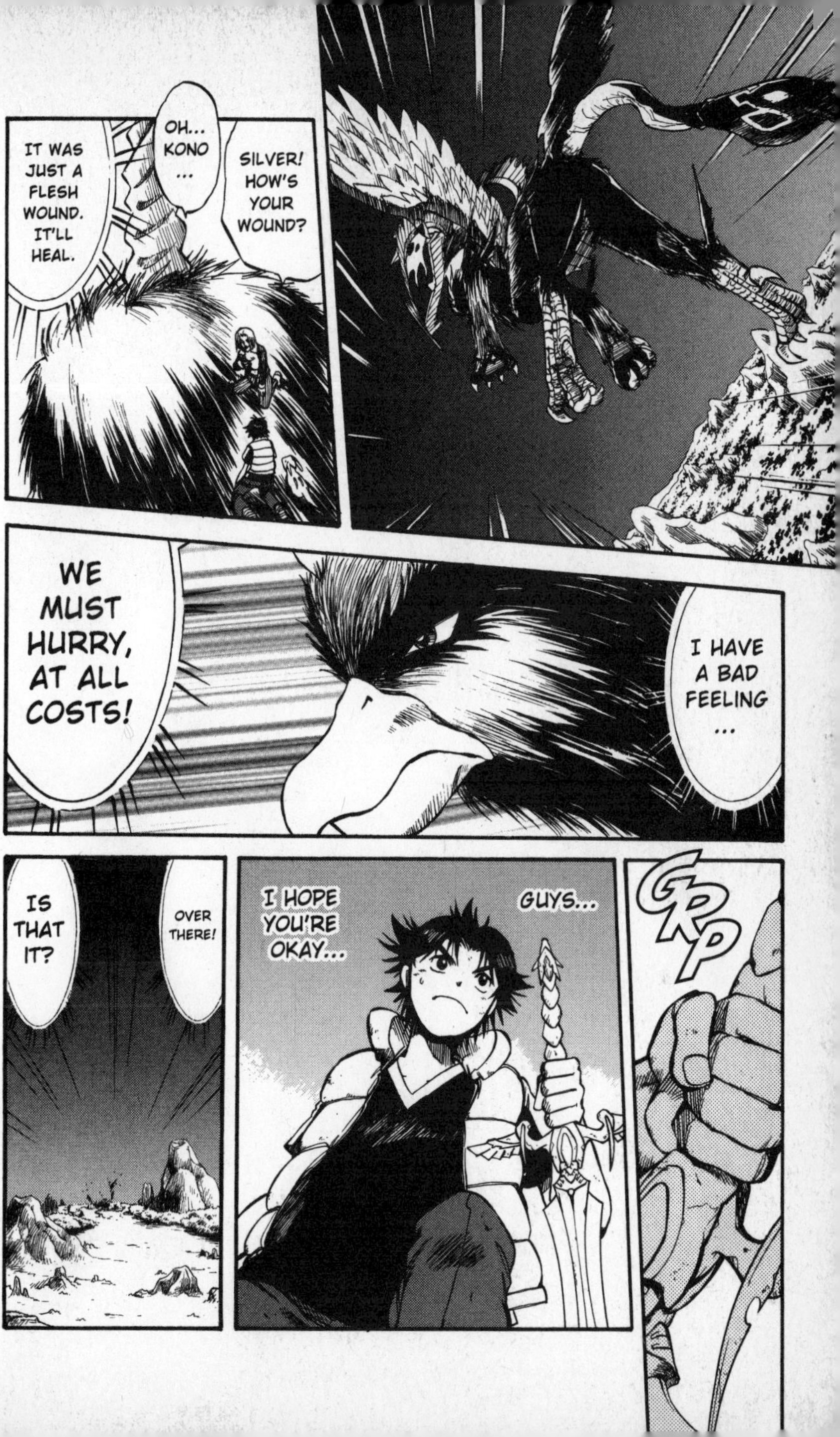
SILVER! HOW'S YOUR WOUND?
OH... KONO ...
IT WAS JUST A FLESH WOUND. IT'LL HEAL.
I HAVE A BAD FEELING ...
WE MUST HURRY, AT ALL COSTS!
GRP
GUYS...
I HOPE YOU'RE OKAY...
OVER THERE!
IS THAT IT?

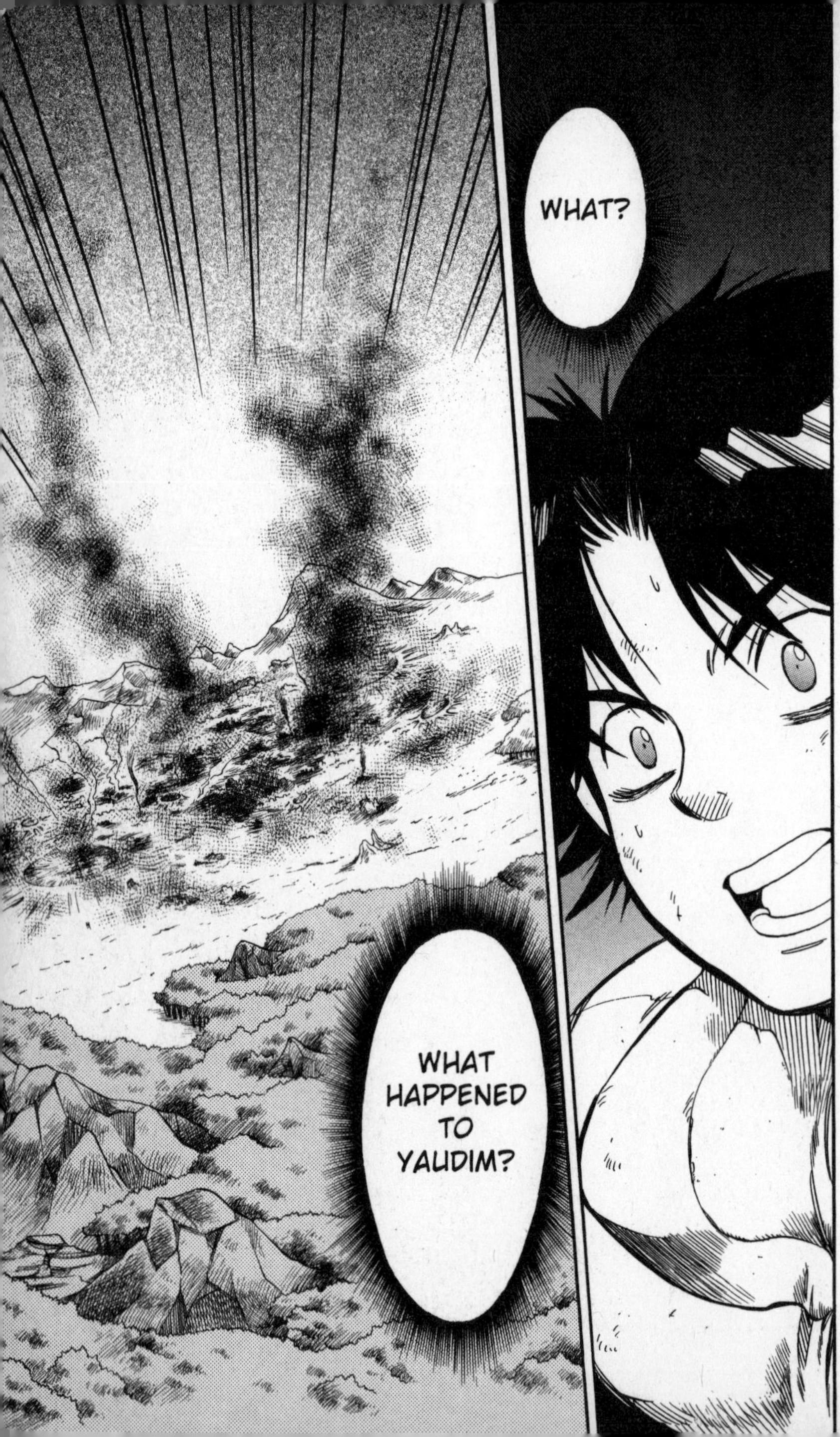
WHAT?
WHAT HAPPENED TO YAUDIM?

GO, PAPA!

BY KIDOCCHI

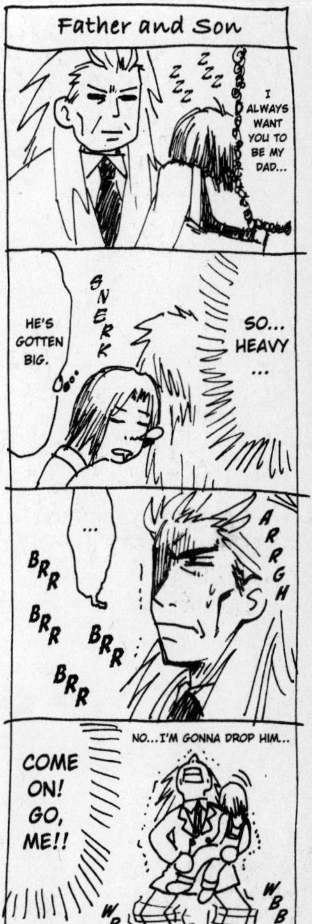
Father and Son
ZZZ
I ALWAYS WANT YOU TO BE MY DAD...
SO... HEAVY ...
SNERK
HE'S GOTTEN BIG.
ARRGH
...
BRR
BRR
BRR
BRR
NO...I'M GONNA DROP HIM...
WBB
COME ON! GO, ME!!
WBB

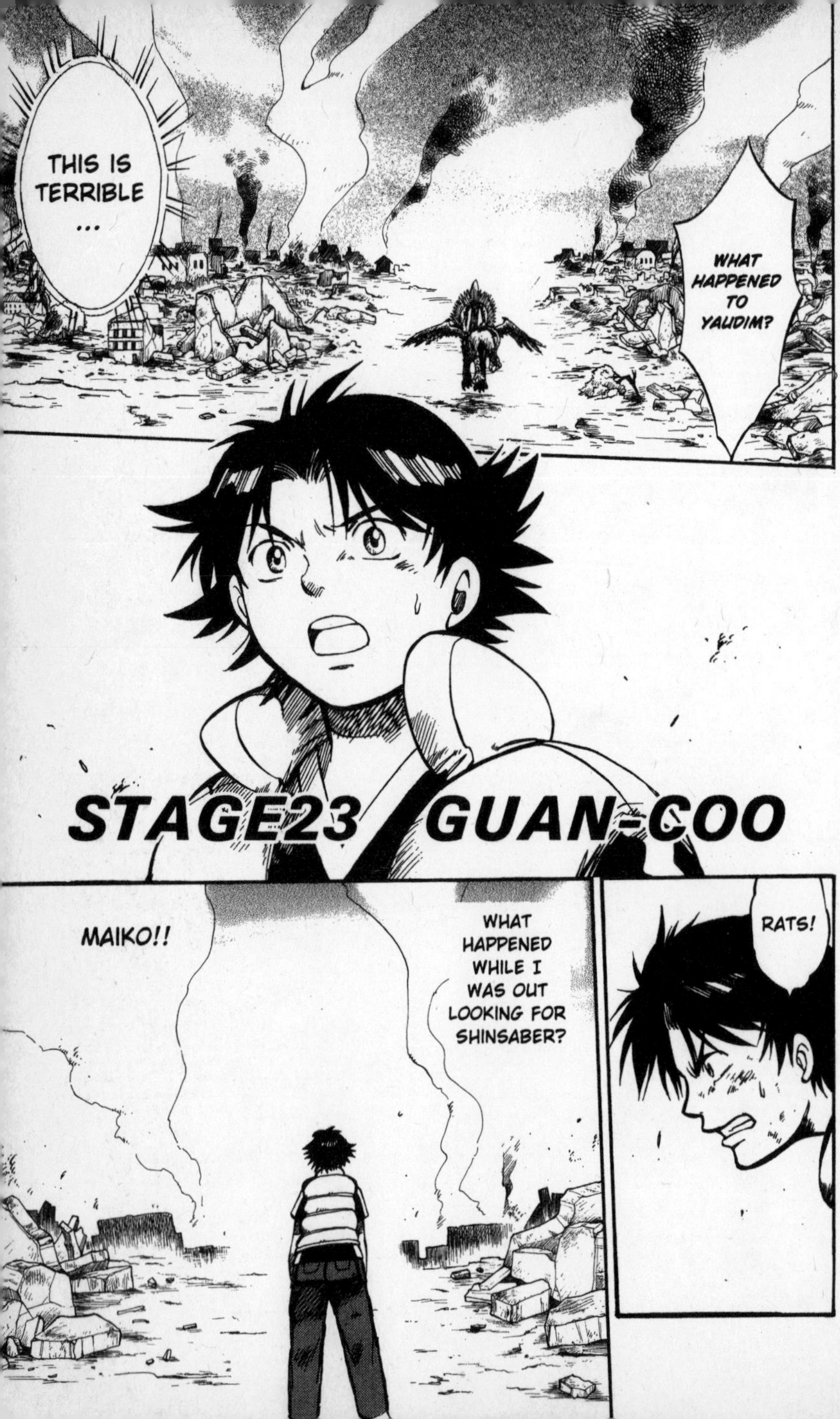
WHAT HAPPENED TO YAUDIM?
THIS IS TERRIBLE ...
STAGE23 GUAN-COO
RATS!
WHAT HAPPENED WHILE I WAS OUT LOOKING FOR SHINSABER?
MAIKO!!

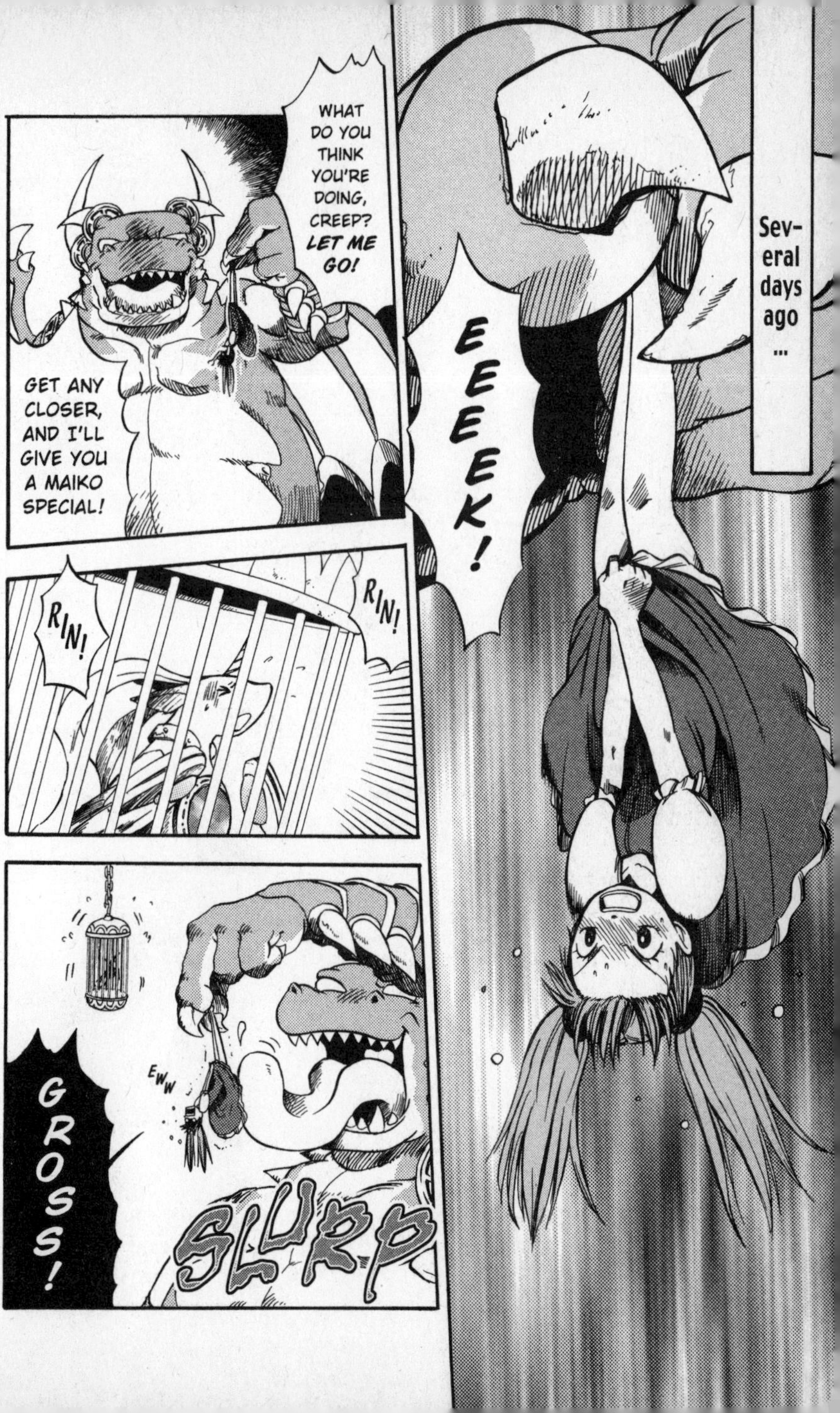
Sev-
eral
days
ago
...
EEEEEK!
WHAT DO YOU THINK YOU'RE DOING, CREEP? LET ME GO!
GET ANY CLOSER, AND I'LL GIVE YOU A MAIKO SPECIAL!
RIN!
RIN!
EWW
GROSS!
SLURP

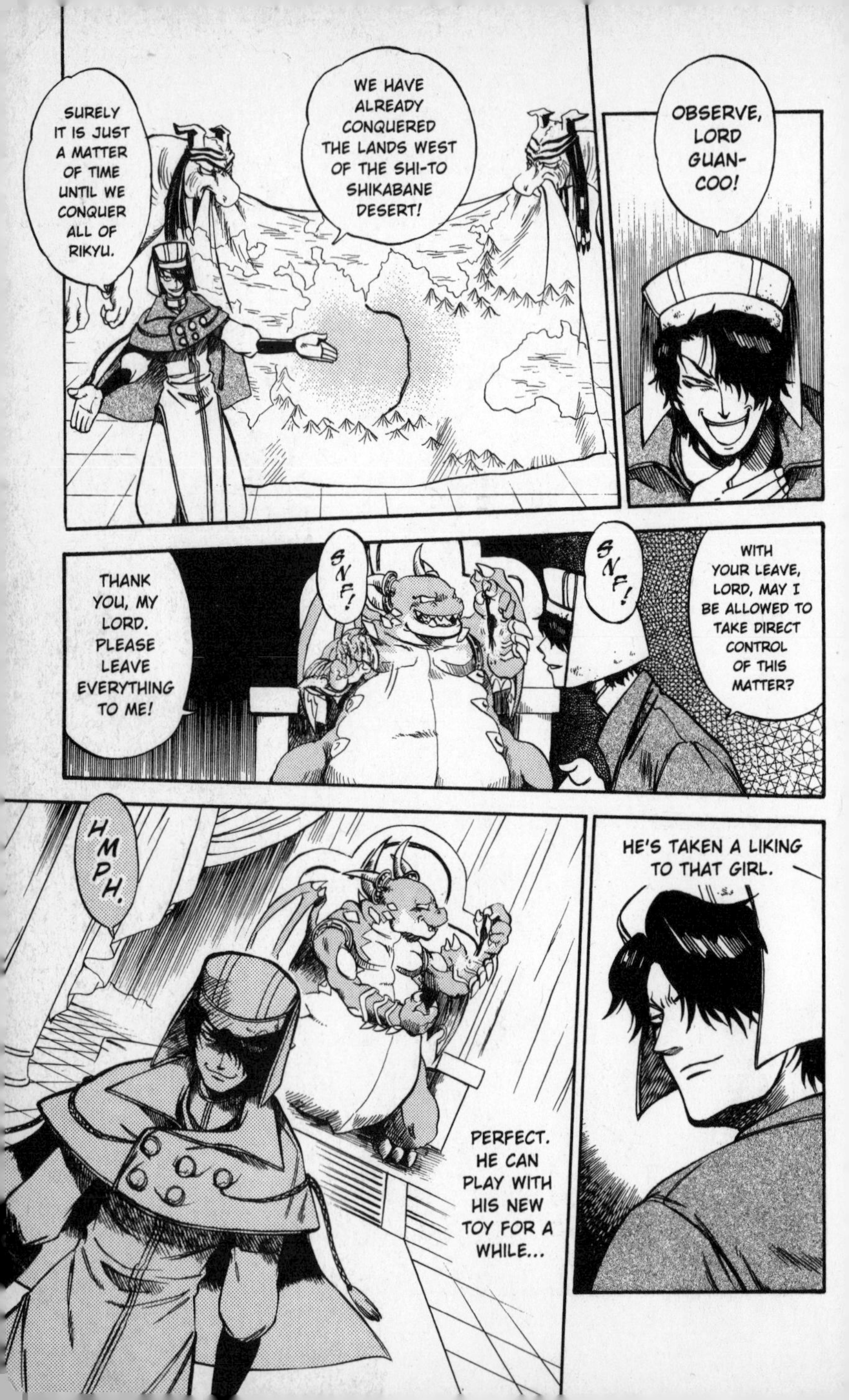
OBSERVE, LORD GUAN-COO!
WE HAVE ALREADY CONQUERED THE LANDS WEST OF THE SHI-TO SHIKABANE DESERT!
SURELY IT IS JUST A MATTER OF TIME UNTIL WE CONQUER ALL OF RIKYU.
WITH YOUR LEAVE, LORD, MAY I BE ALLOWED TO TAKE DIRECT CONTROL OF THIS MATTER?
SNF!
SNF!
THANK YOU, MY LORD. PLEASE LEAVE EVERYTHING TO ME!
HE'S TAKEN A LIKING TO THAT GIRL.
HMPH.
PERFECT. HE CAN PLAY WITH HIS NEW TOY FOR A WHILE...

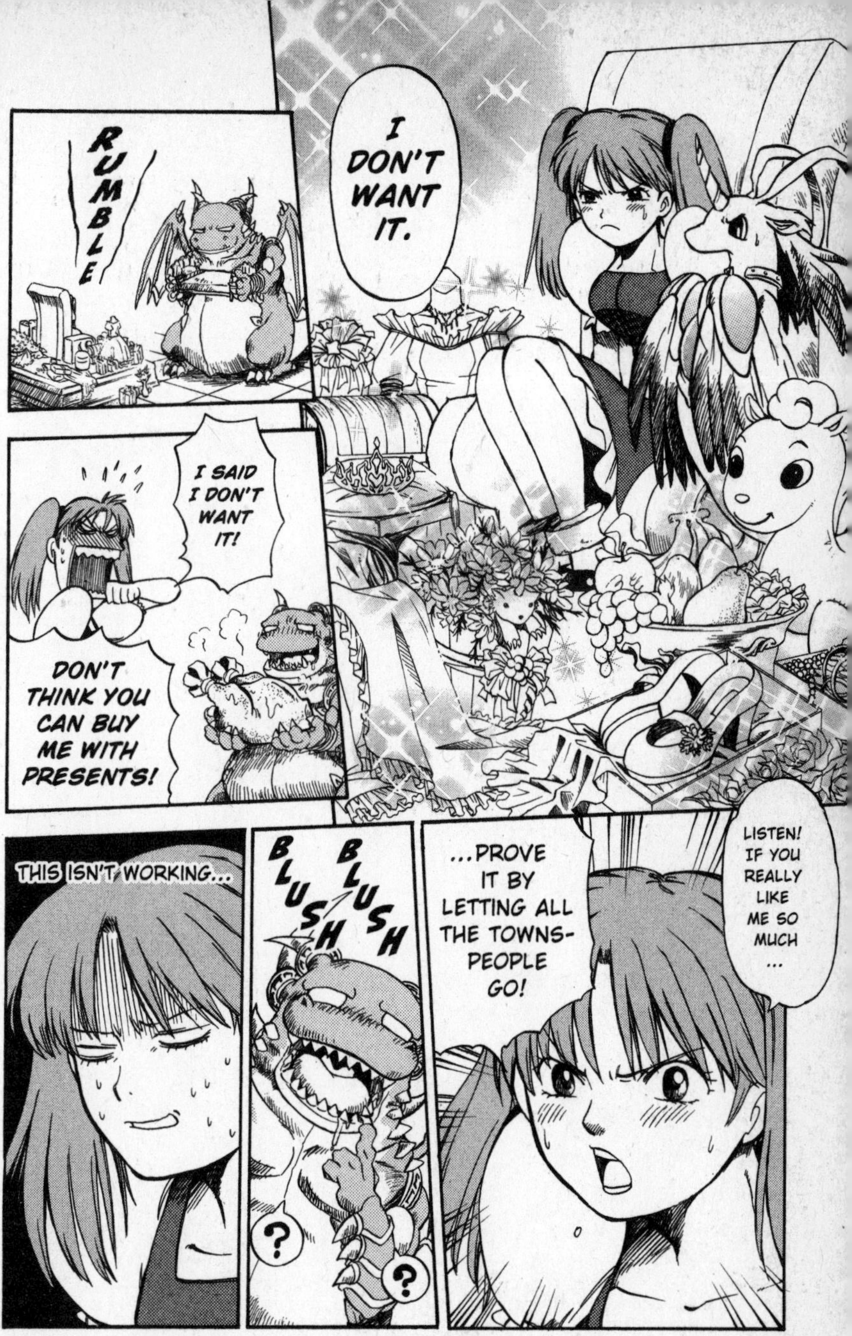
I DON'T WANT IT.
RUMBLE
I SAID I DON'T WANT IT!
DON'T THINK YOU CAN BUY ME WITH PRESENTS!
LISTEN! IF YOU REALLY LIKE ME SO MUCH ...
...PROVE IT BY LETTING ALL THE TOWNS-PEOPLE GO!
BLUSH BLUSH
?
?
THIS ISN'T WORKING...

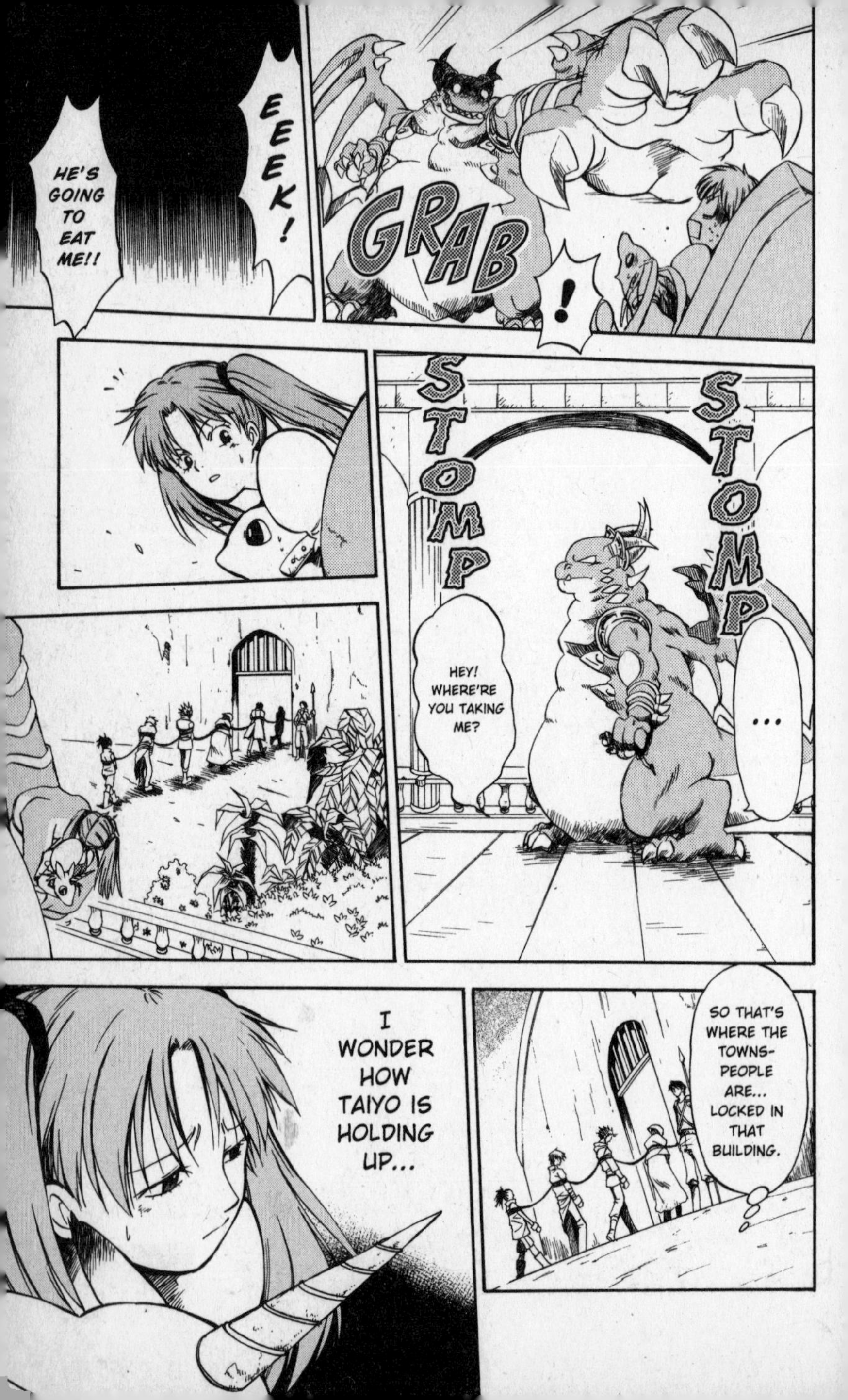
GRAB
!
EEEK!
HE'S GOING TO EAT ME!!
STOMP
STOMP
...
HEY! WHERE'RE YOU TAKING ME?
SO THAT'S WHERE THE TOWNS-PEOPLE ARE... LOCKED IN THAT BUILDING.
I WONDER HOW TAIYO IS HOLDING UP...

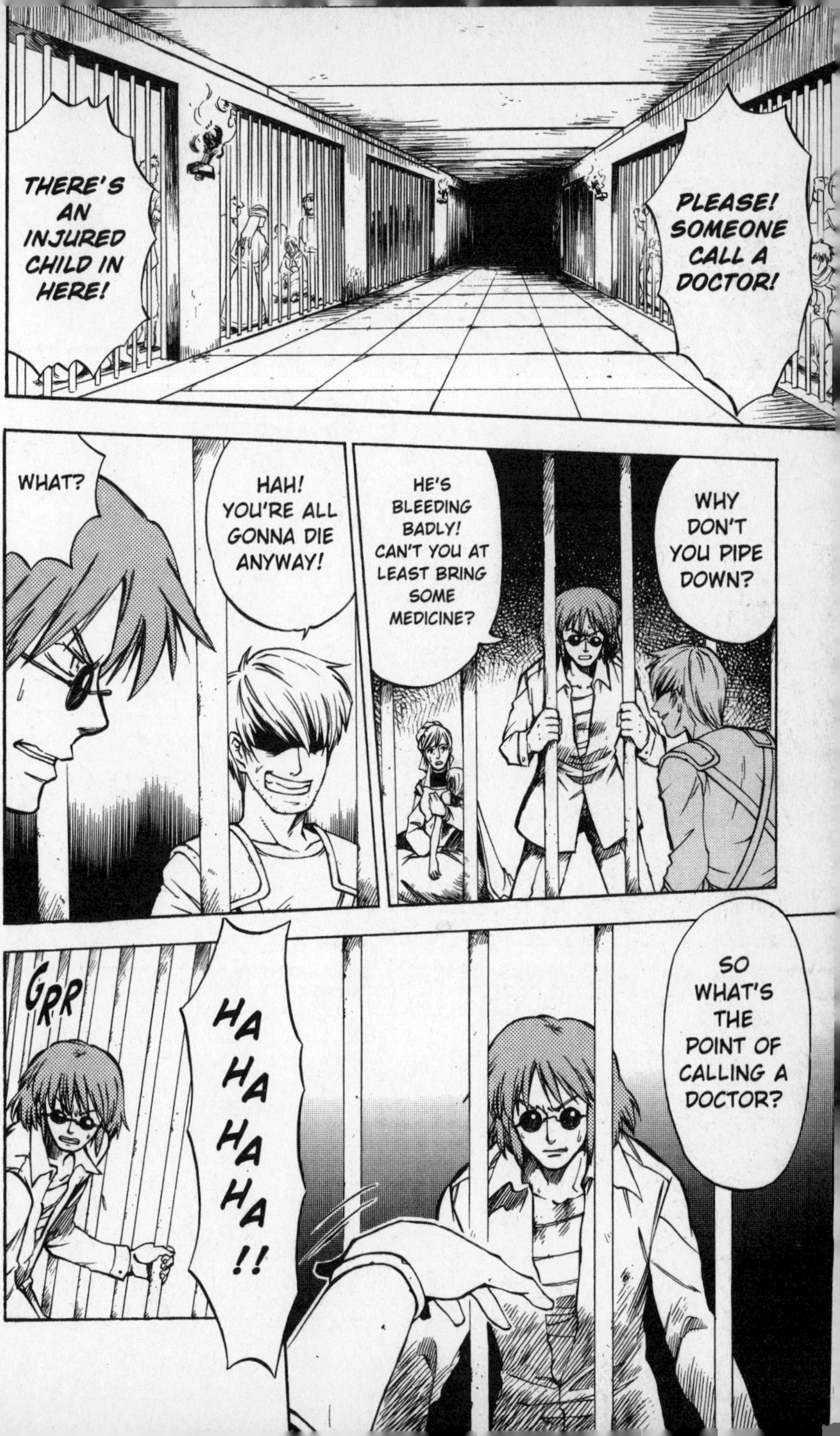
PLEASE! SOMEONE CALL A DOCTOR!
THERE'S AN INJURED CHILD IN HERE!
WHY DON'T YOU PIPE DOWN?
HE'S BLEEDING BADLY! CAN'T YOU AT LEAST BRING SOME MEDICINE?
HAH! YOU'RE ALL GONNA DIE ANYWAY!
WHAT?
SO WHAT'S THE POINT OF CALLING A DOCTOR?
HA HA HA HA HA!!
GRR

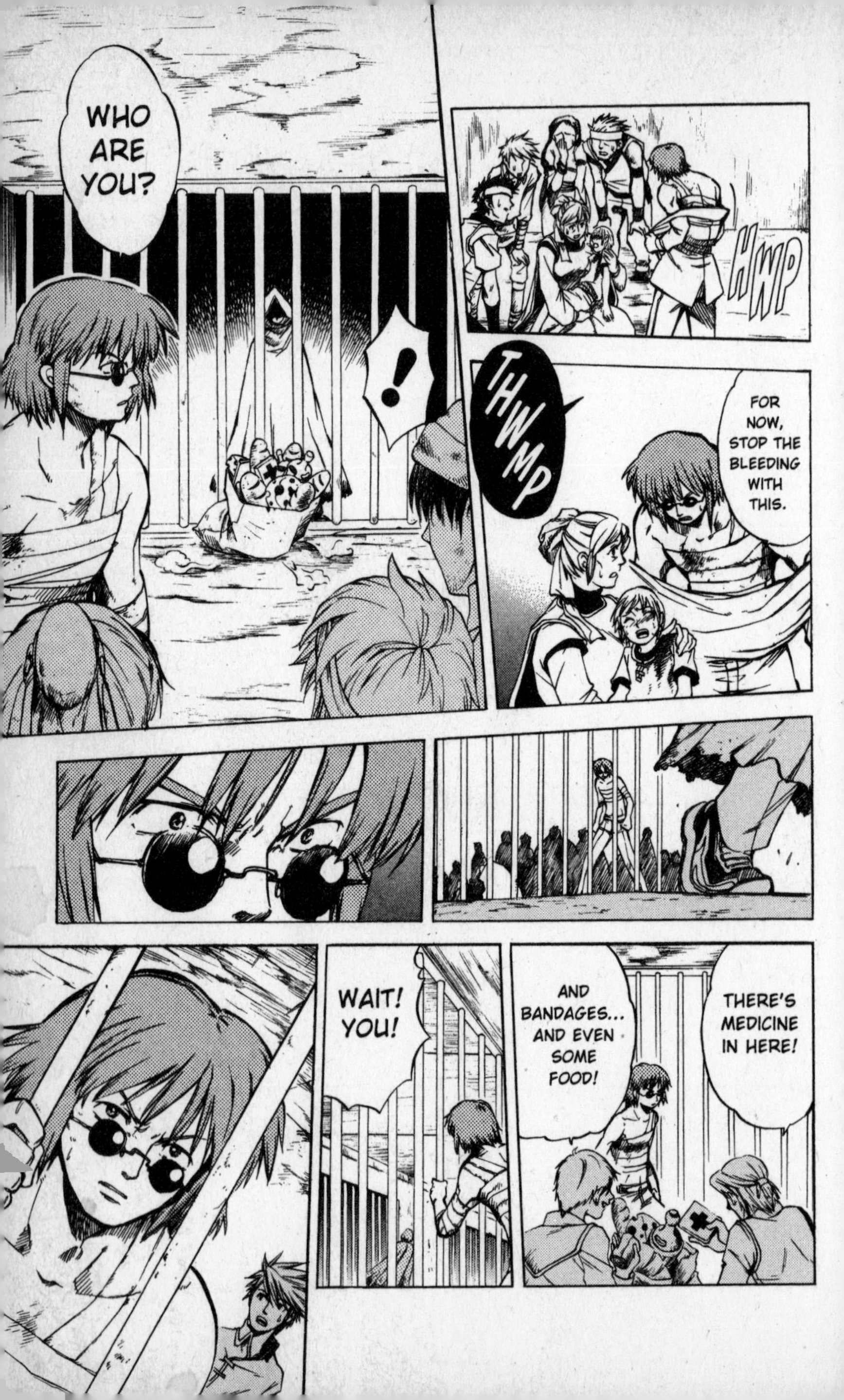
HWP
FOR NOW, STOP THE BLEEDING WITH THIS.
THWMP
WHO ARE YOU?
!
THERE'S MEDICINE IN HERE!
AND BANDAGES... AND EVEN SOME FOOD!
WAIT! YOU!

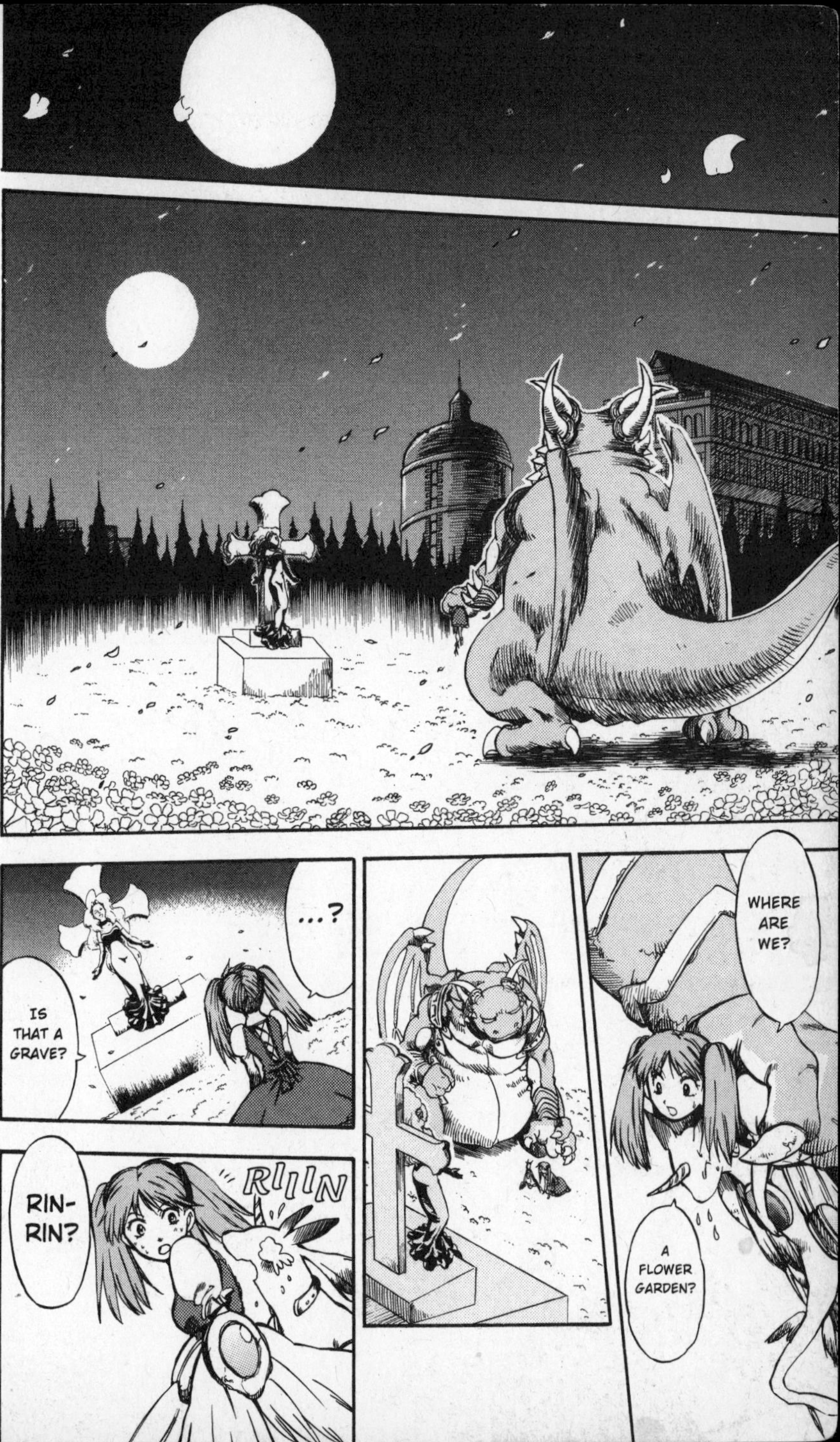
WHERE ARE WE?
A FLOWER GARDEN?
...?
IS THAT A GRAVE?
RIIIN
RIN-RIN?

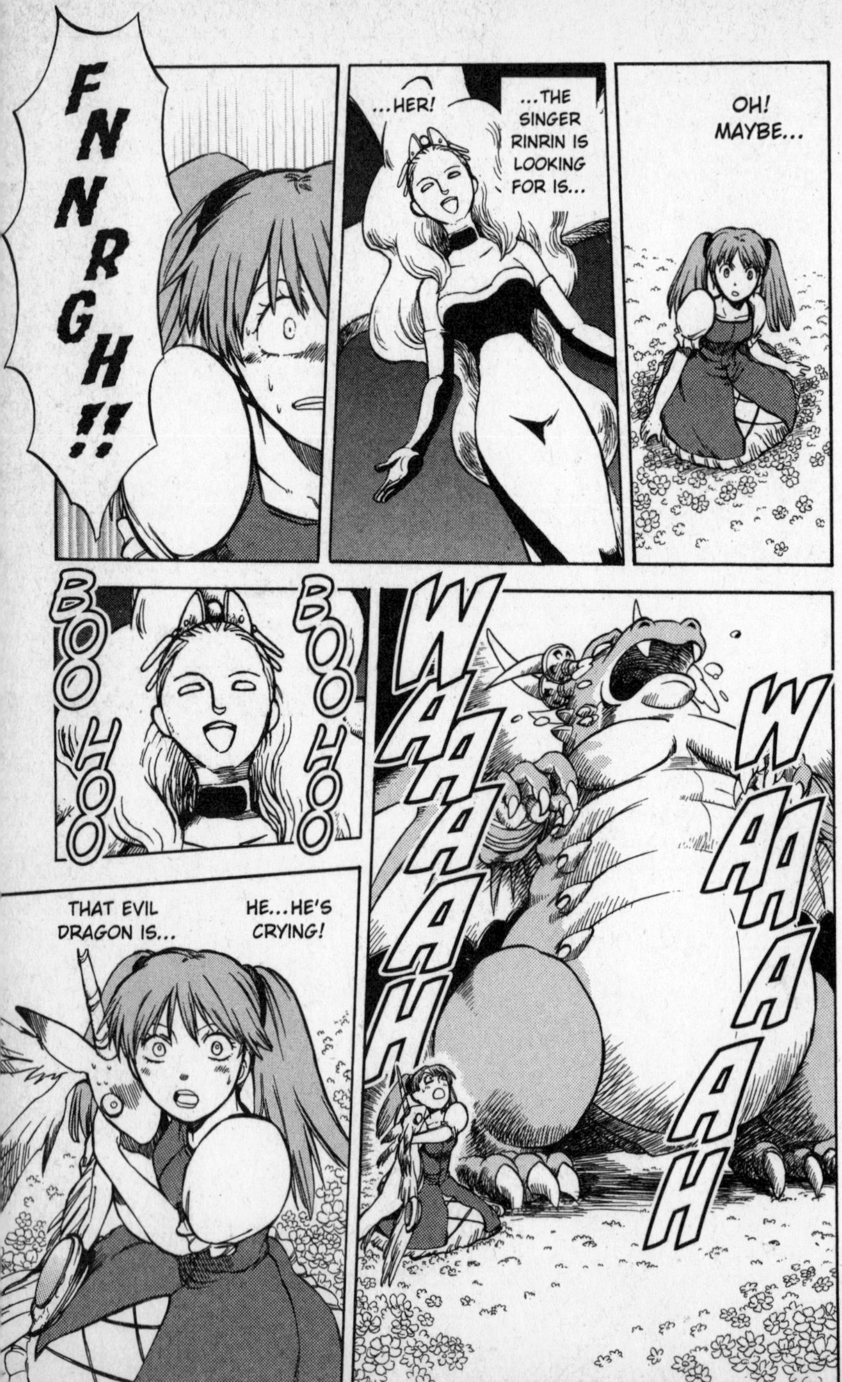
OH! MAYBE...
...THE SINGER RINRIN IS LOOKING FOR IS...
...HER!
FNNRGH!!
WAAAAAH
WAAAAAH
BOOHOOHOO
BOOHOOHOO
HE...HE'S CRYING!
THAT EVIL DRAGON IS...

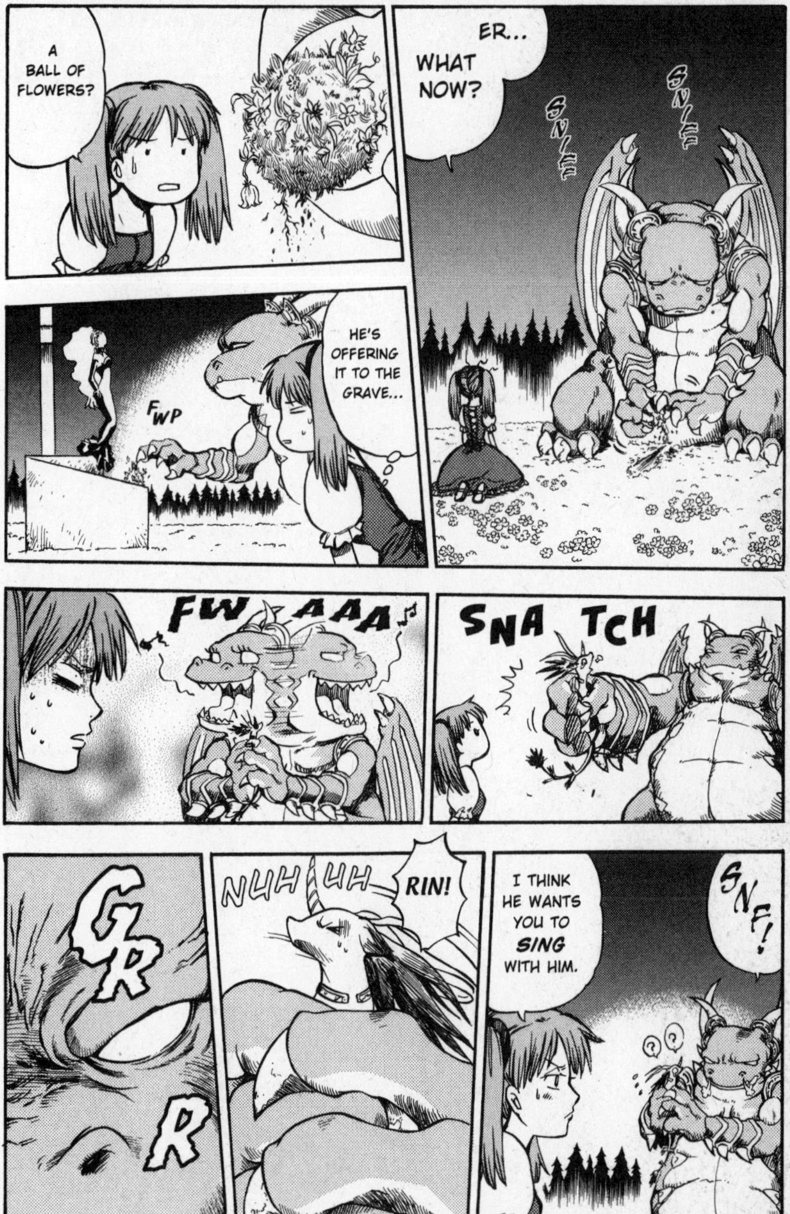
ER... WHAT NOW?
SNIFF
SNIFF
A BALL OF FLOWERS?
HE'S OFFERING IT TO THE GRAVE...
FWP
SNATCH
FWAAAA
I THINK HE WANTS YOU TO SING WITH HIM.
SNF!
NUH UH
RIN!
GRR

READ THIS WAY

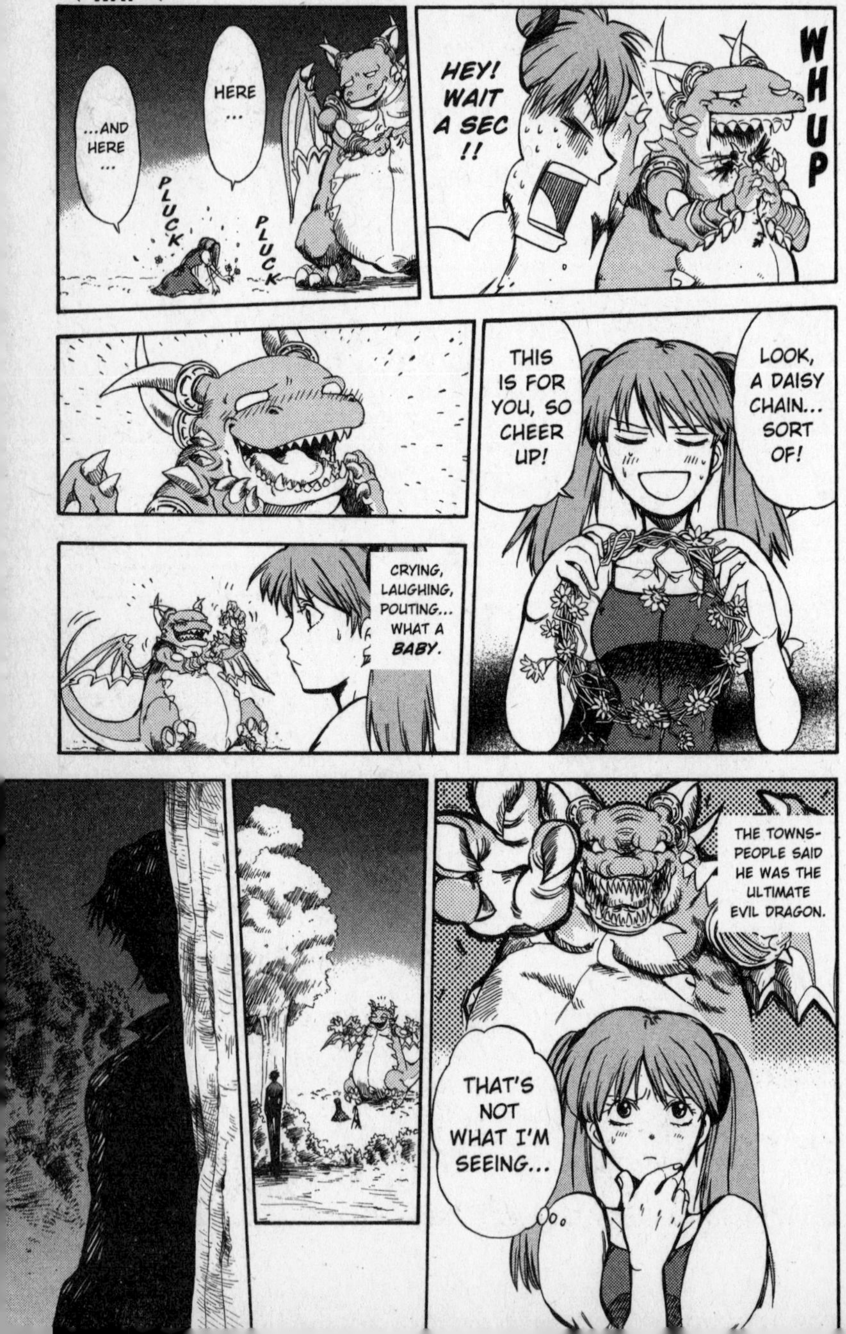

HEY! WAIT A SEC!!
WHUP
HERE...
...AND HERE...
PLUCK
PLUCK
LOOK, A DAISY CHAIN... SORT OF!
THIS IS FOR YOU, SO CHEER UP!
CRYING, LAUGHING, POUTING... WHAT A *BABY*.
THE TOWNS-PEOPLE SAID HE WAS THE ULTIMATE EVIL DRAGON.
THAT'S NOT WHAT I'M SEEING...

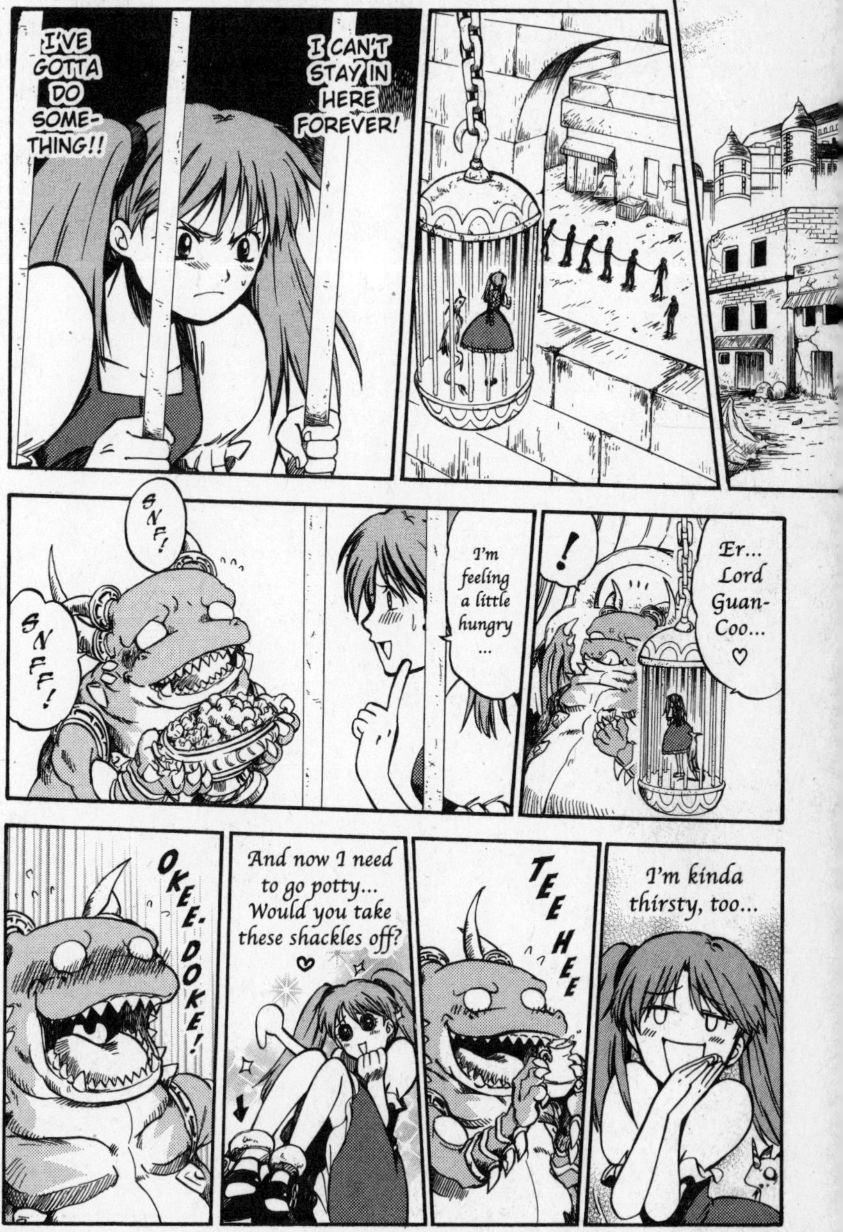
I CAN'T STAY IN HERE FOREVER!
I'VE GOTTA DO SOME-THING!!
!
Er... Lord Guan-Coo... ♡
I'm feeling a little hungry ...
SNF!
SNFF!
I'm kinda thirsty, too...
TEE HEE
And now I need to go potty... Would you take these shackles off? ♡
OKEE-DOKE!

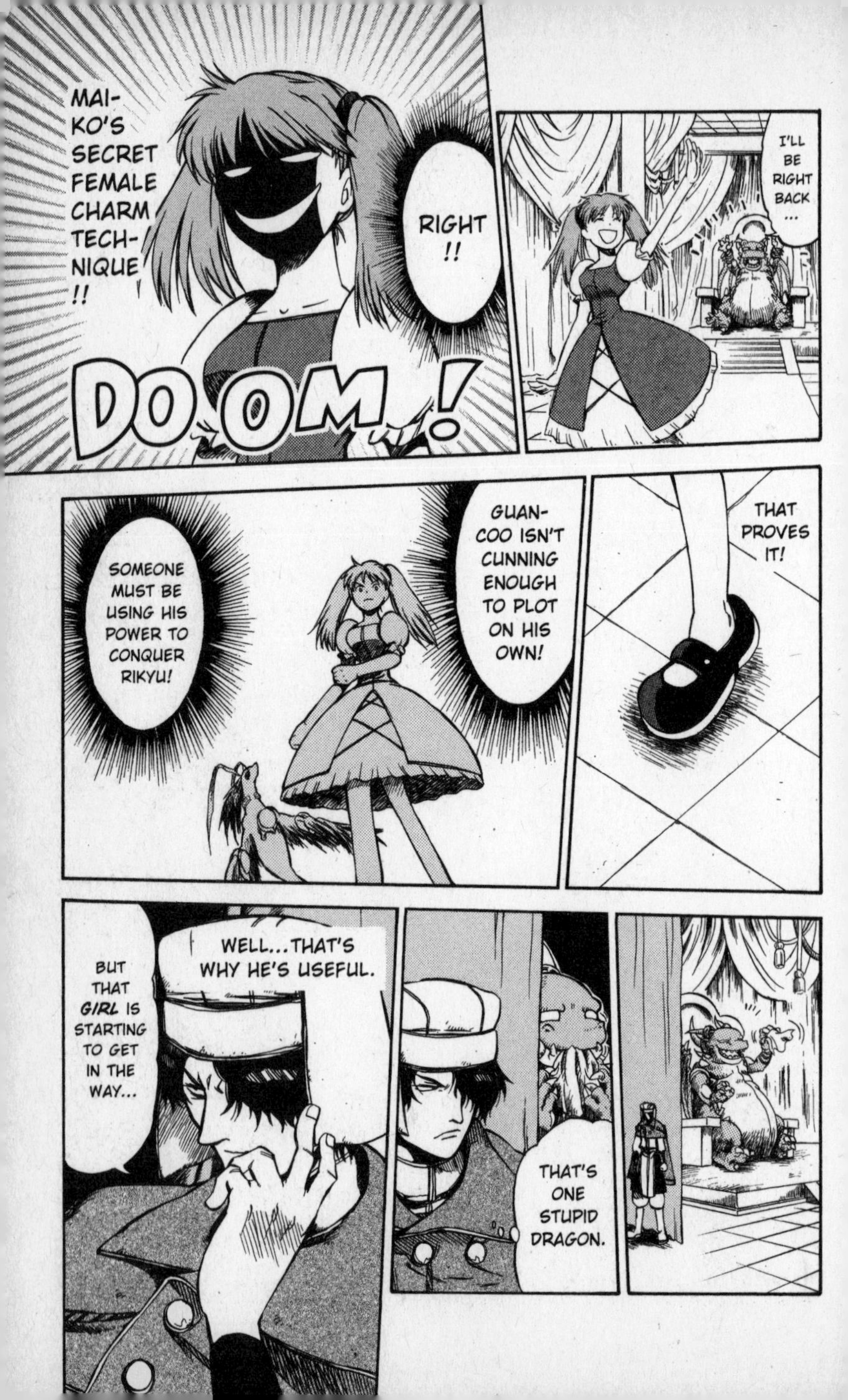
I'LL BE RIGHT BACK ...
RIGHT !!
MAI-KO'S SECRET FEMALE CHARM TECH-NIQUE !!
DOOM!
THAT PROVES IT!
GUAN-COO ISN'T CUNNING ENOUGH TO PLOT ON HIS OWN!
SOMEONE MUST BE USING HIS POWER TO CONQUER RIKYU!
THAT'S ONE STUPID DRAGON.
WELL...THAT'S WHY HE'S USEFUL.
BUT THAT *GIRL* IS STARTING TO GET IN THE WAY...

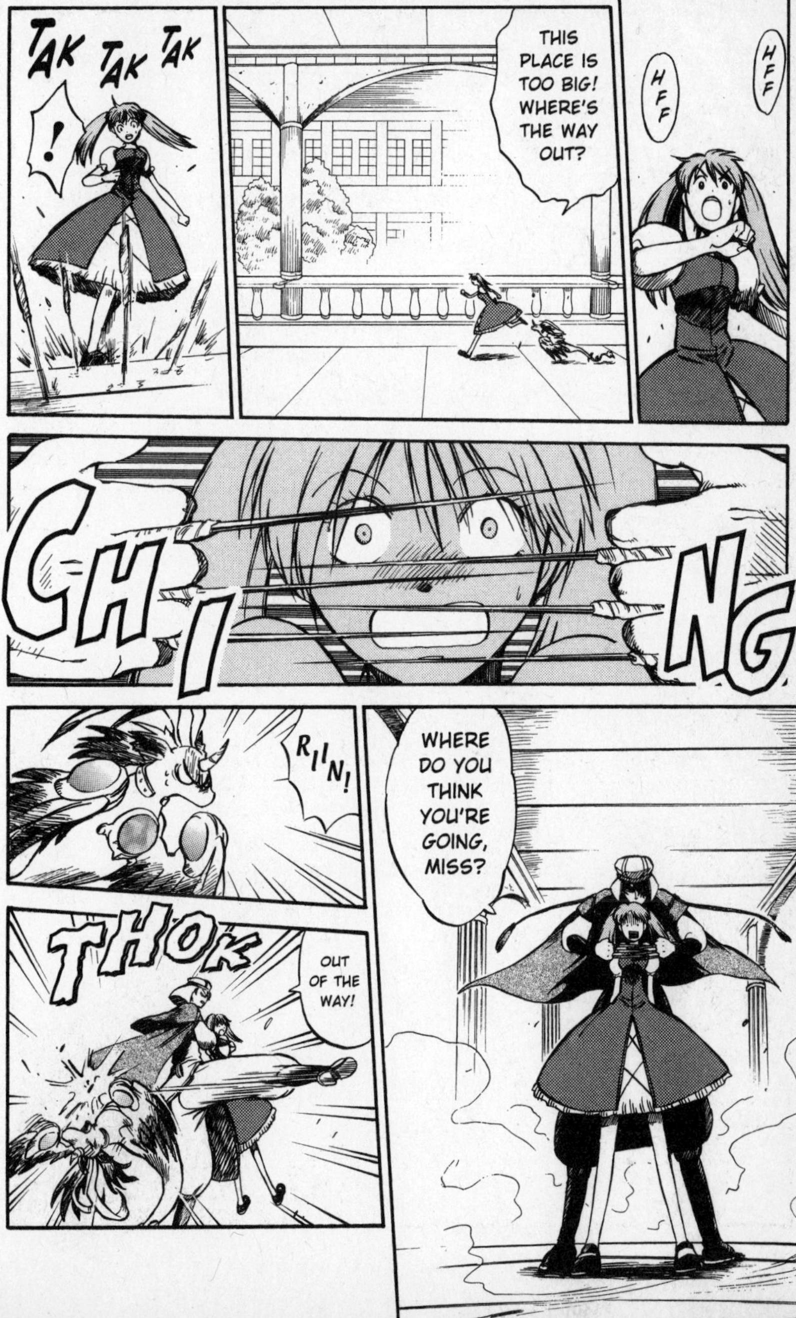
HFF HFF
THIS PLACE IS TOO BIG! WHERE'S THE WAY OUT?
TAK TAK TAK
!
CHIING
RIIN!
WHERE DO YOU THINK YOU'RE GOING, MISS?
THOK
OUT OF THE WAY!

READ THIS WAY

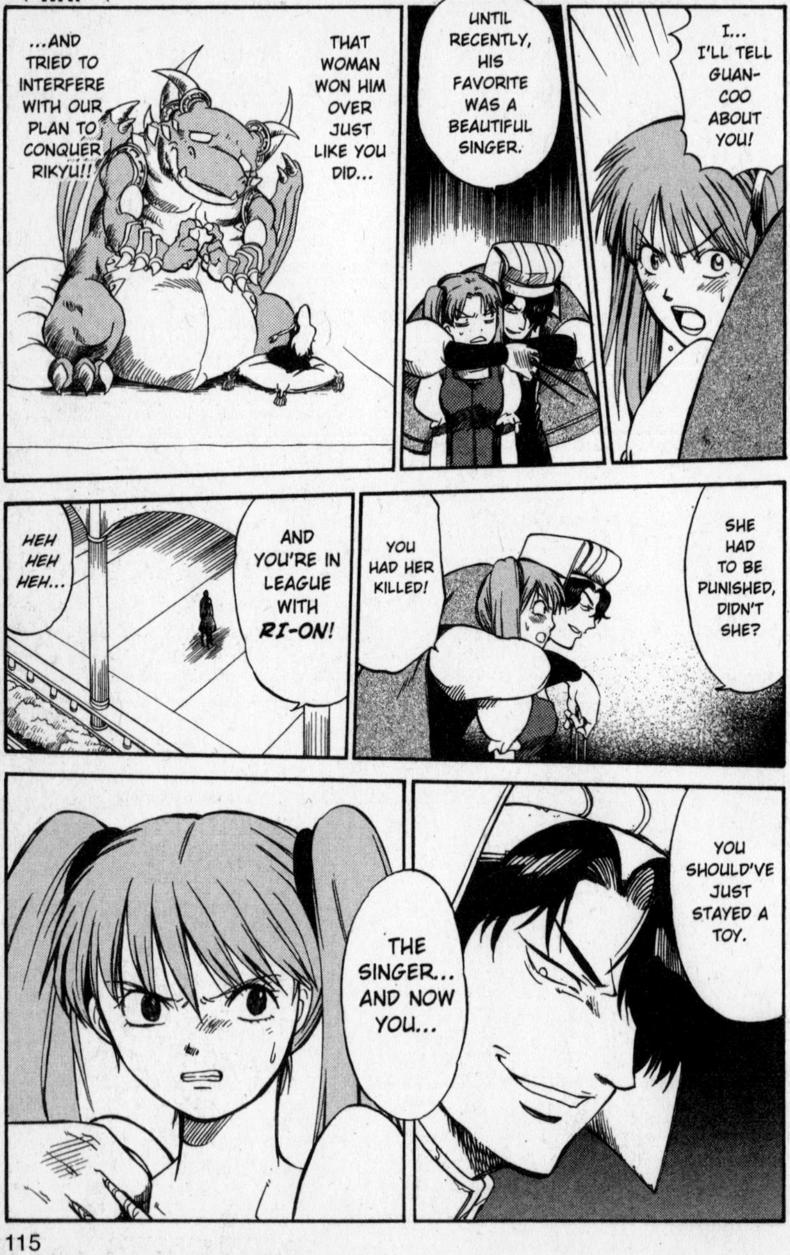
I... I'LL TELL GUAN-COO ABOUT YOU!
UNTIL RECENTLY, HIS FAVORITE WAS A BEAUTIFUL SINGER.
THAT WOMAN WON HIM OVER JUST LIKE YOU DID...
...AND TRIED TO INTERFERE WITH OUR PLAN TO CONQUER RIKYU!!
SHE HAD TO BE PUNISHED, DIDN'T SHE?
YOU HAD HER KILLED!
AND YOU'RE IN LEAGUE WITH RI-ON!
HEH HEH HEH...
YOU SHOULD'VE JUST STAYED A TOY.
THE SINGER... AND NOW YOU...

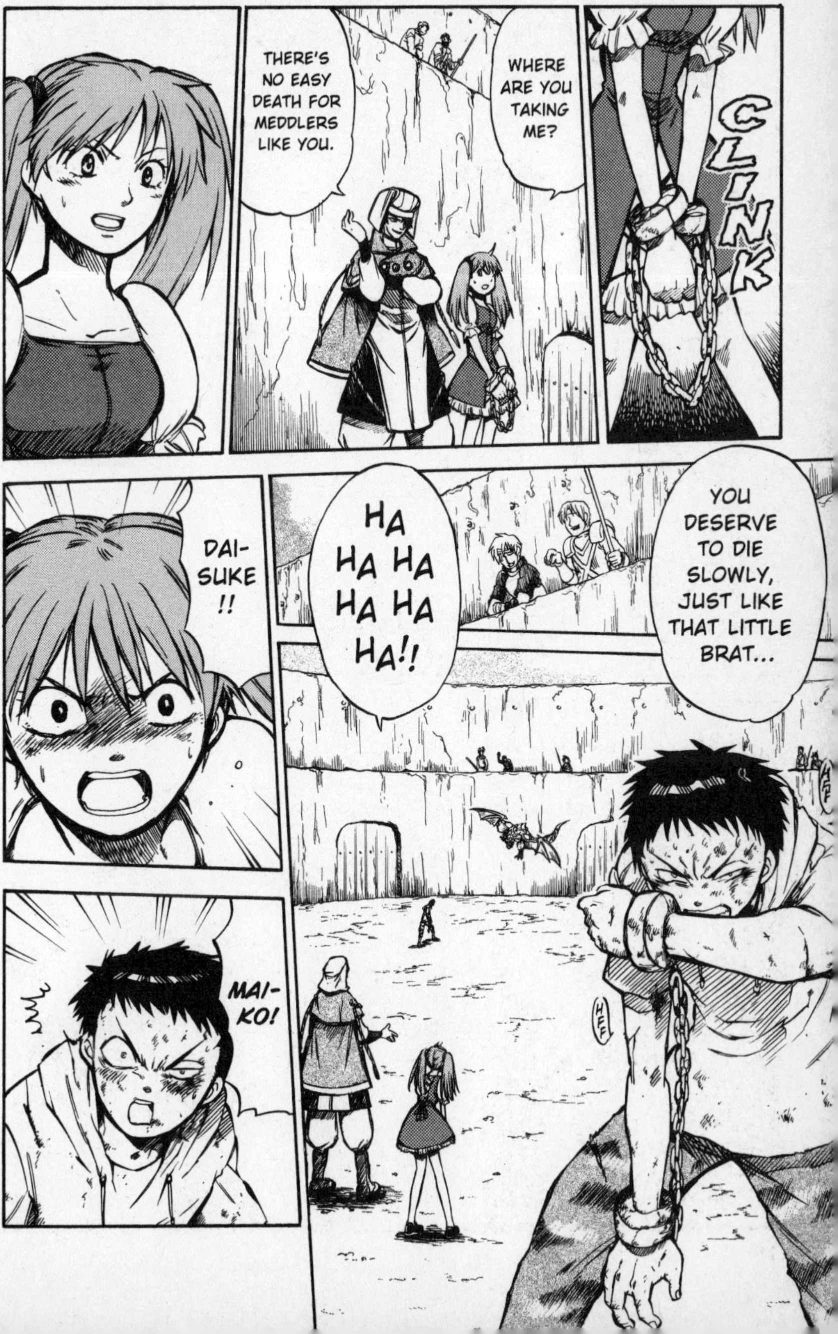
CLINK
WHERE ARE YOU TAKING ME?
THERE'S NO EASY DEATH FOR MEDDLERS LIKE YOU.
YOU DESERVE TO DIE SLOWLY, JUST LIKE THAT LITTLE BRAT...
HA HA HA HA HA HA!!
HEF
HEF
DAI-SUKE!!
MAI-KO!

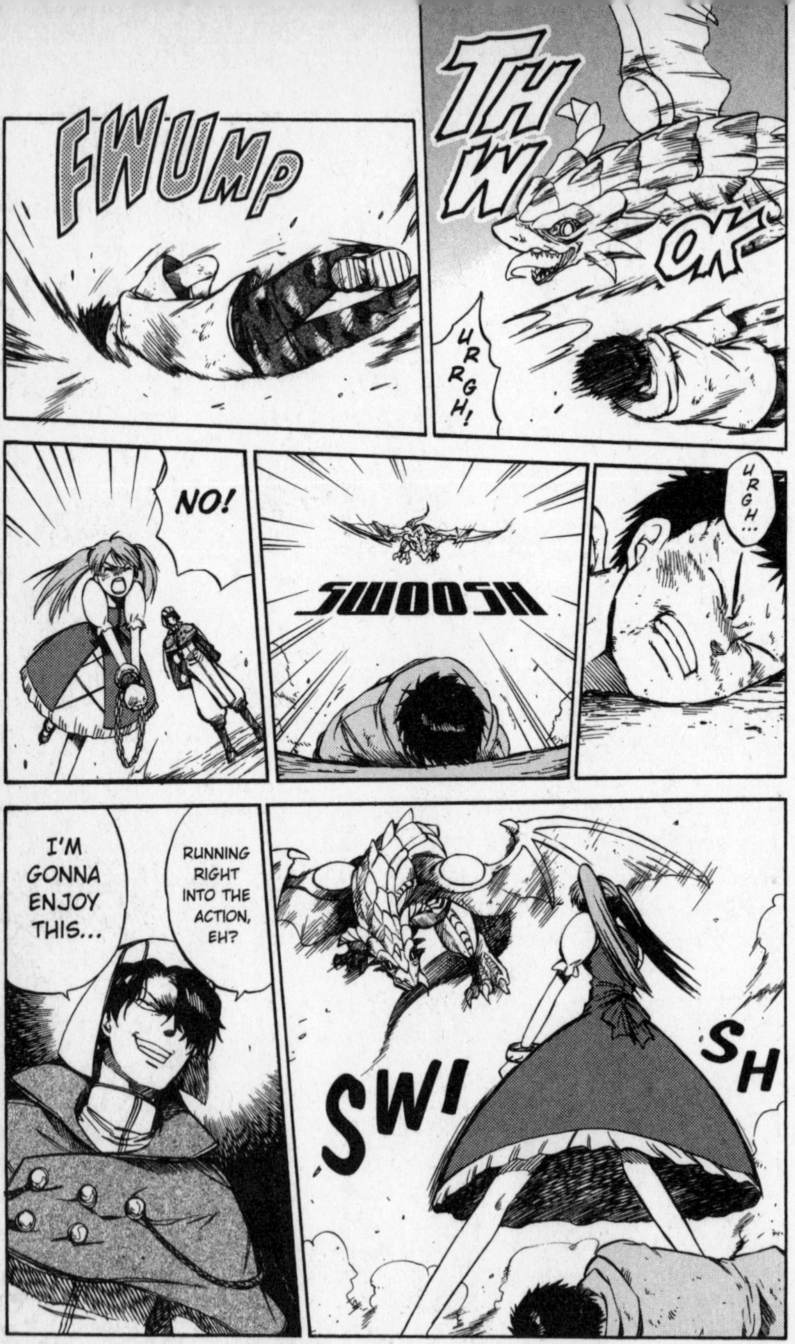
THWOK
URRGH!
FWUMP
URGH...
SWOOSH
NO!
SWISH
RUNNING RIGHT INTO THE ACTION, EH?
I'M GONNA ENJOY THIS...

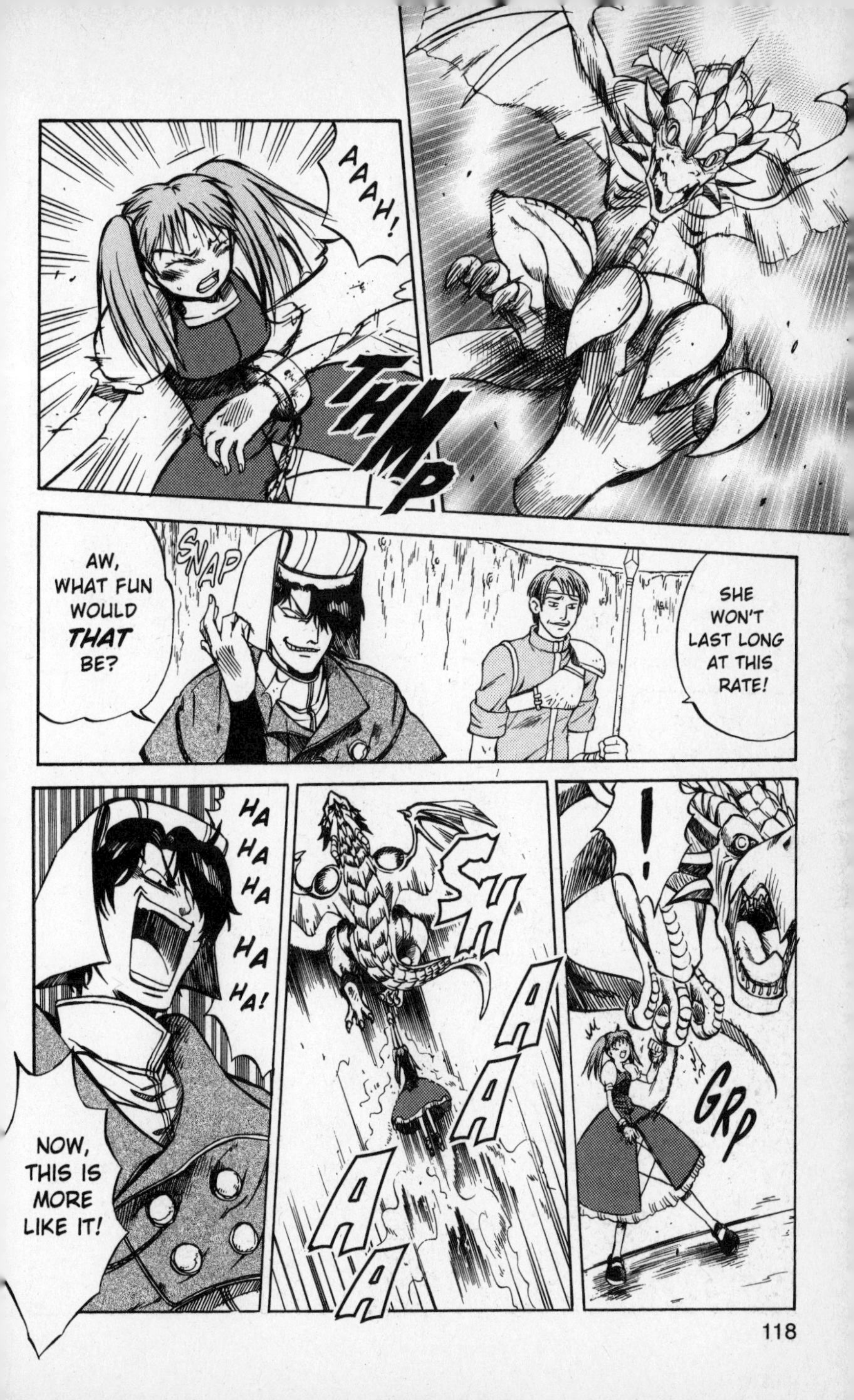
AAAAH!
THMP
SHE WON'T LAST LONG AT THIS RATE!
SNAP
AW, WHAT FUN WOULD THAT BE?
!
GRP
SHA
AAAAAAA
HA HA HA HA HA!
NOW, THIS IS MORE LIKE IT!

READ THIS WAY

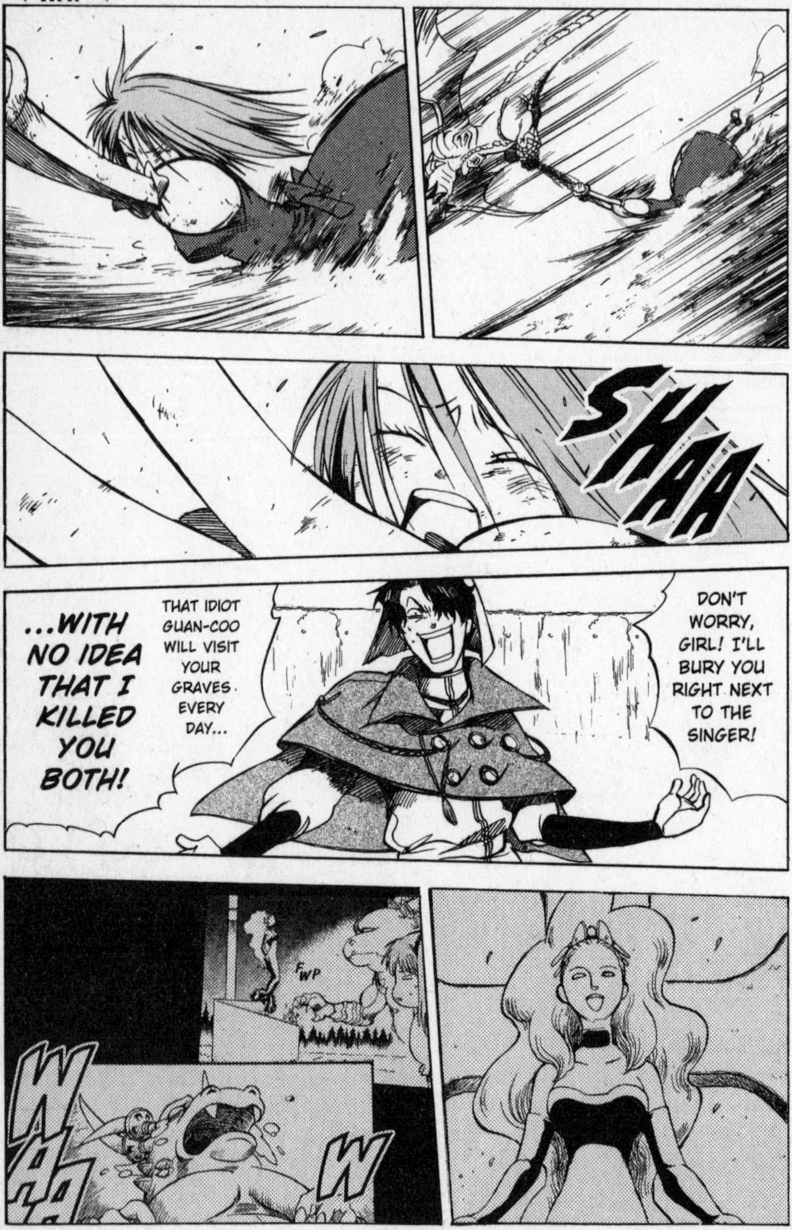
SHAA
DON'T WORRY, GIRL! I'LL BURY YOU RIGHT NEXT TO THE SINGER!
THAT IDIOT GUAN-COO WILL VISIT YOUR GRAVES EVERY DAY...
...WITH NO IDEA THAT I KILLED YOU BOTH!
FWP
WAAA
W

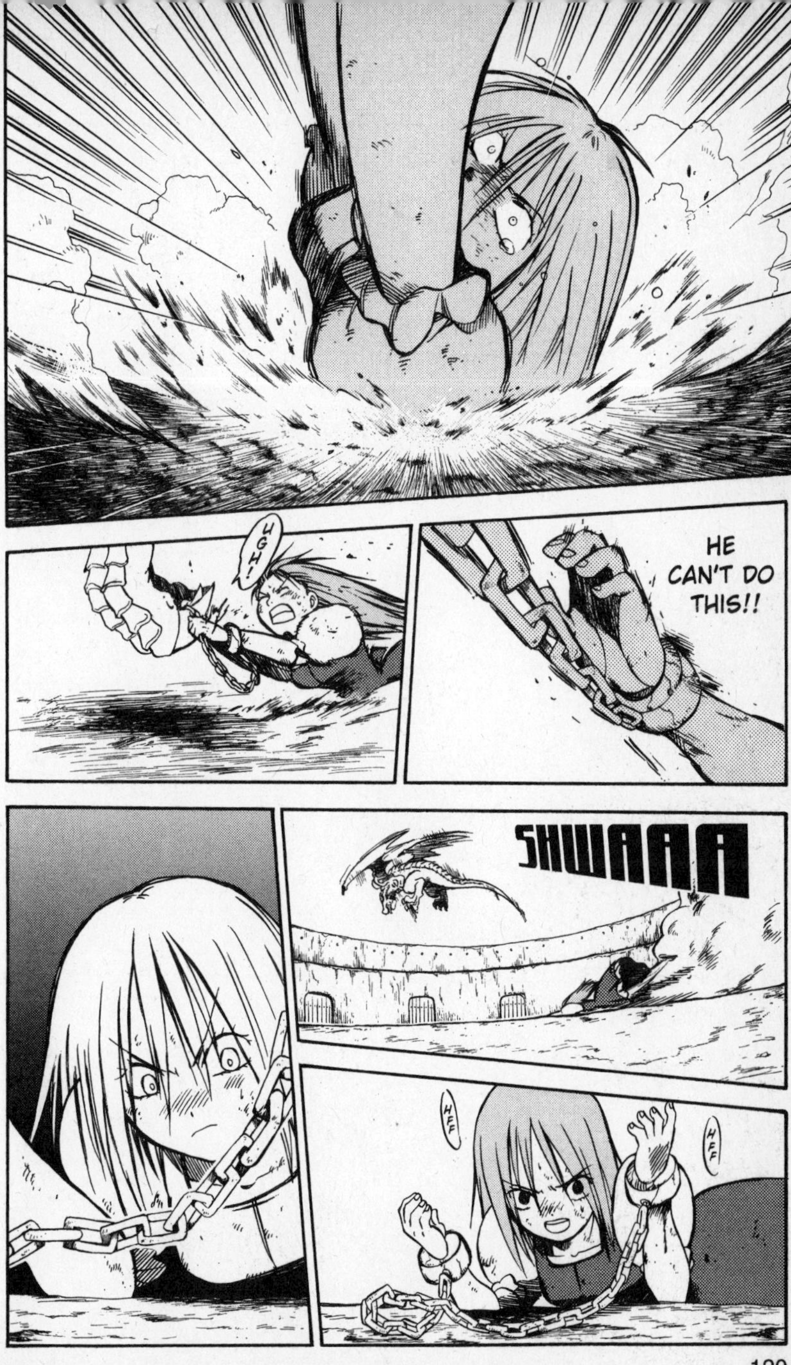
HE CAN'T DO THIS!!
UGH!
SHWAAA
HFF
HFF

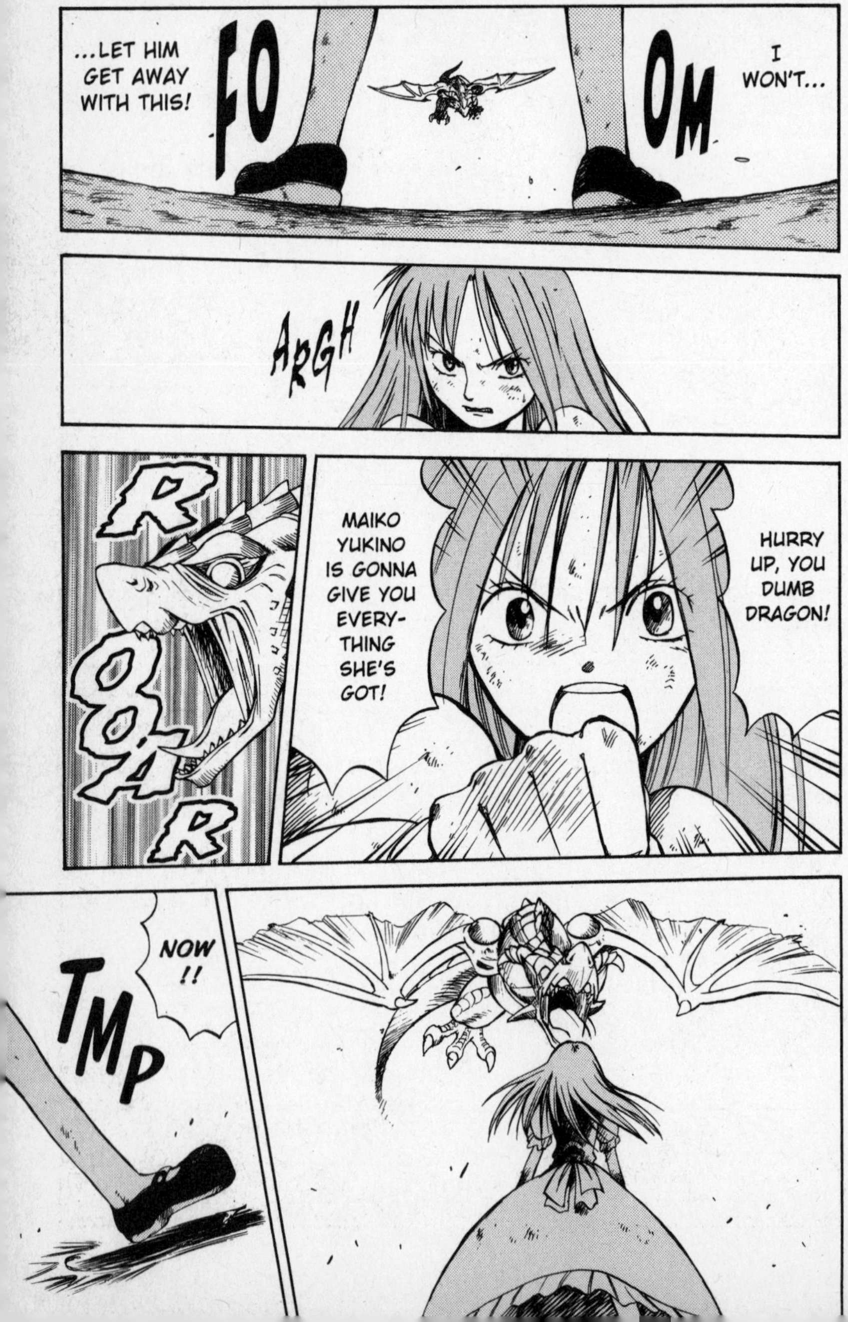
I WON'T...
FOOM
...LET HIM GET AWAY WITH THIS!
ARGH
HURRY UP, YOU DUMB DRAGON!
MAIKO YUKINO IS GONNA GIVE YOU EVERY-THING SHE'S GOT!
ROOAR
NOW !!
TMP

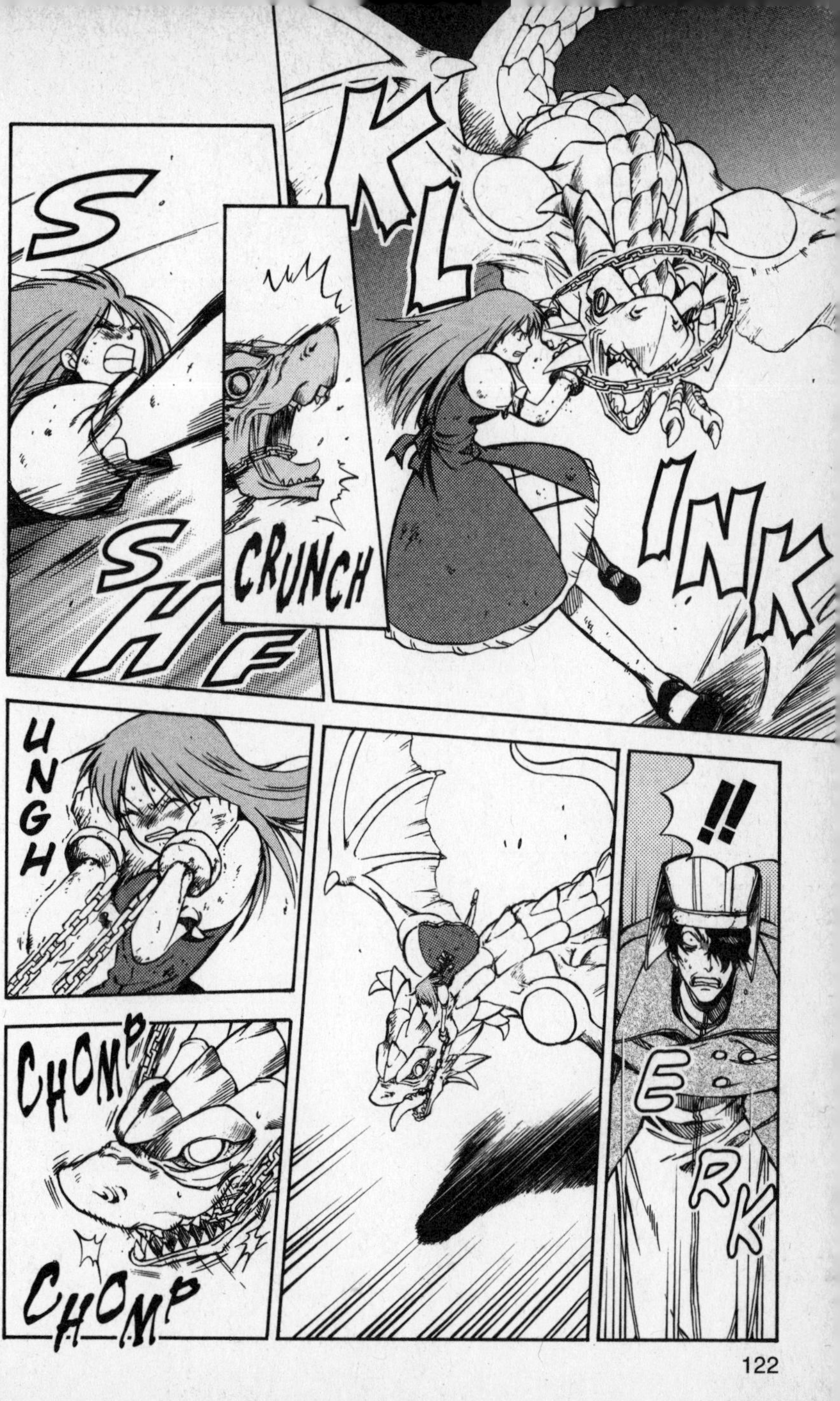
KL
INK
CRUNCH
S
SHF
!!
ERK
UNGH
CHOMP
CHOMP

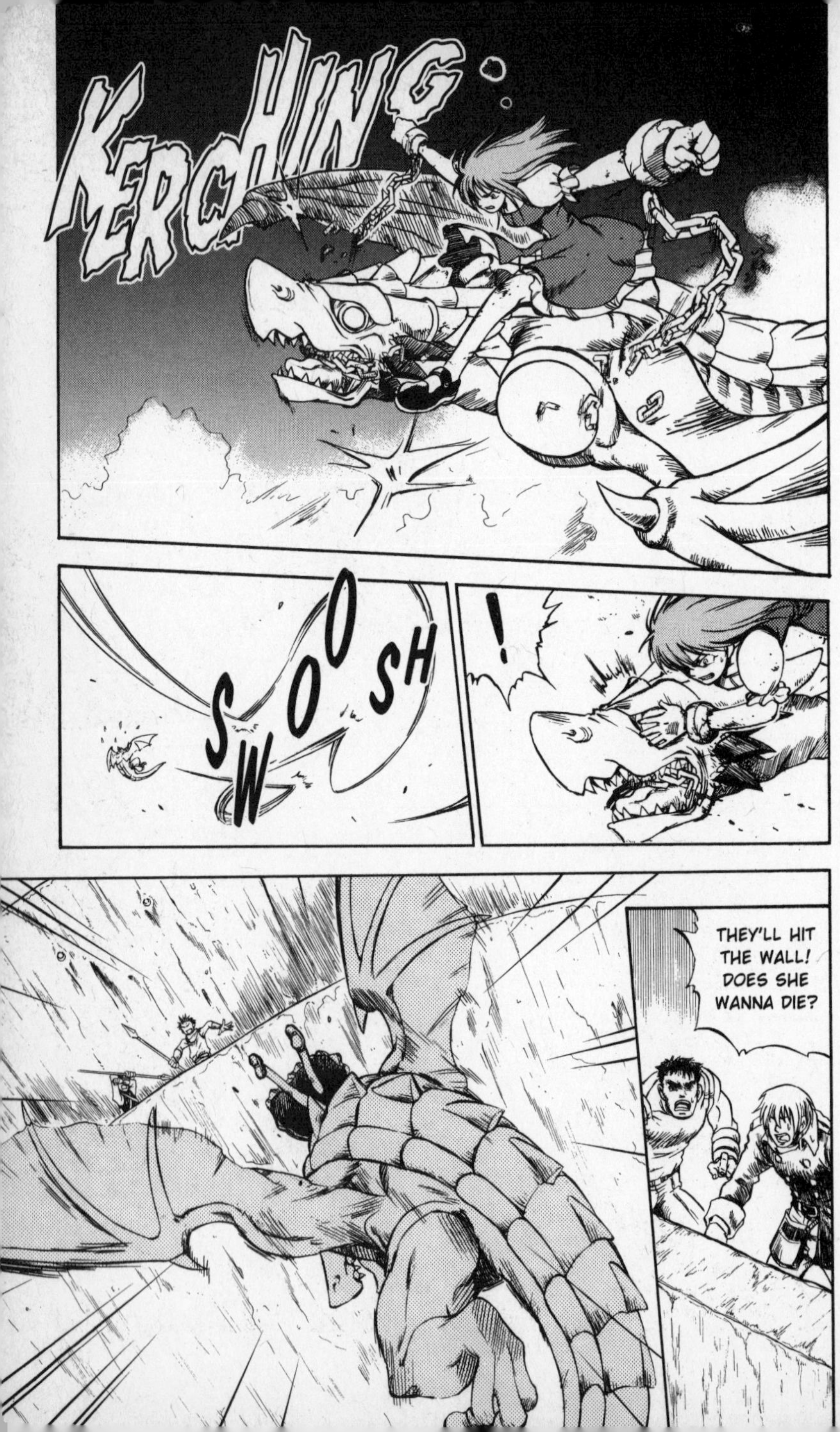
KERCHING
!
SWOOSH
THEY'LL HIT THE WALL! DOES SHE WANNA DIE?

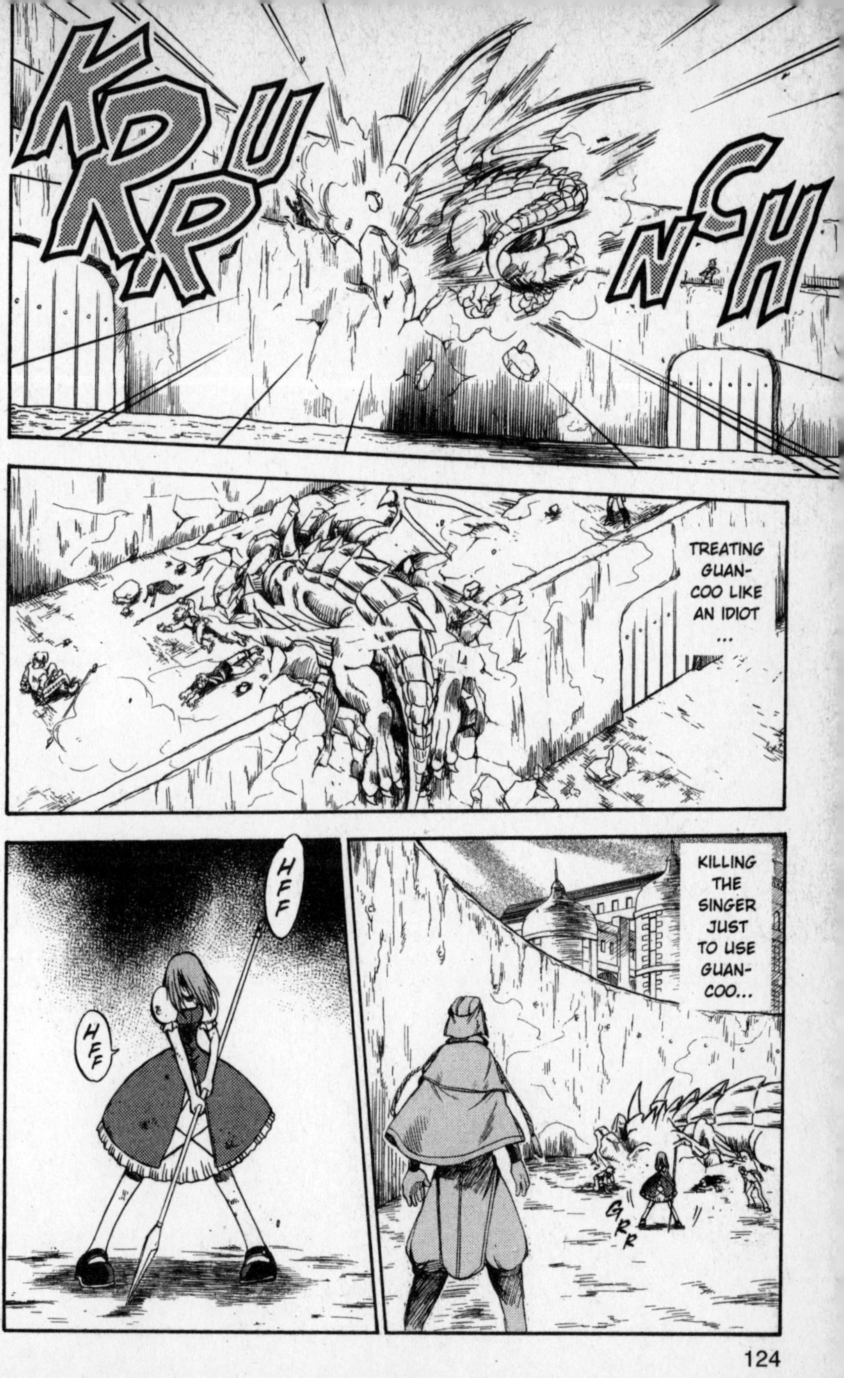
KRUNCH
TREATING GUAN-COO LIKE AN IDIOT ...
KILLING THE SINGER JUST TO USE GUAN-COO...
GRR
HEFF
HEFF

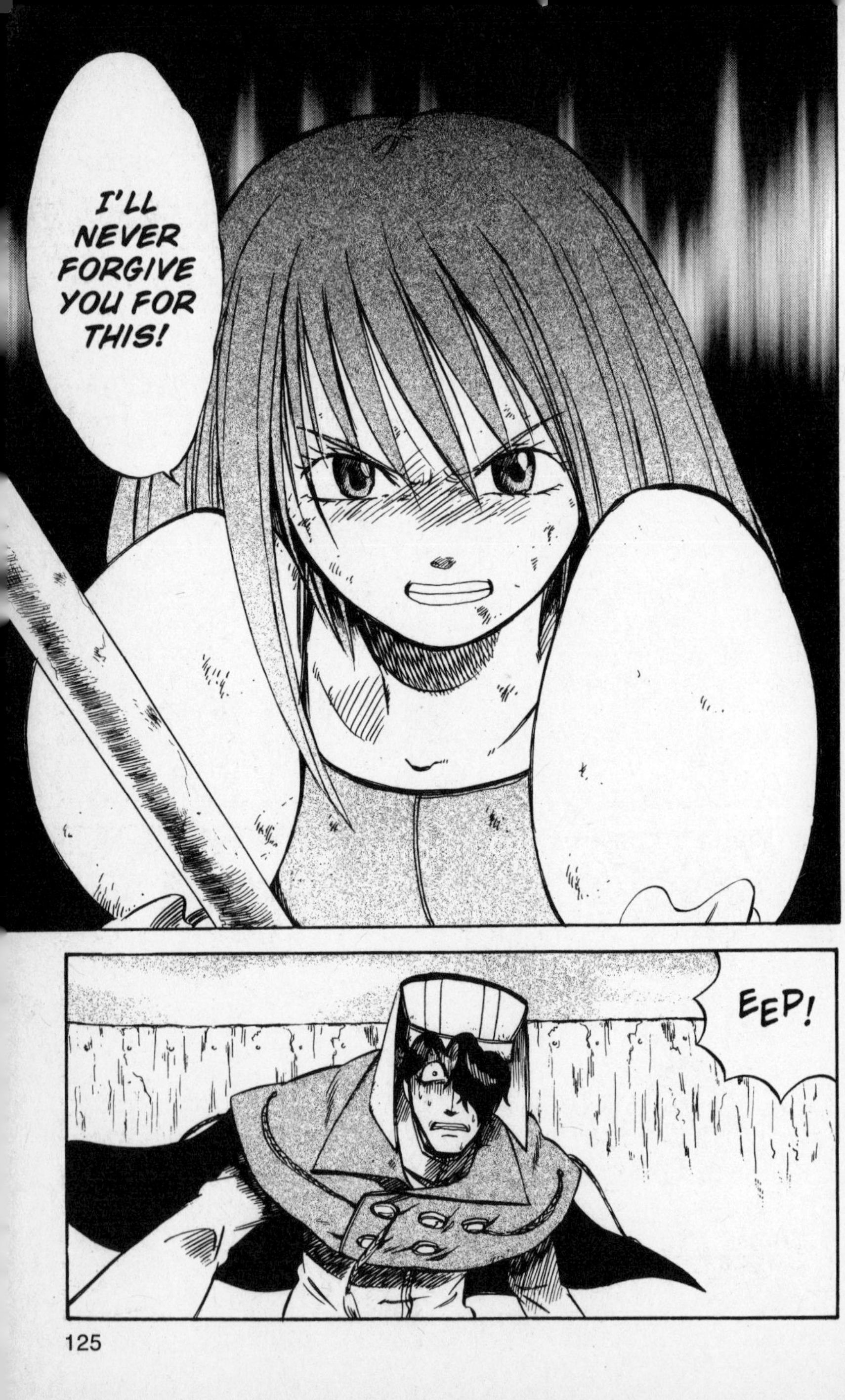
I'LL NEVER FORGIVE YOU FOR THIS!
EEP!

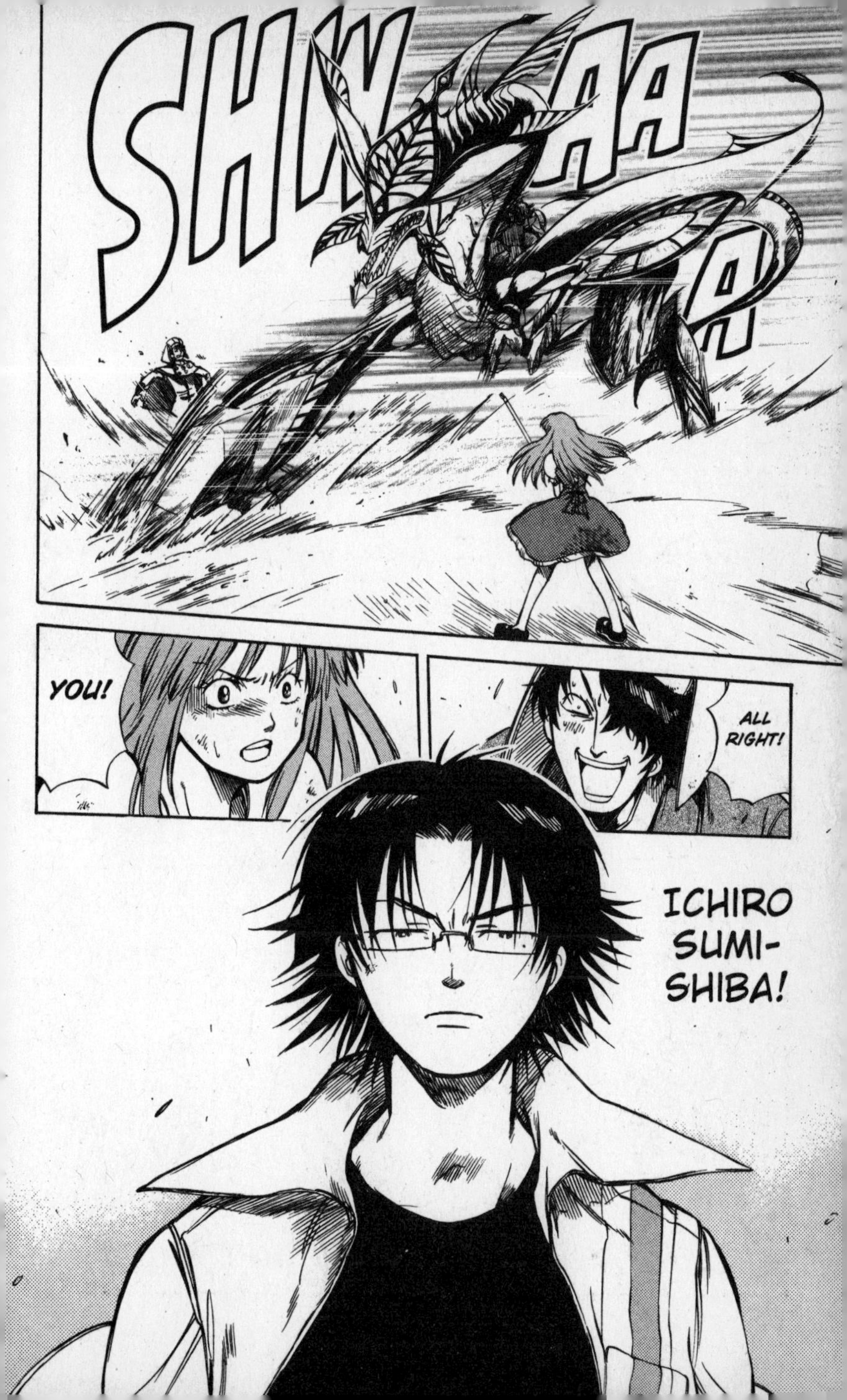
SHWAAA
ALL RIGHT!
YOU!
ICHIRO SUMI-SHIBA!

READ THIS WAY

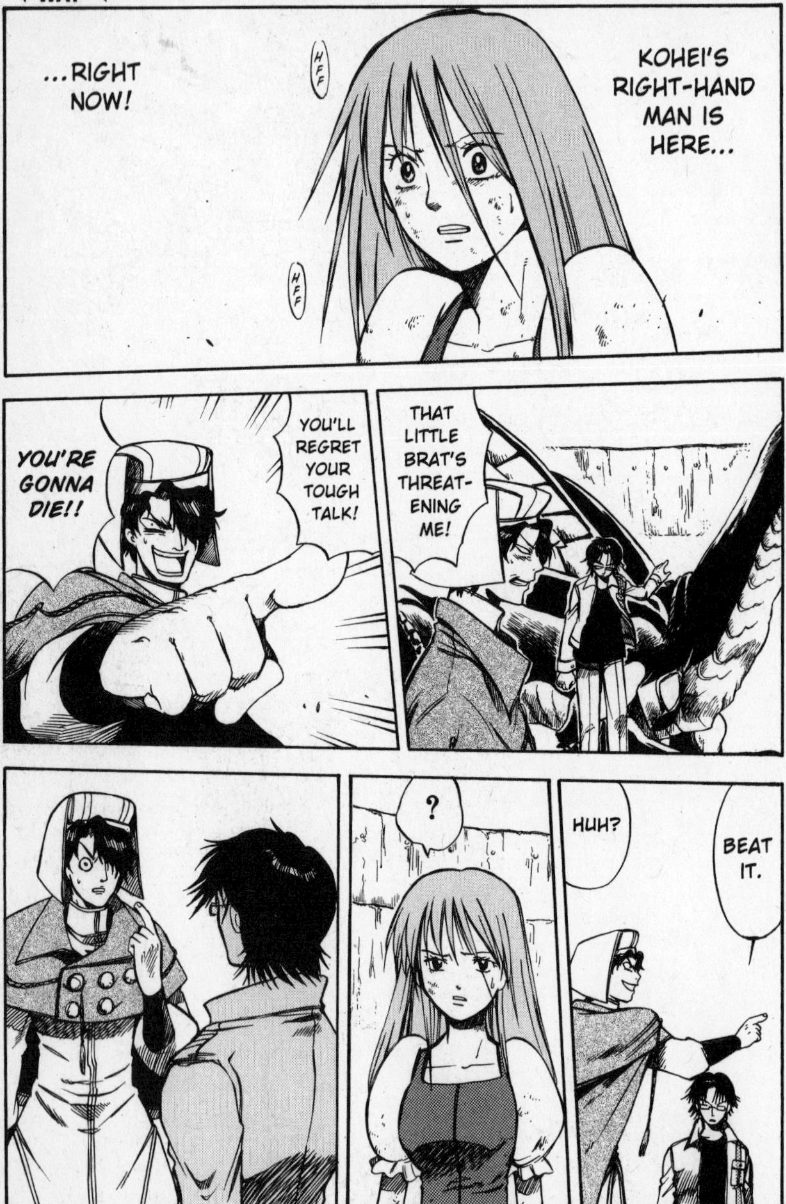
KOHEI'S RIGHT-HAND MAN IS HERE...
HFF
HFF
...RIGHT NOW!
THAT LITTLE BRAT'S THREAT-ENING ME!
YOU'LL REGRET YOUR TOUGH TALK!
YOU'RE GONNA DIE!!
BEAT IT.
HUH?
?

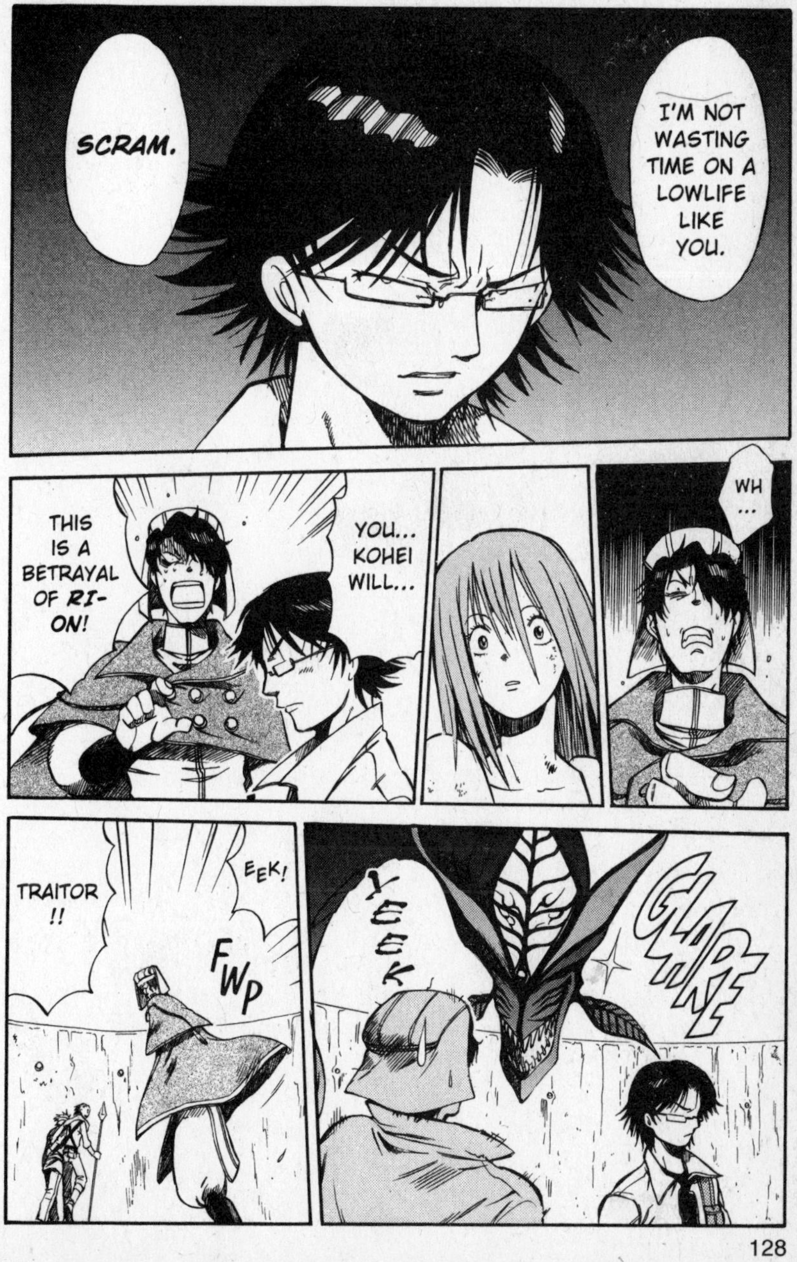
I'M NOT WASTING TIME ON A LOWLIFE LIKE YOU.
SCRAM.
WH ...
YOU... KOHEI WILL...
THIS IS A BETRAYAL OF RI-ON!
GLARE
YEEK
EEK!
TRAITOR !!
FWP

READ THIS WAY

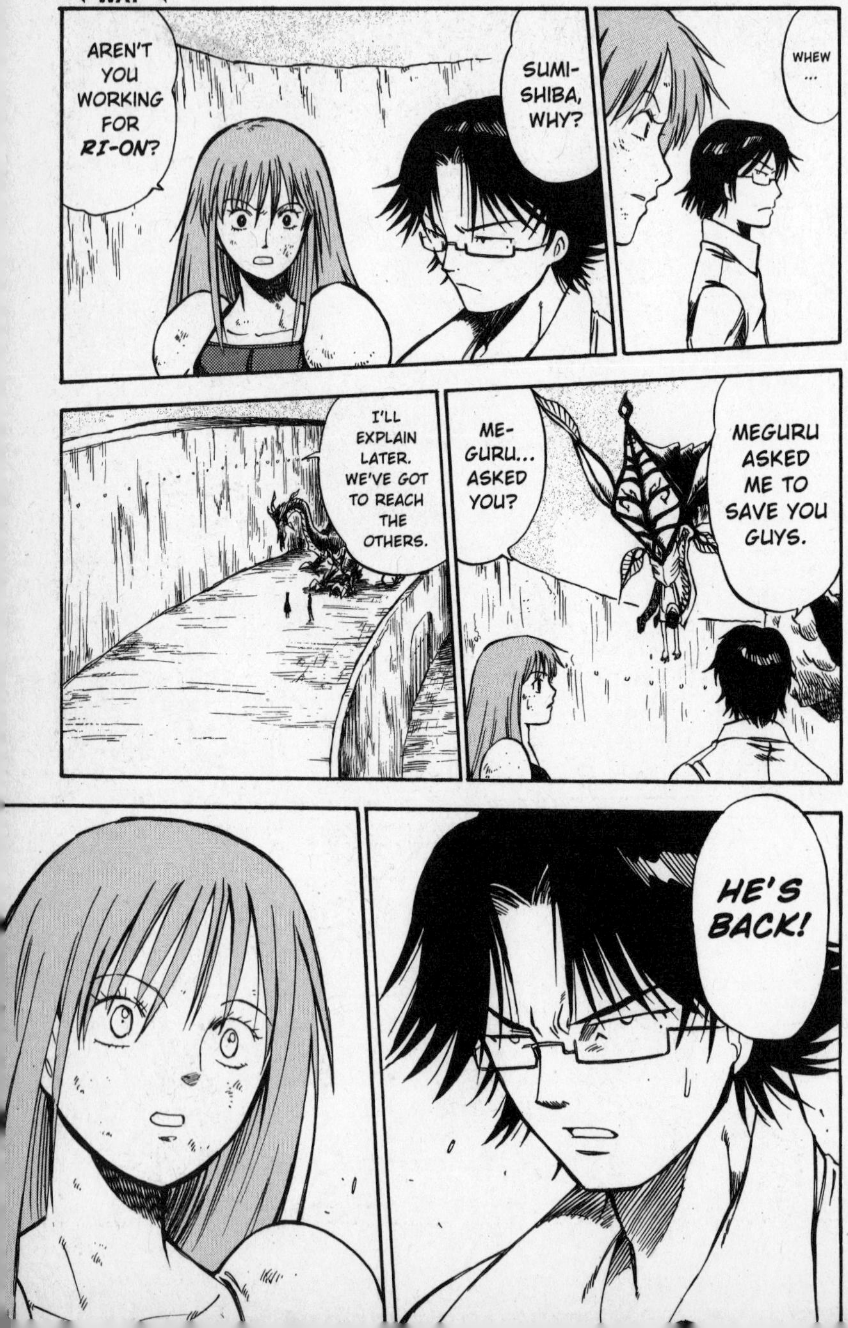
WHEW ...
SUMI-SHIBA, WHY?
AREN'T YOU WORKING FOR *RI-ON*?
MEGURU ASKED ME TO SAVE YOU GUYS.
ME-GURU... ASKED YOU?
I'LL EXPLAIN LATER. WE'VE GOT TO REACH THE OTHERS.
HE'S BACK!

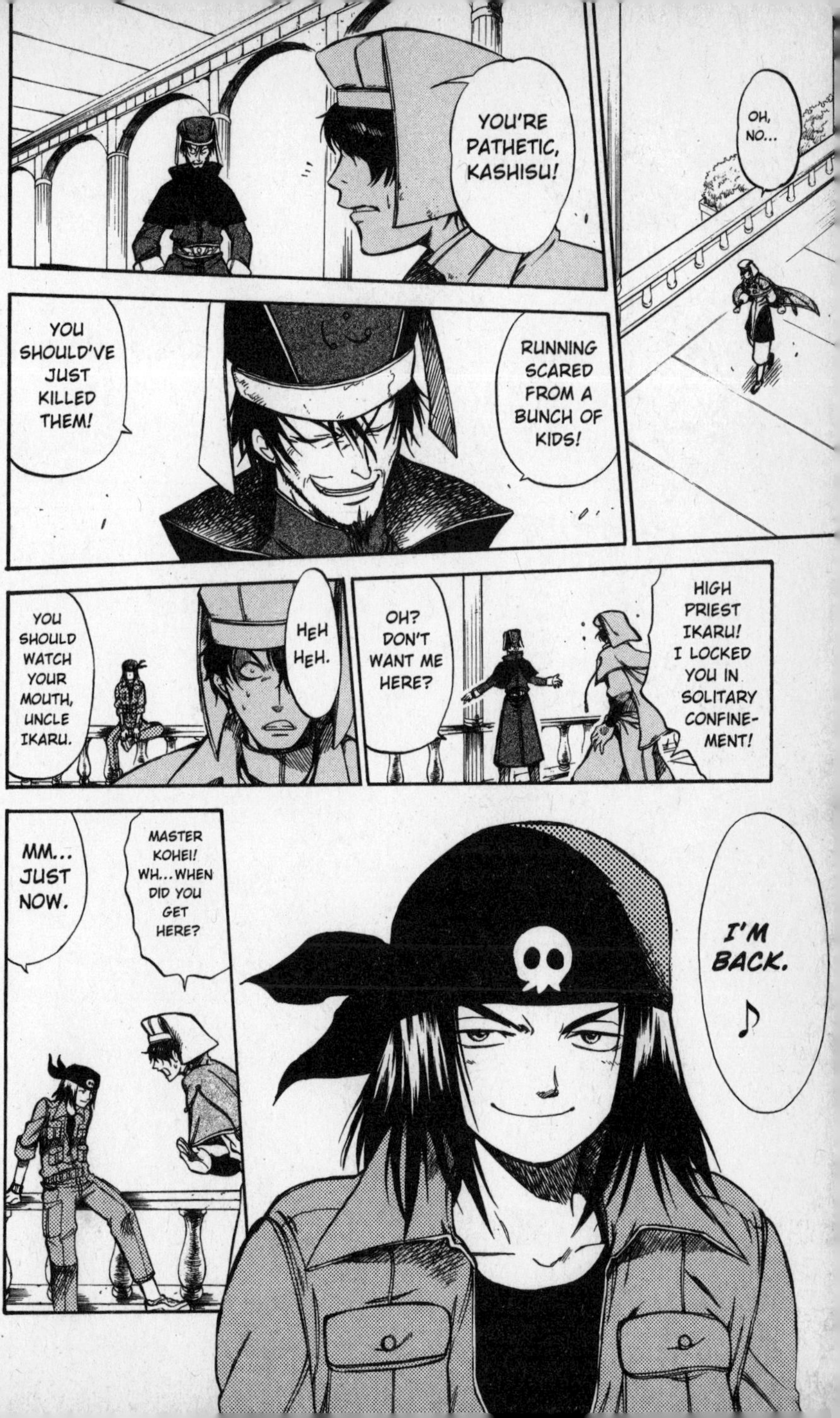
OH, NO...
YOU'RE PATHETIC, KASHISU!
RUNNING SCARED FROM A BUNCH OF KIDS!
YOU SHOULD'VE JUST KILLED THEM!
HIGH PRIEST IKARU! I LOCKED YOU IN SOLITARY CONFINE-MENT!
OH? DON'T WANT ME HERE?
HEH HEH.
YOU SHOULD WATCH YOUR MOUTH, UNCLE IKARU.
I'M BACK. ♪
MASTER KOHEI! WH...WHEN DID YOU GET HERE?
MM... JUST NOW.

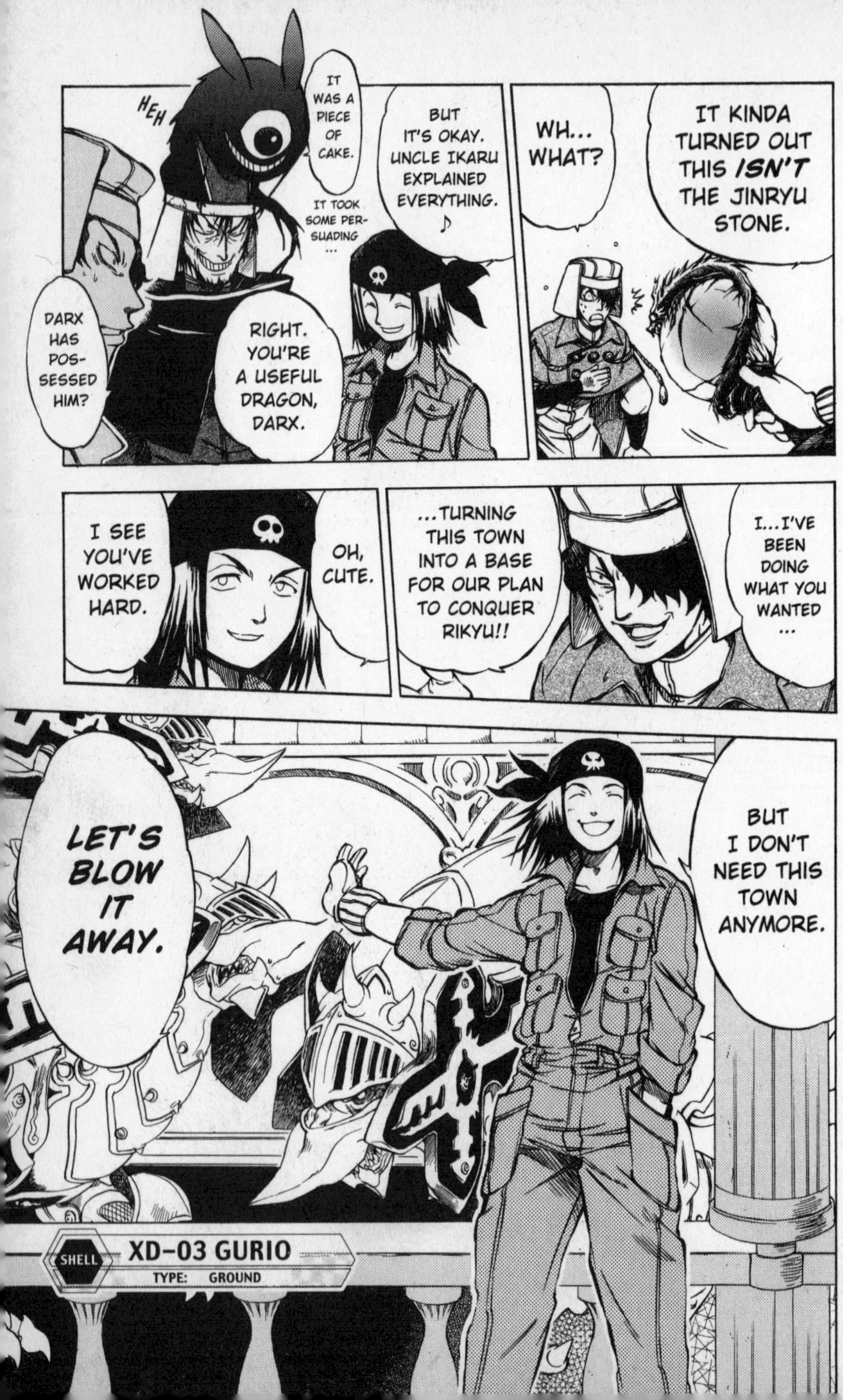
IT KINDA TURNED OUT THIS *ISN'T* THE JINRYU STONE.
WH... WHAT?
BUT IT'S OKAY. UNCLE IKARU EXPLAINED EVERYTHING. ♪
IT WAS A PIECE OF CAKE.
IT TOOK SOME PERSUADING ...
HEH
RIGHT. YOU'RE A USEFUL DRAGON, DARX.
DARX HAS POSSESSED HIM?
I...I'VE BEEN DOING WHAT YOU WANTED ...
...TURNING THIS TOWN INTO A BASE FOR OUR PLAN TO CONQUER RIKYU!!
OH, CUTE.
I SEE YOU'VE WORKED HARD.
BUT I DON'T NEED THIS TOWN ANYMORE.
LET'S BLOW IT AWAY.
SHELL XD-03 GURIO
TYPE: GROUND

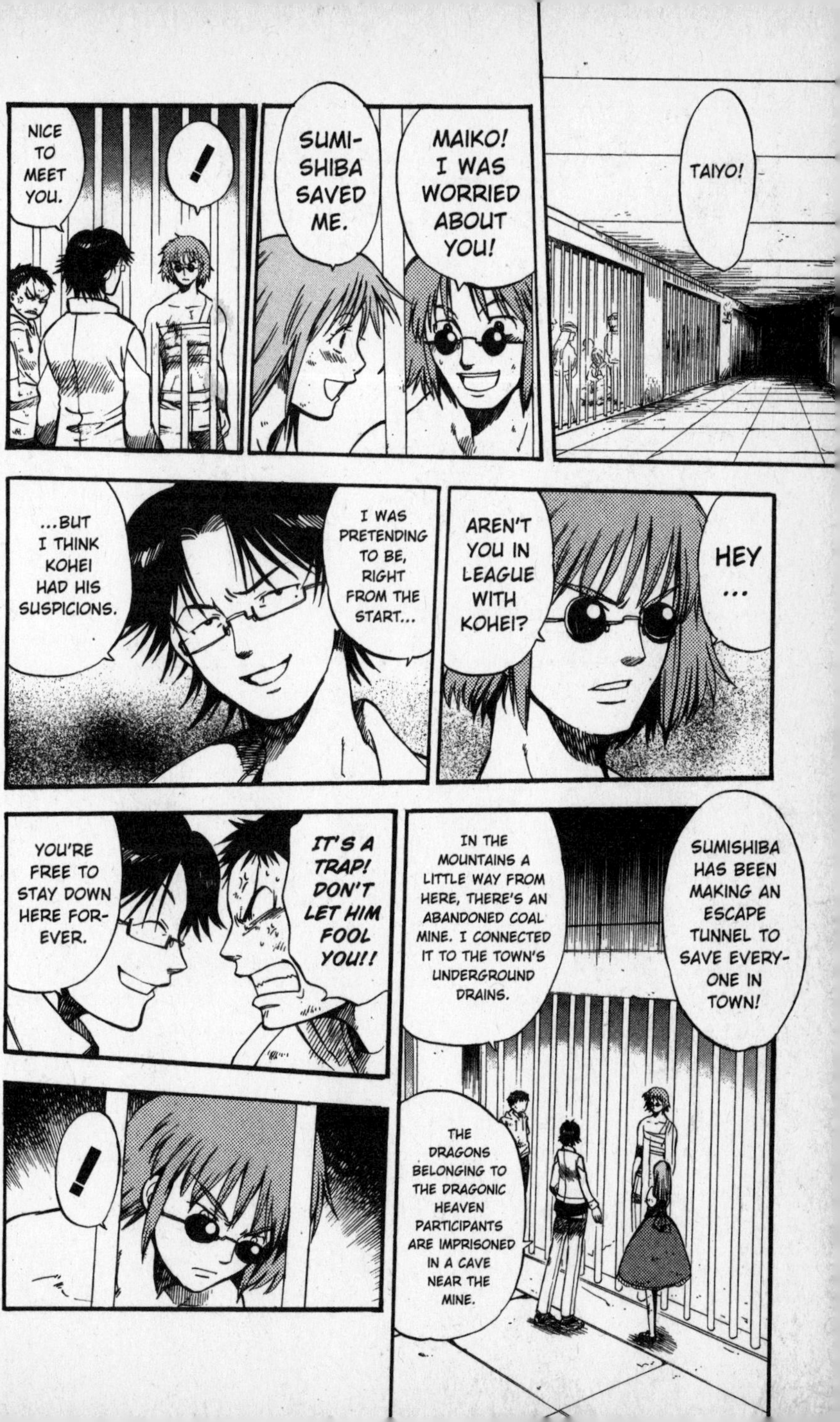
TAIYO!
MAIKO! I WAS WORRIED ABOUT YOU!
SUMI-SHIBA SAVED ME.
!
NICE TO MEET YOU.
HEY ...
AREN'T YOU IN LEAGUE WITH KOHEI?
I WAS PRETENDING TO BE, RIGHT FROM THE START...
...BUT I THINK KOHEI HAD HIS SUSPICIONS.
SUMISHIBA HAS BEEN MAKING AN ESCAPE TUNNEL TO SAVE EVERY-ONE IN TOWN!
IN THE MOUNTAINS A LITTLE WAY FROM HERE, THERE'S AN ABANDONED COAL MINE. I CONNECTED IT TO THE TOWN'S UNDERGROUND DRAINS.
THE DRAGONS BELONGING TO THE DRAGONIC HEAVEN PARTICIPANTS ARE IMPRISONED IN A CAVE NEAR THE MINE.
IT'S A TRAP! DON'T LET HIM FOOL YOU!!
YOU'RE FREE TO STAY DOWN HERE FOR-EVER.
!

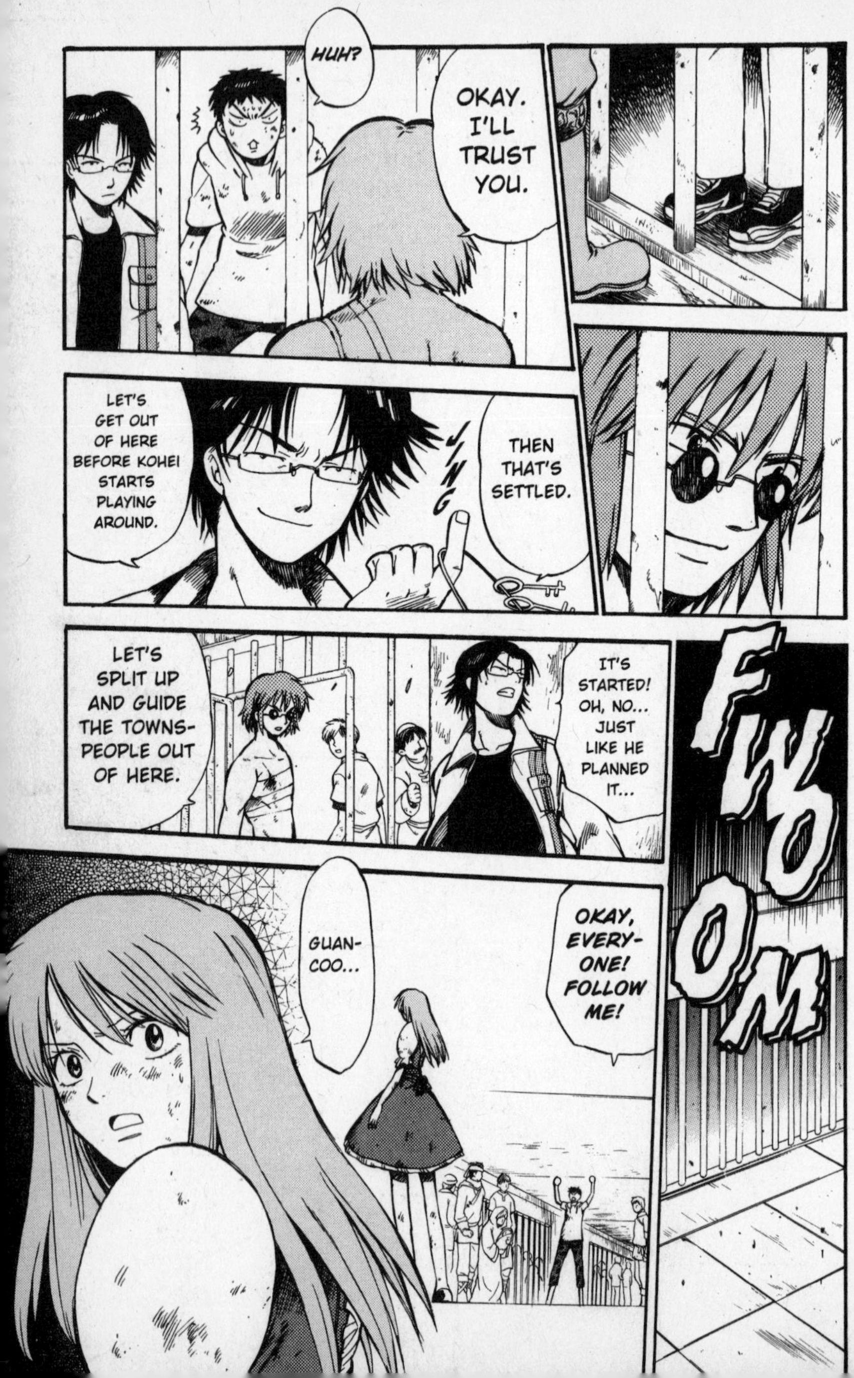
OKAY. I'LL TRUST YOU.
HUH?
THEN THAT'S SETTLED.
JING
LET'S GET OUT OF HERE BEFORE KOHEI STARTS PLAYING AROUND.
FWOOM
IT'S STARTED! OH, NO... JUST LIKE HE PLANNED IT...
LET'S SPLIT UP AND GUIDE THE TOWNS-PEOPLE OUT OF HERE.
OKAY, EVERY-ONE! FOLLOW ME!
GUAN-COO...

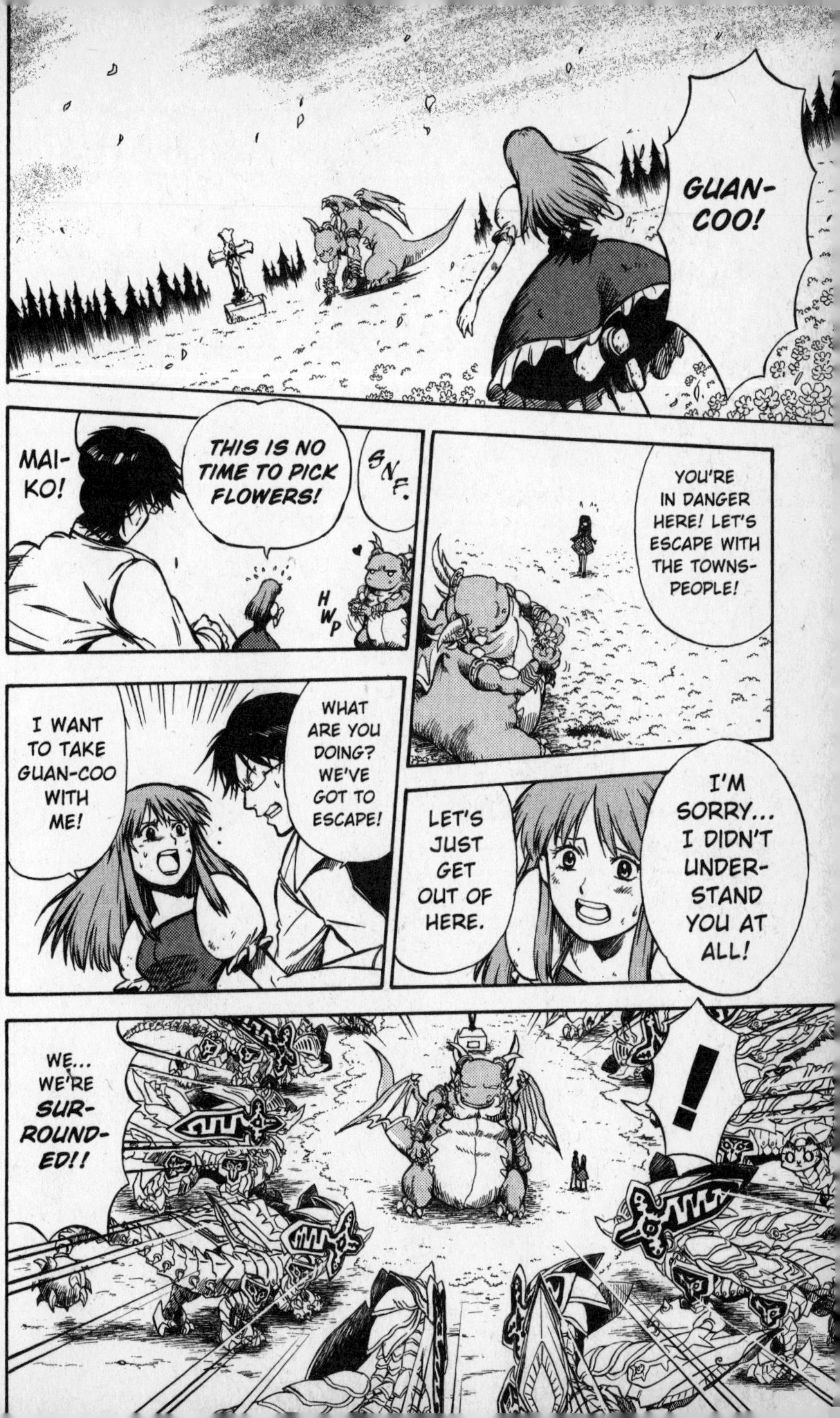
GUAN-COO!
YOU'RE IN DANGER HERE! LET'S ESCAPE WITH THE TOWNSPEOPLE!
I'M SORRY... I DIDN'T UNDERSTAND YOU AT ALL!
LET'S JUST GET OUT OF HERE.
SNF.
THIS IS NO TIME TO PICK FLOWERS!
MAI-KO!
HWP
WHAT ARE YOU DOING? WE'VE GOT TO ESCAPE!
I WANT TO TAKE GUAN-COO WITH ME!
!
WE... WE'RE SURROUNDED!!

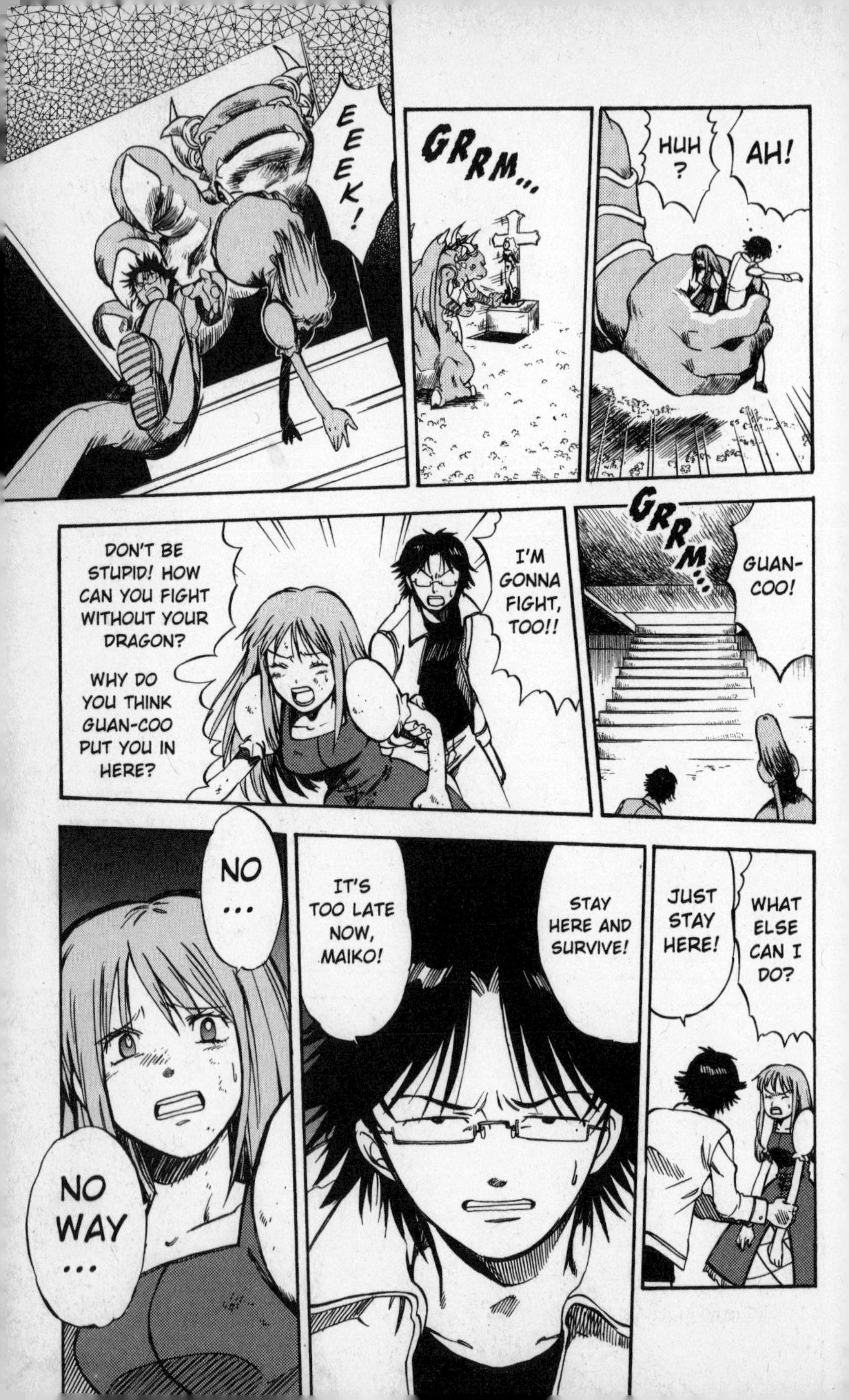
AH!
HUH?
GRRM...
EEEK!
GRRM...
GUAN-COO!
I'M GONNA FIGHT, TOO!!
DON'T BE STUPID! HOW CAN YOU FIGHT WITHOUT YOUR DRAGON?
WHY DO YOU THINK GUAN-COO PUT YOU IN HERE?
WHAT ELSE CAN I DO?
JUST STAY HERE!
STAY HERE AND SURVIVE!
IT'S TOO LATE NOW, MAIKO!
NO...
NO WAY...

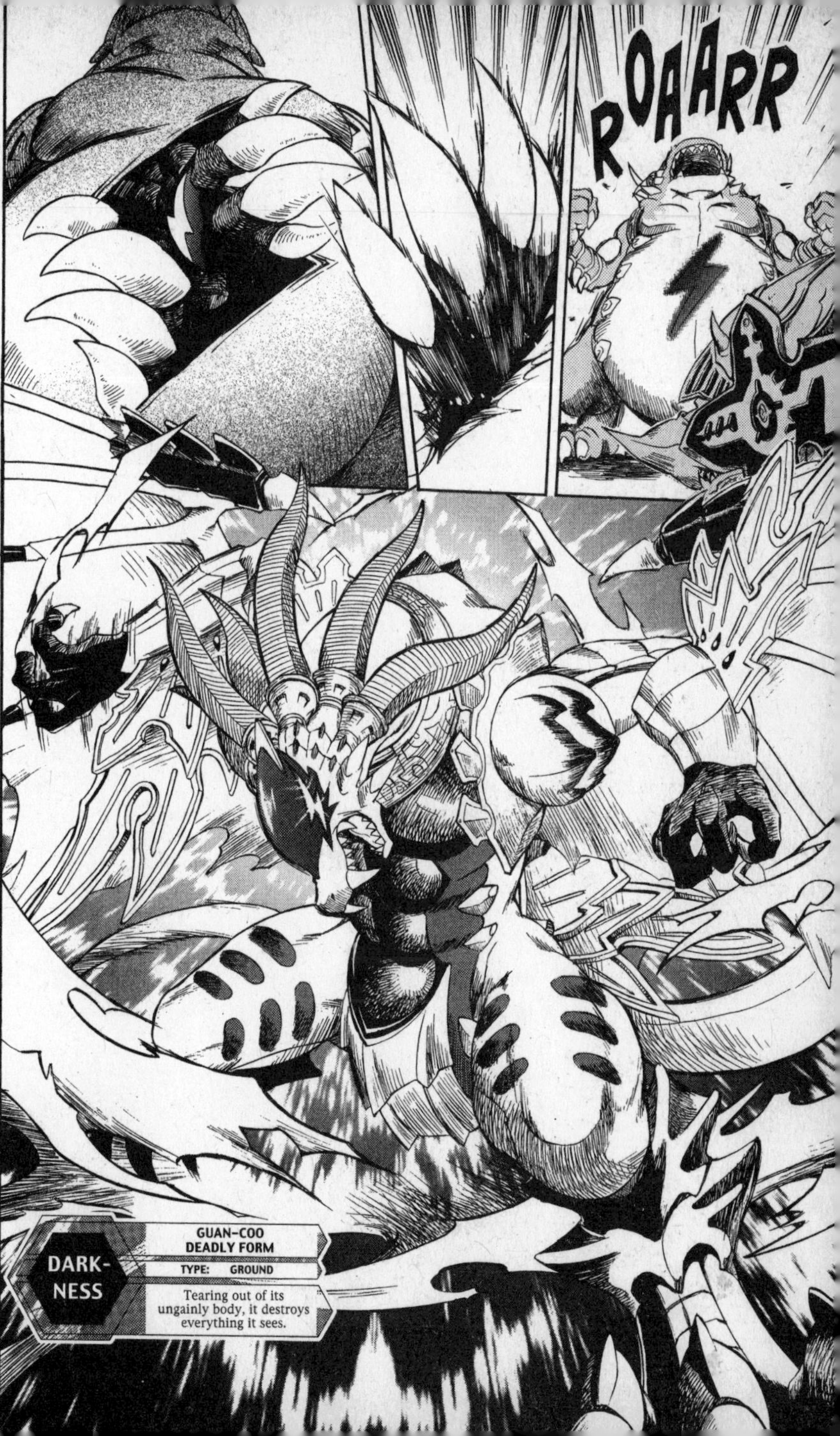
ROAARR
DARK-NESS
GUAN-COO DEADLY FORM
TYPE: GROUND
Tearing out of its ungainly body, it destroys everything it sees.

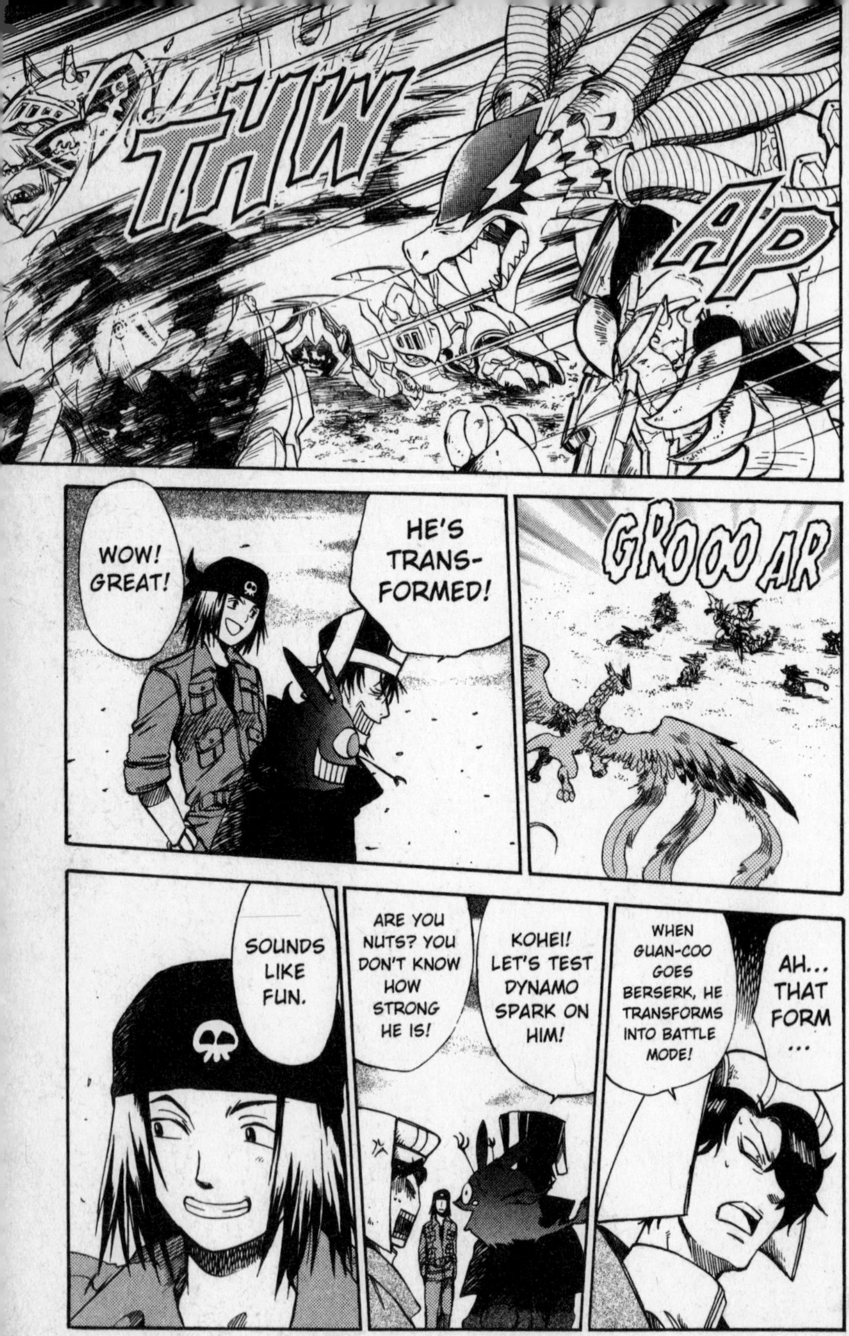
THWAP
GROOO AR
HE'S TRANS-FORMED!
WOW! GREAT!
AH... THAT FORM ...
WHEN GUAN-COO GOES BERSERK, HE TRANSFORMS INTO BATTLE MODE!
KOHEI! LET'S TEST DYNAMO SPARK ON HIM!
ARE YOU NUTS? YOU DON'T KNOW HOW STRONG HE IS!
SOUNDS LIKE FUN.

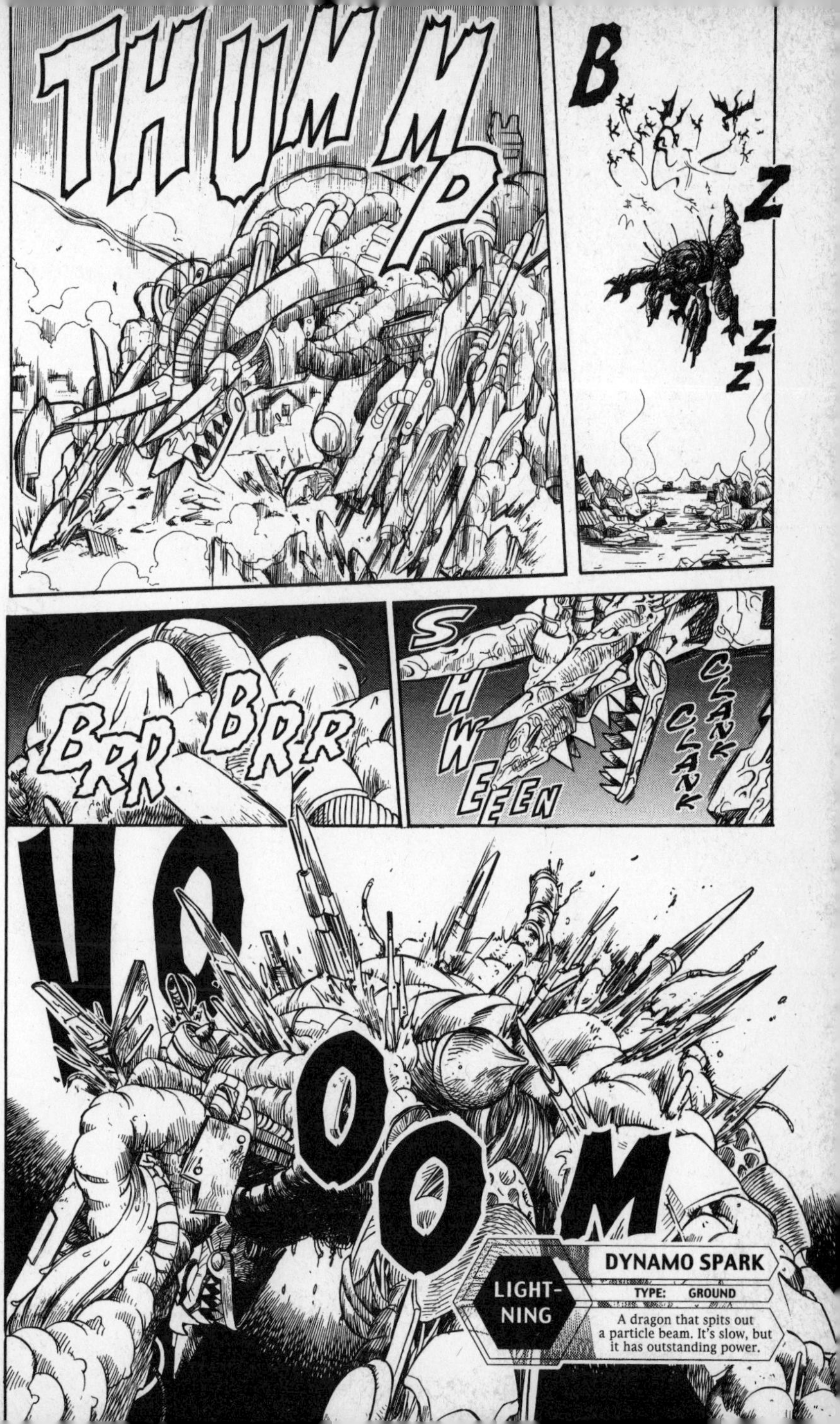

BZZZZ
THUMMP
SHWEEEN
CLANK CLANK
BRR BRR
VOOOM
DYNAMO SPARK
LIGHT-NING
TYPE: GROUND
A dragon that spits out a particle beam. It's slow, but it has outstanding power.

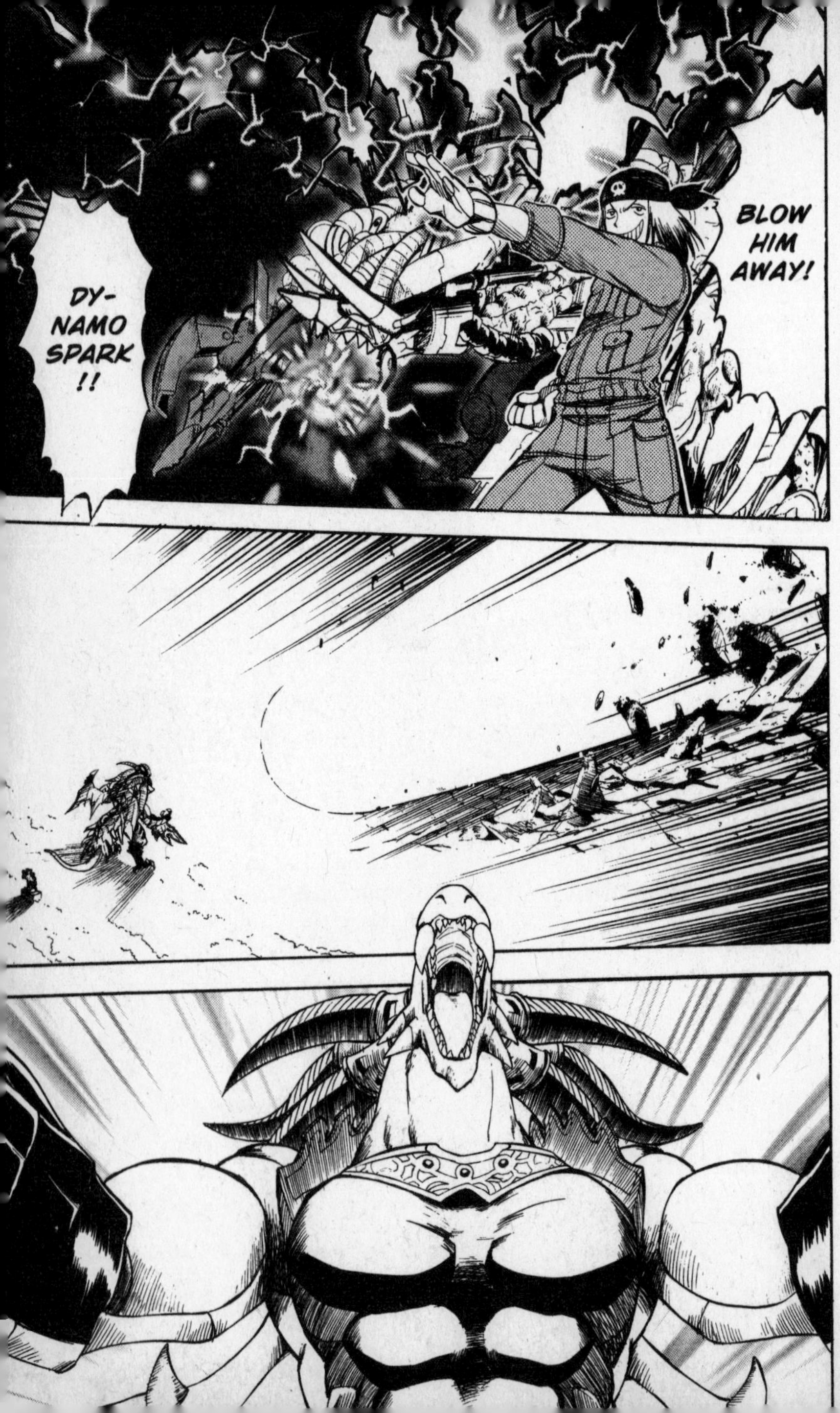
BLOW HIM AWAY!
DY-NAMO SPARK !!

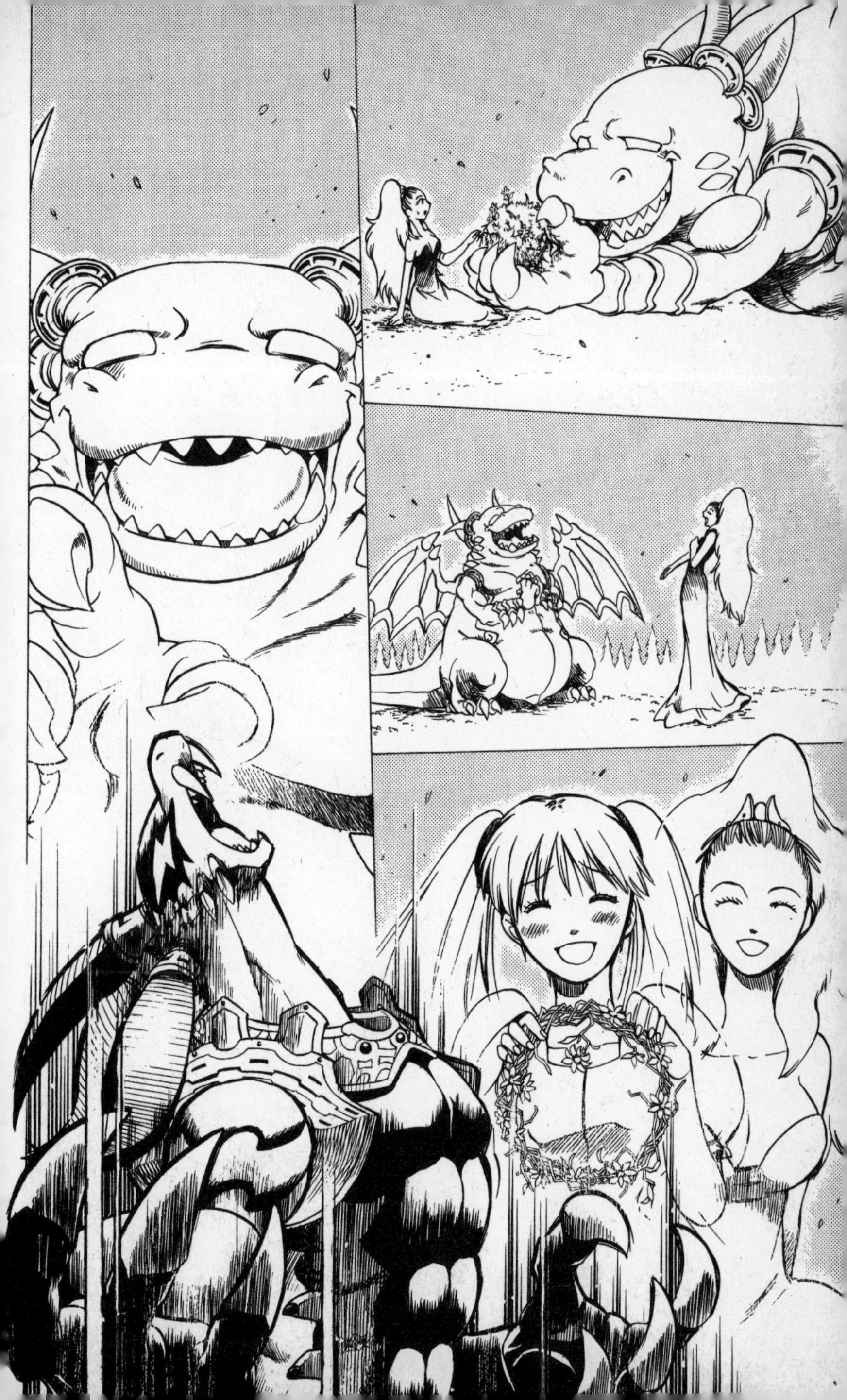

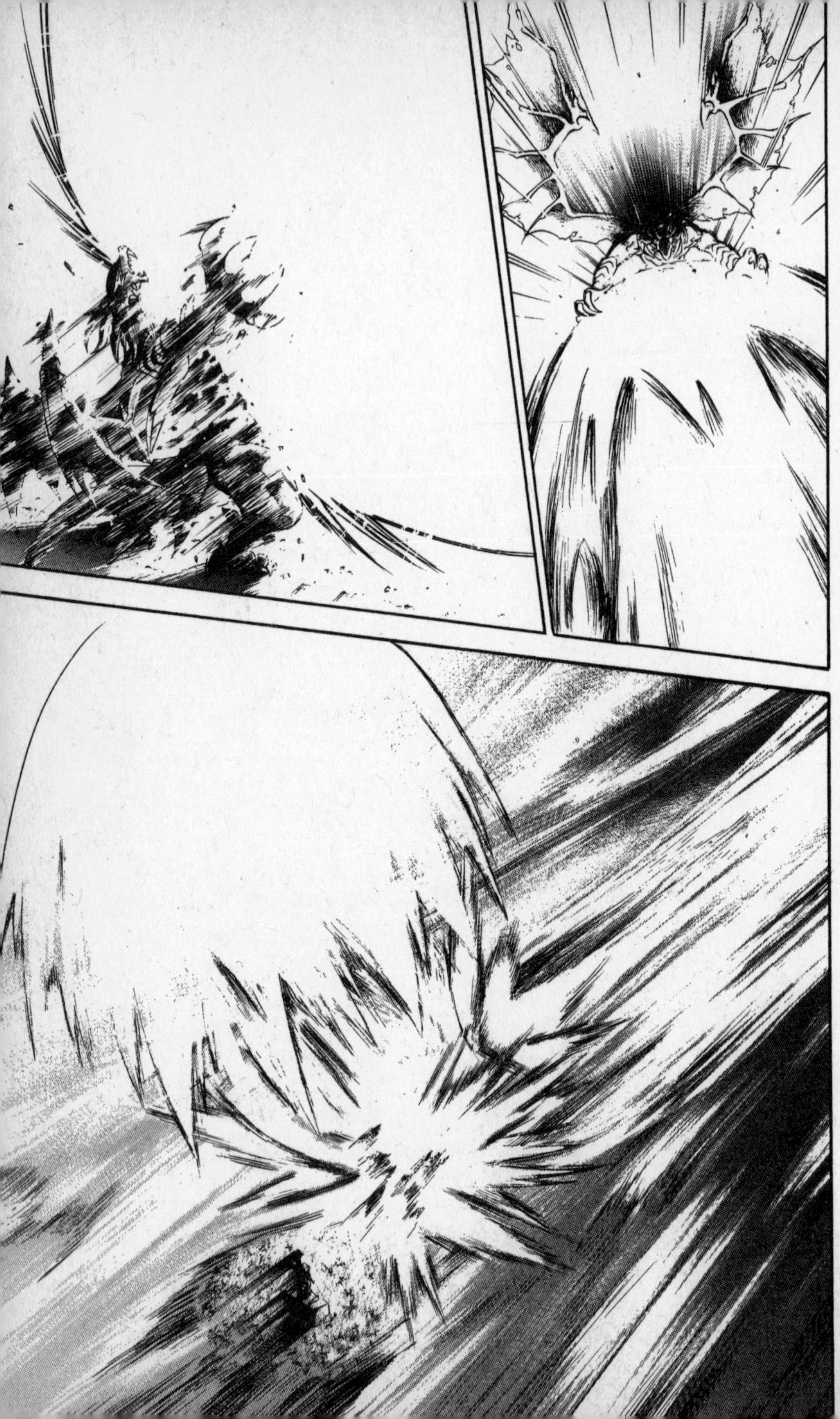

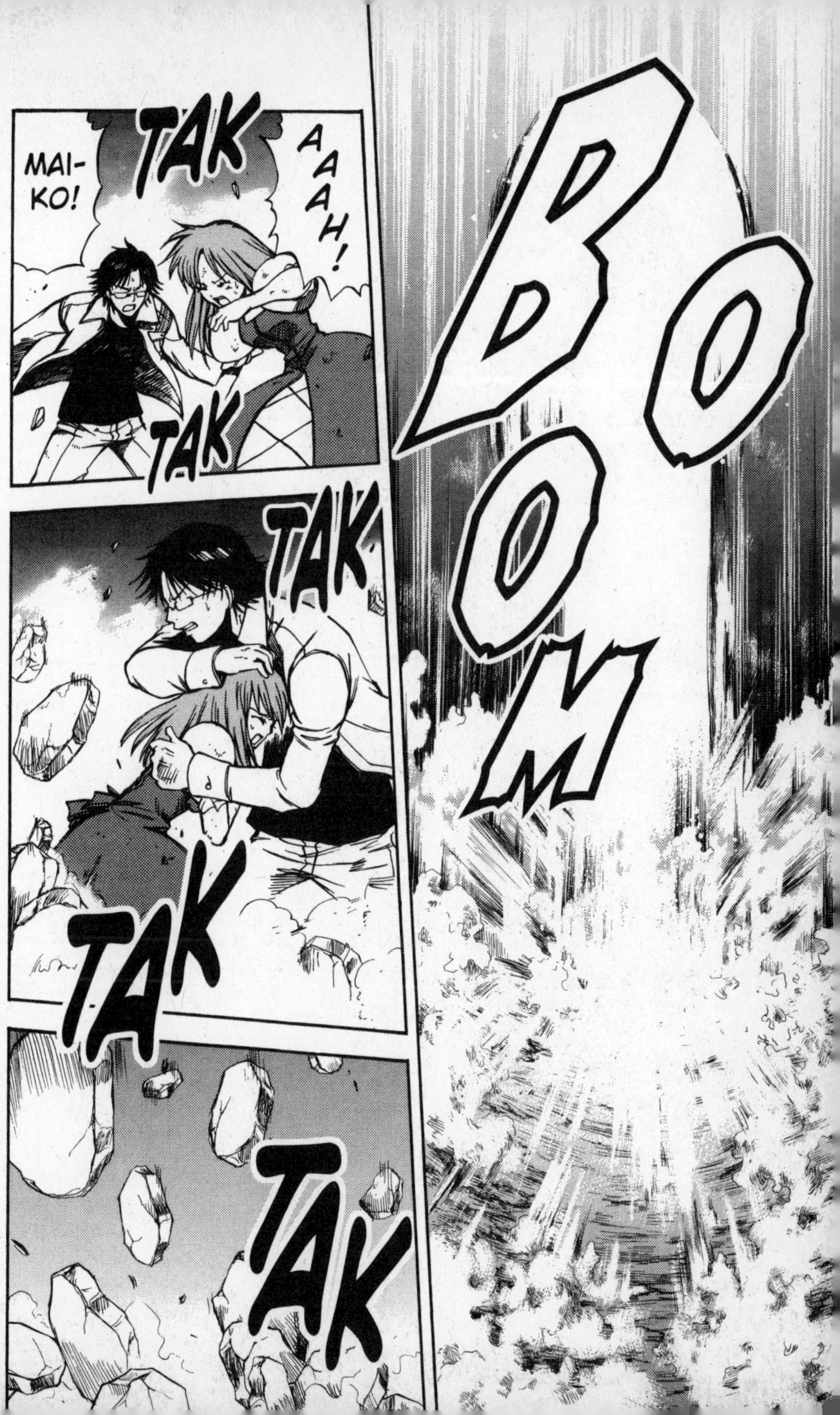
BOOM
AAAAH!
TAK
MAI-KO!
TAK
TAK
TAK
TAK

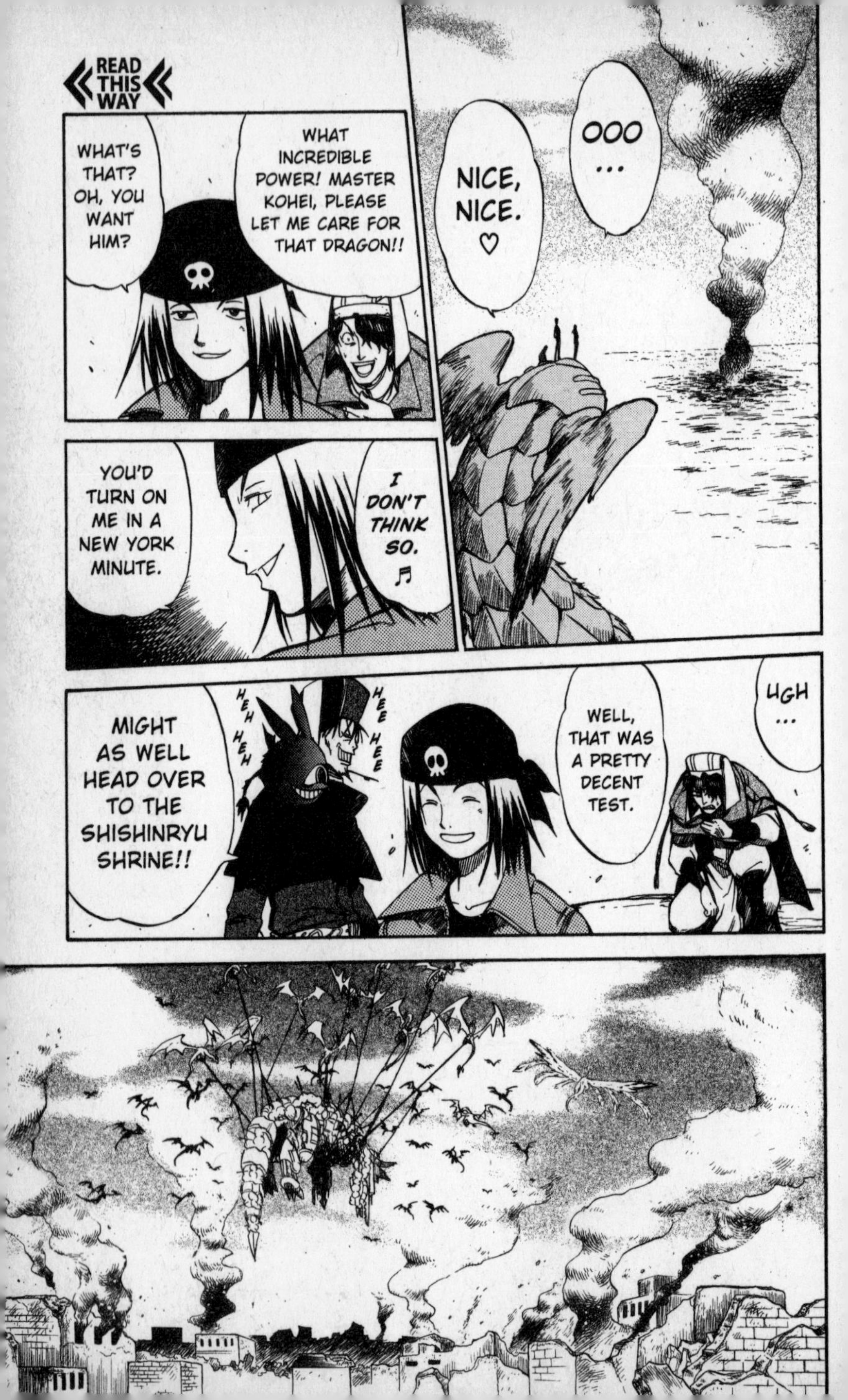
READ THIS WAY
OOO ...
NICE, NICE. ♡
WHAT INCREDIBLE POWER! MASTER KOHEI, PLEASE LET ME CARE FOR THAT DRAGON!!
WHAT'S THAT? OH, YOU WANT HIM?
I DON'T THINK SO. ♬
YOU'D TURN ON ME IN A NEW YORK MINUTE.
UGH ...
WELL, THAT WAS A PRETTY DECENT TEST.
HEE HEE HEE
HEH HEH HEH
MIGHT AS WELL HEAD OVER TO THE SHISHINRYU SHRINE!!

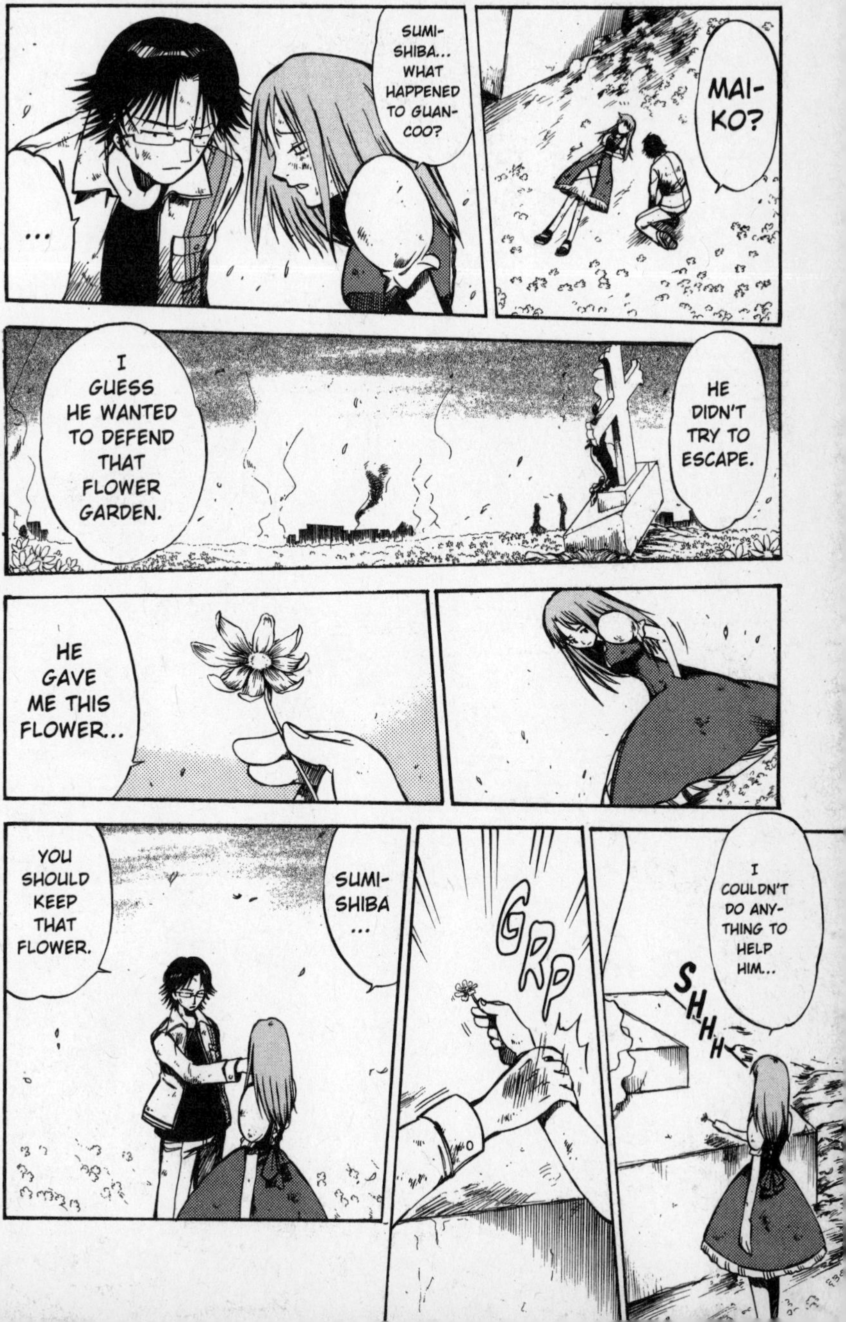
MAI-KO?
SUMI-SHIBA... WHAT HAPPENED TO GUAN-COO?
...
HE DIDN'T TRY TO ESCAPE.
I GUESS HE WANTED TO DEFEND THAT FLOWER GARDEN.
HE GAVE ME THIS FLOWER...
I COULDN'T DO ANY-THING TO HELP HIM...
SHHH
GRP
SUMI-SHIBA ...
YOU SHOULD KEEP THAT FLOWER.

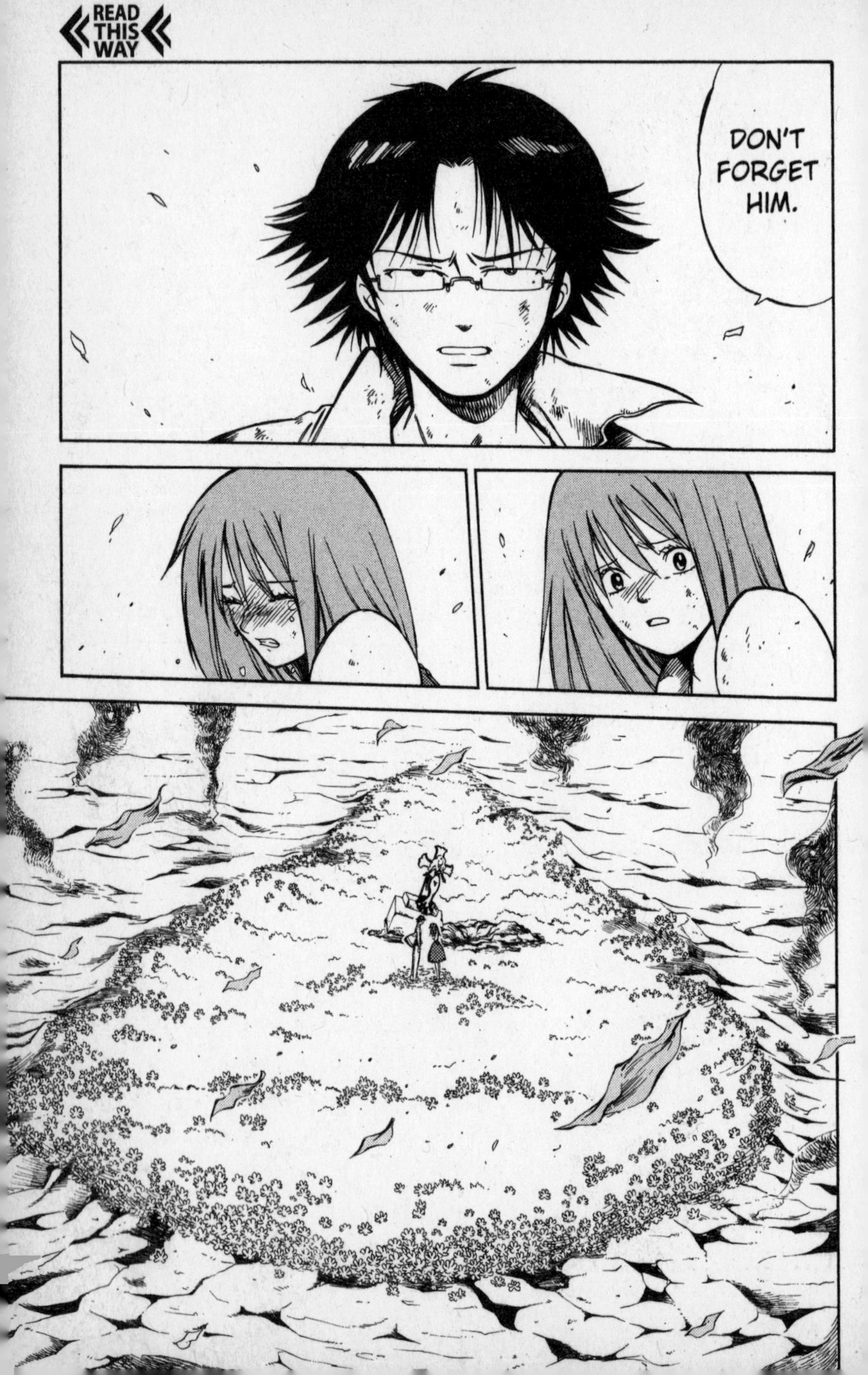
READ THIS WAY
DON'T FORGET HIM.

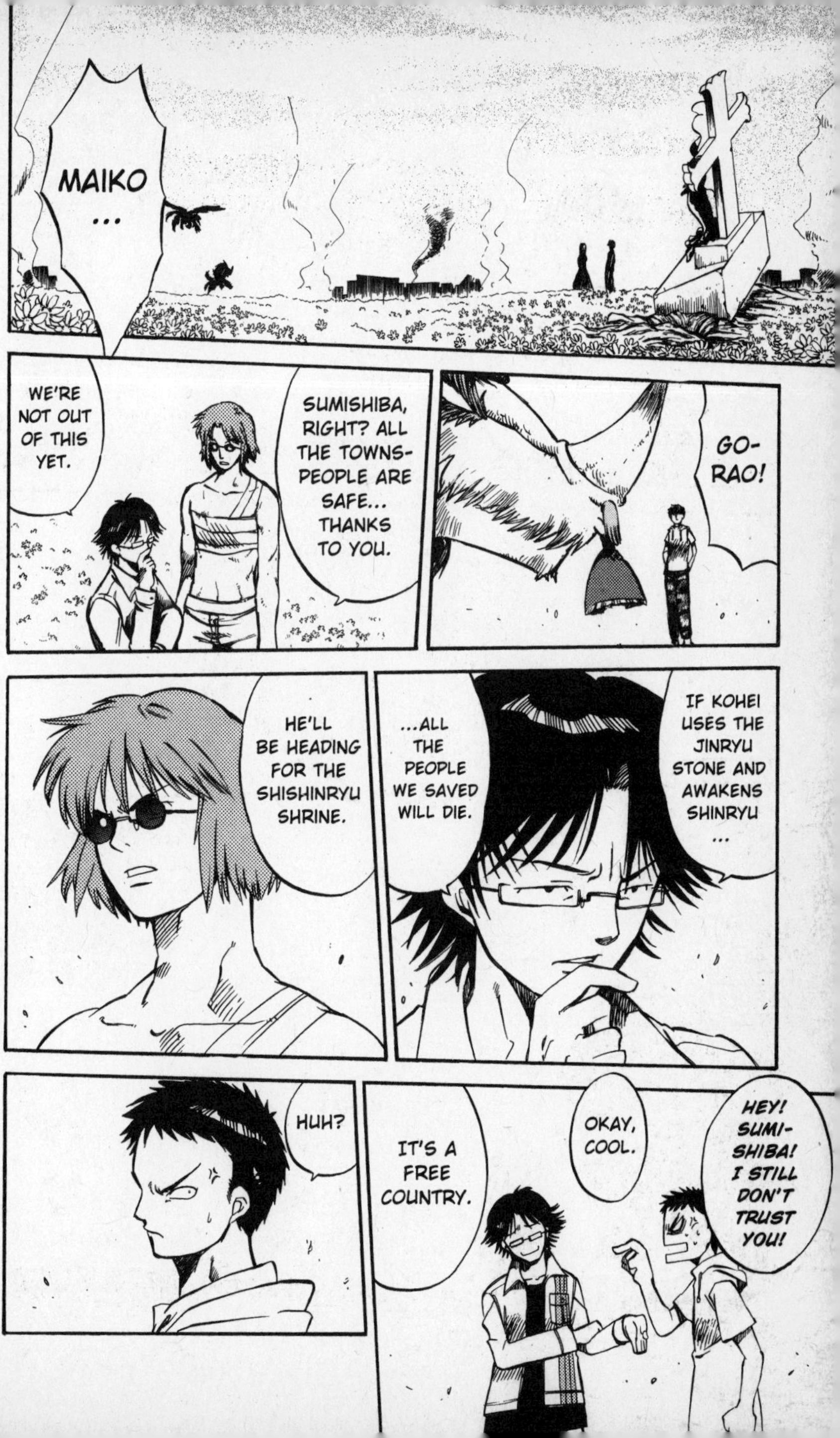
MAIKO ...
GO-RAO!
SUMISHIBA, RIGHT? ALL THE TOWNS-PEOPLE ARE SAFE... THANKS TO YOU.
WE'RE NOT OUT OF THIS YET.
IF KOHEI USES THE JINRYU STONE AND AWAKENS SHINRYU ...
...ALL THE PEOPLE WE SAVED WILL DIE.
HE'LL BE HEADING FOR THE SHISHINRYU SHRINE.
HEY! SUMI-SHIBA! I STILL DON'T TRUST YOU!
OKAY, COOL.
IT'S A FREE COUNTRY.
HUH?

READ THIS WAY

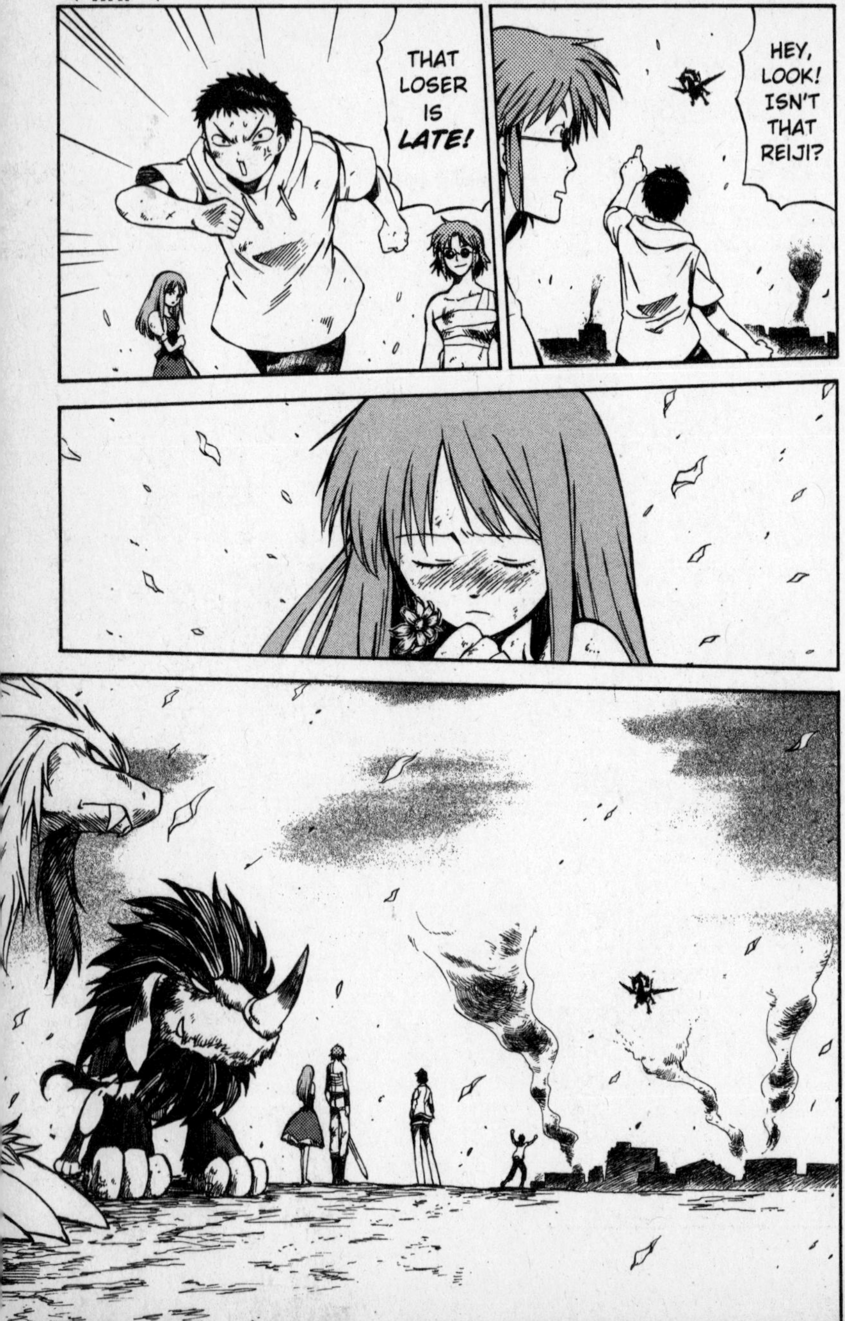
HEY, LOOK! ISN'T THAT REIJI?
THAT LOSER IS *LATE!*

Fight! Agent G!

BY NAGI

NOODLE MANIA!

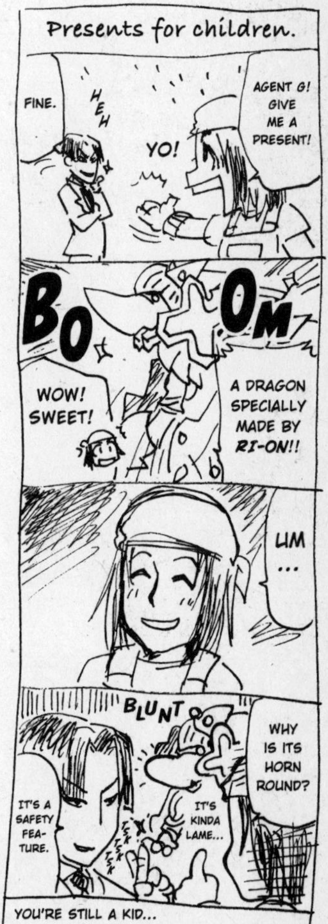
Presents for children.
AGENT G! GIVE ME A PRESENT!
YO!
HEH
FINE.
BOOM
A DRAGON SPECIALLY MADE BY RI-ON!!
WOW! SWEET!
UM ...
BLUNT
WHY IS ITS HORN ROUND?
IT'S KINDA LAME...
TSK TSK TSK
IT'S A SAFETY FEA-TURE.
YOU'RE STILL A KID...

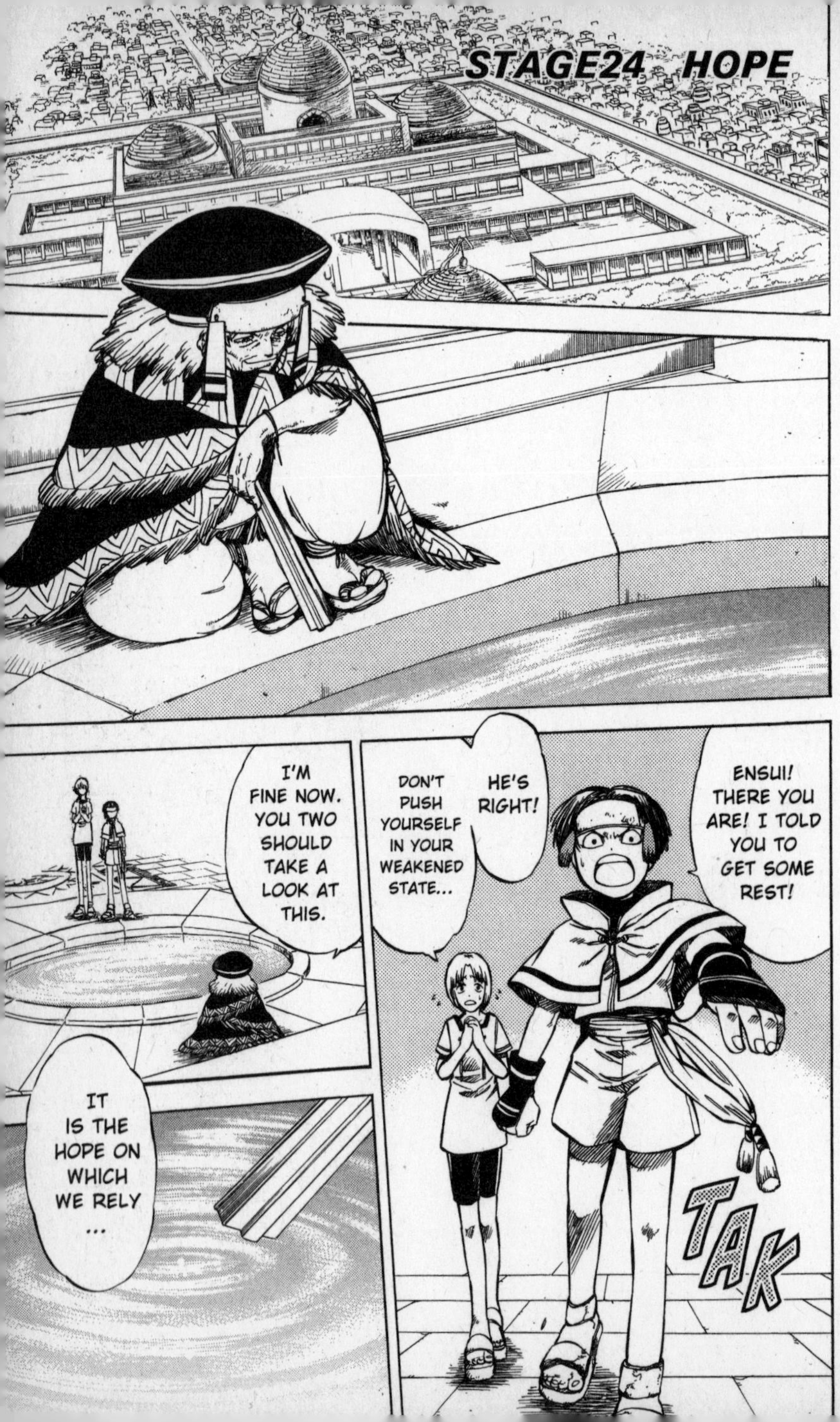
STAGE24 HOPE
ENSUI! THERE YOU ARE! I TOLD YOU TO GET SOME REST!
HE'S RIGHT!
DON'T PUSH YOURSELF IN YOUR WEAKENED STATE...
TAK
I'M FINE NOW. YOU TWO SHOULD TAKE A LOOK AT THIS.
IT IS THE HOPE ON WHICH WE RELY ...

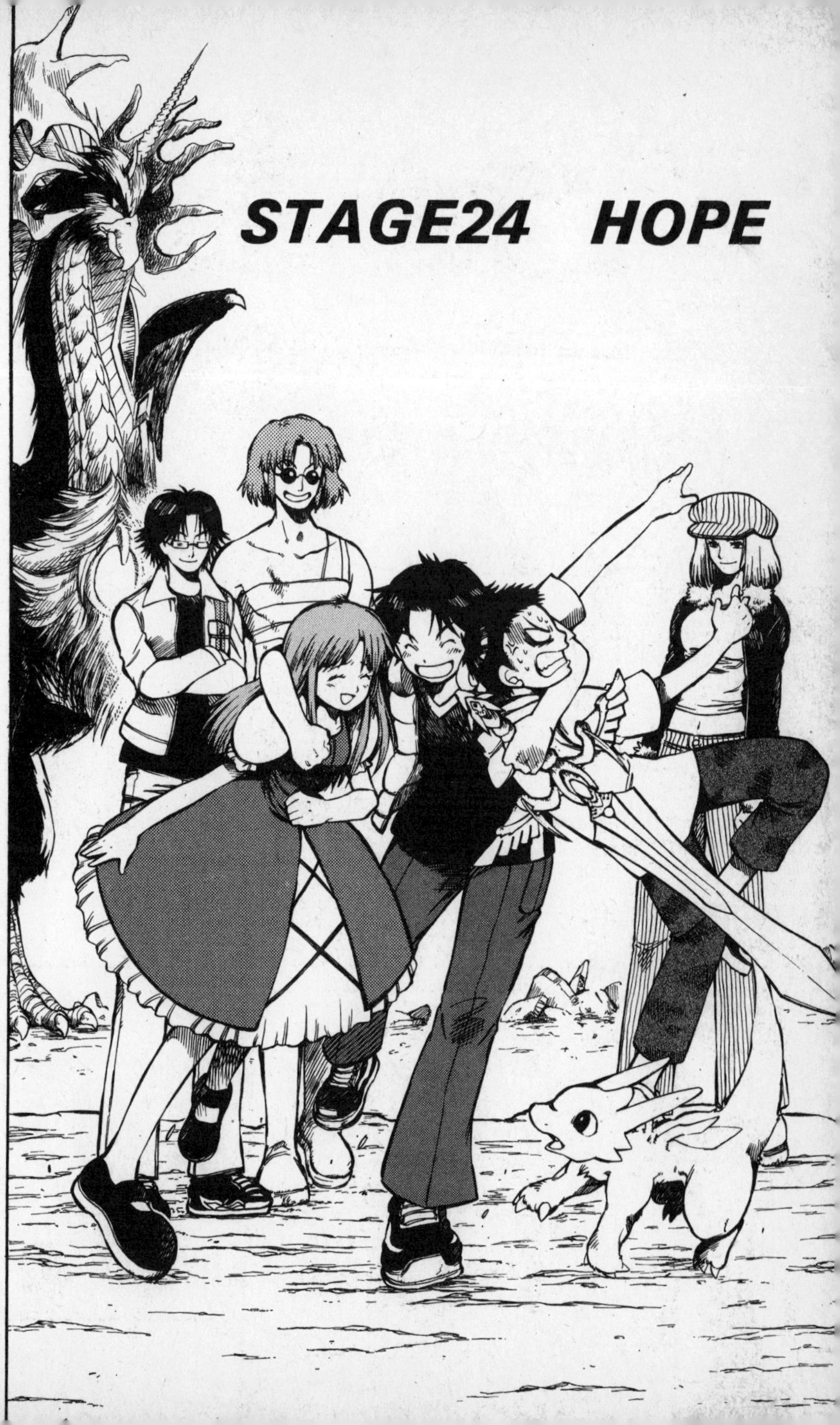
STAGE24 HOPE

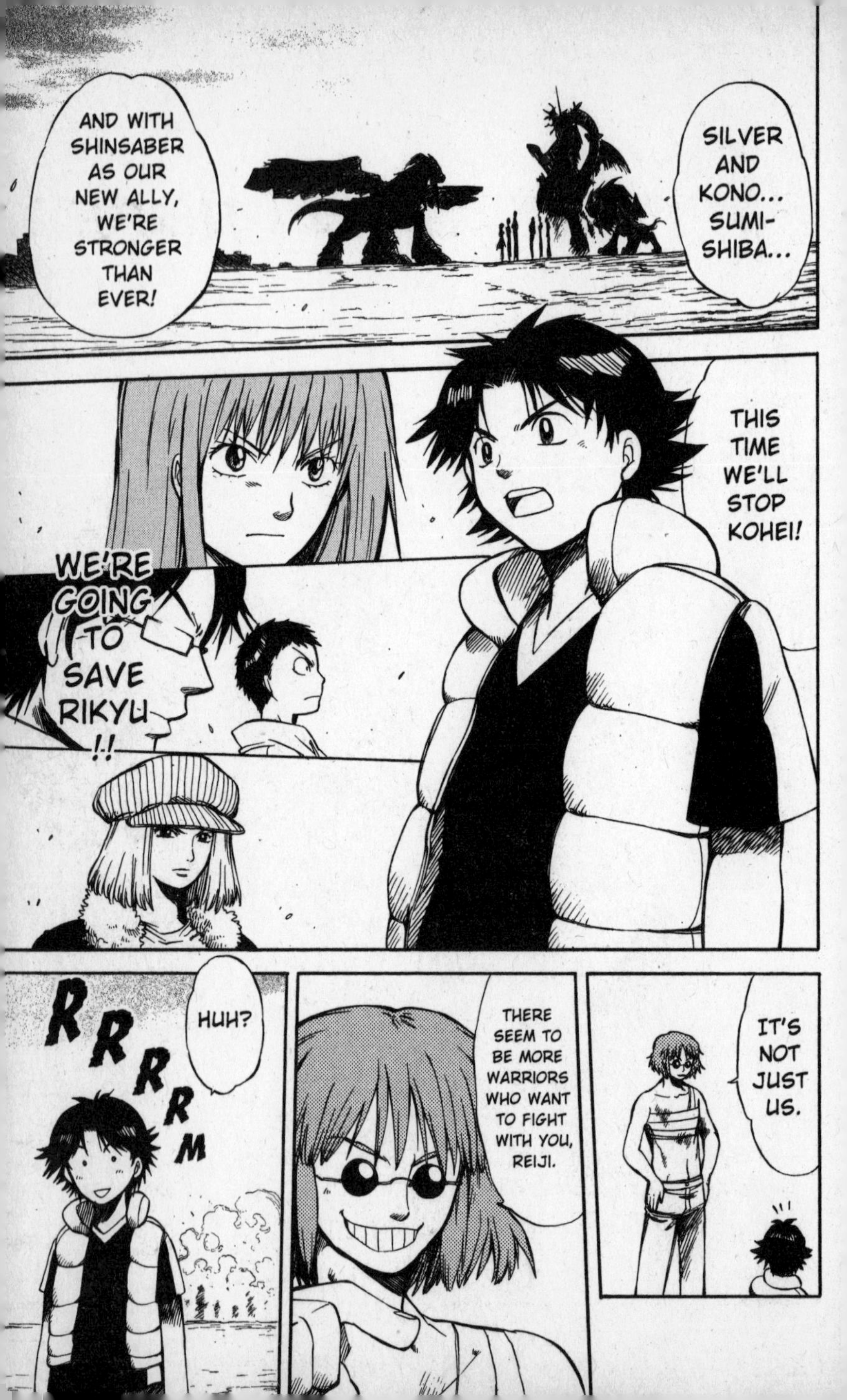
SILVER AND KONO... SUMI-SHIBA...
AND WITH SHINSABER AS OUR NEW ALLY, WE'RE STRONGER THAN EVER!
THIS TIME WE'LL STOP KOHEI!
WE'RE GOING TO SAVE RIKYU!!
IT'S NOT JUST US.
THERE SEEM TO BE MORE WARRIORS WHO WANT TO FIGHT WITH YOU, REIJI.
HUH?
RRRRM

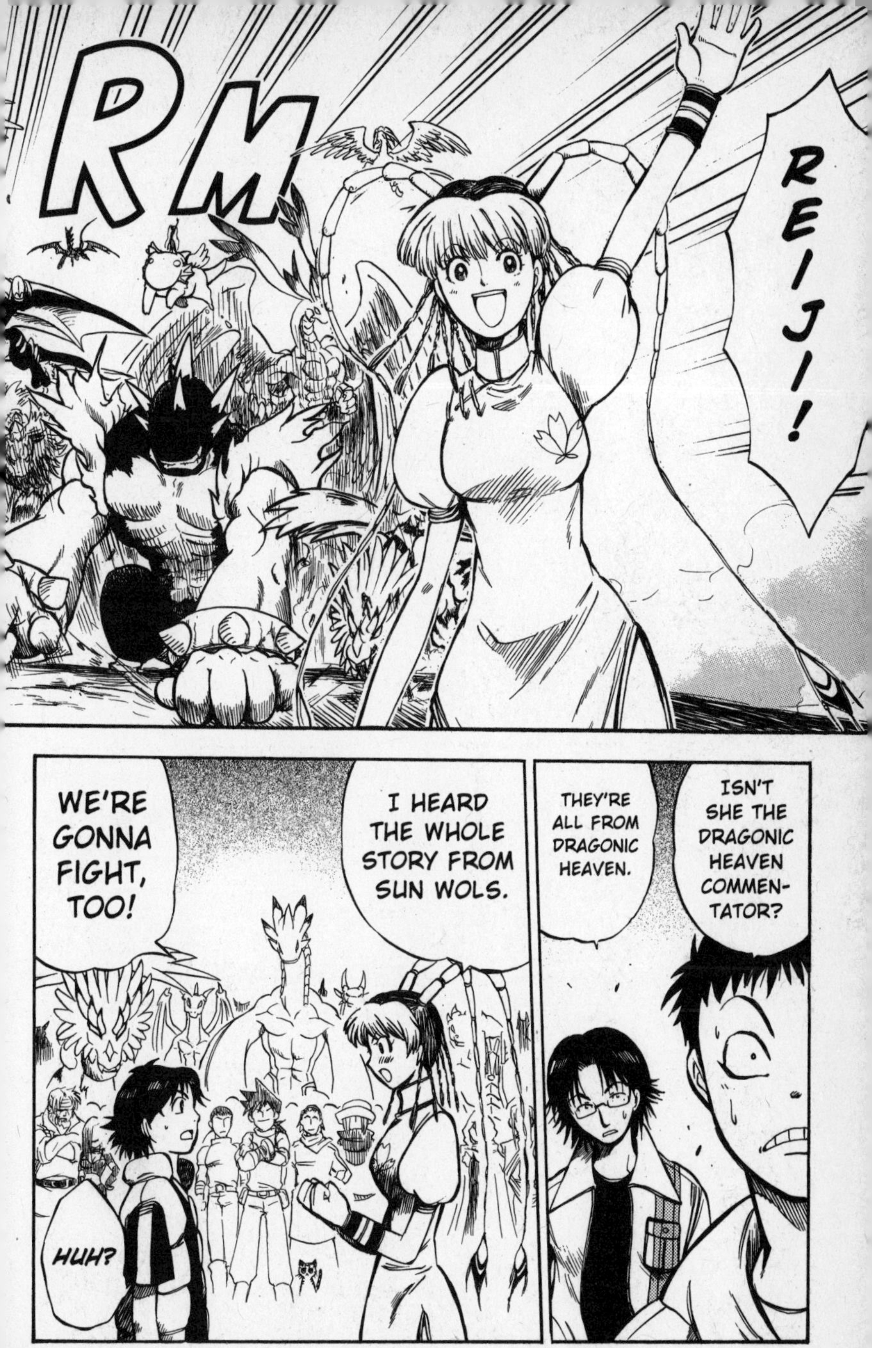
REIJI!
RM
ISN'T SHE THE DRAGONIC HEAVEN COMMENTATOR?
THEY'RE ALL FROM DRAGONIC HEAVEN.
I HEARD THE WHOLE STORY FROM SUN WOLS.
WE'RE GONNA FIGHT, TOO!
HUH?

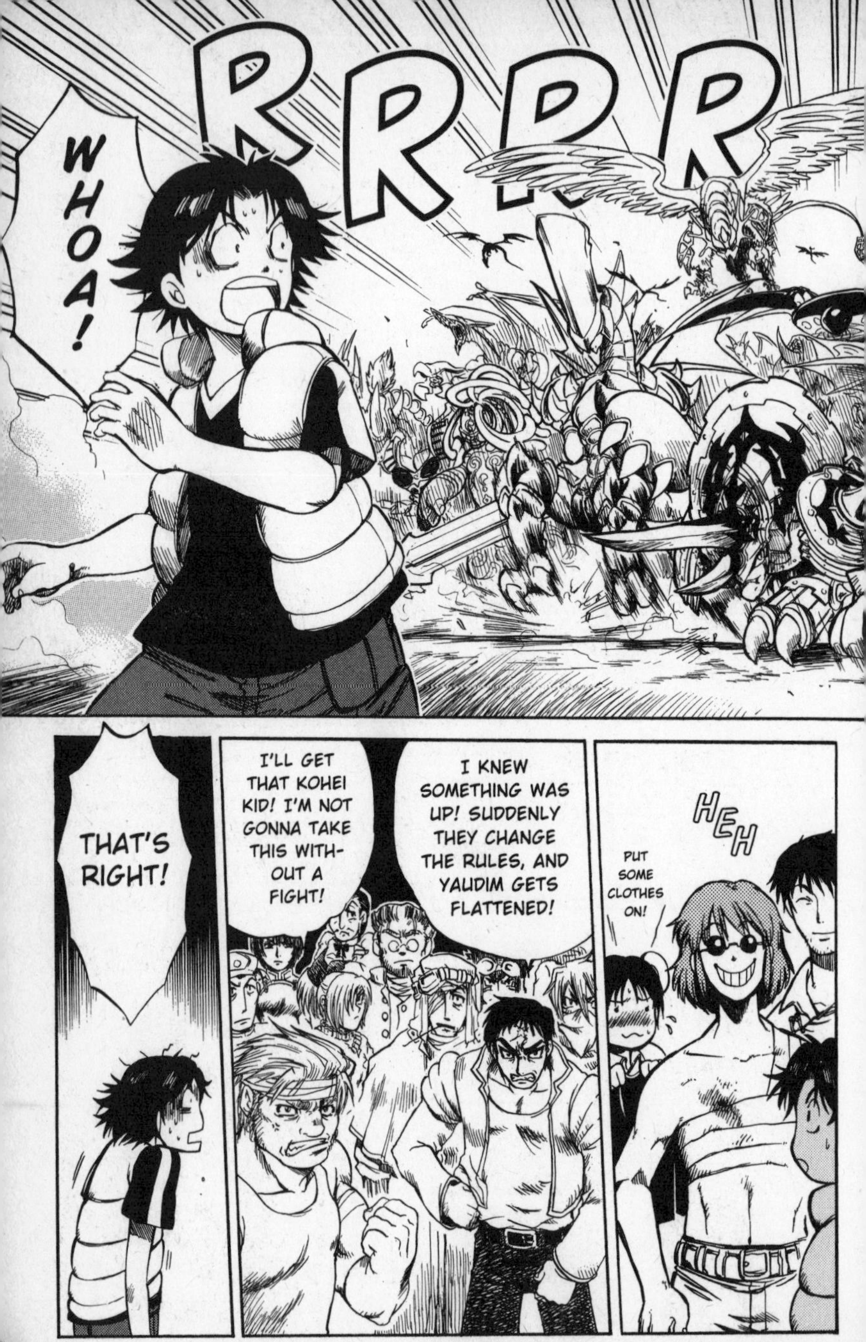
RRRR
WHOA!
HEH
PUT SOME CLOTHES ON!
I KNEW SOMETHING WAS UP! SUDDENLY THEY CHANGE THE RULES, AND YAUDIM GETS FLATTENED!
I'LL GET THAT KOHEI KID! I'M NOT GONNA TAKE THIS WITH-OUT A FIGHT!
THAT'S RIGHT!

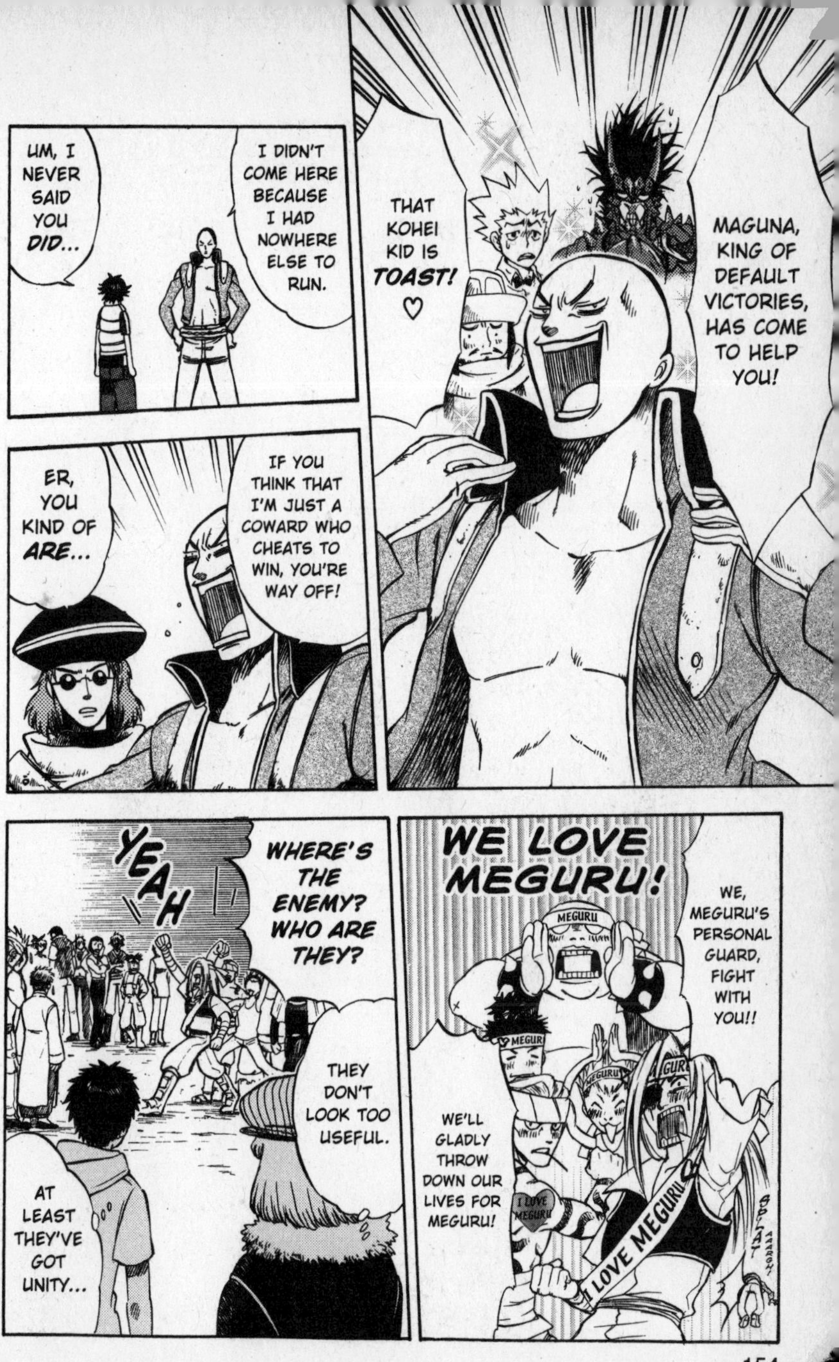
MAGUNA, KING OF DEFAULT VICTORIES, HAS COME TO HELP YOU!
THAT KOHEI KID IS TOAST! ♡
I DIDN'T COME HERE BECAUSE I HAD NOWHERE ELSE TO RUN.
UM, I NEVER SAID YOU DID...
IF YOU THINK THAT I'M JUST A COWARD WHO CHEATS TO WIN, YOU'RE WAY OFF!
ER, YOU KIND OF ARE...
WE LOVE MEGURU!
WE, MEGURU'S PERSONAL GUARD, FIGHT WITH YOU!!
MEGURU
I LOVE MEGURU
SPLAT
WE'LL GLADLY THROW DOWN OUR LIVES FOR MEGURU!
WHERE'S THE ENEMY? WHO ARE THEY?
YEAH
THEY DON'T LOOK TOO USEFUL.
AT LEAST THEY'VE GOT UNITY...

READ THIS WAY

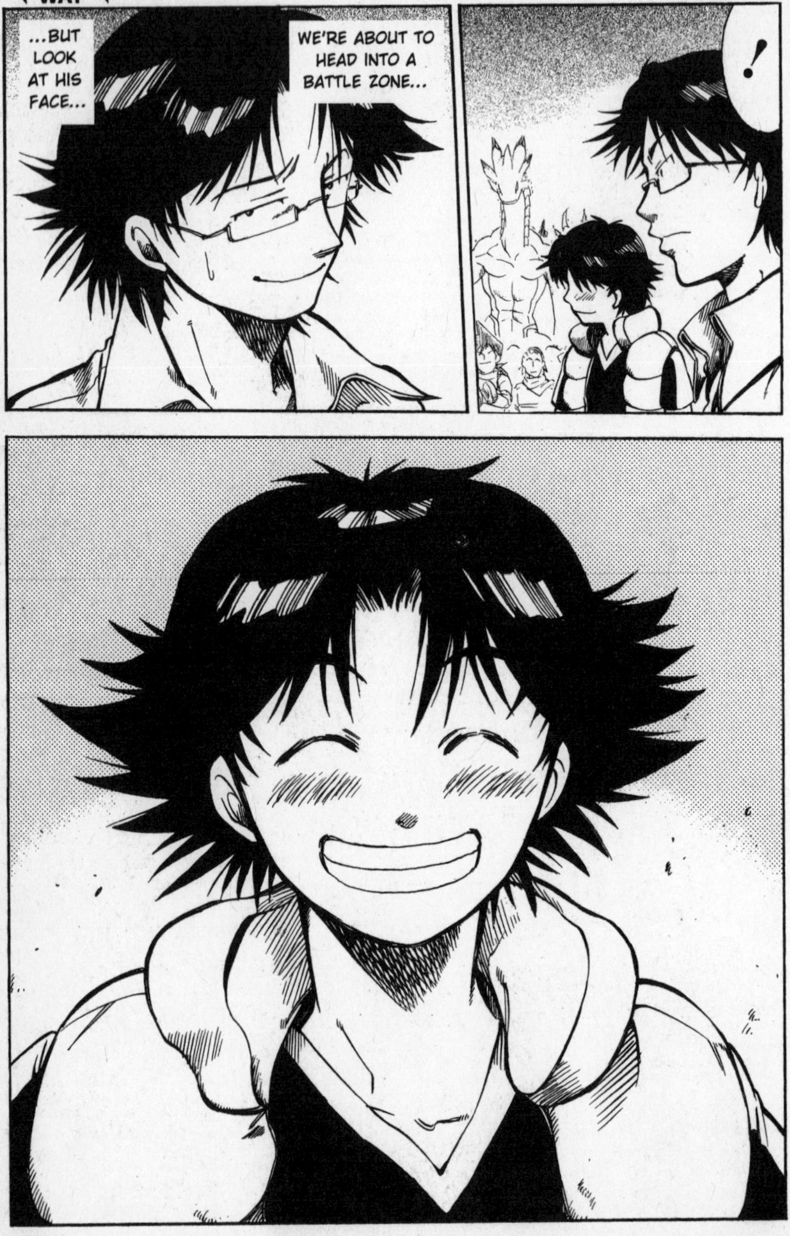
!
WE'RE ABOUT TO HEAD INTO A BATTLE ZONE...
...BUT LOOK AT HIS FACE...

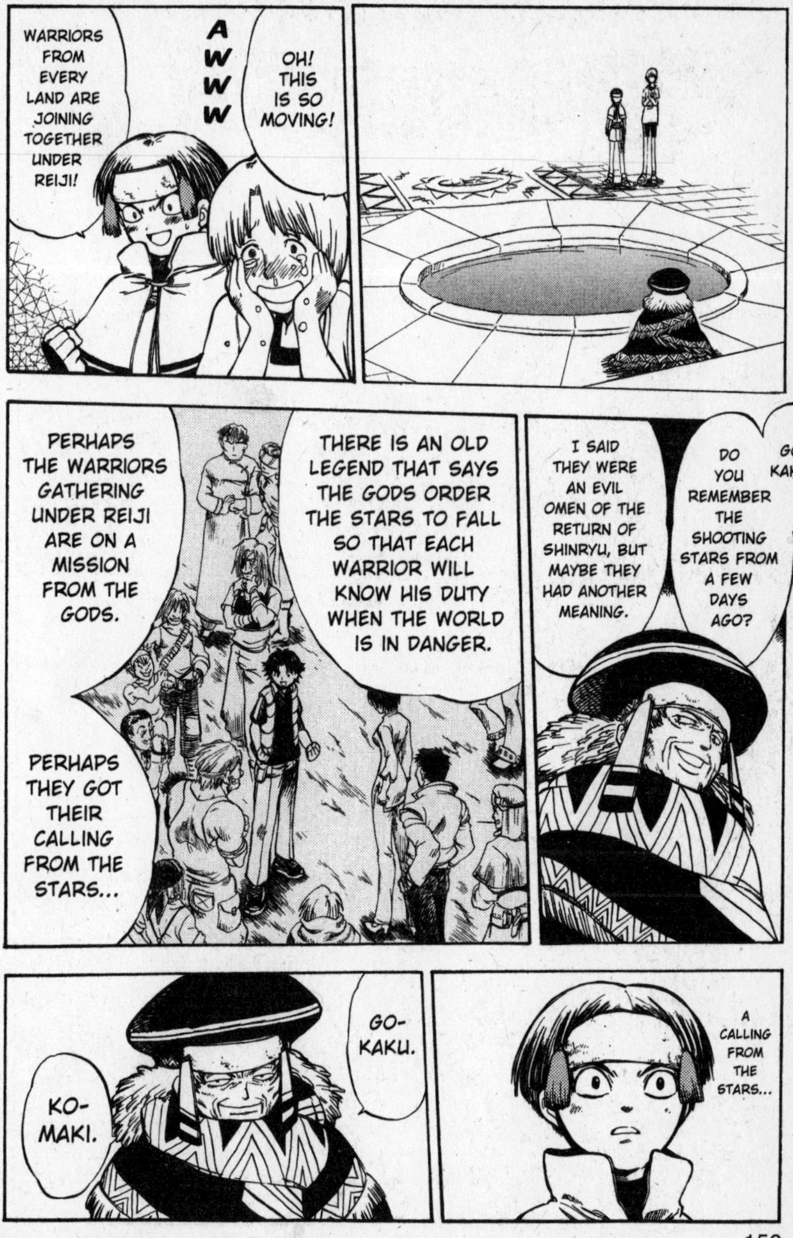
OH! THIS IS SO MOVING!
AWWW
WARRIORS FROM EVERY LAND ARE JOINING TOGETHER UNDER REIJI!
GO-KAKU?
DO YOU REMEMBER THE SHOOTING STARS FROM A FEW DAYS AGO?
I SAID THEY WERE AN EVIL OMEN OF THE RETURN OF SHINRYU, BUT MAYBE THEY HAD ANOTHER MEANING.
THERE IS AN OLD LEGEND THAT SAYS THE GODS ORDER THE STARS TO FALL SO THAT EACH WARRIOR WILL KNOW HIS DUTY WHEN THE WORLD IS IN DANGER.
PERHAPS THE WARRIORS GATHERING UNDER REIJI ARE ON A MISSION FROM THE GODS.
PERHAPS THEY GOT THEIR CALLING FROM THE STARS...
A CALLING FROM THE STARS...
GO-KAKU.
KO-MAKI.

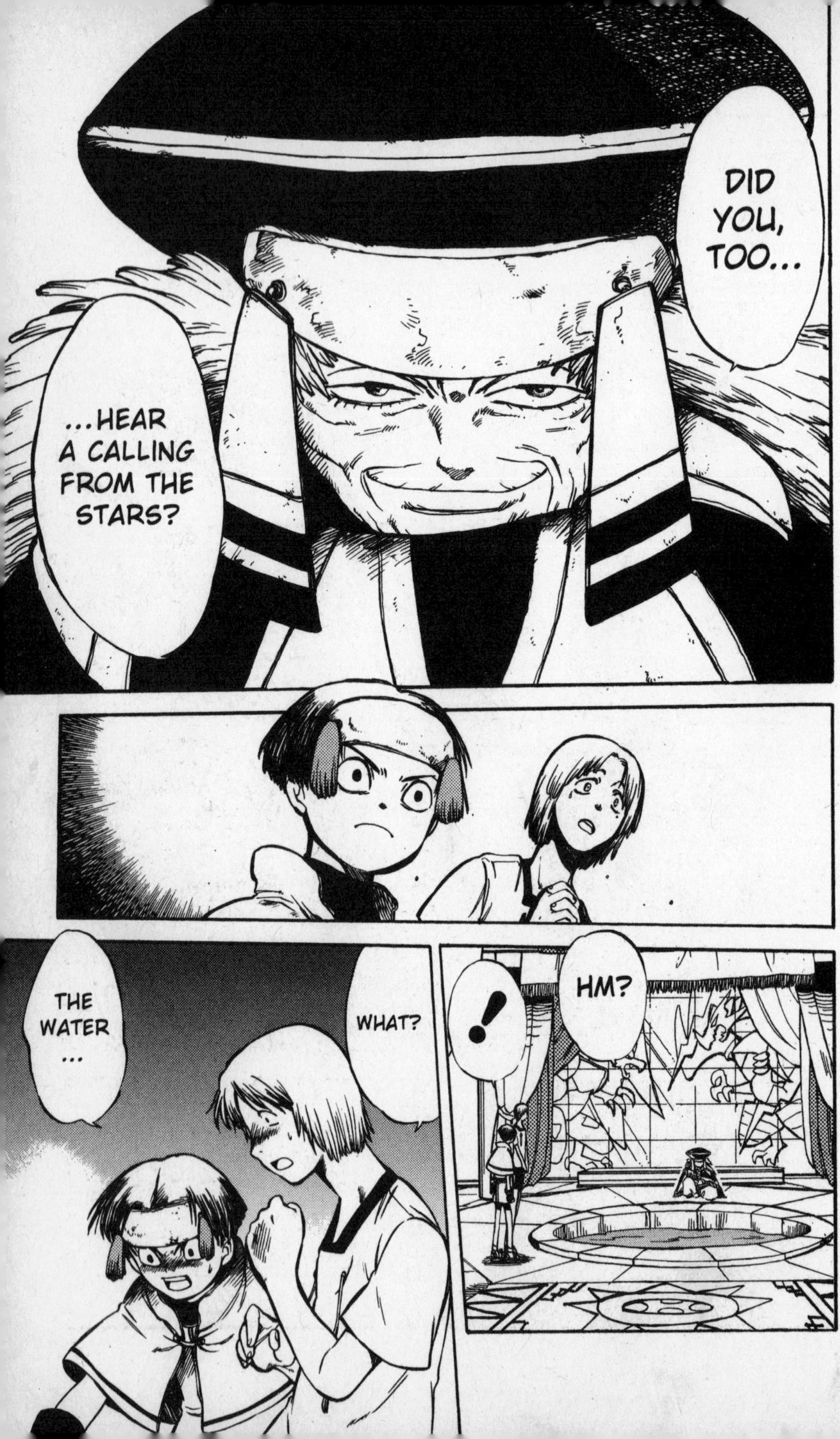
DID YOU, TOO...
...HEAR A CALLING FROM THE STARS?
HM?
!
WHAT?
THE WATER ...

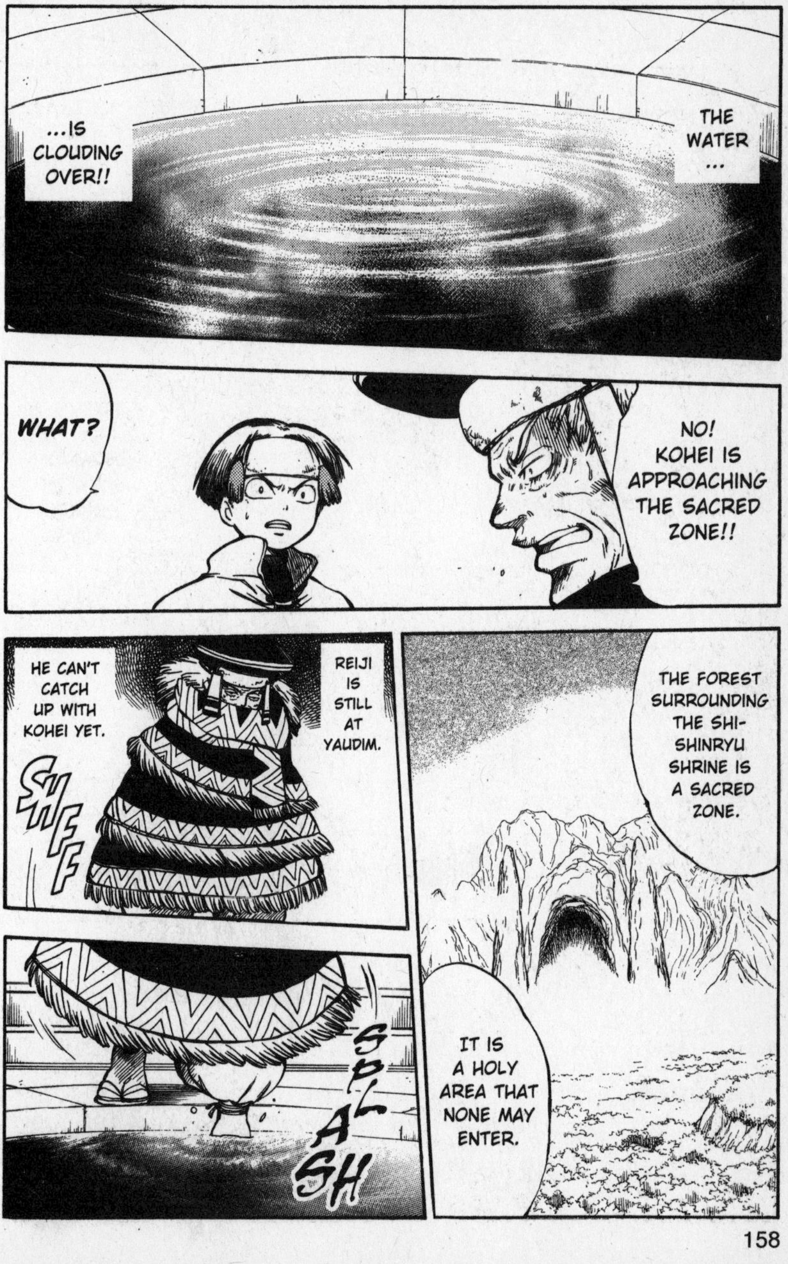
THE WATER ...
...IS CLOUDING OVER!!
NO! KOHEI IS APPROACHING THE SACRED ZONE!!
WHAT?
THE FOREST SURROUNDING THE SHI-SHINRYU SHRINE IS A SACRED ZONE.
IT IS A HOLY AREA THAT NONE MAY ENTER.
REIJI IS STILL AT YAUDIM.
HE CAN'T CATCH UP WITH KOHEI YET.
SHFF
SPLASH

READ THIS WAY

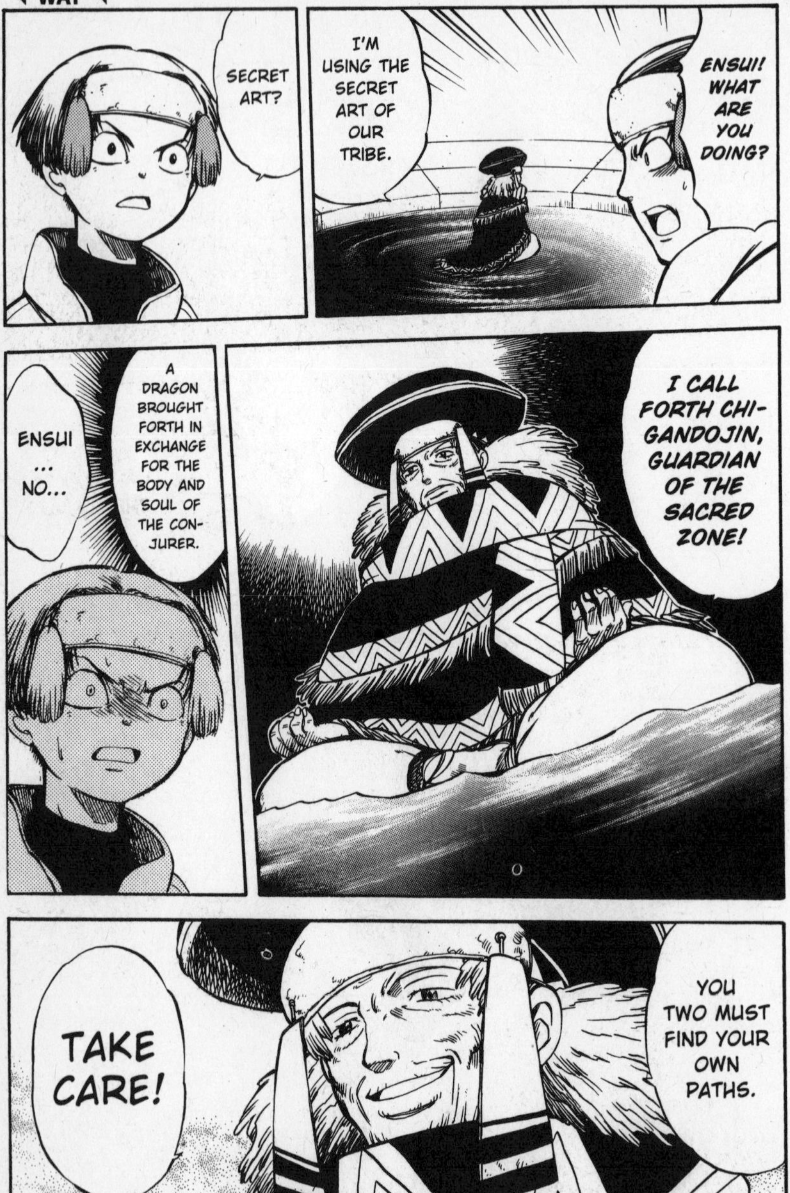
ENSUI! WHAT ARE YOU DOING?
I'M USING THE SECRET ART OF OUR TRIBE.
SECRET ART?
I CALL FORTH CHI-GANDOJIN, GUARDIAN OF THE SACRED ZONE!
A DRAGON BROUGHT FORTH IN EXCHANGE FOR THE BODY AND SOUL OF THE CON-JURER.
ENSUI ... NO...
YOU TWO MUST FIND YOUR OWN PATHS.
TAKE CARE!

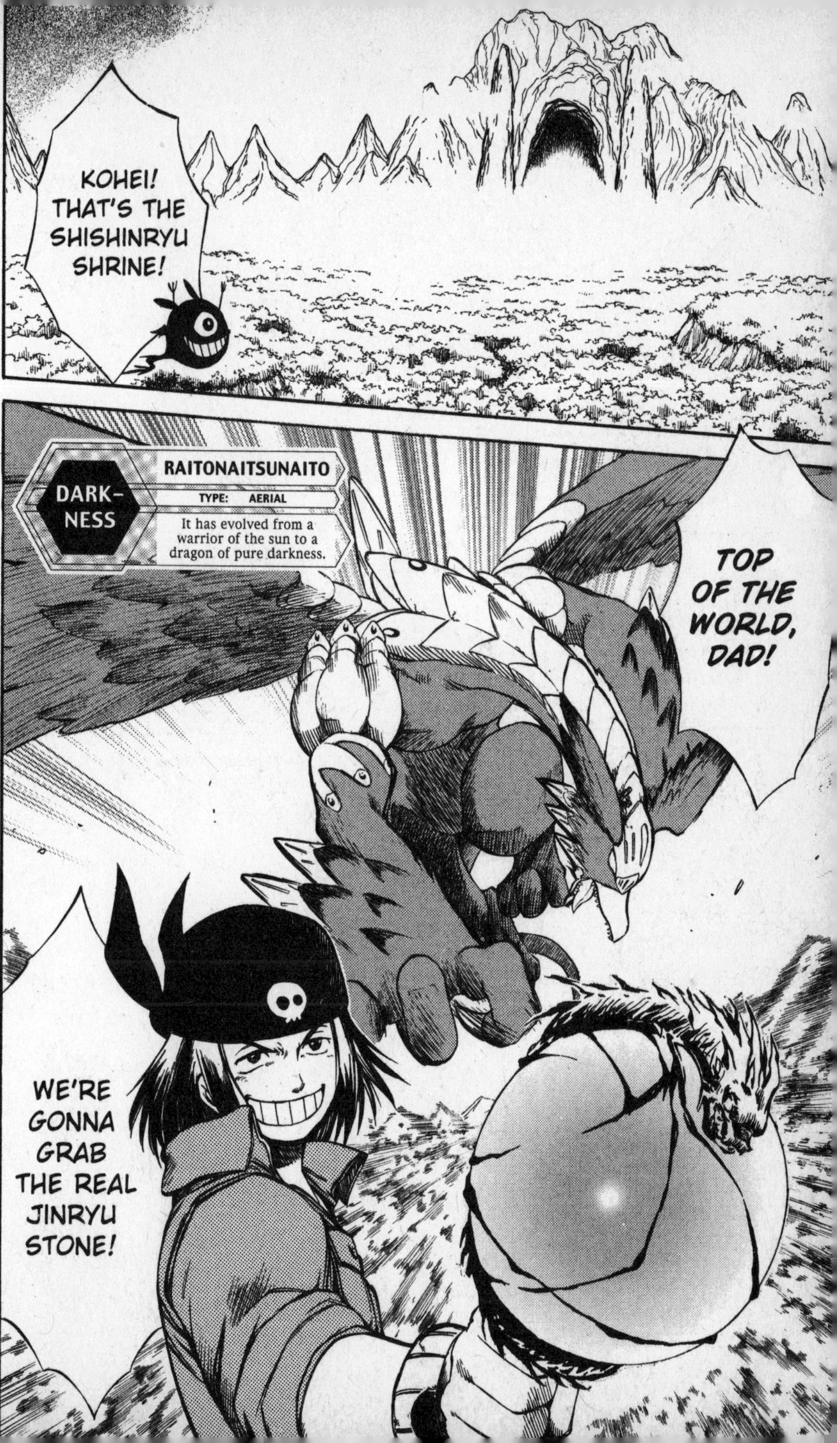
KOHEI! THAT'S THE SHISHINRYU SHRINE!
TOP OF THE WORLD, DAD!
RAITONAITSUNAITO
DARK-NESS
TYPE: AERIAL
It has evolved from a warrior of the sun to a dragon of pure darkness.
WE'RE GONNA GRAB THE REAL JINRYU STONE!

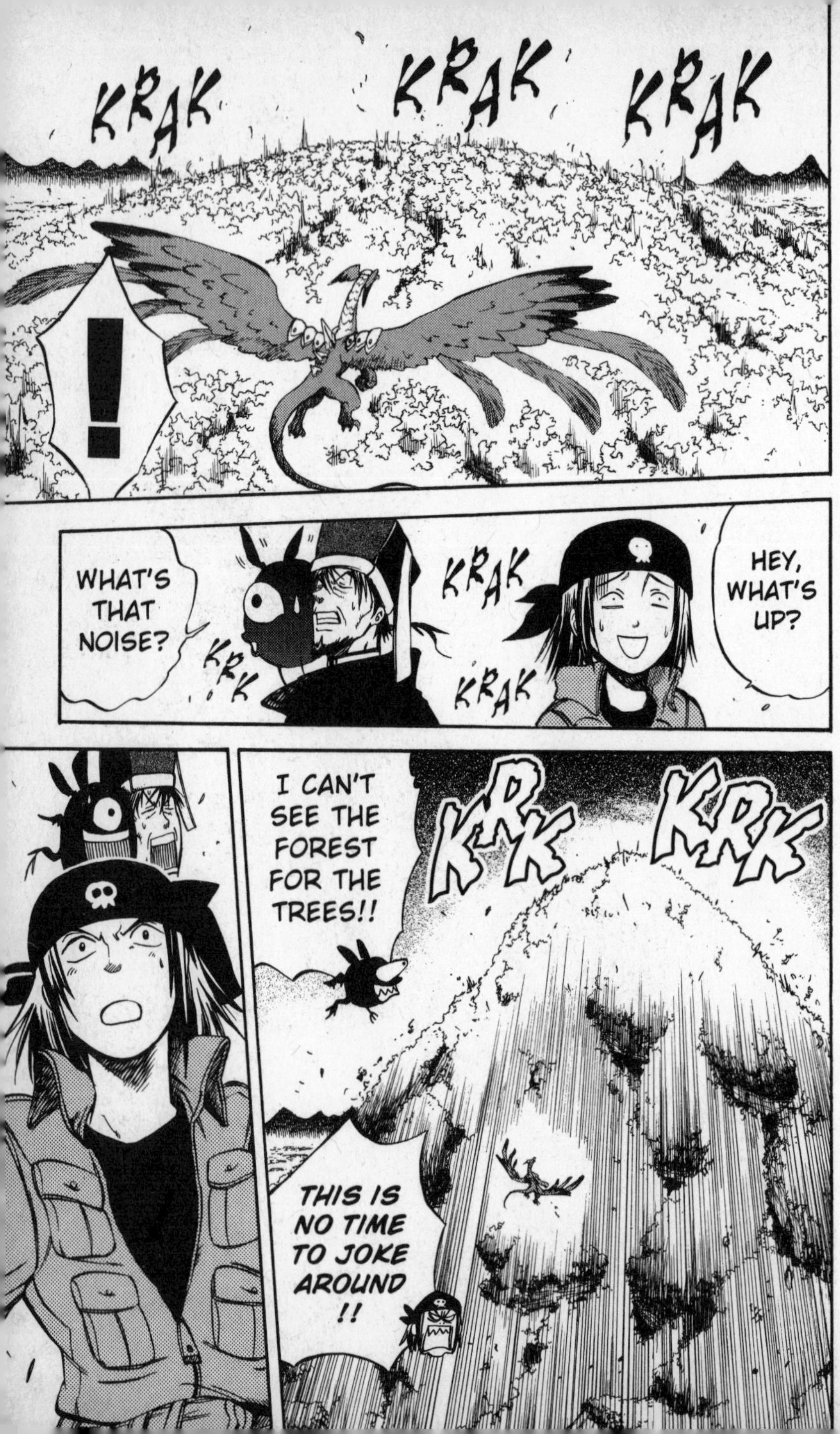
KRAK
KRAK
KRAK
!
HEY, WHAT'S UP?
KRAK
WHAT'S THAT NOISE?
KRAK
KRK
KRK
KRK
I CAN'T SEE THE FOREST FOR THE TREES!!
THIS IS NO TIME TO JOKE AROUND !!

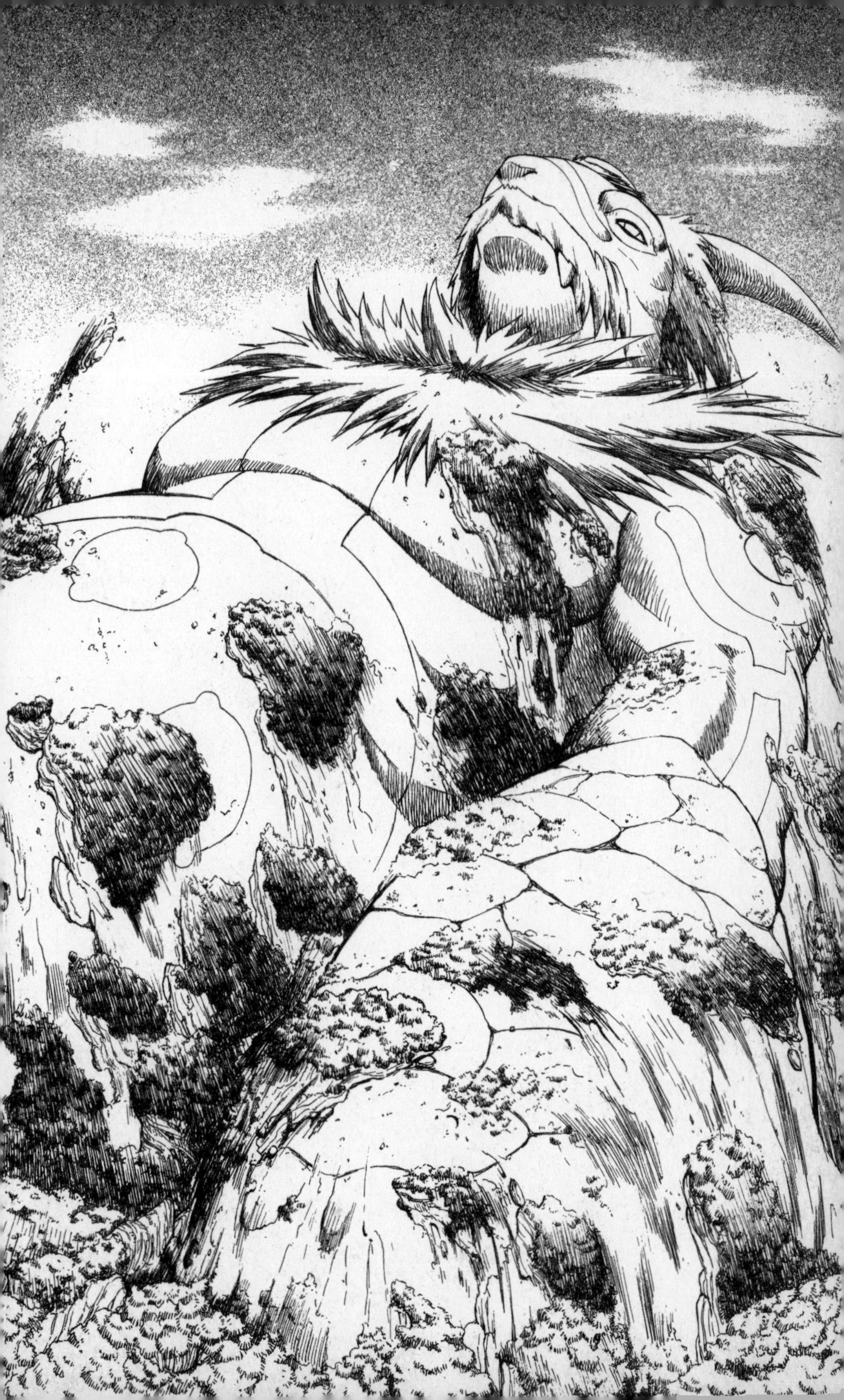

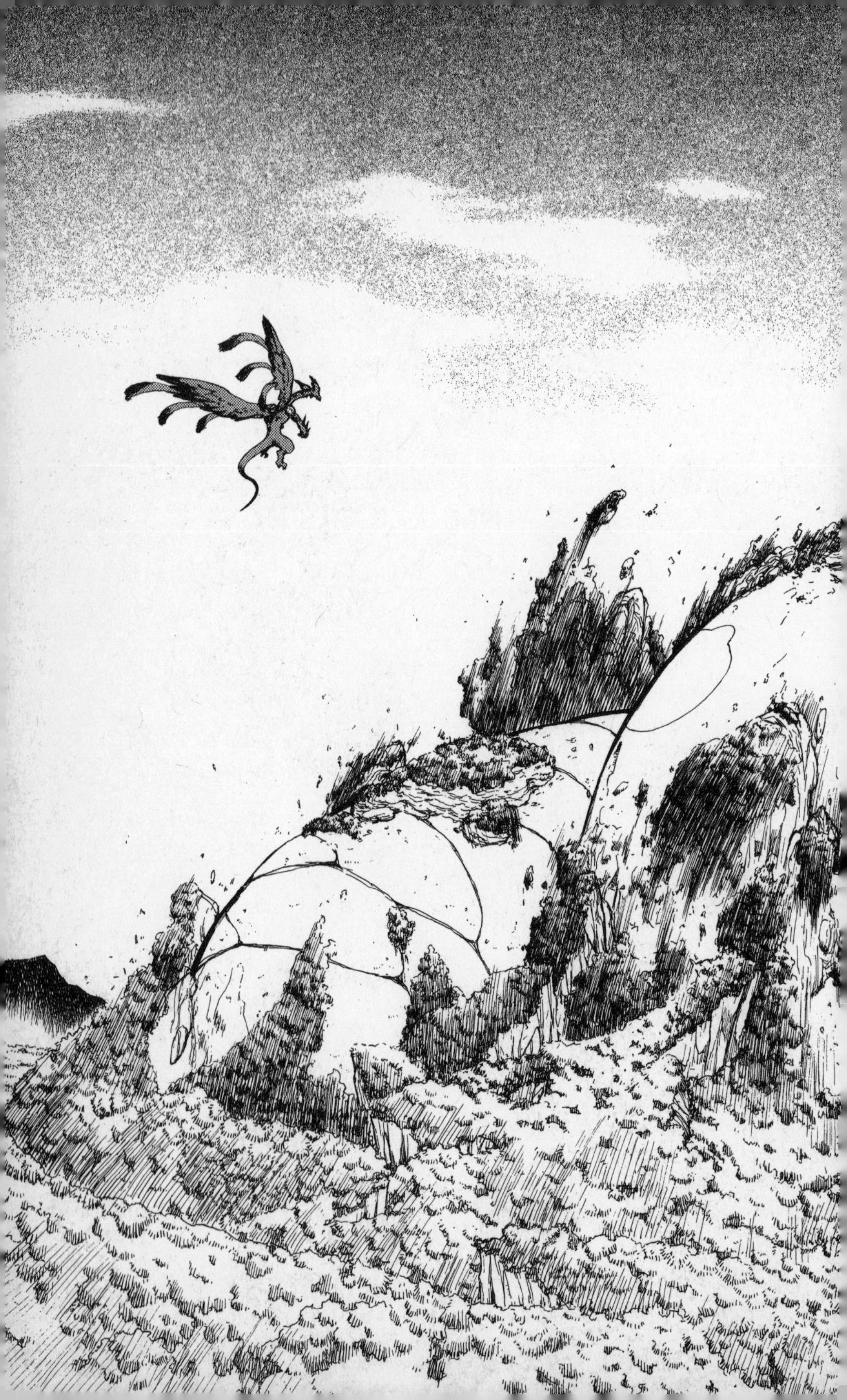

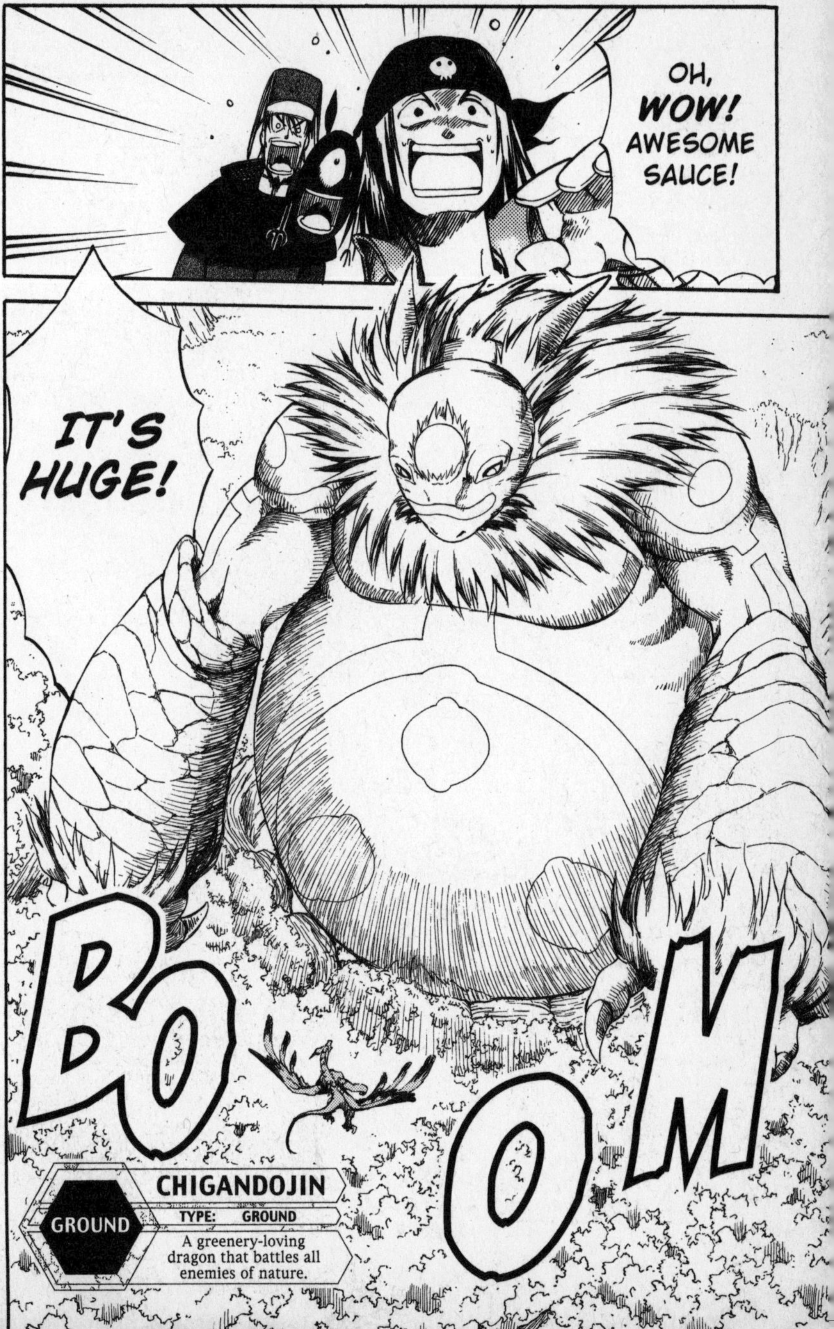
OH, WOW! AWESOME SAUCE!
IT'S HUGE!
BOOM
CHIGANDOJIN
GROUND
TYPE: GROUND
A greenery-loving dragon that battles all enemies of nature.

READ THIS WAY

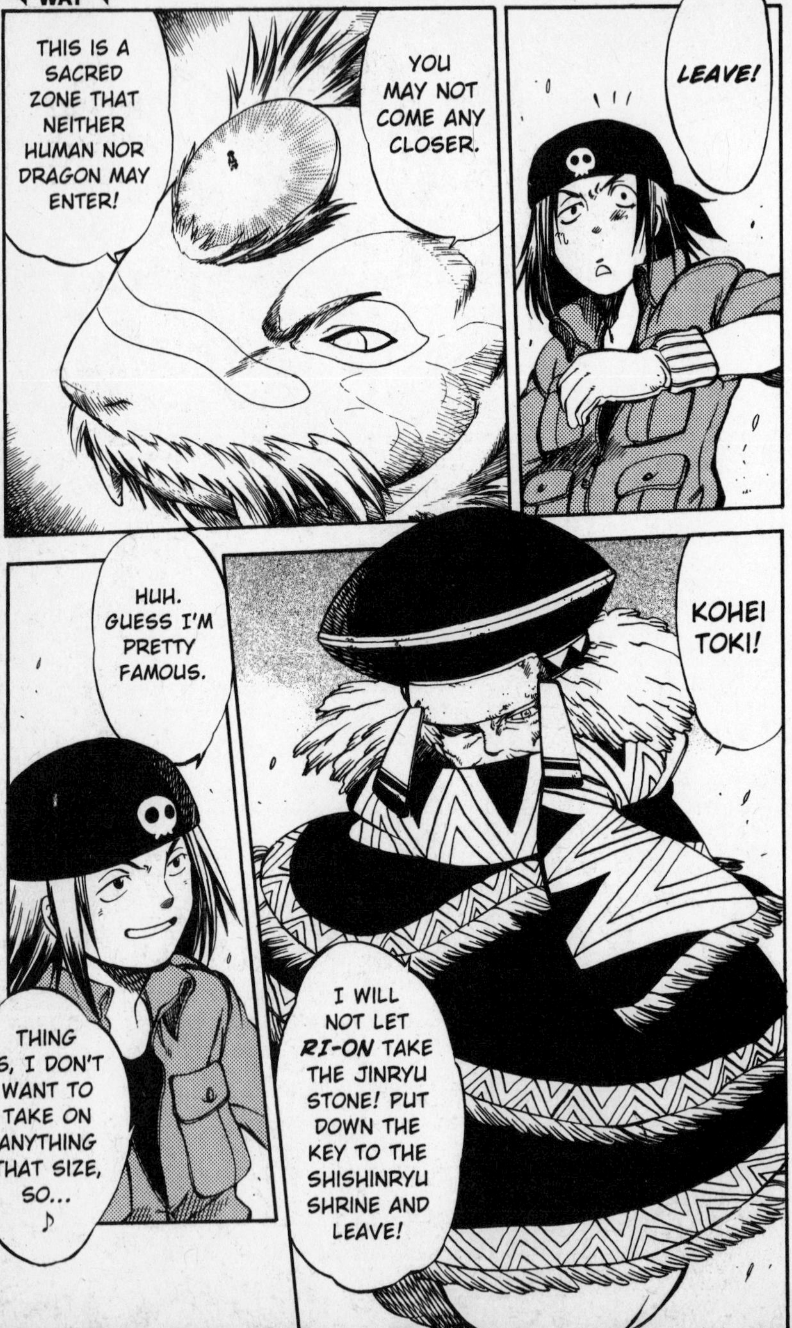

LEAVE!
YOU MAY NOT COME ANY CLOSER.
THIS IS A SACRED ZONE THAT NEITHER HUMAN NOR DRAGON MAY ENTER!
KOHEI TOKI!
I WILL NOT LET *RI-ON* TAKE THE JINRYU STONE! PUT DOWN THE KEY TO THE SHISHINRYU SHRINE AND LEAVE!
HUH. GUESS I'M PRETTY FAMOUS.
THING IS, I DON'T WANT TO TAKE ON ANYTHING THAT SIZE, SO... ♪

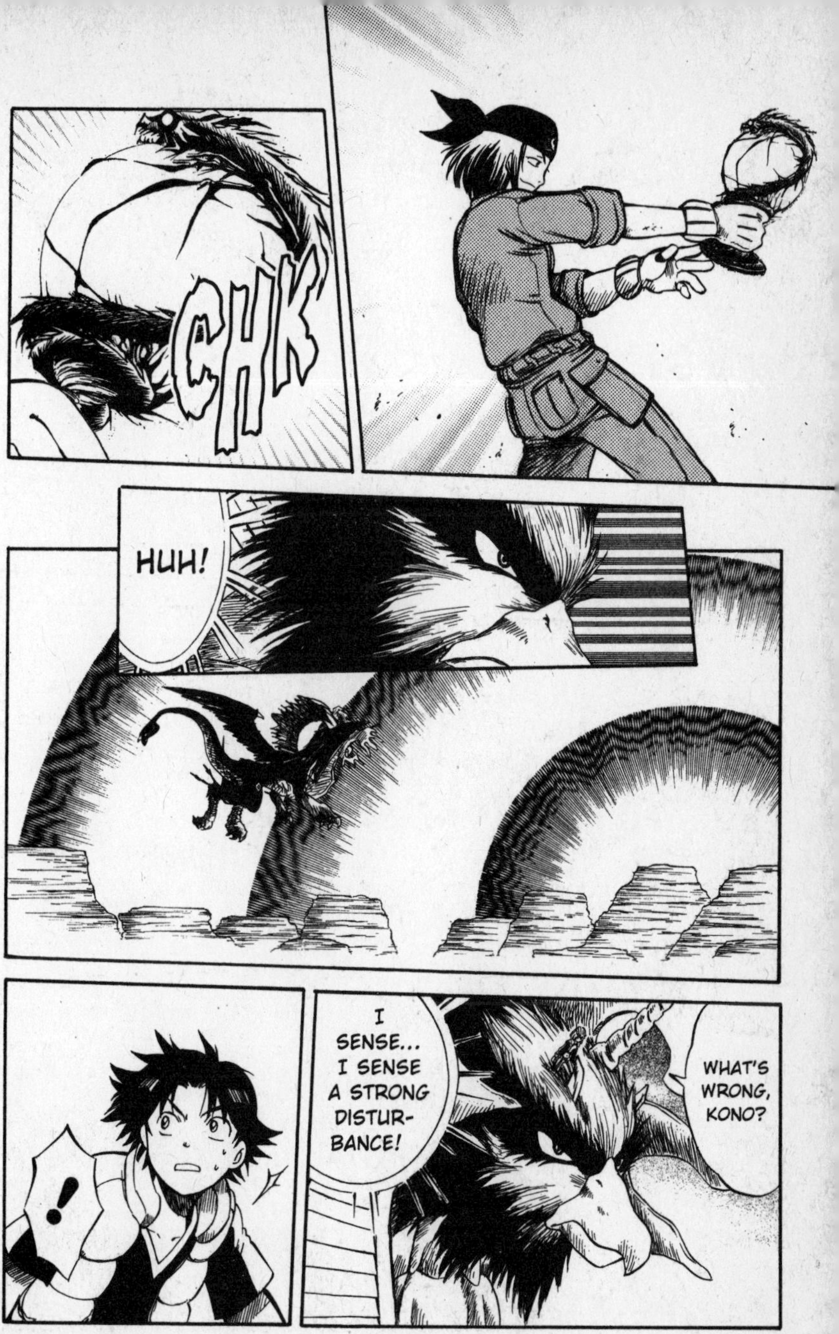
CHK
HUH!
WHAT'S WRONG, KONO?
I SENSE... I SENSE A STRONG DISTUR-BANCE!
!

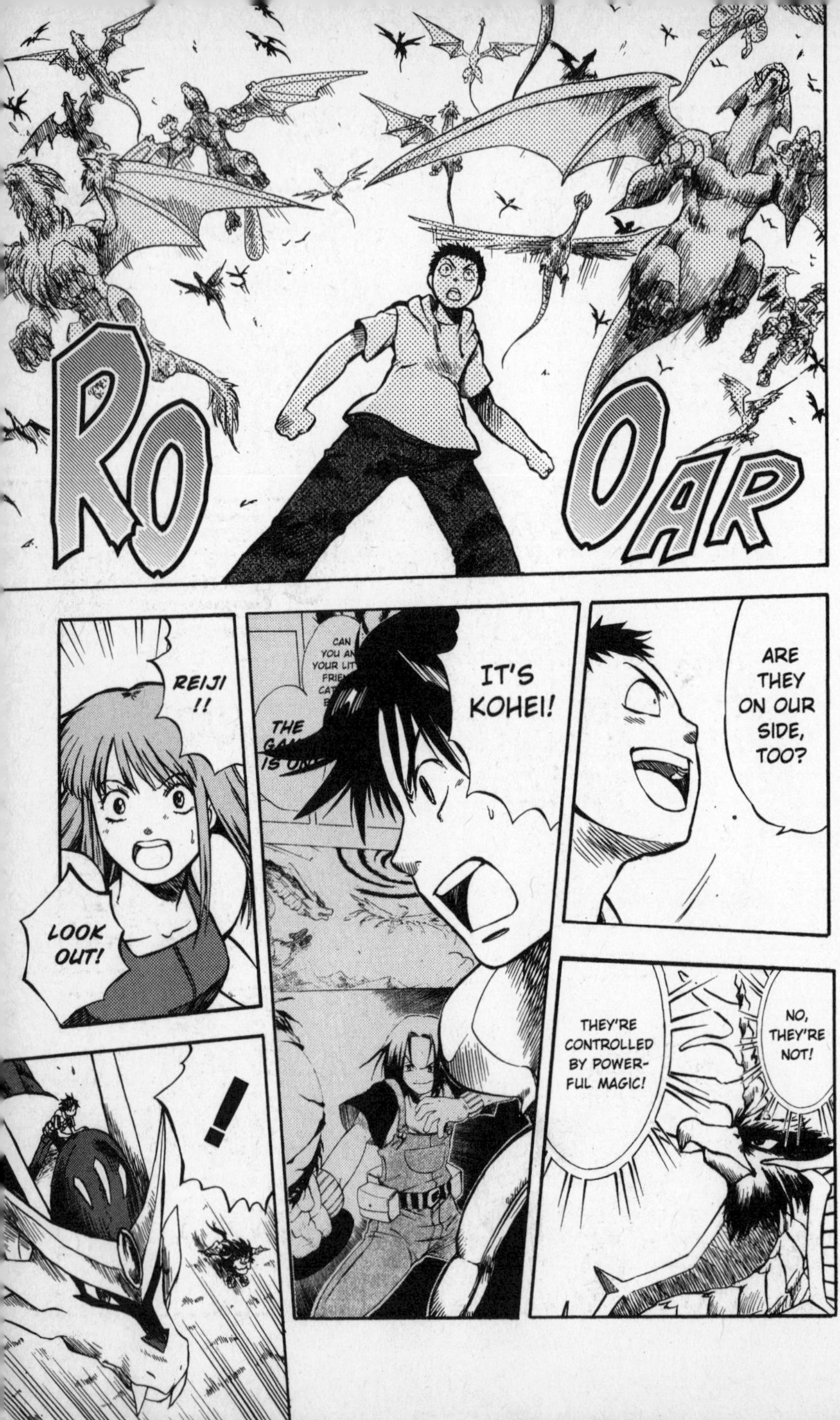
RO
OAR
ARE THEY ON OUR SIDE, TOO?
NO, THEY'RE NOT!
THEY'RE CONTROLLED BY POWER-FUL MAGIC!
IT'S KOHEI!
REIJI !!
LOOK OUT!
!

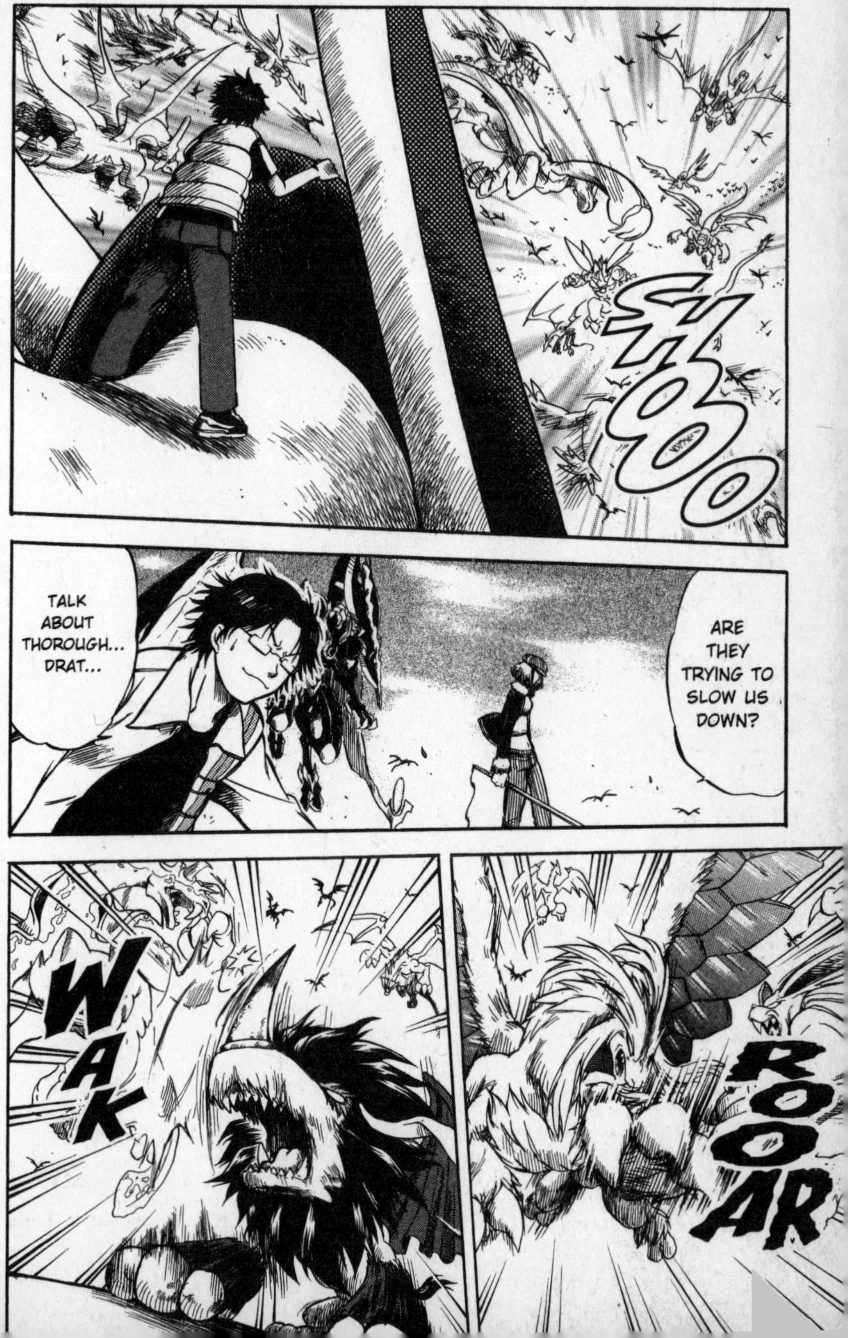
WHOOO
ARE THEY TRYING TO SLOW US DOWN?
TALK ABOUT THOROUGH... DRAT...
ROOOAR
WAK

READ THIS WAY

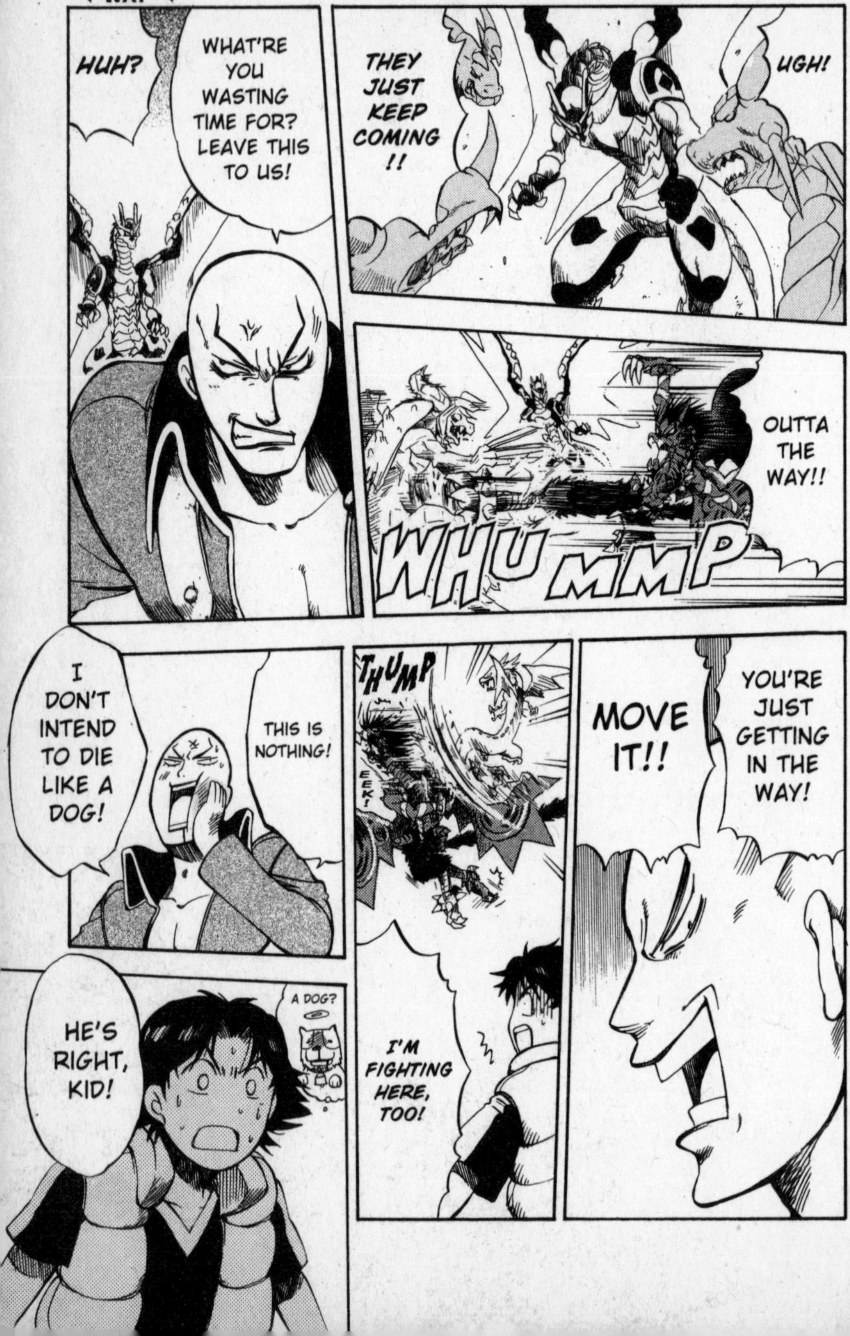
UGH!
THEY JUST KEEP COMING!!
OUTTA THE WAY!!
WHUMMP
WHAT'RE YOU WASTING TIME FOR? LEAVE THIS TO US!
HUH?
YOU'RE JUST GETTING IN THE WAY!
MOVE IT!!
THUMP
EEK!
I'M FIGHTING HERE, TOO!
THIS IS NOTHING!
I DON'T INTEND TO DIE LIKE A DOG!
A DOG?
HE'S RIGHT, KID!

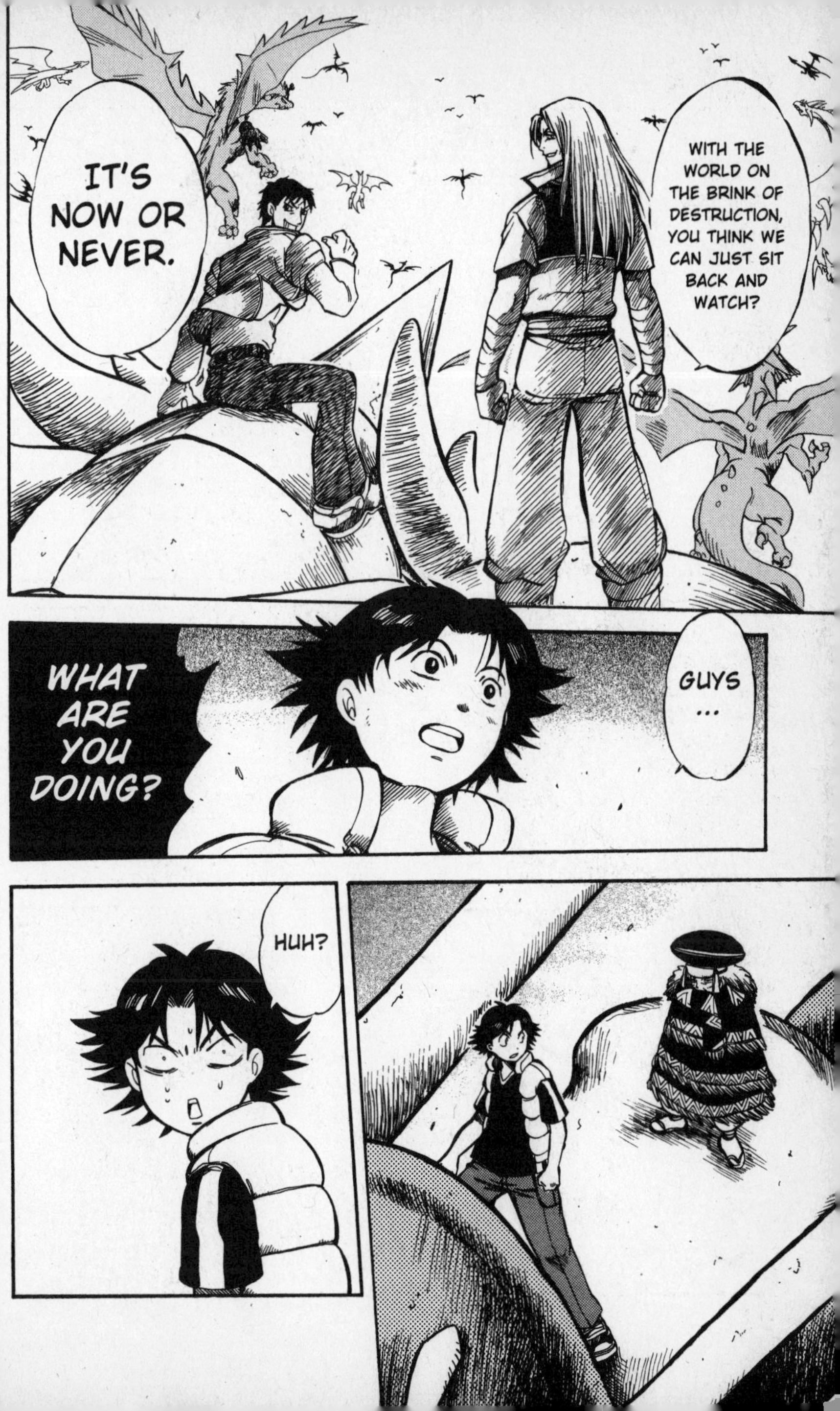
WITH THE WORLD ON THE BRINK OF DESTRUCTION, YOU THINK WE CAN JUST SIT BACK AND WATCH?
IT'S NOW OR NEVER.
GUYS ...
WHAT ARE YOU DOING?
HUH?

READ THIS WAY

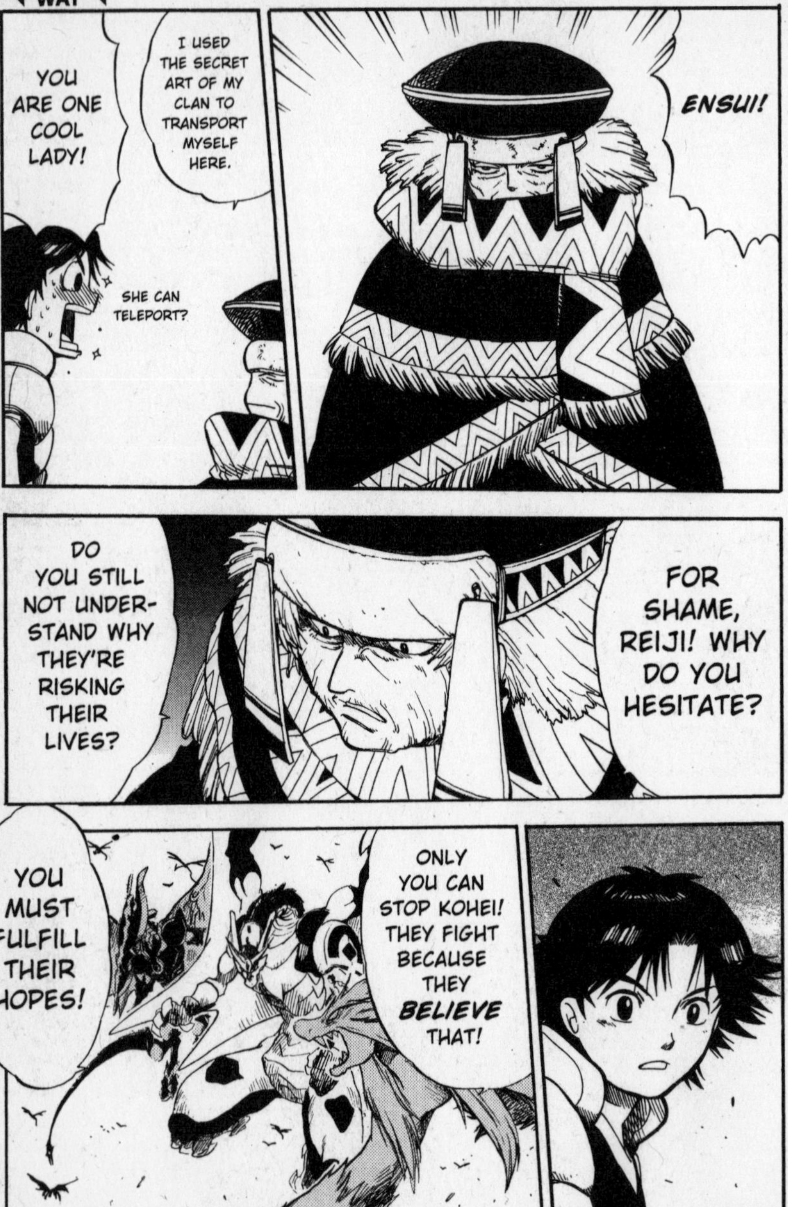

ENSUI!
I USED THE SECRET ART OF MY CLAN TO TRANSPORT MYSELF HERE.
YOU ARE ONE COOL LADY!
SHE CAN TELEPORT?
FOR SHAME, REIJI! WHY DO YOU HESITATE?
DO YOU STILL NOT UNDER-STAND WHY THEY'RE RISKING THEIR LIVES?
ONLY YOU CAN STOP KOHEI! THEY FIGHT BECAUSE THEY *BELIEVE* THAT!
YOU MUST FULFILL THEIR HOPES!

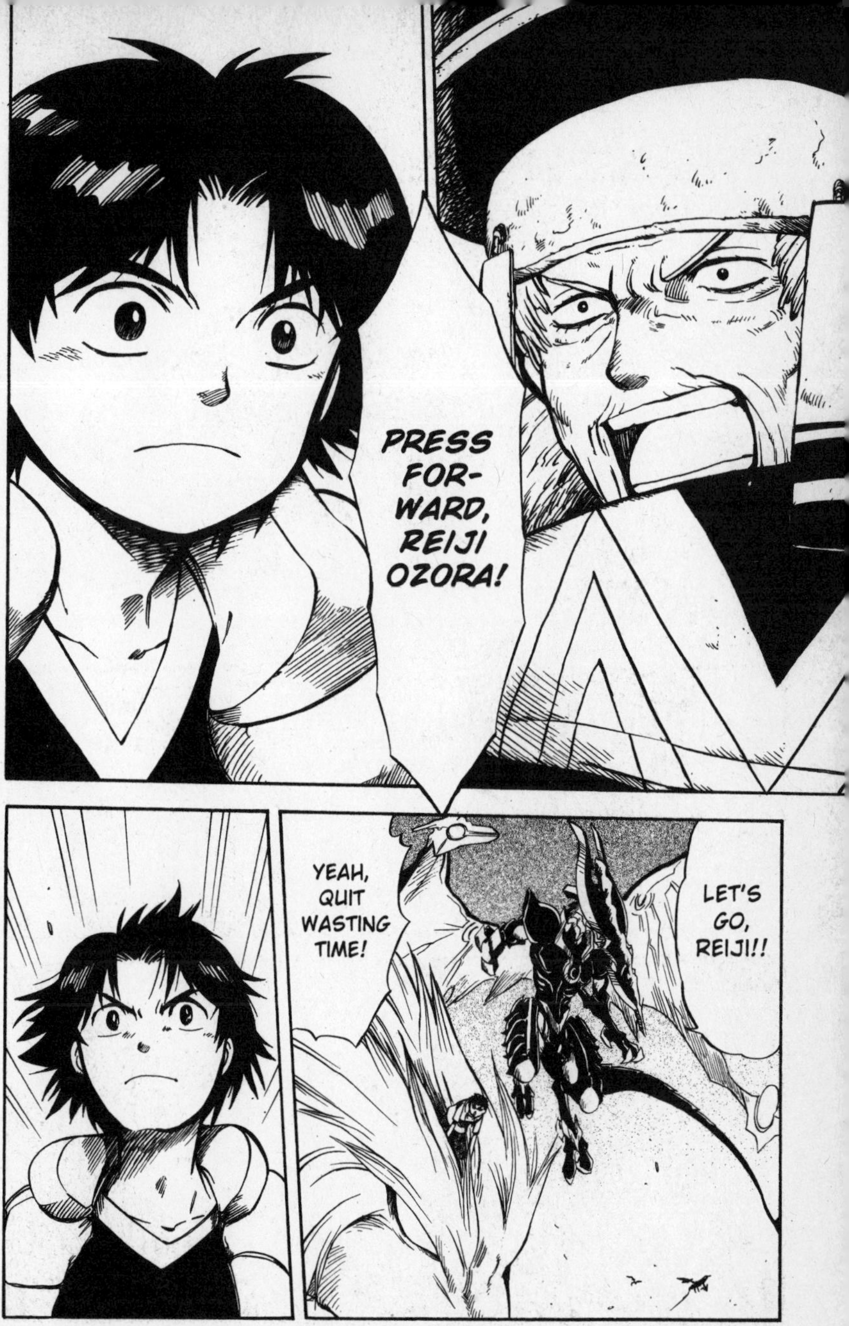
PRESS FOR-WARD, REIJI OZORA!
LET'S GO, REIJI!!
YEAH, QUIT WASTING TIME!

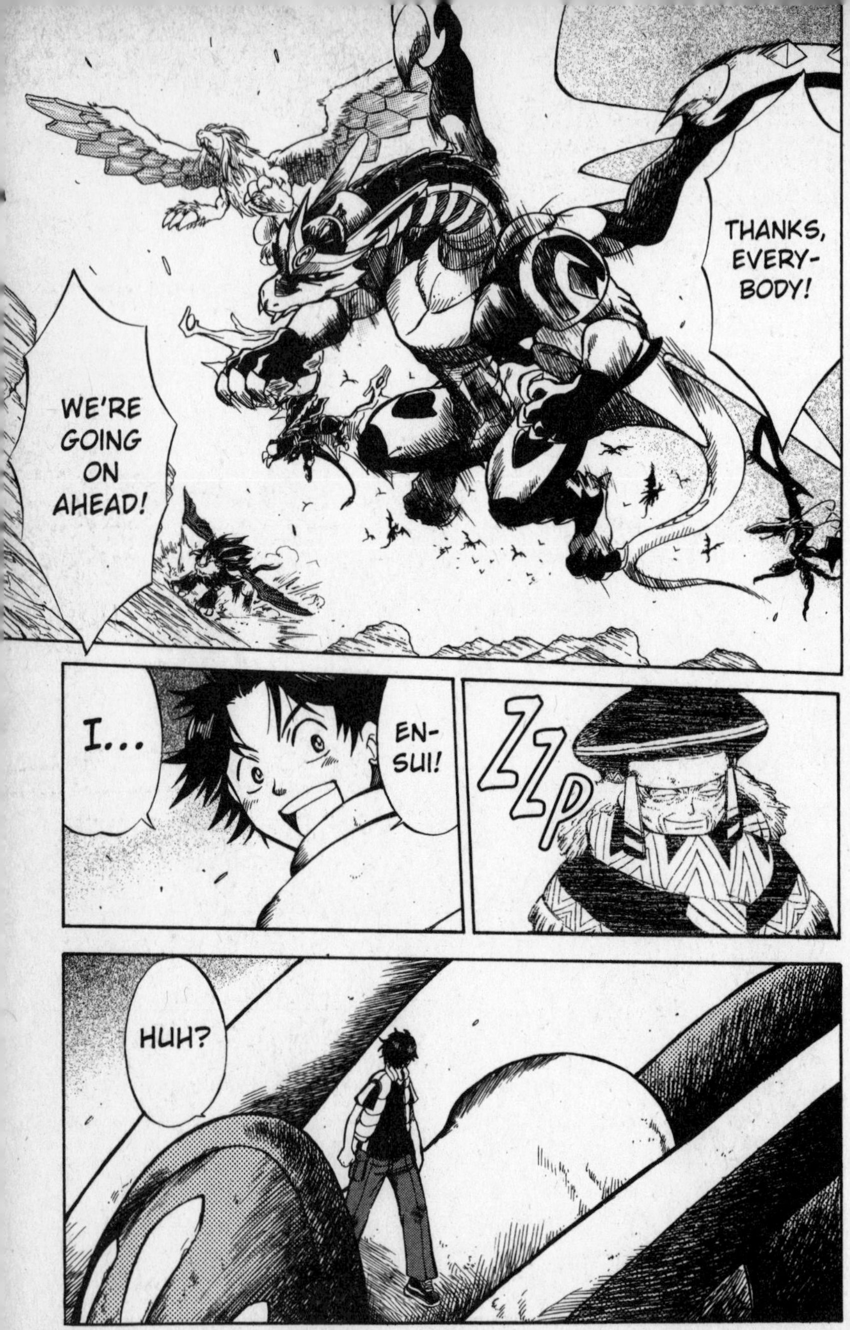
THANKS, EVERY-BODY!
WE'RE GOING ON AHEAD!
ZZP
EN-SUI!
I...
HUH?

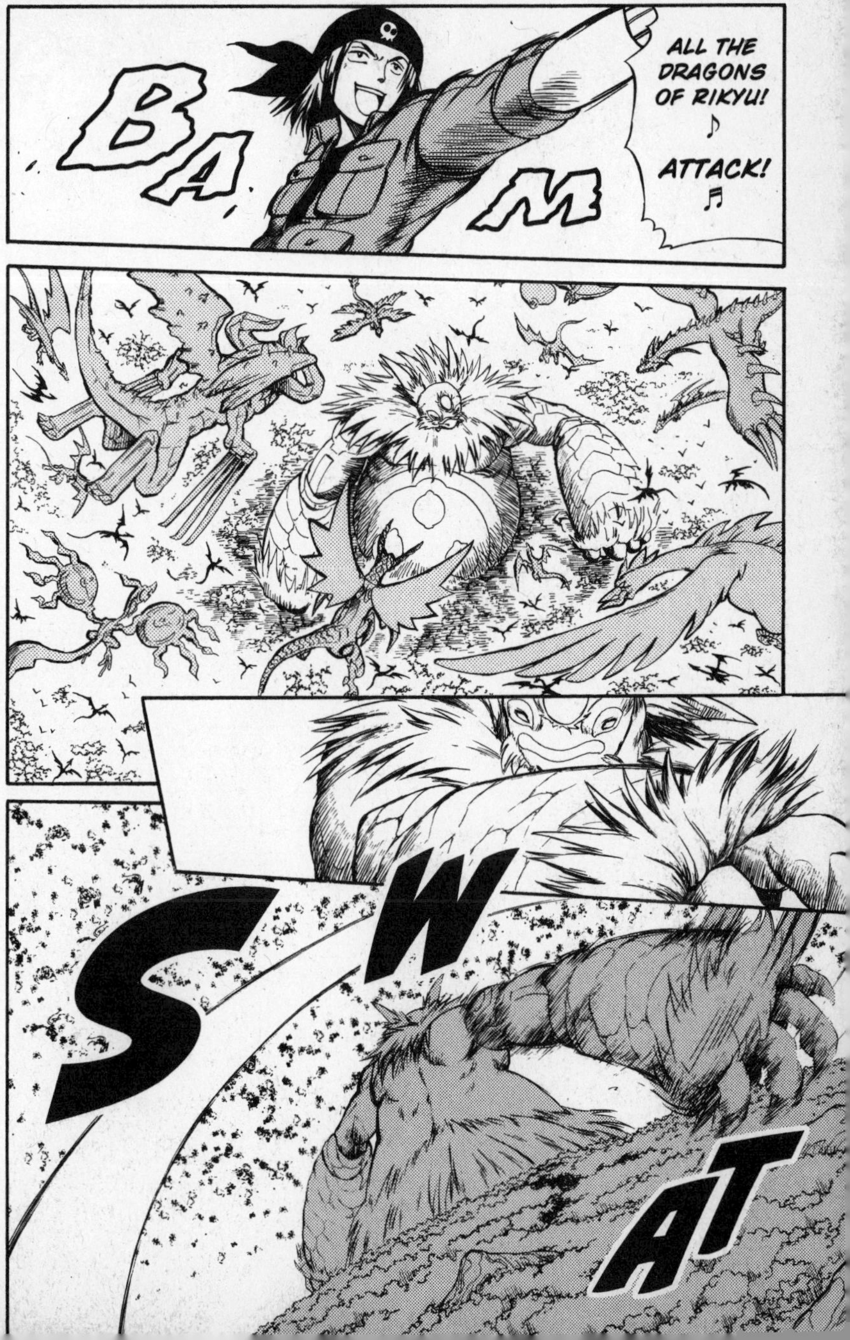
ALL THE DRAGONS OF RIKYU! ♪
ATTACK! ♬
BAM
SWAT

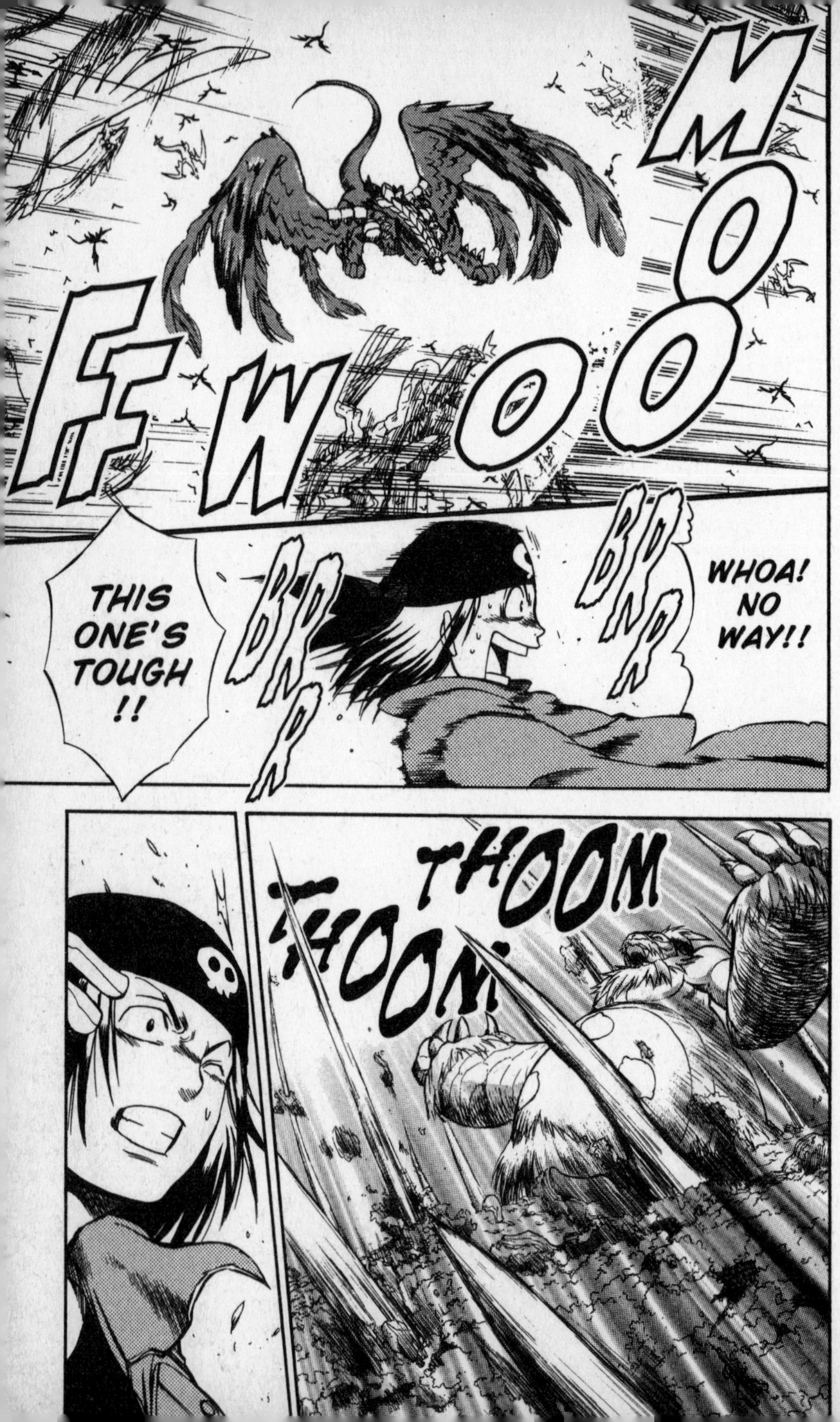
FWOOOOM
BRRR
WHOA! NO WAY!!
BRRR
THIS ONE'S TOUGH!!
THOOM
THOOM

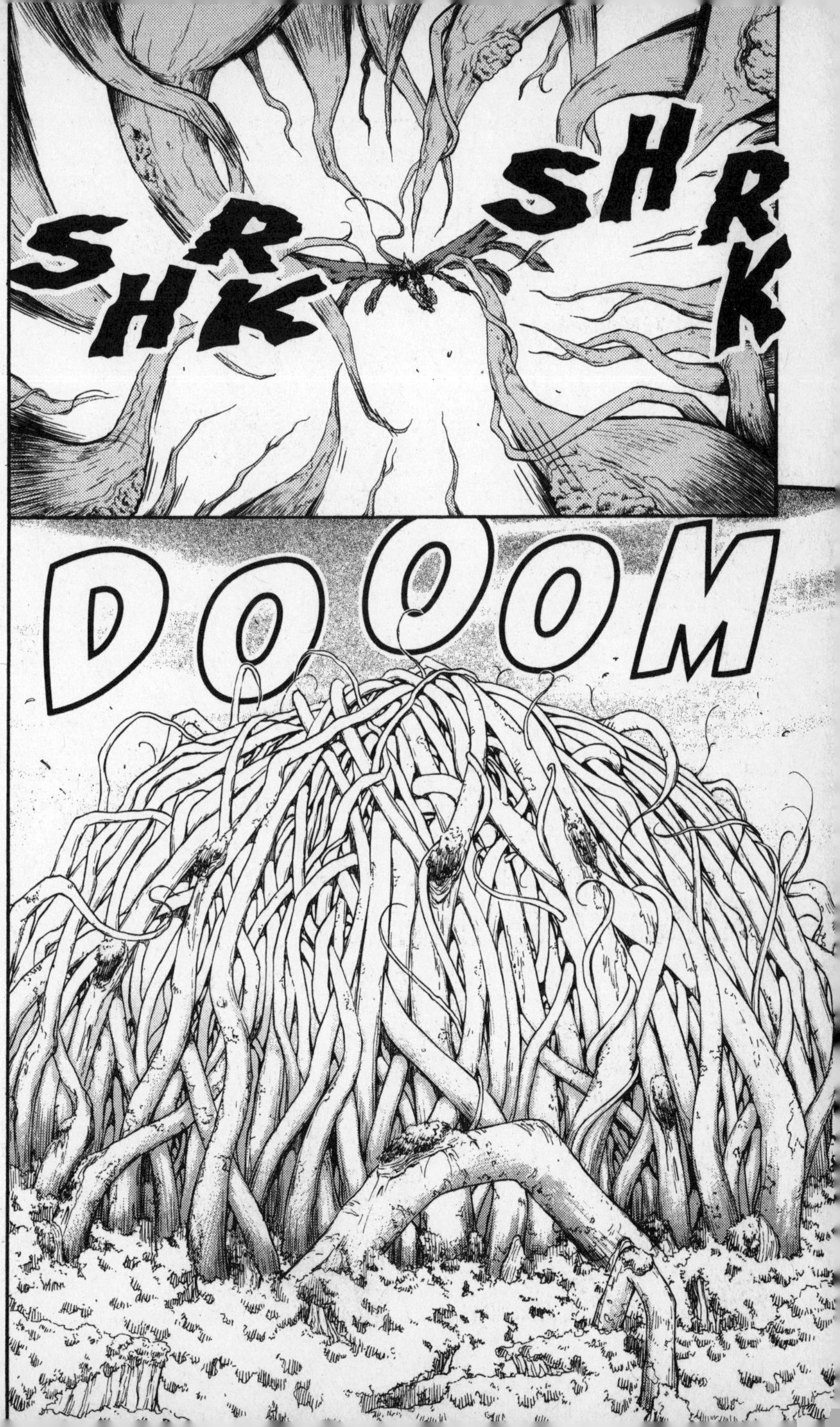
SHRK
SHRK
DOOOM

READ THIS WAY

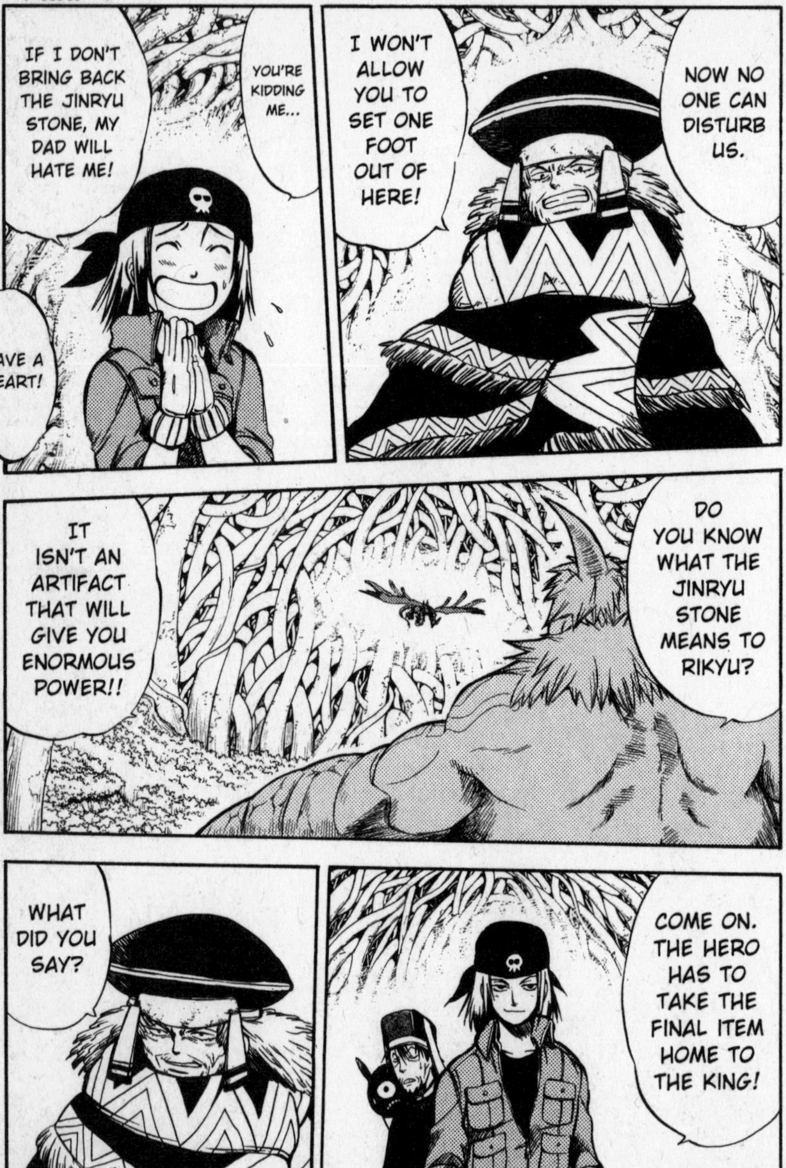
NOW NO ONE CAN DISTURB US.
I WON'T ALLOW YOU TO SET ONE FOOT OUT OF HERE!
YOU'RE KIDDING ME...
IF I DON'T BRING BACK THE JINRYU STONE, MY DAD WILL HATE ME!
HAVE A HEART!
DO YOU KNOW WHAT THE JINRYU STONE MEANS TO RIKYU?
IT ISN'T AN ARTIFACT THAT WILL GIVE YOU ENORMOUS POWER!!
COME ON. THE HERO HAS TO TAKE THE FINAL ITEM HOME TO THE KING!
WHAT DID YOU SAY?

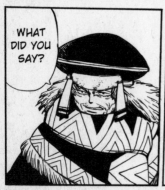

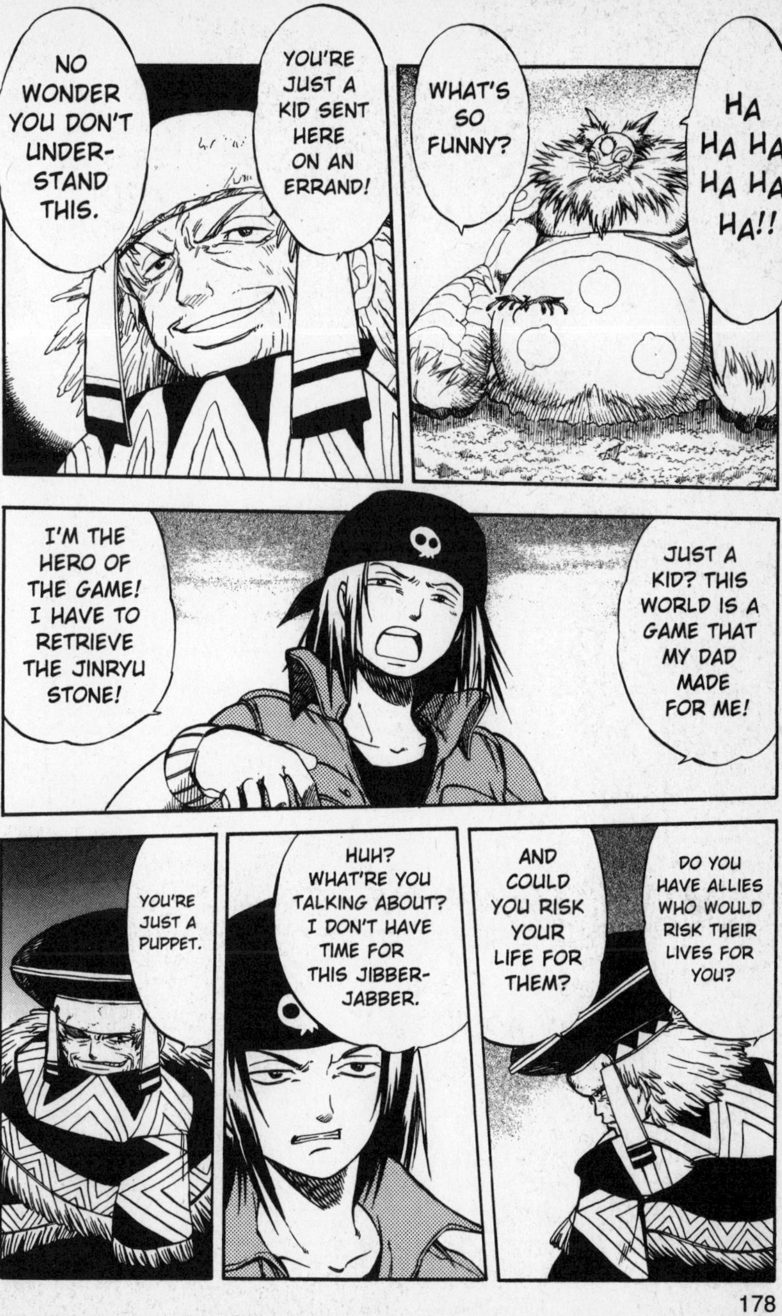
HA HA HA HA HA HA!!
WHAT'S SO FUNNY?
YOU'RE JUST A KID SENT HERE ON AN ERRAND!
NO WONDER YOU DON'T UNDER-STAND THIS.
JUST A KID? THIS WORLD IS A GAME THAT MY DAD MADE FOR ME!
I'M THE HERO OF THE GAME! I HAVE TO RETRIEVE THE JINRYU STONE!
DO YOU HAVE ALLIES WHO WOULD RISK THEIR LIVES FOR YOU?
AND COULD YOU RISK YOUR LIFE FOR THEM?
HUH? WHAT'RE YOU TALKING ABOUT? I DON'T HAVE TIME FOR THIS JIBBER-JABBER.
YOU'RE JUST A PUPPET.

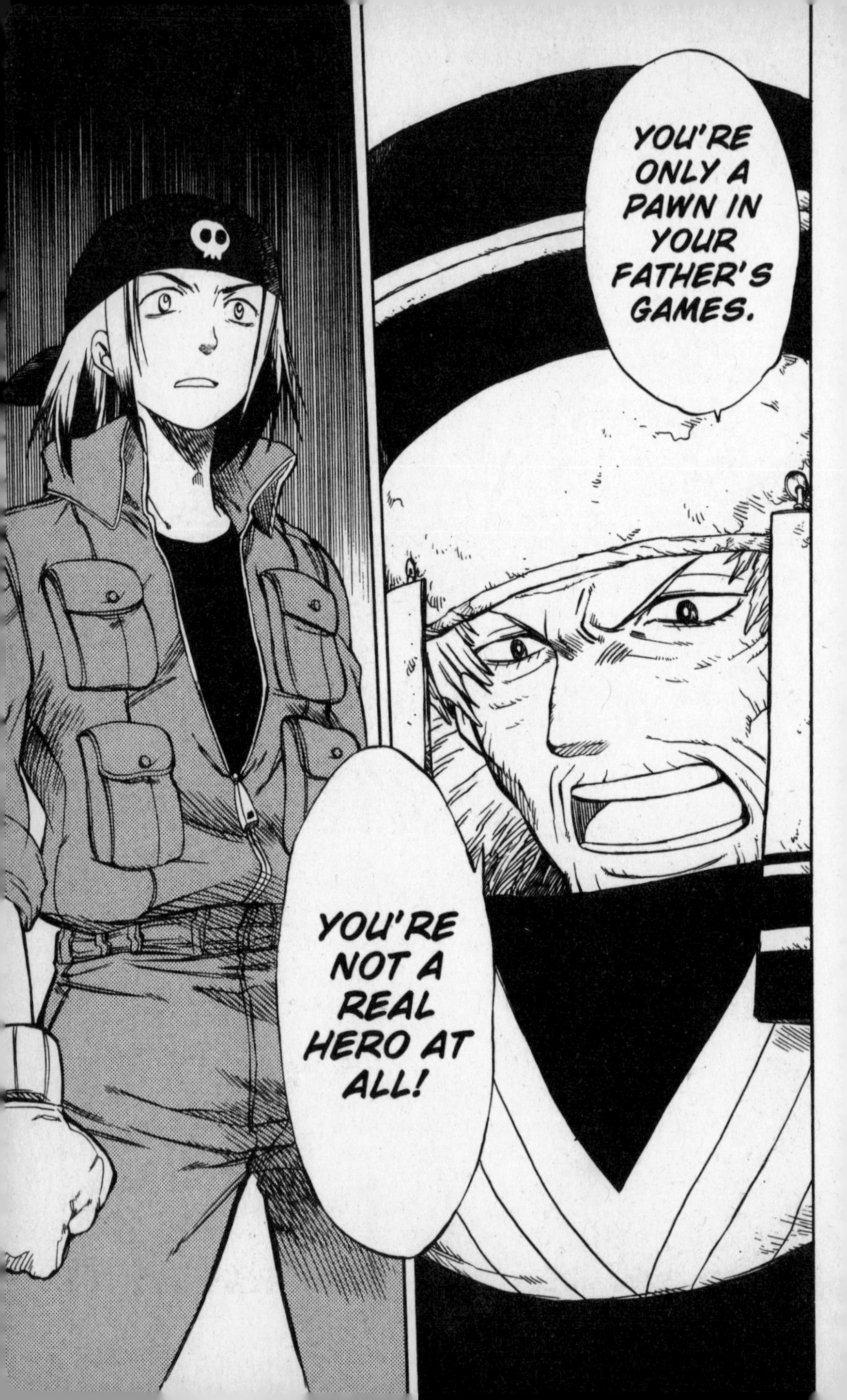
YOU'RE ONLY A PAWN IN YOUR FATHER'S GAMES.
YOU'RE NOT A REAL HERO AT ALL!

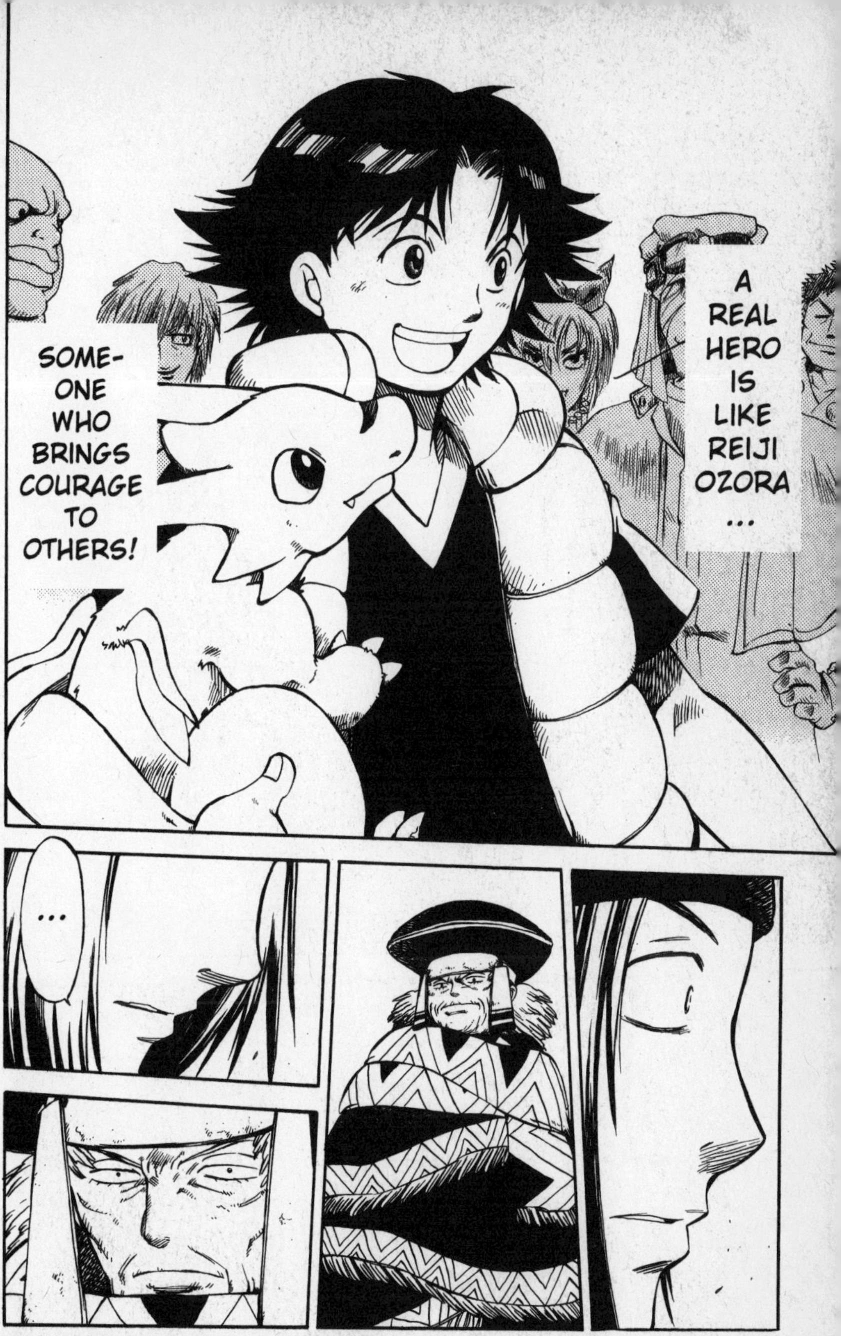
A REAL HERO IS LIKE REIJI OZORA...
SOME-ONE WHO BRINGS COURAGE TO OTHERS!
...

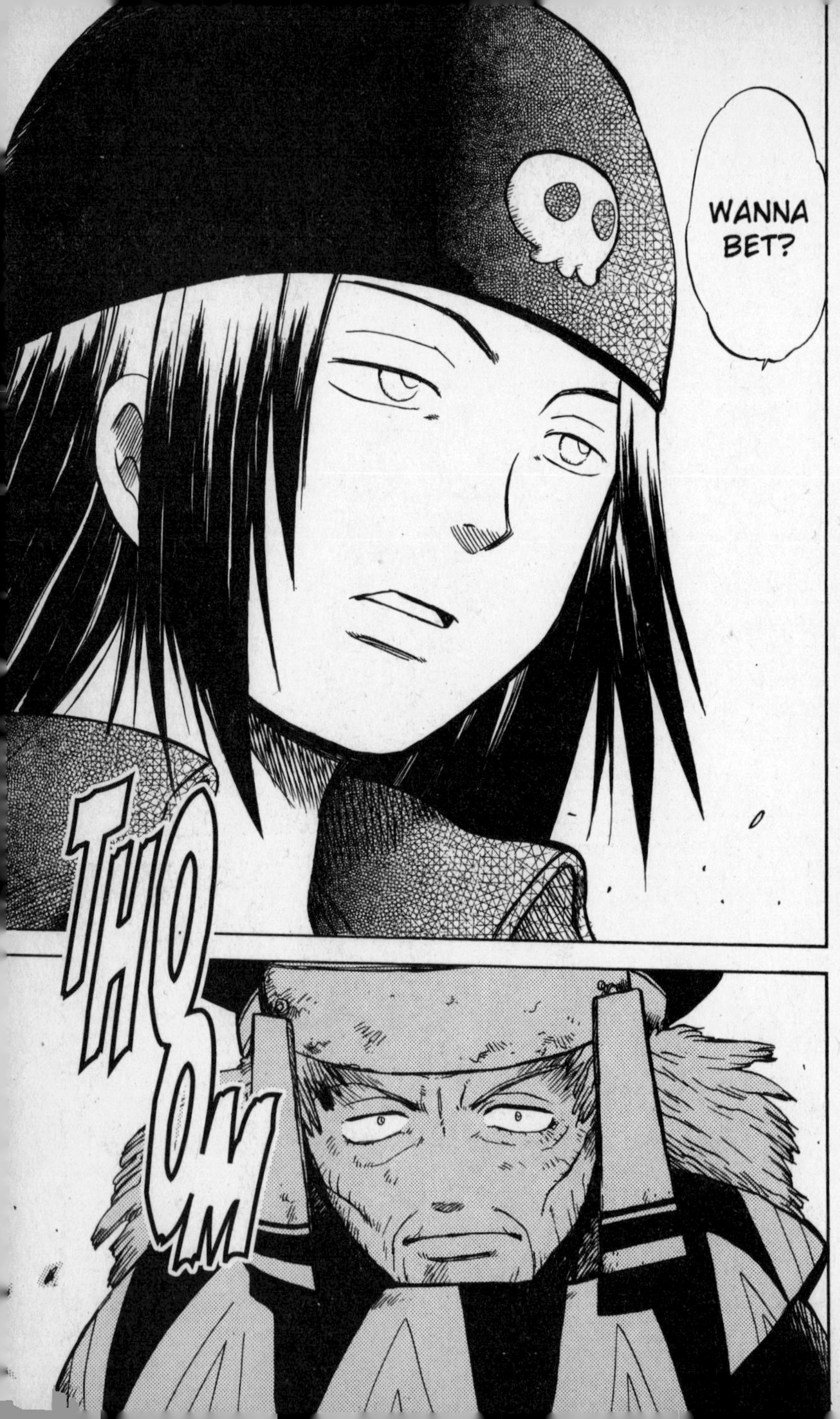
WANNA BET?
THOOM

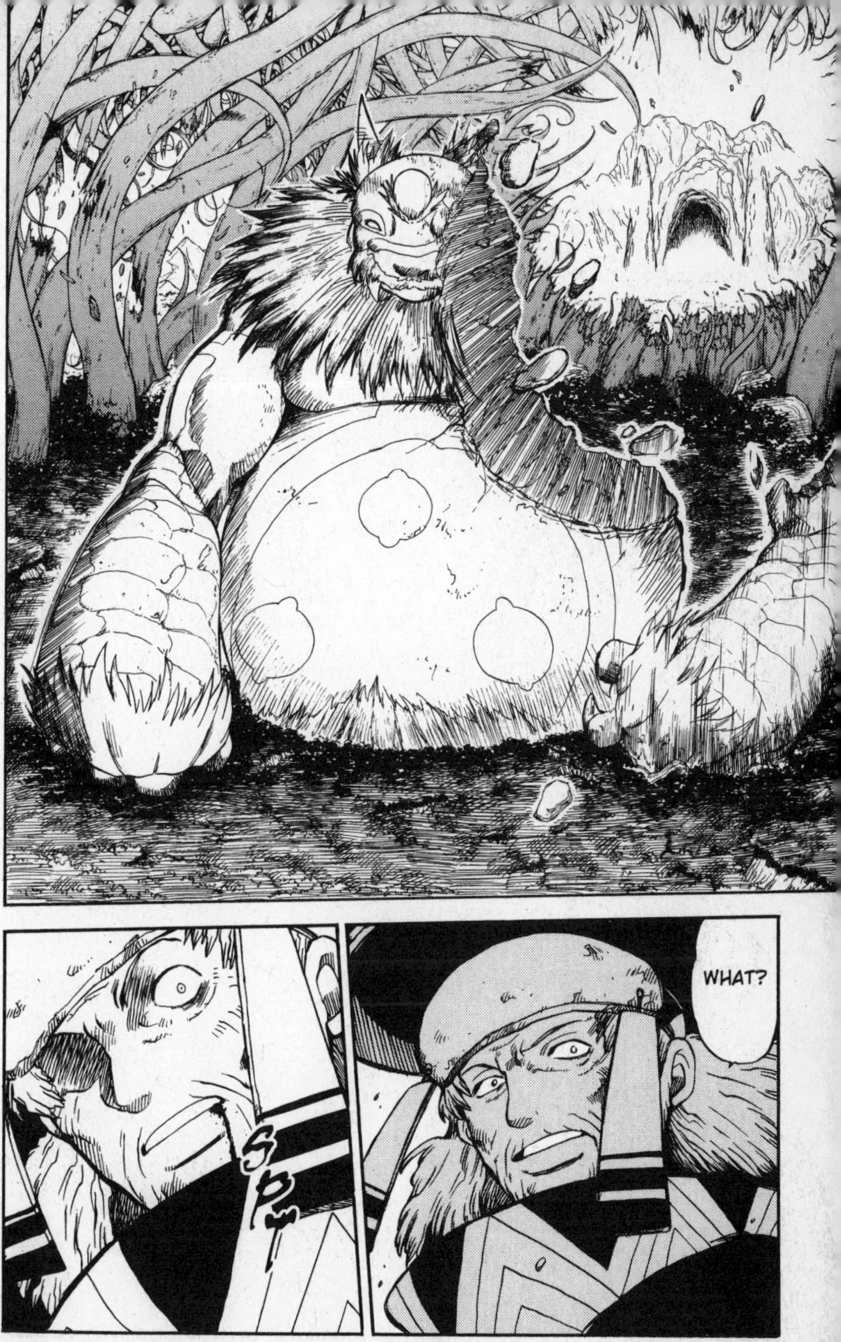
WHAT?

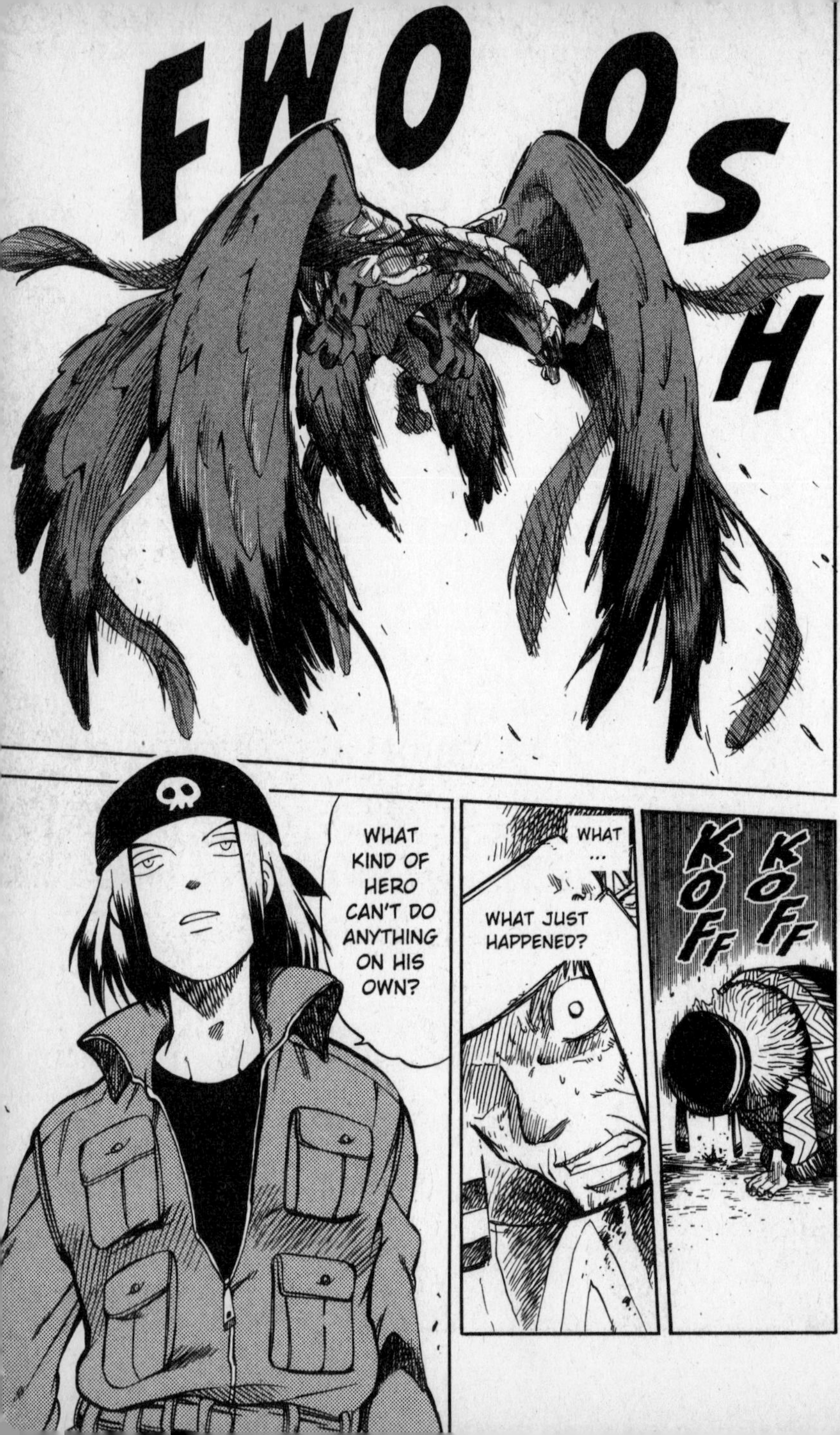
FWOOSH
KOFF KOFF
WHAT ...
WHAT JUST HAPPENED?
WHAT KIND OF HERO CAN'T DO ANYTHING ON HIS OWN?

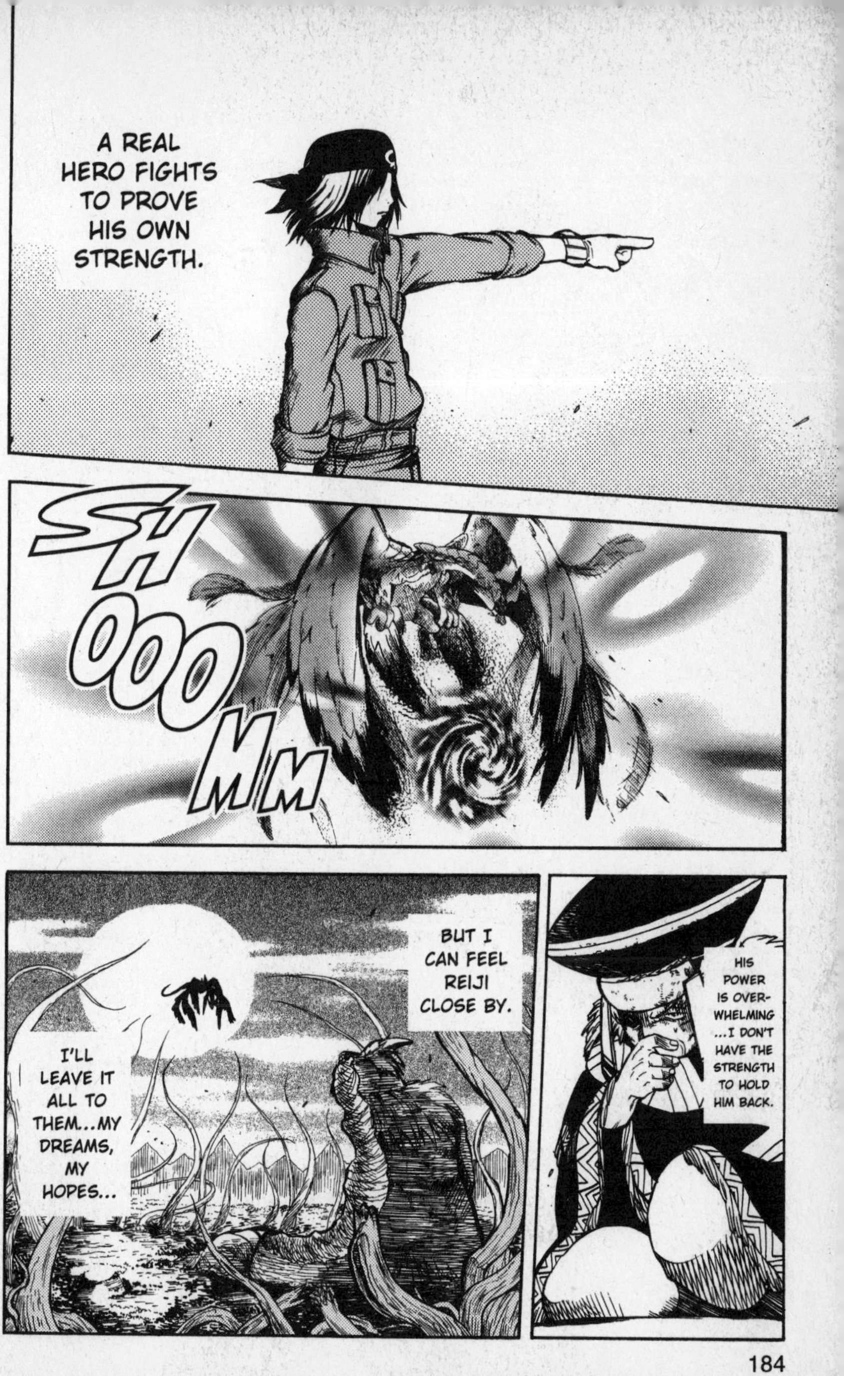
A REAL HERO FIGHTS TO PROVE HIS OWN STRENGTH.
SHOOOMMM
HIS POWER IS OVER-WHELMING ...I DON'T HAVE THE STRENGTH TO HOLD HIM BACK.
BUT I CAN FEEL REIJI CLOSE BY.
I'LL LEAVE IT ALL TO THEM...MY DREAMS, MY HOPES...

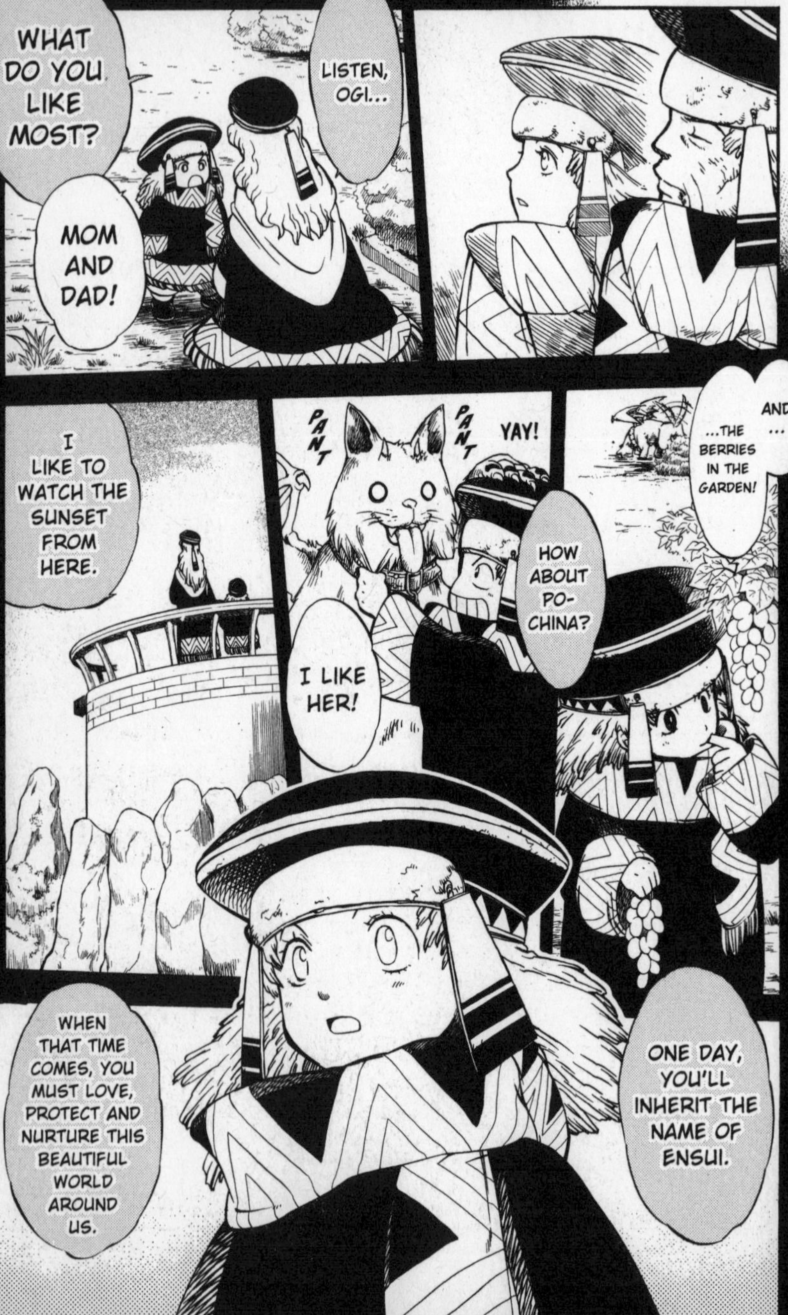
LISTEN, OGI...
WHAT DO YOU LIKE MOST?
MOM AND DAD!
AND ...
...THE BERRIES IN THE GARDEN!
HOW ABOUT PO-CHINA?
PANT PANT
YAY!
I LIKE HER!
I LIKE TO WATCH THE SUNSET FROM HERE.
ONE DAY, YOU'LL INHERIT THE NAME OF ENSUI.
WHEN THAT TIME COMES, YOU MUST LOVE, PROTECT AND NURTURE THIS BEAUTIFUL WORLD AROUND US.

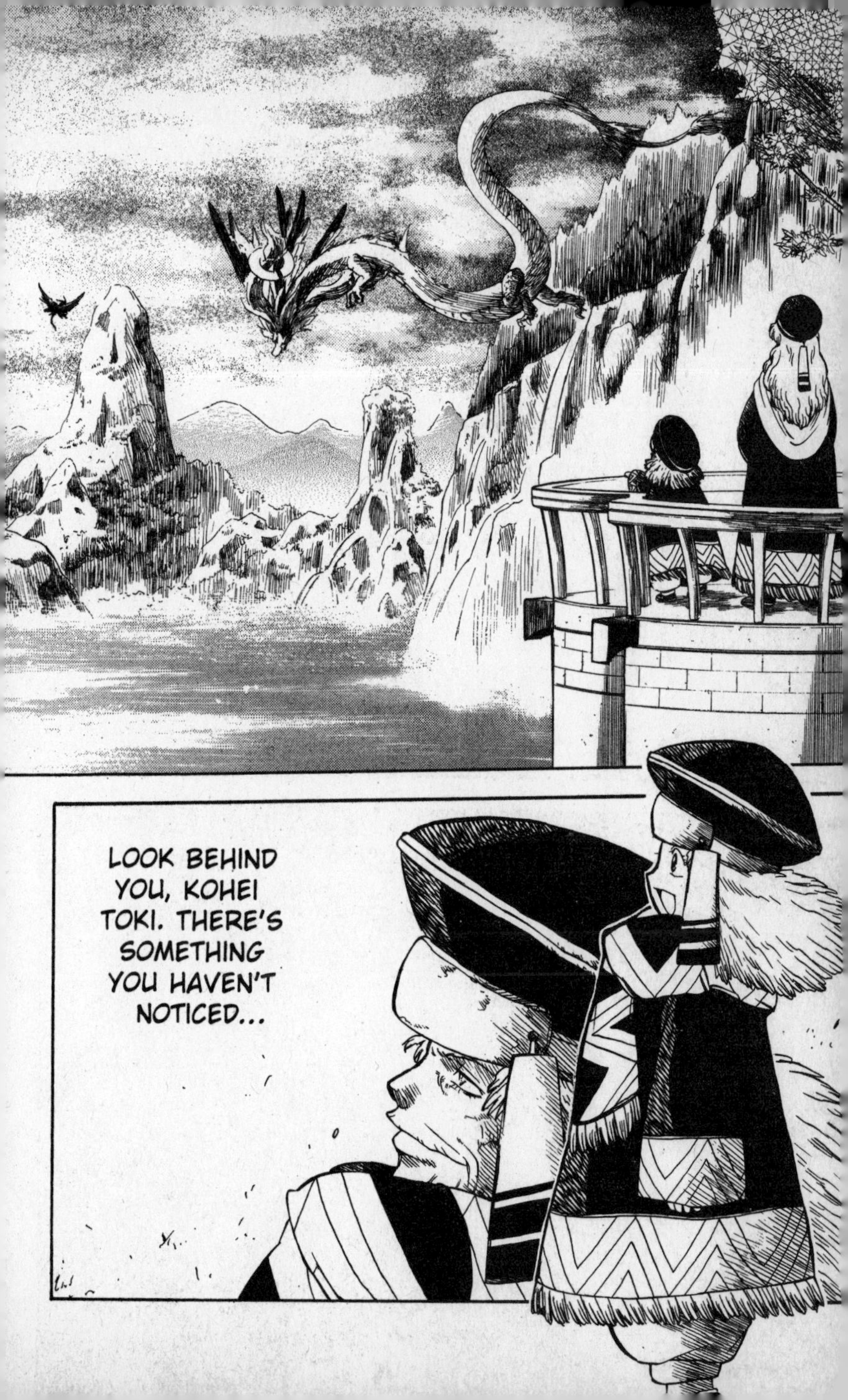
LOOK BEHIND YOU, KOHEI TOKI. THERE'S SOMETHING YOU HAVEN'T NOTICED...

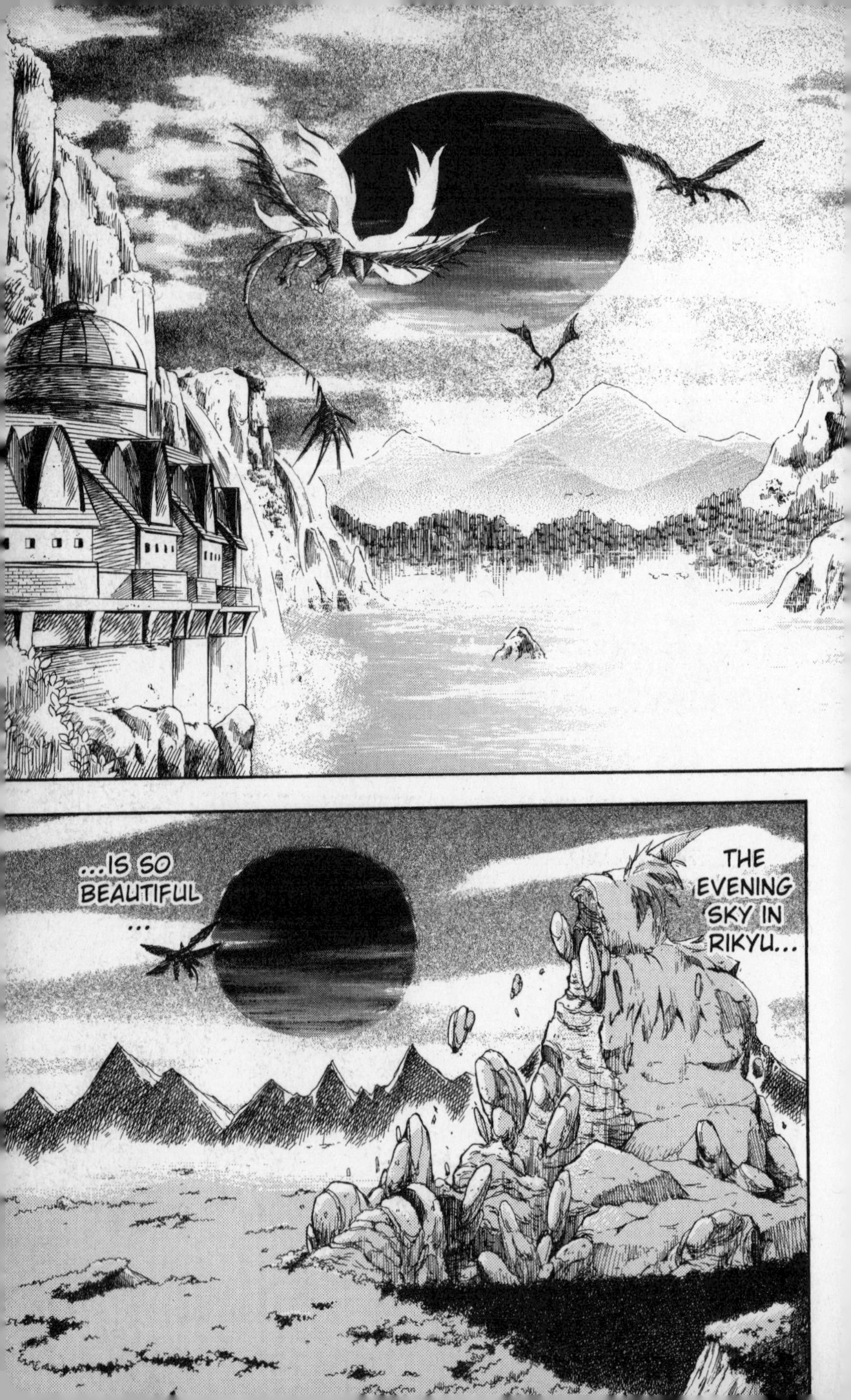
THE EVENING SKY IN RIKYU...
...IS SO BEAUTIFUL ...

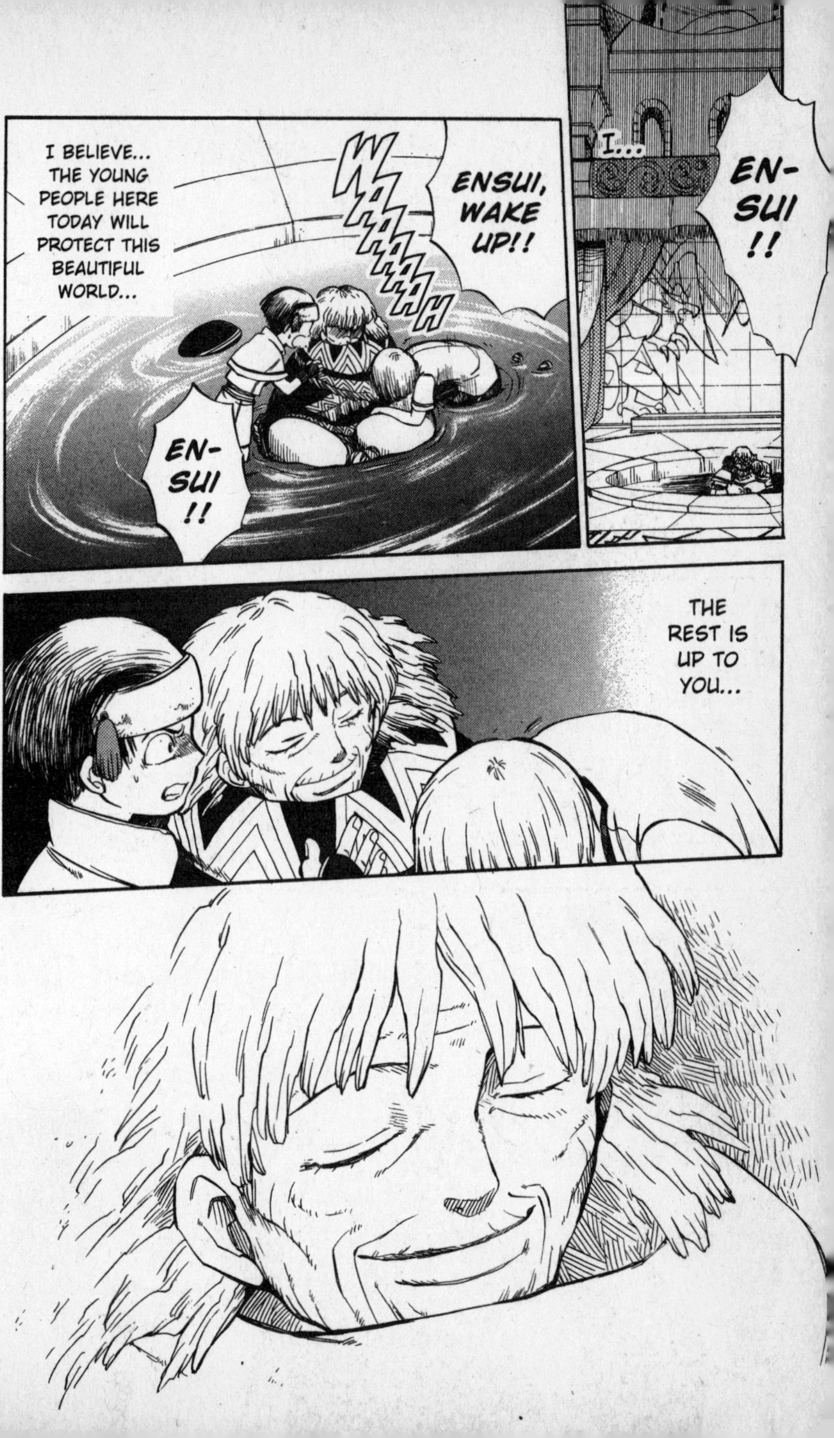
EN-SUI!!
I...
ENSUI, WAKE UP!!
WAAAAAH
I BELIEVE... THE YOUNG PEOPLE HERE TODAY WILL PROTECT THIS BEAUTIFUL WORLD...
EN-SUI!!
THE REST IS UP TO YOU...

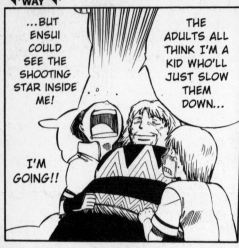

...BUT ENSUI COULD SEE THE SHOOTING STAR INSIDE ME!

THE ADULTS ALL THINK I'M A KID WHO'LL JUST SLOW THEM DOWN...

I'M GOING!!

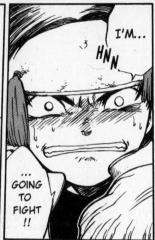

I'M...

HNN

...GOING TO FIGHT!!

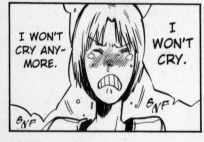

I WON'T CRY ANYMORE.

I WON'T CRY.

SNF

SNF

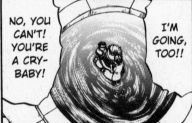

NO, YOU CAN'T! YOU'RE A CRYBABY!

I'M GOING, TOO!!

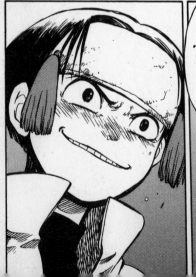

...CAME TO ME, TOO!

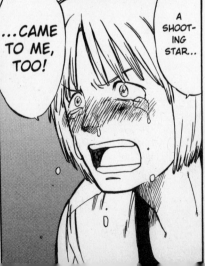

A SHOOTING STAR...

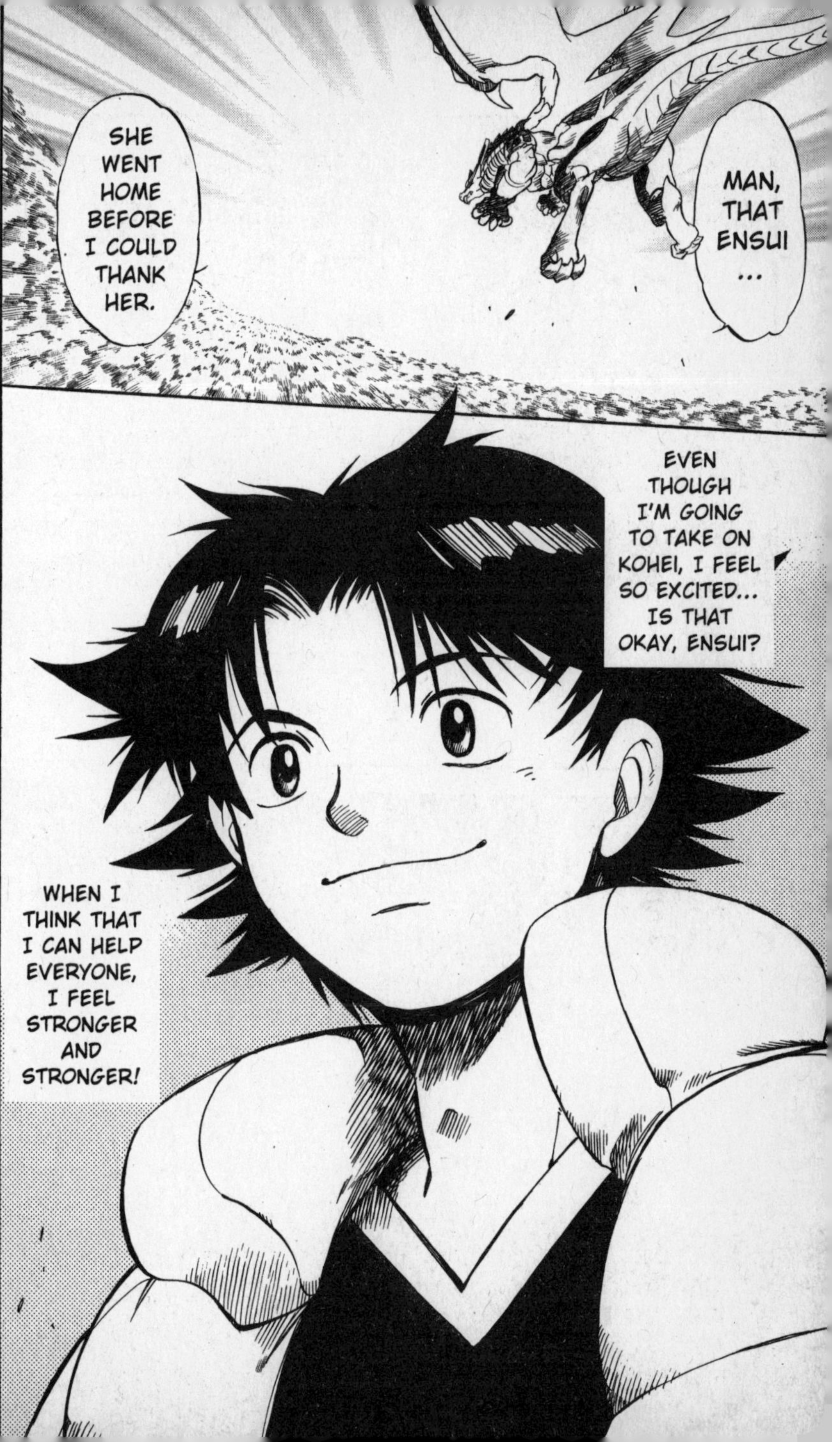
MAN, THAT ENSUI ...
SHE WENT HOME BEFORE I COULD THANK HER.
EVEN THOUGH I'M GOING TO TAKE ON KOHEI, I FEEL SO EXCITED... IS THAT OKAY, ENSUI?
WHEN I THINK THAT I CAN HELP EVERYONE, I FEEL STRONGER AND STRONGER!

READ THIS WAY

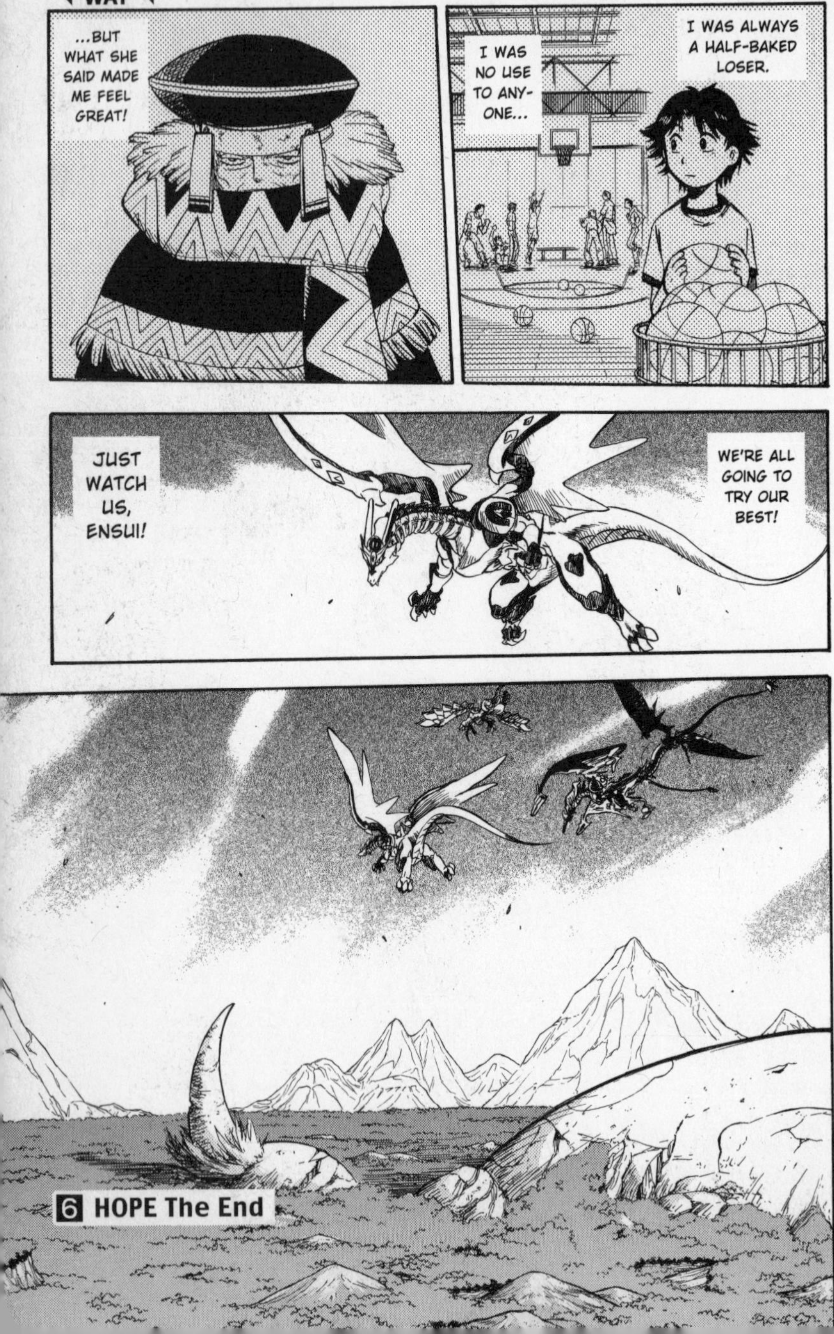
I WAS ALWAYS A HALF-BAKED LOSER.
I WAS NO USE TO ANY-ONE...
...BUT WHAT SHE SAID MADE ME FEEL GREAT!
WE'RE ALL GOING TO TRY OUR BEST!
JUST WATCH US, ENSUI!
6 HOPE The End

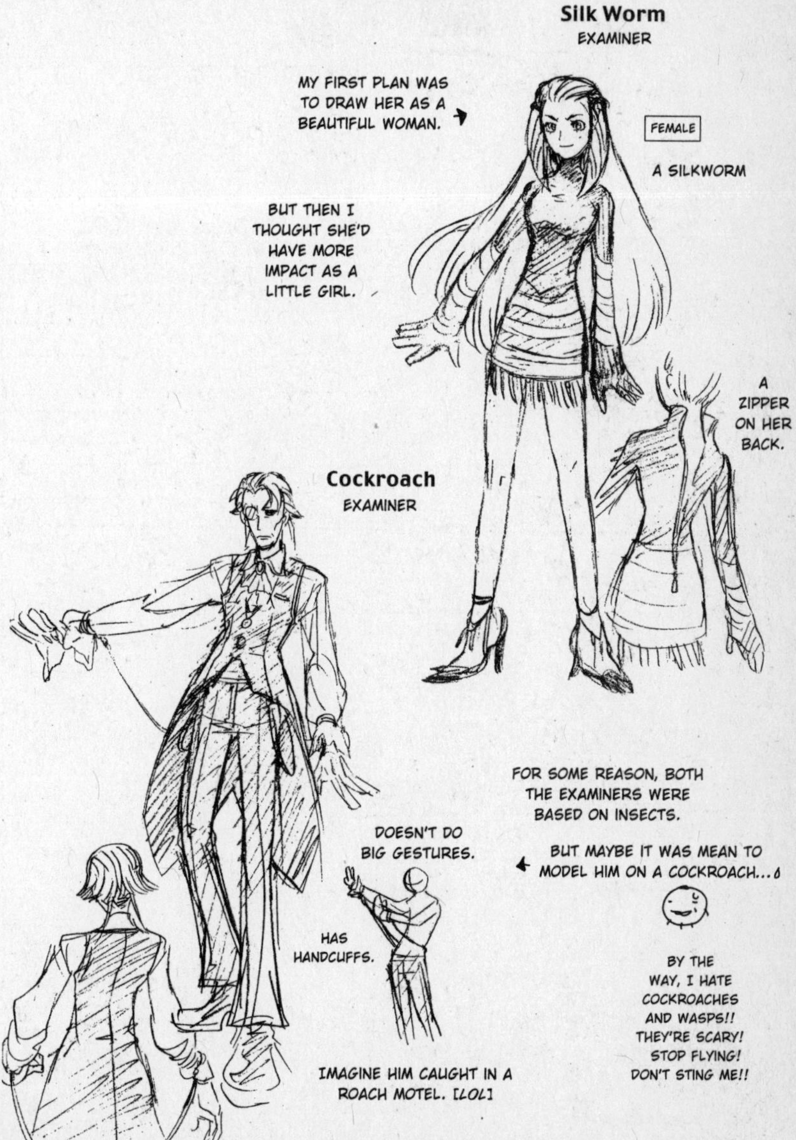
Silk Worm
EXAMINER
MY FIRST PLAN WAS TO DRAW HER AS A BEAUTIFUL WOMAN.
FEMALE
A SILKWORM
BUT THEN I THOUGHT SHE'D HAVE MORE IMPACT AS A LITTLE GIRL.
A ZIPPER ON HER BACK.
Cockroach
EXAMINER
FOR SOME REASON, BOTH THE EXAMINERS WERE BASED ON INSECTS.
BUT MAYBE IT WAS MEAN TO MODEL HIM ON A COCKROACH...
DOESN'T DO BIG GESTURES.
HAS HANDCUFFS.
BY THE WAY, I HATE COCKROACHES AND WASPS!! THEY'RE SCARY! STOP FLYING! DON'T STING ME!!
IMAGINE HIM CAUGHT IN A ROACH MOTEL. [LOL]

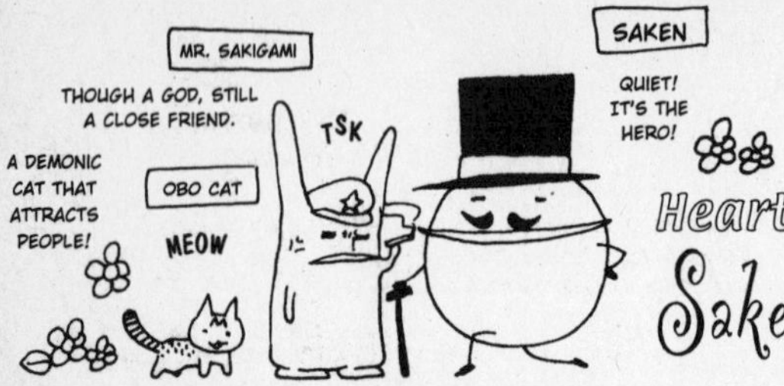
SAKEN
QUIET! IT'S THE HERO!
MR. SAKIGAMI
THOUGH A GOD, STILL A CLOSE FRIEND.
TSK
OBO CAT
A DEMONIC CAT THAT ATTRACTS PEOPLE!
MEOW

Heartwarming Saken Theater

BY KEN-ICHI SAKURA

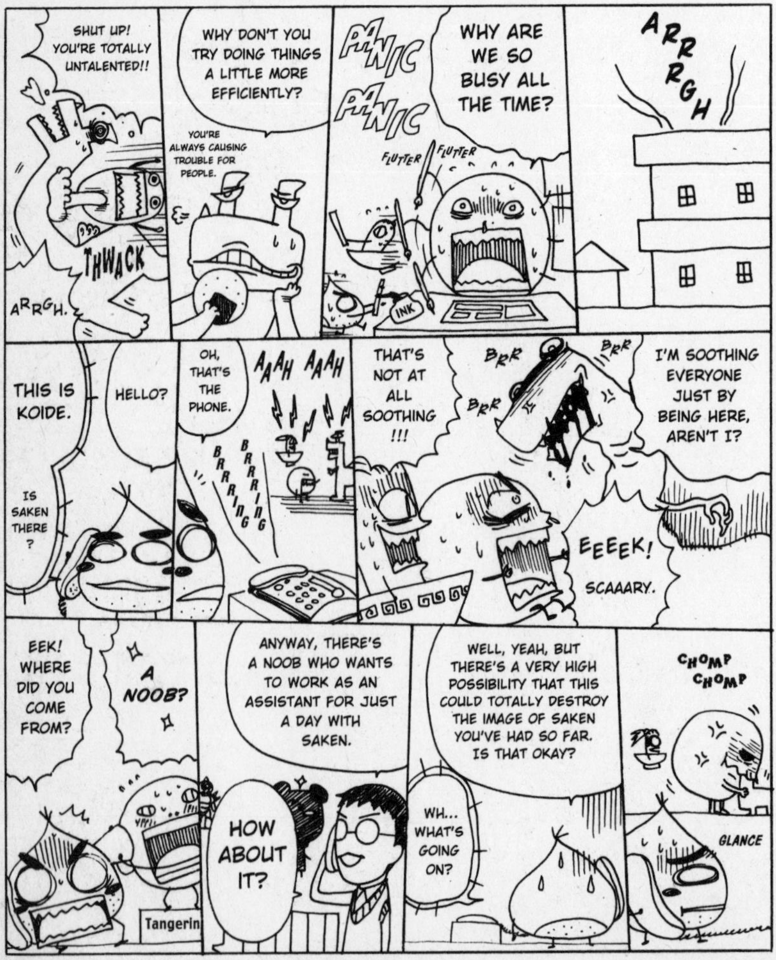
ARRRGH
PANIC
PANIC
WHY ARE WE SO BUSY ALL THE TIME?
FLUTTER
FLUTTER
INK
WHY DON'T YOU TRY DOING THINGS A LITTLE MORE EFFICIENTLY?
YOU'RE ALWAYS CAUSING TROUBLE FOR PEOPLE.
SHUT UP! YOU'RE TOTALLY UNTALENTED!!
THWACK
ARRGH.
I'M SOOTHING EVERYONE JUST BY BEING HERE, AREN'T I?
BRR
BRR
BRR
EEEEK!
SCAAARY.
THAT'S NOT AT ALL SOOTHING!!!
OH, THAT'S THE PHONE.
AAAH AAAH
BRRRRING
BRRRRING
HELLO?
THIS IS KOIDE.
IS SAKEN THERE?
CHOMP CHOMP
GLANCE
WELL, YEAH, BUT THERE'S A VERY HIGH POSSIBILITY THAT THIS COULD TOTALLY DESTROY THE IMAGE OF SAKEN YOU'VE HAD SO FAR. IS THAT OKAY?
WH... WHAT'S GOING ON?
ANYWAY, THERE'S A NOOB WHO WANTS TO WORK AS AN ASSISTANT FOR JUST A DAY WITH SAKEN.
HOW ABOUT IT?
A NOOB?
EEK! WHERE DID YOU COME FROM?
Tangerin

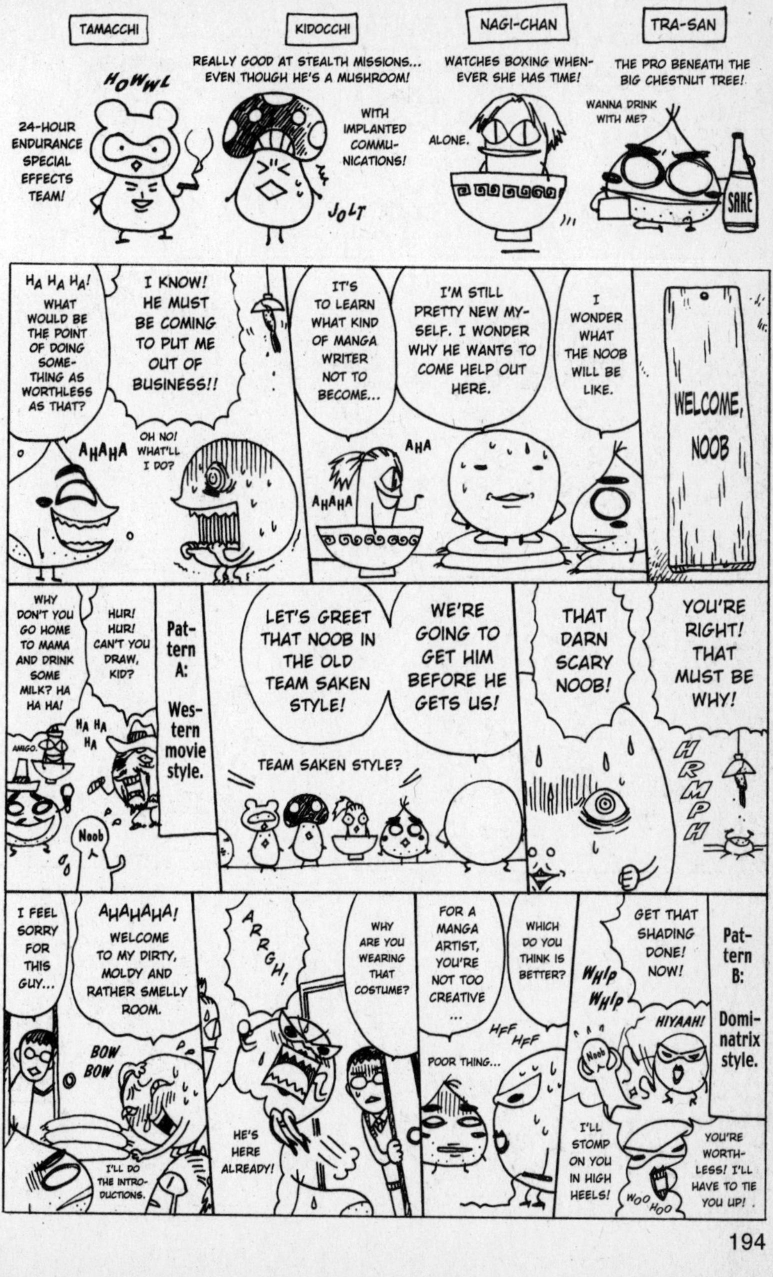
TRA-SAN
THE PRO BENEATH THE BIG CHESTNUT TREE!
WANNA DRINK WITH ME?
SAKE
NAGI-CHAN
WATCHES BOXING WHENEVER SHE HAS TIME!
ALONE.
KIDOCCHI
REALLY GOOD AT STEALTH MISSIONS... EVEN THOUGH HE'S A MUSHROOM!
WITH IMPLANTED COMMUNICATIONS!
JOLT
TAMACCHI
HOWWL
24-HOUR ENDURANCE SPECIAL EFFECTS TEAM!
WELCOME, NOOB
I WONDER WHAT THE NOOB WILL BE LIKE.
I'M STILL PRETTY NEW MYSELF. I WONDER WHY HE WANTS TO COME HELP OUT HERE.
IT'S TO LEARN WHAT KIND OF MANGA WRITER NOT TO BECOME...
AHA
AHAHA
I KNOW! HE MUST BE COMING TO PUT ME OUT OF BUSINESS!!
OH NO! WHAT'LL I DO?
HA HA HA! WHAT WOULD BE THE POINT OF DOING SOMETHING AS WORTHLESS AS THAT?
AHAHA
YOU'RE RIGHT! THAT MUST BE WHY!
HRMPH
THAT DARN SCARY NOOB!
WE'RE GOING TO GET HIM BEFORE HE GETS US!
LET'S GREET THAT NOOB IN THE OLD TEAM SAKEN STYLE!
TEAM SAKEN STYLE?
Pattern A: Western movie style.
HUR! HUR! CAN'T YOU DRAW, KID?
WHY DON'T YOU GO HOME TO MAMA AND DRINK SOME MILK? HA HA HA!
HA HA HA
AMIGO.
Noob
Pattern B: Dominatrix style.
GET THAT SHADING DONE! NOW!
WHIP WHIP
HIYAAH!
Noob
YOU'RE WORTHLESS! I'LL HAVE TO TIE YOU UP!
I'LL STOMP ON YOU IN HIGH HEELS!
WOO HOO
WHICH DO YOU THINK IS BETTER?
FOR A MANGA ARTIST, YOU'RE NOT TOO CREATIVE...
HFF HFF
POOR THING...
WHY ARE YOU WEARING THAT COSTUME?
ARRGH!
HE'S HERE ALREADY!
AHAHAHA! WELCOME TO MY DIRTY, MOLDY AND RATHER SMELLY ROOM.
I FEEL SORRY FOR THIS GUY...
BOW BOW
I'LL DO THE INTRODUCTIONS.

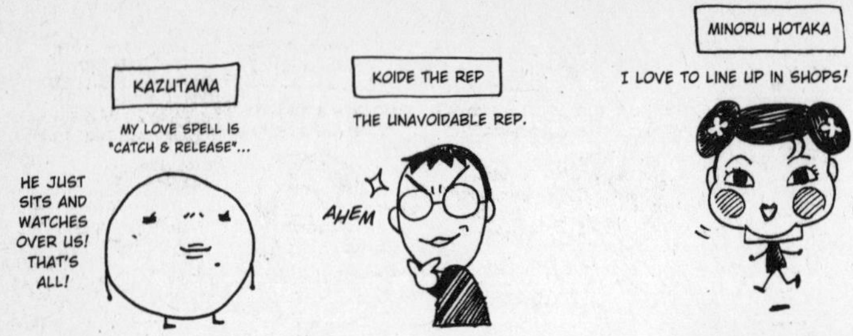
MINORU HOTAKA
I LOVE TO LINE UP IN SHOPS!
KOIDE THE REP
THE UNAVOIDABLE REP.
AHEM
KAZUTAMA
MY LOVE SPELL IS "CATCH & RELEASE"...
HE JUST SITS AND WATCHES OVER US! THAT'S ALL!

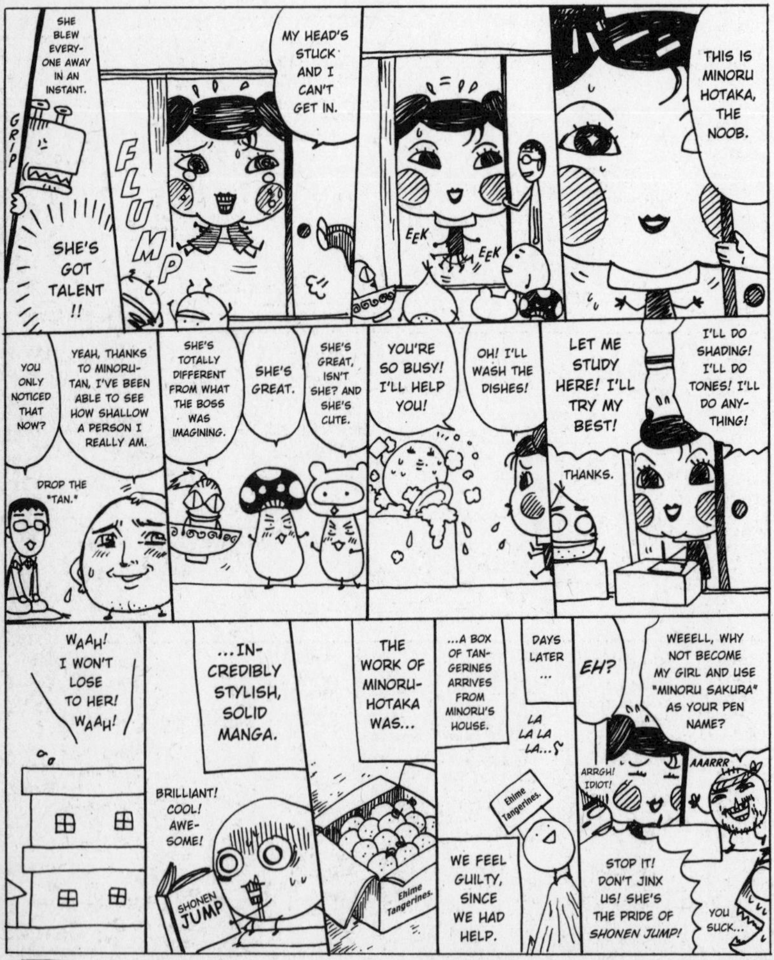
THIS IS MINORU HOTAKA, THE NOOB.
EEK
EEK
MY HEAD'S STUCK AND I CAN'T GET IN.
FLUMP
SHE BLEW EVERYONE AWAY IN AN INSTANT.
GRIP
SHE'S GOT TALENT!!
I'LL DO SHADING! I'LL DO TONES! I'LL DO ANYTHING!
LET ME STUDY HERE! I'LL TRY MY BEST!
THANKS.
OH! I'LL WASH THE DISHES!
YOU'RE SO BUSY! I'LL HELP YOU!
SHE'S GREAT, ISN'T SHE? AND SHE'S CUTE.
SHE'S GREAT.
SHE'S TOTALLY DIFFERENT FROM WHAT THE BOSS WAS IMAGINING.
YEAH, THANKS TO MINORU-TAN, I'VE BEEN ABLE TO SEE HOW SHALLOW A PERSON I REALLY AM.
YOU ONLY NOTICED THAT NOW?
DROP THE "TAN."
WEEELL, WHY NOT BECOME MY GIRL AND USE "MINORU SAKURA" AS YOUR PEN NAME?
EH?
AAARRR
ARRGH! IDIOT!
STOP IT! DON'T JINX US! SHE'S THE PRIDE OF SHONEN JUMP!
YOU SUCK...
DAYS LATER...
LA LA LA LA...
Ehime Tangerines.
...A BOX OF TANGERINES ARRIVES FROM MINORU'S HOUSE.
WE FEEL GUILTY, SINCE WE HAD HELP.
THE WORK OF MINORU-HOTAKA WAS...
...INCREDIBLY STYLISH, SOLID MANGA.
Ehime Tangerines.
BRILLIANT! COOL! AWESOME!
SHONEN JUMP
WAAH! I WON'T LOSE TO HER! WAAH!

The End

COMING NEXT VOLUME...

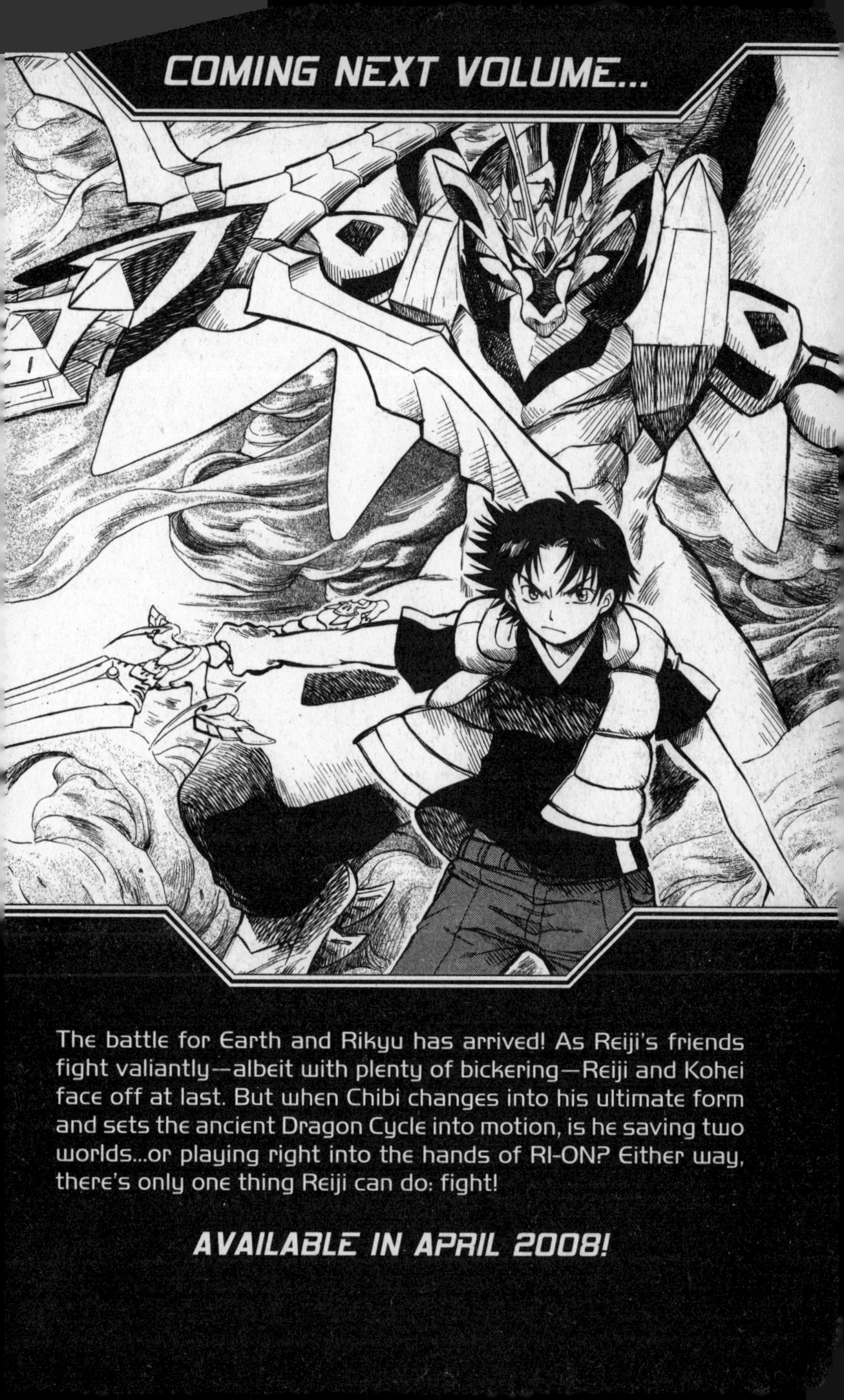

The battle for Earth and Rikyu has arrived! As Reiji's friends fight valiantly—albeit with plenty of bickering—Reiji and Kohei face off at last. But when Chibi changes into his ultimate form and sets the ancient Dragon Cycle into motion, is he saving two worlds...or playing right into the hands of RI-ON? Either way, there's only one thing Reiji can do: fight!

AVAILABLE IN APRIL 2008!

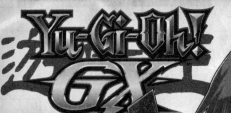
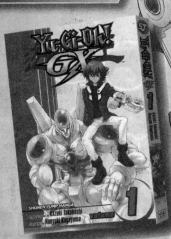
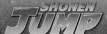

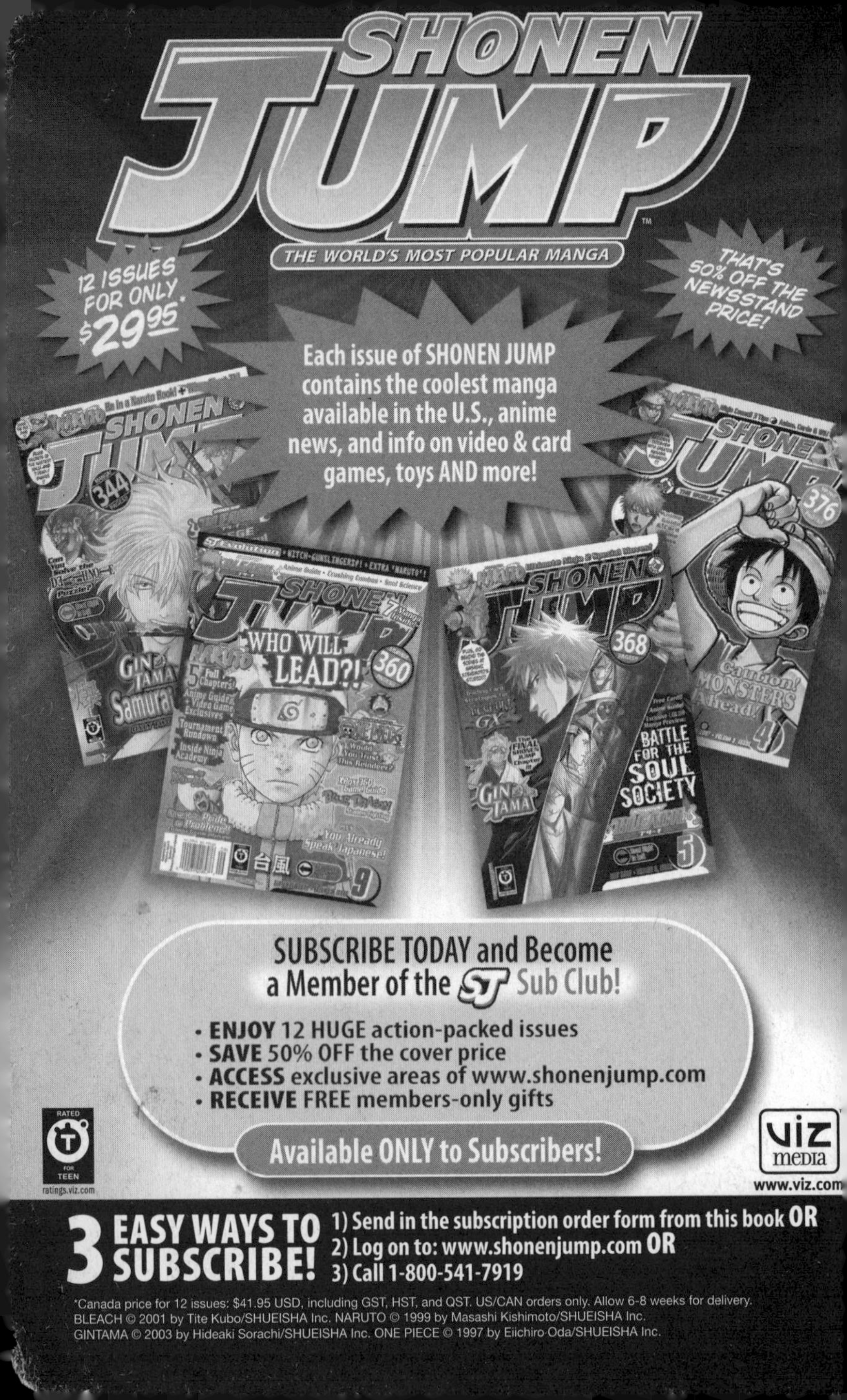
SHONEN JUMP
THE WORLD'S MOST POPULAR MANGA
12 ISSUES FOR ONLY $29.95*
THAT'S 50% OFF THE NEWSSTAND PRICE!
Each issue of SHONEN JUMP contains the coolest manga available in the U.S., anime news, and info on video & card games, toys AND more!
SUBSCRIBE TODAY and Become a Member of the SJ Sub Club!
• ENJOY 12 HUGE action-packed issues
• SAVE 50% OFF the cover price
• ACCESS exclusive areas of www.shonenjump.com
• RECEIVE FREE members-only gifts
Available ONLY to Subscribers!
RATED T FOR TEEN
ratings.viz.com
viz media
www.viz.com
3 EASY WAYS TO SUBSCRIBE!
1) Send in the subscription order form from this book OR
2) Log on to: www.shonenjump.com OR
3) Call 1-800-541-7919
*Canada price for 12 issues: $41.95 USD, including GST, HST, and QST. US/CAN orders only. Allow 6-8 weeks for delivery.
BLEACH © 2001 by Tite Kubo/SHUEISHA Inc. NARUTO © 1999 by Masashi Kishimoto/SHUEISHA Inc.
GINTAMA © 2003 by Hideaki Sorachi/SHUEISHA Inc. ONE PIECE © 1997 by Eiichiro Oda/SHUEISHA Inc.

Save **50% OFF**

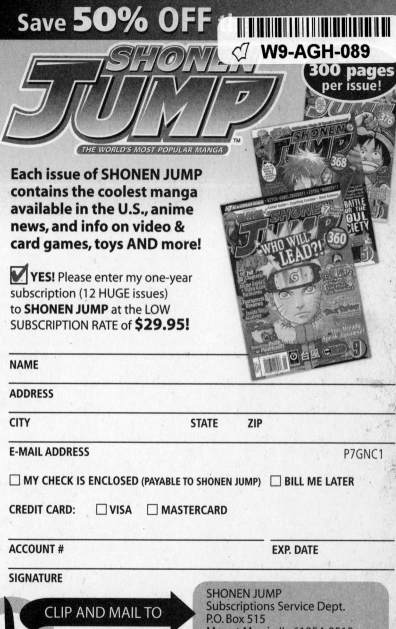

W9-AGH-089

SHONEN JUMP
THE WORLD'S MOST POPULAR MANGA™

300 pages per issue!

Each issue of SHONEN JUMP contains the coolest manga available in the U.S., anime news, and info on video & card games, toys AND more!

☑ **YES!** Please enter my one-year subscription (12 HUGE issues) to **SHONEN JUMP** at the LOW SUBSCRIPTION RATE of **$29.95!**

NAME _____

ADDRESS _____

CITY _____ STATE ___ ZIP ___

E-MAIL ADDRESS _____ P7GNC1

☐ **MY CHECK IS ENCLOSED** (PAYABLE TO SHONEN JUMP)   ☐ **BILL ME LATER**

CREDIT CARD: ☐ **VISA**   ☐ **MASTERCARD**

ACCOUNT # _____ **EXP. DATE** _____

SIGNATURE _____

CLIP AND MAIL TO ➡

SHONEN JUMP
Subscriptions Service Dept.
P.O. Box 515
Mount Morris, IL 61054-0515

Make checks payable to: **SHONEN JUMP**. Canada price for 12 issues: $41.95 USD, including GST, HST and QST. US/CAN orders only. Allow 6-8 weeks for delivery.

BLEACH © 2001 by Tite Kubo/SHUEISHA Inc. NARUTO © 1999 by Masashi Kishimoto/SHUEISHA Inc. ONE PIECE © 1997 by Eiichiro Oda/SHUEISHA Inc.

RATED **T** / TEEN
ratings.viz.com